Computer and Information Security

Computer and Information Security

Edited by **Audrey Coon**

WILLFORD PRESS
New York

Published by Willford Press,
118-35 Queens Blvd., Suite 400,
Forest Hills, NY 11375, USA
www.willfordpress.com

Computer and Information Security
Edited by Audrey Coon

International Standard Book Number: 978-1-68285-108-1 (Hardback)

Printed in the United States of America.

Contents

Preface

This comprehensive book provides a global overview of computer and information security. It offers an in-depth analysis of theories, technology and applications of this field. This book focuses on the emerging topic of security informatics. It brings forth some innovative research applications and rigorous case studies from around the globe under one umbrella. It includes contributions of renowned experts in the areas of cyber warfare and security, system security and data storage. This text will serve as a valuable reference to experts, IT engineers and interested readers.

This book unites the global concepts and researches in an organized manner for a comprehensive understanding of the subject. It is a ripe text for all researchers, students, scientists or anyone else who is interested in acquiring a better knowledge of this dynamic field.

I extend my sincere thanks to the contributors for such eloquent research chapters. Finally, I thank my family for being a source of support and help.

Editor

Knowledge encapsulation framework for technosocial predictive modeling

Michael C Madison[1*], Andrew J Cowell[1], R Scott Butner[1], Keith Fligg[1], Andrew W Piatt[1], Liam R McGrath[1] and Peter C Ellis[2]

Abstract

Analysts who use predictive analytics methods need actionable evidence to support their models and simulations. Commonly, this evidence is distilled from large data sets with significant amount of culling and searching through a variety of sources including traditional and social media. The time/cost effectiveness and quality of the evidence marshaling process can be greatly enhanced by combining component technologies that support directed content harvesting, automated semantic annotation, and content analysis within a collaborative environment, with a functional interface to models and simulations. Existing evidence extraction tools provide some, but not all, the critical components that would empower such an integrated knowledge management environment. This paper describes a novel evidence marshaling solution that significantly advances the state of the art. Its embodiment, the Knowledge Encapsulation Framework (KEF), offers a suite of semi-automated and configurable content harvesting, vetting, annotation and analysis capabilities within a wiki-enabled and user-friendly visual interface that supports collaborative work across distributed teams of analysts. After a summarization of related work, our motivation, and the technical implementation of KEF, we will explore the model for using KEF and results of our research.

Keywords: Semantic web, Technosocial predictive analytics, Predictive analytics, Knowledge management, Knowledge encapsulation framework, Semantic MediaWiki, Web-based interaction, Collaborative computing environments, Data mining, Web harvesting, Natural language processing

Introduction

Information analysts and researchers across many domains in academia, industry, and government have the onerous task of culling and searching through large data sets of traditional and social media to support their research in their domain. While the internet has simplified distance collaboration and increased many facets of an individual's or team's productivity [1], it has also significantly increased the number of possible traditional (e.g., journal articles, conference papers, technical reports, etc.) and social media (e.g., blogs, Twitter, etc.) sources that the analyst must locate, fact check, and leverage in a meaningful way [2]. The *Washington Post* helps to illustrate the quantity of data that can be accumulated rapidly when social media is combined with traditional media surrounding a topic with a recent blog

post focusing on Twitter volume during the 2012 Republican Presidential primary. Well over 200,000 tweets were made about the front-running 2012 Republican candidates in *a single day* [3]. This is, of course, insignificant to the amount of social media data churned out daily by Twitter alone (approximately 140,000,000 tweets per day as of this writing [4]), in addition to Facebook, LinkedIn, Google+, and the other prominent social networking sites.

The analyst, who's research is enabled by this mountain of data, is now responsible for combining the various sources, fact checking each record, marshaling the evidence, and aligning it with models for predicting future events. This analyst's job can be made simpler through the use of state-of-the art data mining and harvesting applications, which can automatically locate and combine disparate data repositories into a single, much larger repository. The analyst can then go to a single location to search for relevant evidence instead of searching multiple locations. Once harvested, these data can

* Correspondence: michael.madison@pnnl.gov
[1]Pacific Northwest National Laboratory, 902 Battelle Boulevard, 999, MSIN K7-28 Richland, WA 99352, USA
Full list of author information is available at the end of the article

be fed through other analytical applications to find relevant named entity, location, or event mentions that would be of interest to the analyst or the models. Finally, the analyst can use existing collaborative tools to interact with peers who might be doing similar research. Unfortunately, these solutions have not yet been integrated into a single tool, leaving much of the burden on the analyst for moving data between applications and noticing relevant information once it's been collected. For example, environments such as IBM SPSS and SAS Analytics, which are the instruments of choice for predictive analysis, provide tools for data collection through surveys, data mining, and presentation but do not offer a collaborative framework with capabilities for harvesting content from the internet and automated semantic annotation.

Why does a predictive analyst need such powerful features combined in a single tool? Consider the diversity of the research that a predictive analyst might face in today's world:

- What does the use of social media tools such as Facebook and Twitter in the recent "Arab Spring" uprisings tell us about the regimes in the region that are most vulnerable to similar rebellions? How might cultural differences affect the translation of these phenomena to other parts of the world?
- Assuming that the high incidence of 100-degree days in much of the southern United States during the summer of 2011 is a long-term trend, what are the likely implications for U.S. power grid operations? Will any of the anticipated changes in electrical load create new vulnerabilities in the grid? Where are these vulnerabilities likely to be concentrated? How might they be mitigated?
- How would one recognize the "early warning signs" of an emerging terrorist network that has the goal of building a nuclear weapon? How could these warning signs be differentiated from activities resulting from peaceful use of nuclear power?

Though each of these sets of questions represents a focus on different technical domains and social phenomena, each illustrates the interconnectedness of technological and social systems that characterizes our modern world. It is within this intersection of technology and society that Technosocial Predictive Analytics (TPA) [5] exists. The goal of TPA is to "create decision advantage in support of natural decision making through a process of analytical transformation that integrates psychosocial and physical models by leveraging insights from both the social and natural sciences" [6]. In the information security domain, TPA helps the analyst anticipate and counter threats to national security and social well being that originate through this interaction of society and

technology. Whether these threats are man-made or natural, malicious or unintended, our ability to create computer models that help us think robustly about plausible future scenarios is increasingly being used to improve our understanding of the consequences emerging from the complex intersection of human society, technology, and the physical environment.

In this paper, we describe the Knowledge Encapsulation Framework (KEF) [7], a platform for managing information, marshaling evidence, empowering collaboration, and automatically discovering relevant data. After discussing related work, our motivation for developing KEF, and its technical implementation, we will explore both the general KEF model for applying the framework and its real-world experiences.

Related work

The underlying research behind KEF is based on research done in a number of domains over a number of years. Experts systems research [8,9] have tried to capture the tacit knowledge residing within a specific domain (usually through the elicitation of that knowledge from subject matter experts [SMEs]) so this information can be shared and transferred to other members [10]. KEF itself does not attempt to master or understand the SMEs' knowledge and evidence as a learning system might. KEF instead focuses on streamlining the research and modeling processes by creating a collaborative environment for SMEs to come together, organize and share information, and provide transparency to help connect research, data, and the types of dialog that occur naturally between researchers. KEF therefore is an environment that allows for the discussion and evolution of new knowledge and ideas and not a more anthropomorphic representation that may appear to have human form and can listen and talk to the user [11].

There is also often a significant amount of effort placed in engineering the knowledge structure in expert systems so that reasoning can occur to handle unforeseen situations. While KEF does attempt to annotate semantic relationships identified within the data sources, these are not hard-coded ontologies – rather, we build up a categorization scheme based on the content identified [10]. Finally, typical expert systems focus on a very narrowly defined domain such as Mycin [12] and CADUCEUS [13] (both medical diagnosis systems), NetEXPERT [14] (network operations automation system), KnowledgeBench [15] (new product development applications), and Dipmeter Advisor [16] (oil exploration system). KEF, while similar in many regards to these other examples, is distinctly different as it is specifically designed to be widely applicable to many domains allowing for customization to meet specific domain needs and requirements.

Collaborative problem solving environments (CPSE) are another analogy for this concept. The Pacific Northwest National Laboratory (PNNL) has a long history of building CPSEs for U.S. Department of Energy (DOE) scientists [17], such as the DOE2000 Electronic Notebook Project [18] and Velo [19]. Watson [20] reviewed a number of organizations pursuing CPSEs including other DOE sites (e.g., the Common Component Architecture, Collaboratory Interoperability Framework, and Corridor One Project) as well as the U.S. Department of Defense (e.g., Gateway), NASA (e.g., the Intelligent Synthesis Environment, Collaborative Engineering Environment, and Science Desk) and numerous university efforts (Rutgers University's Distributed System for Collaborative Information Processing and Learning, the University of Michigan's Space Physics and Aeronomy Research Collaboratory, and Stanford's Interactive Workspaces). Shaffer [21], in his position statement on CPSEs, defined them as a "system that provides an integrated set of high level facilities to support groups engaged in solving problems from a proscribed domain." These facilities – for example, components to enable three-dimensional molecular visualization for biologists – are most often directly related to the domain.

There are a number of domain-specific applications that a predictive analyst might use. IBM SPSS [22] and SAS Analytics [23] are both marketed towards a business analytics/business intelligence audience and provide capabilities such as text analysis, data mining, visualization, model integration, and statistics. Palantir [24] also markets to business clients, but also has a growing reputation in the intelligence community for being able to mine data from disparate sources (e.g., CIA and FBI databases) and combine them into a single, structured repository. Each of these examples represents widely used predictive analytics applications; however, each is lacking in key areas. Specifically, they do not offer a collaborative framework with capabilities for harvesting content from the internet and automated semantic annotation. They also have not addressed the growing need for being able to combine traditional data repositories with social media data.

Perhaps the most currently available technologies most similar to KEF are "web 2.0" information stores. Examples include encyclopedic resources such as Wikipedia and Knol that rely on the "wisdom of the crowds [25]" to build and maintain a knowledge base of information. Such resources rarely utilize automated processes to extract semantic relations and add these as additional metadata that can aid in the discovery process. Like KEF, some of these systems use tags to provide an informal taxonomy, but the domain scale is typically very wide (in the case of Wikipedia, the goal is to provide an encyclopedia's worth of knowledge). Project Halo [26] is a specific instance of an information store that aims to develop an application capable of answering novel questions and solving advanced problems in a broad range of scientific disciplines (e.g., biology, physics, and chemistry). The mechanism for inserting knowledge into the data store (i.e., using graduate students with domain knowledge) requires significant effort, however. The KEF approach is to share the load between automated information extraction tools and domain experts. While we acknowledge the limitations of automated information extraction technologies, we believe an approach that leverages automated means while encouraging users to make corrections and provide their own annotations provides significant semantic markup and encourages SME engagement.

Motivation for this work

Our work on KEF is motivated by two goals – one specific to the task of TPA, the other more general. The first goal is to provide a framework that meets the specific knowledge management requirements imposed by the multi-disciplinary character of TPA, supporting the ability to:

- collaborate across multiple disciplines
- marshal evidence in support of model design and calibration
- provide transparency into the models being used

Our implementation of features supporting these requirements is discussed in detail in subsequent sections of this paper.

A second, more general goal of this work is to provide a framework that shifts the focus of analysts towards tasks that add value to their data and away from the more mechanical aspects of data collection. It is not uncommon for intelligence analysts (a specific type of knowledge worker with whom the authors have experience) to spend 80% of their time collecting material for their task, thanks in part to the previously mentioned access to publications on the internet, leaving only 20% of time for the analysis [27]. In the research described herein, we aim to address the data quantity problem as well as making use of electronic media to increase collaboration and productivity. We do this through a collaborative wiki environment designed to find and filter input data, allow for user input and annotations, and provide a collaborative workspace for team members. This framework is also designed to establish provenance, linking data from sources directly to a research area for maximum productivity and pedigree.

Technical implementation

At its core, KEF is a blending of open source software projects and custom development. KEF seamlessly integrates these separate components into a single environment, providing users with a suite of features and capabilities that no single KEF component can provide on its own.

MediaWiki [28], the same software that powers Wikipedia, forms the foundation of KEF. The wiki provides KEF with many standard web content management system (CMS) features and functionality such as user account management; the ability to easily create, edit, and delete content; a customizable theme engine; attribution of authors for not only the creation of content but all edits and deletions; and perhaps most importantly, a framework for importing community and custom created extensions. As each piece of content is created, MediaWiki creates a new web-based "page" to store its contents. All data from the wiki are stored in a MySQL database. For the author and any subsequent editors, the wiki provides a version control system, ensuring that any subsequent edits, deletions, or moves are preserved for provenance.

Despite being a powerful CMS, these features alone are not sufficient to accomplish the goals set forth by the KEF project. Even though MediaWiki stores its content in a database, each page of content is stored as a single field of text. To a user reading the page, this is acceptable because the user has no direct interaction with the database or underlying functionality. However, for a user who wishes to perform advanced queries across multiple pages, it is less than adequate. Krötzsch et. al. [29] created an extension called Semantic MediaWiki (SMW) that integrates semantic features into the base MediaWiki framework. Extending MediaWiki in this way provided the capability to rapidly sift through the content in the wiki based on the semantically tagged text. KEF uses the Semantic Forms [30] extension to provide manual semantic markup within the wiki pages. Not only does this alleviate the need for a user to learn wiki syntax, a web programming language similar to HTML, but by providing user-friendly forms for data entry, it ensures consistency because semantic properties are applied automatically when wiki pages are created. In addition to properties, each page in the wiki is associated with a template, which controls what information is displayed to the user and how it appears, and a category, which groups similar types of pages together (e.g., all journal articles might be in a "publications" category).

For example, an analyst might have a collection of publications that needs to be tracked with KEF. Some of these publications might be journal articles, books, conference papers, technical articles, technical reports, etc., and as a result, each might have quite different information associated with it. The publication category therefore would be used to group like content together, but each type of publication would have a custom form to capture its information and a custom template to display its information properly.

In a traditional MediaWiki environment, a security analyst could still create a series of pages, each representing a different type of publication in a publication category. The analyst could also perform text-based searches to locate a particular string of text located within one or more of the pages in the wiki. This is how many commercial wikis, such as Wikipedia, function. Within KEF however, that same analyst would have access to much more powerful searching mechanism. Each field that is filled out with the semantic form can be converted into a facet in a faceted browser, [31] a method of filtering and reducing quantities of information, to rapidly filter the collection of publications to a more manageable subset based on a selection of semantic properties. Instead of the traditional "search results" page, the page would be a dynamically updating one where the analyst has the ability to drill down into the content and more easily find relevant information.

For example, as seen in Figures 1, 2 and 3, the analyst would be presented with a set of results in the faceted browser. From here, the analyst may select a particular author, publication date, or interesting phrase to explore the results in a manageable way. If the analyst selected the date "1995-01-01" in Figure 3, all but 2 of the original 145 results would be filtered out. Any of the metadata collected during content entry may be exposed as a facet, giving a high degree of customization to these interfaces and allowing them to be molded to most accurately represent the content to be explored.

KEF blends community and custom extensions to facilitate this faceted browsing capability. Exhibit [18], a

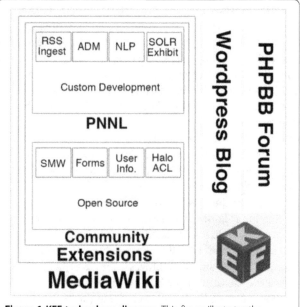

Figure 1 KEF technology diagram. This figure illustrates the various components that have been brought together to create KEF.

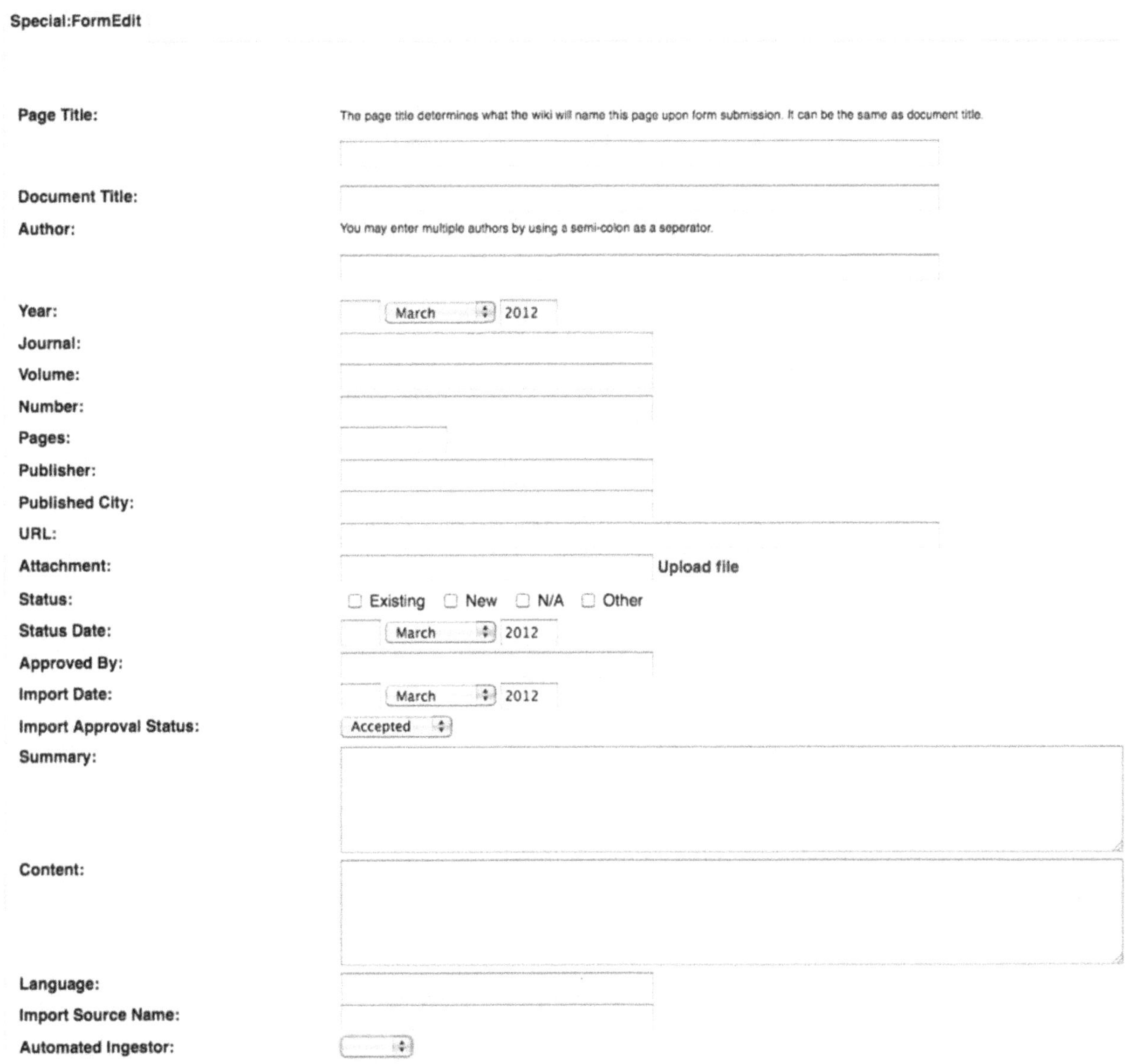

Special:FormEdit

Page Title:

The page title determines what the wiki will name this page upon form submission. It can be the same as document title.

Document Title:

Author:

You may enter multiple authors by using a semi-colon as a seperator.

Year: March ⬍ 2012

Journal:

Volume:

Number:

Pages:

Publisher:

Published City:

URL:

Attachment: Upload file

Status: ☐ Existing ☐ New ☐ N/A ☐ Other

Status Date: March ⬍ 2012

Approved By:

Import Date: March ⬍ 2012

Import Approval Status: Accepted ⬍

Summary:

Content:

Language:

Import Source Name:

Automated Ingestor: ⬍

Figure 2 Journal article entry form. This screenshot illustrates the form that aids the analyst when creating a journal article.

product of the SIMILE project at the Massachusetts Institute of Technology (MIT), provides a number of simple visualizations for the semantic data such as a Timelines, Table, Map (powered by Google Maps), and Calendar. The value of these visualizations is amplified by the faceted browsing technique, allowing the user to remove any of the pages that do not match their filters. KEF updates the visualization with each new selection, reducing the amount of data that the user must actively view. The KEF development team has integrated the research done at MIT on the Exhibit project with Apache SOLR [32] technology to significantly improve the scaling of Exhibit, giving the user instantaneous access to the data contained in their KEF site, even when there are tens of thousands of pages in the wiki.

Beyond providing basic content and user management, KEF serves as a collaborative environment, fostering discussion and the sharing of information. Several enhancements are necessary to facilitate this capability in the wiki. We have introduced the concept of User Profiles into KEF through a customized version of the community extension Social Profile [33]. These profiles might contain the standard "social networking" type of information such as name, email address, interests, skills, etc. They also commonly include research interests, publications, projects, and other information that might not be shared on a traditional social networking site (e.g., Facebook, LinkedIN), but would still be of interest to internal collaborators. We have also bolstered the security system within the wiki environment to adequately protect the users and their

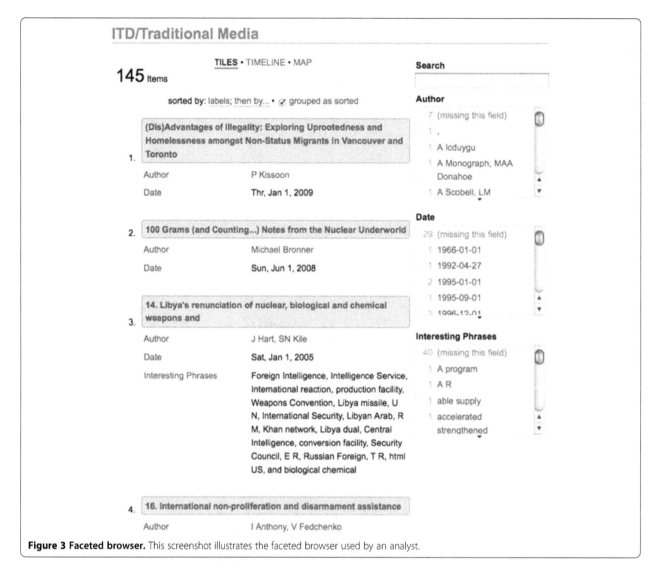

Figure 3 Faceted browser. This screenshot illustrates the faceted browser used by an analyst.

research. A wiki, at its core, is an open collaborative environment. Because of the sensitive nature of some analysts' research, it is often necessary to provide safeguards and access restrictions on their KEF installations. The community extension HaloACL [34] was integrated into KEF to provide security for these cases. This extension provides the capability of hiding complete pages and sub-page elements from users outside a particular user class. For example, a team of analysts might be spread across several institutions, requiring that their KEF installation live on a publicly available web server. While a brief welcome screen and general explanation of the project might be available for public consumption, none of the research, discussion, or modeling that goes on within KEF should be available publicly. Through HaloACL, that installation can be secured so that only registered and approved users that belong to the team of analysts can view or edit the sensitive data in KEF. On some installations, that is all of the data while others only protect a small subset.

Other community extensions add functionality such as the ability to construct widgets for commonly used code (e.g., embedding social video such as YouTube), add new semantic views for data (e.g., a sortable, printable, color-coded spreadsheet), use simple programmatic functions in wiki markup (e.g., if statements and arrays), a What You See is What You Get (WYSIWYG) editor, etc. In addition to custom development already highlighted in this section, the KEF team has created a significant number of extensions to facilitate specific functionality. These extensions will be covered in more detail in the KEF Model section below.

KEF relies heavily on MediaWiki for content management, but MediaWiki is not the only component within the framework. PHPbb [35] (PHP Bulletin Board) is a web-based forum application. While an analyst could easily share links to content in the wiki through an email or instant messaging client, these solutions are often lacking when it comes to recalling the conversation in the future or sharing it with other collaborators. A discussion forum provides a central resource that anyone with the appropriate access can view, engage, and share. As we will outline, the ability to discuss the activities in the wiki with other members of a research team to solicit feedback and knowledge sharing is critical to the success of the KEF model. KEF also uses Wordpress [36], a web-based blogging engine. A wiki is designed to have infinite layers of content, while a blog is designed to give users a chronological view of new information. Many KEF installations use the "blog" feature as an announcements or tasking platform to disseminate changes or new information rapidly among the user community. The KEF Model

Figure 4 illustrates the collaborative process followed by a team using KEF. Each numbered section represents a collaborative effort that is part of the KEF process. The specific example in Figure 4 focuses on a demonstration of KEF's capabilities that studies nuclear proliferation and illicit trafficking. This model focuses not on managing existing evidence (although KEF can play that role), but on discovering new evidence, fostering the collaboration of SMEs, aligning evidence with data models, and analyzing these data and evidence.

At its simplest, this process is:

1. Set Up Environment
2. Automated Discovery Process
3. Evidence Marshaling
4. Evidence-Model Alignment
5. Analytical Gaming / Analysis

Throughout each stage in this process, KEF steps outside of the standard wiki model to fuel collaboration. To that extent, KEF's discussion forum allows team members to flesh out ideas and participate in threaded conversations. Team members are automatically notified via email when new topics or replies are posted, ensuring that busy team members are kept in the loop even if they do not view the forum regularly. KEF's blog allows a team member to reach out to the rest of the team and alert them to new content in the wiki or a new discussion in the forum. Team members receive announcements from the blog either as a subscribed RSS feed or via email.

Stage 1: Set up environment

When starting a new instantiation of the environment, the KEF team meets with the SMEs and modelers to understand more about the domain (Stage 1 in Figure 4).

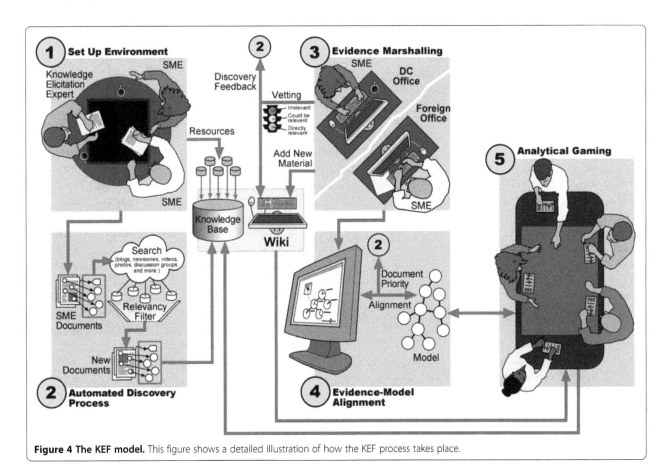

Figure 4 The KEF model. This figure shows a detailed illustration of how the KEF process takes place.

The KEF team is composed of computer scientists, designers, and developers. As a result, projects rarely are in a domain that matches the team's experience. These initial meetings with SMEs provide critical insight into the problem space and the desired outcome of the project. Key resources such as data sets, specific databases, important documents (e.g., journal articles, technical reports, etc.), and social media sources (e.g., specific users, topics, or sources) are gathered as the team seeks an understanding of the major domain concepts.

Based on the requirements outlined by the SMEs and modelers, KEF is customized based on project-specific requirements to easily incorporate the project's key resources. A typical KEF environment is deployed to a web server for development using a custom continuous build system. As the members of the research and KEF teams work on the site, changes in content (which are primarily stored in the MySQL database) and changes in the underlying framework (which are primarily stored on the web server) can be made simultaneously, allowing for the rapid development process that is often necessary in a research environment.

Once the environment is set up, the KEF team usually creates a series of Semantic Forms for the SME to use for manually entering content. As this new content is added to the wiki, the underlying semantics = mark up the text. Semantic Forms itself allows for basic markup, using each of the different fields in the form to represent a semantic property once the page has been created. KEF has also introduced a series of custom Natural Language Processing (NLP) tools that search through the submitted text adding additional annotations. The goal of these annotations to the unstructured data is to assist the SME in adding additional structure to the unstructured data that will support discovery and alignment of evidence. The current set of automated annotations includes:

- named entity mentions
- automated categorization
- statistically improbably phrases
- sentiment analysis
- event recognition

Named entity mentions annotations are used to indicate where entities of certain types of interest are referred to in a document. For recognizing named entities such as proper names, dates, times, and locations, we use two approaches: a statistical approach to provide coverage for general entity types (e.g., Person, Location, and Organization) and a dictionary-based approach to provide precision for domain-specific types. KEF's statistical named entity recognizer (NER) annotator can also use the Stanford NER tagger to tag people, organizations, and locations based on a linear chain Conditional

Random Field sequence classifier. The dictionary-based NER annotator uses lists of terms provided by the SME to tag entities relevant to the particular domain, such as specific types of people, organizations, or technologies.

Automated categorization annotations identify documents belonging to particular categories. The process for determining these categories starts with the SME providing some example documents. A maximum likelihood estimator (provided by LingPipe [37]) is trained on these categories and documents. As new documents are added, KEF can automatically place them into the appropriate category.

Statistically improbable phrase annotations identify phrases in a document that are deemed unlikely as compared to some background corpus. The sort of phrases identified can vary based on the background corpus used. For example, a general-purpose background corpus is used with a similar approach for Amazon's Statistically Improbable Phrases [38] to produce domain- or topic-specific terms in books. Similarly, a same-domain corpus of earlier documents can identify emerging themes and terms over time as used by Google News and similar tools. The functionality of our statistically improbable phrases annotator is based on LingPipe. As a background corpus for each document we use a collection of public domain novels, providing a generic model that allows topic-relevant terminology to emerge.

Sentiment analysis is performed to identify polarity (positive or negative) of documents or passages. This is driven by lexicons, which may be customized for specific domains. These annotations can be used for searching for evidence supporting specific opinions.

Event recognition is used to automatically annotate mentions of events of interest and the entities that that have roles in the events. Events and entities are identified using an information extraction pipeline and labeled according to types defined in an ontology. Event ontologies can be centered around domains – such as terrorism or technology [39] – or types of evidence – such as rhetoric [40].

With the structure given by these automated annotations, features of the semantic wiki such as the faceted search and summary views can be used by the SME to home in on specific content or pieces of content of interest for identifying evidence. For example, to identify the current state of networks of interest, the SME can search for mentions of entity types representing people of interest (e.g., Denied Person).

A threaded discussion forum and blog are also often deployed with the wiki in the earliest stages of the KEF development cycle. The forum will house discussions related to the models and data being gathered within the wiki. We begin with the forum in place to ensure that as content is manually entered in Stage 1, automatically harvested in Stage 2, integrated with the wiki in Stage 3, and aligned with data models in Stage 4, the SMEs will have a consistent area for holding collaborative discussions. Even during the analysis stage, a SME can return to the same discussion space to resume a discussion from a previous portion of the project. We also use the blog to highlight new features, or pieces of content, that might be of interest to other members of the team.

At the end of Stage 1, KEF has a functional blog, wiki, and forum and is available for the research team to begin collaborating, although at this time the amount of content is limited to only those documents manually entered. For example, this could include those reports and other documents considered to be excellent examples of the types of information the SME's and modelers hope to use to drive their models. In addition, this could also include structured data sets.

Stage 2: Automated discovery process

In Stage 2, we introduce the automated discovery mechanism (ADM). This suite of tools enables the SME to use the content entered during Stage 1 to automatically locate content on the internet (and other, potentially secure or otherwise restricted data sources) that may be statistically relevant. Through the semantic markup that was done as these "seed documents" were created, the ADM captures the essence of those documents (e.g., named entity mentions, automated categorization, statistically improbably phrases, sentiment analysis, event recognition) and searches across other data sources to identify potentially relevant material, covering both traditional and social media, such as:

- Google Scholar
- Opensource.gov
- CNS Nonproliferation Databases
- Microblogs (e.g., Twitter)
- Blogs dedicated to nuclear nonproliferation discussions
- The Nuclear Suppliers Group Trigger and Dual Use list
- The U.S. munitions list (category I-IV)

For each document identified, a relevancy metric (specifically, binary term occurrence) is computed to evaluate whether the document is truly related and not just a copy of the same document or too distinct to be useful. A researcher interested in expanding the search into new domains or topics of interest can add additional seed documents to KEF, which will in turn cause the ADM to expand its search to include those new concepts. Each document discovered through the ADM is harvested into KEF, passing through the same NLP tools as content that was manually entered and stored in a temporary repository while it awaits review by a SME.

Stage 3: Evidence marshaling

In Stage 3, users make use of KEF's faceted interface and summaries to browse the harvested content from Stage 2 and manually vet each piece of content, allowing the SMEs to decide which pieces of evidence should be introduced into the wiki. We recognize that no matter how thorough our NLP tools are, an automated harvesting process will inevitably find data that are not of interest to the SMEs. The goal here is that their vetting decisions can be fed back to the discovery mechanism to help improve the quality of the ADM process.

The faceted interface will load a series of documents that the ADM has harvested. A summary of information (e.g., source, title, categories, named entities, etc.) will be shown to the SME, and a series of facets will be available with similar content. The SME can rapidly go through the content and mark which documents should be accepted into KEF and which should be deleted. At any time, SMEs continue to add their own material into the environment adding to the vetted documents being harvested by the ADM.

Stage 4: Evidence-model alignment

In Stage 4, users can upload their model structure to the wiki and the environment will parse the structure and associated properties. Currently, this feature is in place for Bayesian Analysis of Competing Hypotheses (BACH) [41] models that are represented in XML, but similar visualizations can be added for other types of models. The user can then select specific parts of documents to connect to parts of the model (e.g., a paragraph of a known nuclear trafficking suspect entering the country could be aligned with the model node entitled "Suspect Geographically Linked to Target"). With large numbers of users, the goal is that the system will start automatically classifying the textual annotations linked to a particular node. These can be used to recommend other documents that the user should examine within the wiki and prioritize incoming material. This is especially important when the corpus of discovered documents is large. Specifically, the system attempts to classify the piece of text that users align with model nodes in order to characterize their linguistic structure so that it can try to identify this signature elsewhere.

This approach is based on research done by Y. Li et al. [42] in which two sentences are semantically compared using the WordNet [43] ontology, weighted by the frequency of the words in a large corpus and further combined with the similarity of word order among the sentences. We have expanded their research by preprocessing the sentences in order to semantically compare the words in those sentences. The first preprocessing step is to tag the various parts of speech (nouns, verbs, adjectives, etc.). The next step is to disambiguate the word sense of each of the words as outlined by Kolhatkar [44] so that "blue" in "I'm feeling blue" and that found in "The sky is blue" are considered separate with distinct meanings. The third step is to do a lookup to convert the form of the words to that found in WordNet. All words whose parts of speech or word sense cannot be determined, as well as those not found in WordNet, are removed before the sentence comparison is attempted.

The results of our research are promising. For example, the sentence "The threat that terrorists could acquire and use a nuclear weapon in a major U.S. city is real and urgent" was compared against a document containing 141 sentences. The most similar sentence retrieved was worded: "A dangerous gap remains between the urgency of the threat of nuclear terrorism and the scope and pace of the U.S. and world response." The first sentence talks about a real and urgent threat of nuclear terrorism while the second suggests that the international community's pace to respond to that threat is insufficient compared to the urgency of the threat. The next step is to expand from

sentences to paragraphs while maintaining the level of accuracy experienced at the sentence level [45].

We are currently researching novel methods to expand this concept to dynamically assign evidence as new content is fed into the corpus as well as learning from the analyst's responses whether or not the evidence that the automated process finds is relevant. The algorithm will then use this feedback to further improve the discovery mechanism.

Stage 5: Analytical gaming/Analysis

In Stage 5, the model, fully parameterized with attached evidence, can be exported from the wiki environment and used within a separate analytical tool suite. Figure 4 shows a serious game that enables decision- and policy-makers to perform "what if?" analysis. The game can reach back into the KEF environment to utilize real content and push results and decisions back into KEF for retrospective analysis. KEF can also be used to inject material directly into a running game in order to change the focus and bring the game back on track. Figures 5

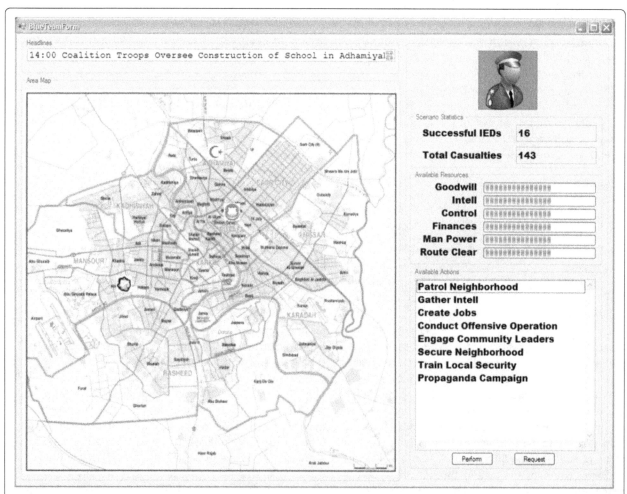

Figure 5 The IED Game. This screenshot shows a portion of the Analytical Game used in the Illicit Trafficking Demonstration (ITD), which will be discussed in the next section.

and 6 show some examples of how this linkage has been exercised with an Improvised Explosive Devices (IED) serious game [46] and an Energy Infrastructure Security serious game [47].

KEF also includes a basic chart and graph API, allowing users to visualize data sets metadata about evidence (e.g., comparing the number of pieces of evidence from a series of categories).

Case Study: The illicit trafficking demonstration

The Illicit Trafficking Demonstration (ITD) was intended as a showcase of the capacities provided by KEF, particularly its integration with the BACH and Analytical Gaming [48] frameworks. The demonstration showcases KEF's handling of the interaction between SMEs, the documents they have entered into KEF, and the analytical models built from those documents. The end goal of the demonstration was to present a cohesive environment where SMEs, analysts, and other interested parties could collaborate on the construction and execution of a particular analytical model within a single environment. We describe the implementation of KEF within PNNL's Technosocial Predictive Analytics Initiative (TPAI) [5] capstone demonstration below.

ITD was constructed for analysts working in the domain of nuclear trafficking and nonproliferation. As a regular part of their job, these analysts are often asked to research the formation of illicit nuclear trafficking networks, how nuclear materials might move and proliferate through those networks, and the relative likelihood that particular countries or political actors might engage in nuclear trafficking activities. A possible outcome of this research is a model describing the likelihood that a particular type of nuclear material might be transported into the United States. During our research, we found that many of the analysts we interacted with were overwhelmed by the amount of data they could interact with in their current toolset [6]. These data primarily comprised web search results obtained through a variety of sources.

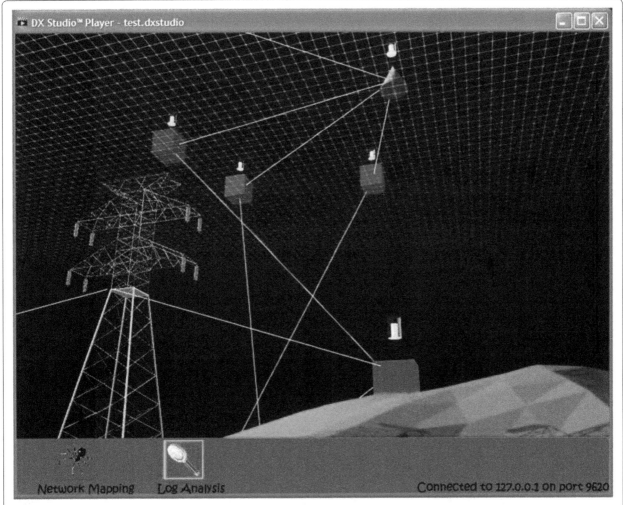

Figure 6 The Energy Infrastructure Security Game. This screenshot shows a portion of the Energy Infrastructure Security Game.

To help offset this overload, the KEF Model (specifically Stages 2 and 3) is formulated to streamline the information capture and analysis process.

When analysts visit the ITD site, they can see at a glance the various types of content that have already been harvested and incorporated into KEF. In Figure 7, the majority of the data has come from social media sources, primarily blogs. There is, however, also a series of traditional journal articles, books, conference papers, and presentations, some of which were entered manually as seed documents to aid in the ADM. Analysts can select a particular type of document (e.g., social media) and load a faceted browser, as seen in Figure 8, to drill down into that data.

All of these social media data have been automatically harvested by KEF. A SME has already vetted these data and allowed it to be entered into the wiki. After using the faceted browser to narrow down the original results (in

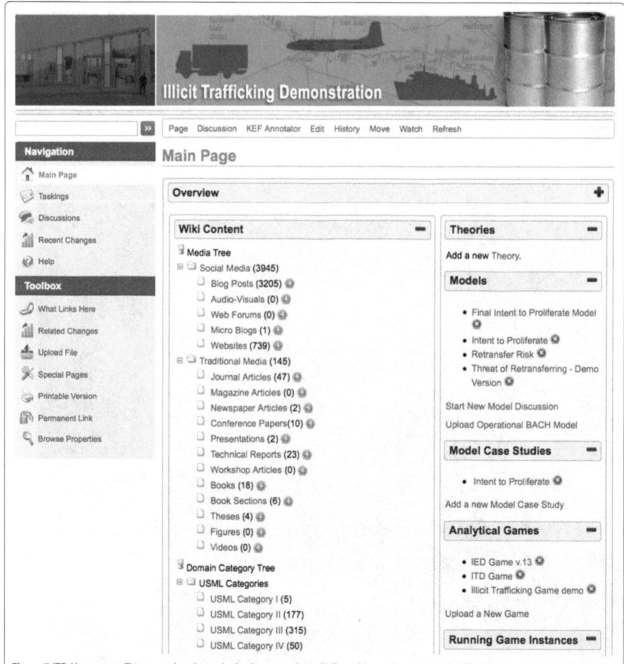

Figure 7 ITD Homepage. This screenshot shows the landing page that a SME would see when visiting the ITD KEF site, including links to the various types of documents, available models, analytical games, and the collaborative discussion forum and taskings areas.

Figure 8 ITD social media faceted browser. This screenshot shows the ability to filter social media content based on a series of criteria such as author, date, and interesting phrases.

this case, we started with approximately 4000 documents), the SME can select a single entry to view the document, as seen in Figure 9, as it was harvested from the web.

This example of an individual record in KEF contain several key pieces of information and capabilities:

- key information about the article (e.g., title, author, source)
- metadata about the article (e.g., KEF project, number of comments, and whether this document is used to seed future harvests from the ADM)
- the original content

- history of the article within KEF (to preserve provenance of harvest, edits, and modifications)

From this individual blog post, the SME has several options. The KEF Annotator (as seen in Figure 10), was custom developed by the KEF team to enable analysts to further semantically mark up the document by highlighting phrases that are of particular interest. The discussion option will transport the user to the threaded discussion area of KEF, as seen in Figure 11, where the SME can join an existing discussion surrounding this particular article or start a new one.

Figure 9 ITD blog post. This screenshot shows harvested content from a blog after it has been placed into the KEF environment.

If the analyst instead decides to focus on an existing model, they could go into a data model directly from the homepage. KEF is not, itself, a modeling framework. However, we have built the capability into KEF to visualize models and associate evidence with particular nodes from the model. Figure 12 shows a BACH model being viewed in the model visualizer.

This model visualizer is accompanied by pages of documentation that explain each node. KEF also allows for the alignment of evidence, both manually entered and harvested through the ADM, with any part of the model.

KEF evolution since the illicit trafficking demonstration
ITD was very precisely targeted at one domain, nuclear trafficking and nonproliferation. Since KEF's inception we have completed projects in a number of other domains such as cyber security [49], renewable energy [50], biomedical nanotechnology, signature discovery [51], multiscale science, semantic technologies, carbon

sequestration [52], microbial communities [53], visual analytics, mass spectrometry, and computer supported cooperative work (CSCW). We have found, over the past three years, that our original concept of "what KEF is" to an analyst has evolved somewhat. We find that the overarching concept of KEF, that collection of open source applications, community extensions, and custom development, is largely the same. However, we have also found that KEF implementations can be successful even when they omit some elements of the framework, depending on the needs of the project and the subject domain. These needs have also driven the development of new options in the framework, including the internal management of modeling data and the integration discussion topics in-line with wiki content.

Management of data for models
Multiple projects, across a number of domains, have recently approached us about KEF's data modeling capability. In the past, it was assumed that KEF would be used

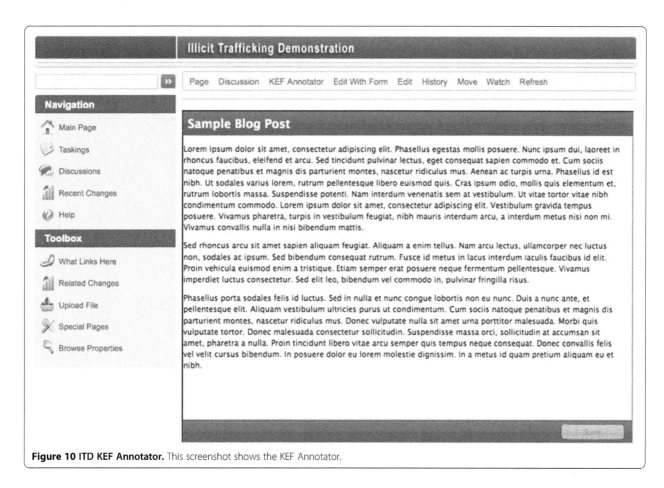

Figure 10 ITD KEF Annotator. This screenshot shows the KEF Annotator.

as a way of marshaling evidence to support models, but this modeling would not necessarily be done in the KEF environment. Current development is aimed not only at aligning evidence with these models (e.g., BACH) but also managing the data itself:

- Recent work with projects dealing with radical rhetoric [54], business intelligence, and building component data has modified analyst workflows. For example, through KEF, an analyst can start with a large data set, use the faceted browser to filter out unwanted or unneeded data, and then send that data directly into a modeling framework running in parallel with the wiki environment. Users can control the data that they run through models much more accurately, thanks to the filtering they apply in KEF before exporting the data into the model.
- Similar work is being pursued to allow data maintained in KEF to be exported directly into visualization tools such as Scalable Reasoning System (SRS) [55] or IN-SPIRE™ [56], giving users access to additional analytical tools beyond the existing gaming and charting frameworks.
- KEF's growing capabilities for managing large quantities of structured data in a user-friendly way

give SMEs and other users easy access to data that they might not otherwise locate.
- This increasing use of KEF in managing model data also highlights the benefit of working with SMW, as the wiki already has an established programming language for interacting with its data and allowing external applications to gain access to it.

Discussion threads in-line with content

It is uncommon, unfortunately, for users of KEF to take full advantage of the current implementation of discussion forums. Web analytical data from KEF sites and responses from project managers after deployments often indicate that a discussion forum topic about content in the wiki will see significantly less traffic than the wiki content page itself. The responses to the discussion topic are typically even fewer than the number of "reads" that the topic receives. In an effort to better engage users in meaningful discussions, we developed an in-line discussion feature that allows content contained on a wiki page to be discussed in an integrated, threaded discussion located on the same wiki page. We believe that the threaded discussion forum still has value, as it gives users a view of "what has been discussed since I was last here." We also believe, based on our analytical data and

View unanswered posts I View active topics   View new posts I View your posts

Board Index			All times are UTC - 8 hours [DST]

[Moderator Control Panel]

Mark all forums read

Forum	Topics	Posts	Last post
ITD Model Discussions	13	24	Wed Oct 20, 2010 2:41 pm Roderick Riensche
Other Model Discussions	0	0	No posts
ITD Scenario Discussions	0	0	No posts
Gaming Discussions	0	0	No posts
KEF Discussions	15	52	Wed Aug 18, 2010 5:05 pm Andrew Piatt
Initiative Discussions	0	0	No posts
ITD Feedback	5	8	Thu May 06, 2010 8:49 am Andrew Piatt

Delete all board cookies I The team

Who is online

In total there is **1** user online :: 1 registered, 0 hidden and 0 guests (based on users active over the past 5 minutes)

Most users ever online was 5 on Fri Jul 30, 2010 8:25 am

Registered users: Michael Madison

Legend :: Administrators, Global moderators

Statistics

Total posts **84** I Total topics **32** I Total members **29** I Our newest member Mikhail Akopov

Figure 11 ITD discussion forums. This screenshot shows the discussion forums.

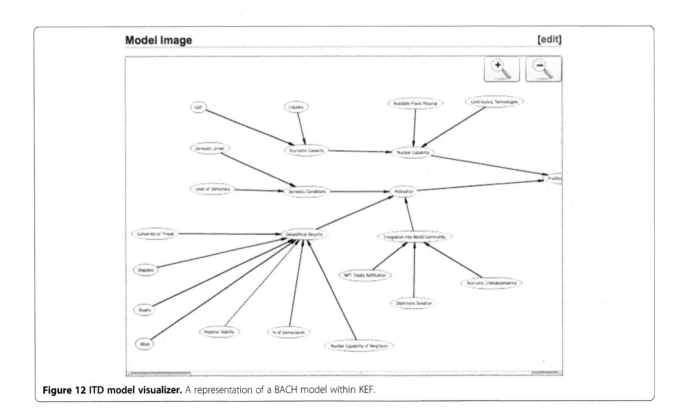

Figure 12 ITD model visualizer. A representation of a BACH model within KEF.

user interactions, that by placing the discussion in-line with the content, more users will be exposed to the conversation and encouraged to participate.

Increased data scaling

In the original KEF model, we expected that analysts would be harvesting a combination of traditional and social media. However, some years ago, the volume of social media data was significantly less than it is at the time of this writing. Clients also have become interested in exploring large data sets (tens of thousands of records) within KEF, using its faceted browser and visualization tools to explore these data. As a result, KEF regularly must increase the scale of the data we can handle. Additional work with Apache SOLR, as well as continued tweaking of the MySQL database, is continually underway to allow for increasing quantities of data to be hosted seamlessly within the KEF environment.

Conclusions

The Knowledge Encapsulation Framework represents a leap forward in the collaborative process of teams across many domains. We have presented a collaborative workspace for analysts to gather, automatically discover, annotate, and store relevant information. The combination of automatically harvested material with user vetting helps the researcher effectively handle the potentially large quantities of data available while providing a measure of quality control. The use of the faceted browser allows users to explore large quantities of data, filtering the total number of results down into a more easily managed subset.

As we interact with an increasing number of domains, we find that the ease of use of the Semantic Forms throughout our sites greatly increases the quality of data that our users provide. Many of our projects start with relatively unstructured data, and after working with KEF, users have an easily managed and searchable repository of data.

We are continuing to evolve and mature the technology described in this paper. We already anticipate that work with evolving and new forms of social media, visual analytic tools, mobile devices, and additional collaborative tools (e.g., Drupal [57]) will continue to play an important role in our current and future projects.

Abbreviations

ADM: Automated Discovery Mechanism; BACH: Bayesian Analysis of Competing Hypotheses; BioCat: National Biosurveillance Integration System; CBR: Chemical Biological and Radiological; CMS: Content Management System; CPSE: Collaborative Problem Solving Environments; CSCW: Computer Supported Cooperative Work; DHS: Department of Homeland Security; DOE: Department Of Energy; EERE: Department of Energy's Office of Energy Efficiency and Renewable Energy; EPRI: Electric Power Research Institute; IED: Improvised Explosive Devices; ITD: Illicit Trafficking Demonstration; KEF: Knowledge Encapsulation Framework; MHK: Marine HydroKinetic; MIT: Massachusetts Institute of Technology; NER: Named Entity Recognizer; NLP: Natural Language Processing; PHPBB: PHP Bulletin Board; PNNL: Pacific Northwest National Laboratory; RSS: Really Simple Syndication; SME: Subject Matter Expert; SMW: Semantic Media Wiki; SRS: Scalable Reasoning System; TPA: Technosocial Predictive Analytics; TPAI: Technosocial Predictive Analytics Initiative; UNCC: University of North Carolina Charlotte; WYSIWYG: What You See Is What You Get.

Competing interests
The authors declare that they have no competing interests.

Authors' contributions
MM did provided significant contribution throughout the journal article and drafted the manuscript. AC and KF did much of the underlying research, and provided the information on the KEF process. RB provided the introduction, and information on other domain application. AP and PE provided use case and background information throughout. LM provided underlying research on NLP and provided information for the KEF model section. All authors read and approved the final manuscript.

Acknowledgements
This work was supported in part by the Pacific Northwest National Laboratory (PNNL) Technosocial Predictive Analytics Initiative. PNNL is operated by Battelle for the U.S. Department of Energy under Contract DE-AC06-76RL01830. The authors are indebted to reviewers and editors that have helped refine this paper and the associated research. PNNL Information Release No. PNWD-SA-9613.

Author details
[1]Pacific Northwest National Laboratory, 902 Battelle Boulevard, 999, MSIN K7-28 Richland, WA 99352, USA. [2]State of Washington, 735B Desoto Ave, Tumwater, WA 98512, USA.

References
1. F Barjak, Research productivity in the internet era. Scientometrics **68**, 343–360 (2006)
2. KM Oliver, GL Wilkinson, LT Bennett, Evaluating the quality of internet information sources, in *ED-MEDIA & ED-TELECOM 97, June 14-19, 1997* (Association for the Advancement of Computing in Education, Calgary, 1997). http://www.eric.ed.gov/PDFS/ED412927.pdf
3. N Jennings, Twitter volume on the most tumultuous day of the campaign. Washington Post Blog (2012). 1/21/2012. Washington DC. Web. 3/12/2012. http://www.washingtonpost.com/blogs/election-2012/post/twitter-volume-on-the-most-tumultuous-day-of-the-campaign-atmentionmachine/2012/01/20/gIQAkHVEGQ_blog.html
4. Twitter, *Twitter Numbers* (Twitter Blog, San Francisco, 2011). Web. 3/12/2012. http://blog.twitter.com/2011/03/numbers.html
5. A Sanfilippo, *Technosocial Predictive Analytics Initiative* (Pacific Northwest National Laboratory, Richland, 2011). Web.3/12/2012. http://predictiveanalytics.pnnl.gov
6. A Sanfilippo, AJ Cowell, L Malone, R Riensche, J Thomas, S Unwin, P Whitney, PC Wong, Technosocial predictive analytics in support of naturalistic decision making, in *9th Bi-annual international conference on naturalistic decision making (NDM9)* (BCS, London, 2009)
7. MC Madison, AK Fligg, AW Piatt, AJ Cowell, *Knowledge Encapsulation Framework* (Pacific Northwest National Laboratory, Richland, 2011). Web. 3/12/2012. http://kef.pnnl.gov
8. JP Ignizio, *Introduction to expert systems: The development and implementation of rule-based expert systems* (McGraw Hill, New York, 1991)
9. P Jackson, *Introduction to expert systems* (Addison Wesley, Boston, 1998)
10. AJ Cowell, ML Gregory, EJ Marshall, LR McGrath, Knowledge encapsulation framework for collaborative social modeling, in *Association for the advancement of artificial intelligence (AAAI)* (AAAI Press, Chicago, 2009)
11. AJ Cowell, KM Stanney, Manipulation of non verbal interaction style and demographic embodiment to increase anthropomorphic computer character credibility. Int J Hum Comput Stud Spec Issue: Subtle Expressivity for Characters and Robots **62**(2), 281–306 (2005)
12. EH Shortliffe, *Computer-based medical consultations MYCIN* (Elsevier, New York, 1976)
13. H Pople, *CADUCEUS An experimental expert system for medical diagnosis* (MIT Press, Cambridge MA, 1984)

14. R Sanguesa, J Pujol, Netexpert: Agent-based expertise location by means of social and knowledge networks, in *Knowledge management and organizational memories*, ed. by R. Dieng-Kuntz, N. Matta, First Editionth edn. (Springer, New York, 2002), pp. 159–168

15. P Dean, T Hoverd, D Howlett, *KnowledgeBench* (Cambridgeshire, United Kingdom,). Web. 3/12/2012. http://www.knowledgebench.com

16. RG Smith, JD Baker, The dipmeter advisor system: a case study in commercial expert system development, in *Proceedings of the eighth international joint conference on artificial intelligence (IJCAI'83), August 8-12, 1983; Karlsruhe, Germany* (Morgan Kaufmann Publishers Inc, San Francisco, 1983)

17. D Gracio, *Knowledge foundations & collaboratories: Bringing together people, tools, and science* (Pacific Northwest National Laboratory, Richland, 2008). http://www.pnl.gov/science/highlights/highlight.asp?id=225

18. RT Kouzes, JD Myers, WA Wulf, Collaboratories: doing science on the Internet. Computer **29**(8), 40–46 (1996)

19. I Gorton, C Sivaramakrishnan, G Black, S White, S Purohit, C Lansing, M Madison, K Schuchardt, Y Liu, A Velo, Knowledge-Management Framework for Modeling and Simulation. Computing Sci Eng **14**(2), 12–23 (2012)

20. VR Watson, Supporting scientific analysis within collaborative problem solving environments, in *HICSS 34 Minitrack on Collaborative Problem Solving Environments, January 3-6, 2001* (IEEE, Maui, 2001)

21. CA Shaffer, *Collaborative problem solving environments* (Virginia Tech, Blacksburg, 2008). Web. 3/12/2012. http://people.cs.vt.edu/~shaffer/Papers/DICPMShaffer.html

22. D Vesset, HD Morris, *The business value of predictive analytics* (IBM SPSS, San Jose, California, 2011)

23. SAS Institute Inc, *SAS architecture for business analytics* (SAS Institute Inc, Cary, NC, 2010)

24. A Vance, B Stone, Palantir the War on Terror's Secret Weapon, in *Business Week* (2011). Web. 3/12/2012. http://www.businessweek.com/magazine/palantir-the-vanguard-of-cyberterror-security-11222011.html

25. A Kittur, RE Kraut, Harnessing the wisdom of crowds in Wikipedia: quality through coordination, in *CSCW '08 Proceedings of the 2008 ACM conference on Computer supported cooperative work ACM, November 8-12, 2008; San Diego* (ACM, New York, 2008)

26. NS Friedland, PG Allen, G Matthews, M Witbrock, D Baxter, J Curtis, B Shepard, P Miraglia, J Angele, S Staab, E Moench, H Oppermann, D Wenke, D Israel, V Chaudhri, B Porter, K Barker, J Fan, SY Chaw, P Yeh, D Tecuci, P Clark, Project Halo: towards a digital Aristotle. AI Mag. **25**(4), 29–48 (2004)

27. S Singh, J Allanach, H Tu, K Pattipati, P Willett, Stochastic modeling of a terrorist event via the ASAM system, in *2004 IEEE International Conference on Systems Man and Cybernetics, October 10-13, 2004; The Hague, The Netherlands* (IEEE, Piscataway, 2004)

28. WikiMedia Project, Welcome to MediaWiki.org. (2012). Web. 3/12/2012. http://www.mediawiki.org

29. M Krötzsch, D Vrandečić, M Völkel, Semantic MediaWiki. Lecture Notes in Computer Science **4273**, 935–942 (2006)

30. Y Koren, *Semantic Forms* (2012). Web. 3/12/2012. http://www.mediawiki.org/wiki/Extension:Semantic_Forms

31. M Stefaner, User interface design, in *Dynamic taxonomies and faceted search: Theory,practice, and experience*, ed. by G. Sacco, Y. Tzitzikas. The Information Retrieval Series, Vol. 25 (Springer, New York, 2009)

32. Apache, *Apache SOLR*. Web. 3/12/2012. http://lucene.apache.org/solr/

33. D Pean, A Wright, J Phoenix, *Social Profile*, 2012. Web. 3/12/2012. http://www.mediawiki.org/wiki/Extension:SocialProfile

34. Ontoprise GmbH, *HaloACL* (, 2012). Web. 3/12/2012. http://www.mediawiki.org/wiki/Extension:Access_Control_List

35. *PHPBB*. (2012). Web. 3/12/2012. http://www.phpbb.com/

36. *Wordpress*. Web. 3/12/2012. http://wordpress.com/

37. B Carpenter, Phrasal queries with LingPipe and Lucene, in *Proceedings of the 13th Meeting of the Text Retrieval Conference (TREC), November 16-19, 2004; Gaithersburg, Maryland* (National Institute of Standards and Technology, Gaithersburg, 2004)

38. Amazon.com, Inc, *Amazon.com statistically improbable phrases*. Web. 3/12/2012. http://www.amazon.com/gp/search-inside/sipshelp.html

39. ML Gregory, LR McGrath, EB Bell, K O'Hara, K Domico, Domain independent knowledge base population from structured and unstructured data sources, in *Association for the Advancement of Artificial Intelligence* (AAAI Press, San Francisco, 2011)

40. A Sanfilippo, LR Franklin, S Tratz, GR Danielson, N Mileson, R Riensche, L McGrath, Automating frame analysis in social computing behavioral modeling and prediction, in *Social Computing, Behavioral Modeling, and Prediction*, ed. by H. Liu, J.J. Salerno, M.J. Young (Springer, New York, 2008), pp. 239–248

41. A Sanfilippo, B Baddeley, C Posse, P Whitney, A layered dempster-shafer approach to scenario construction and analysis intelligence and security informatics, in *IEEE International Conference on Intelligence and Security Informatics 2007 (ISI 2007), May 23-24, 2007; New Brunswick, NJ* (IEEE, Piscataway, NJ, 2007), pp. 95–102

42. Y Li, D McLean, ZA Bandar, JD O'Shea, K Crockett, Sentence similarity based on semantic nets and corpus statistics. IEEE Trans on Knowledge and Data Engineering **18**(8), 1138–1150 (2006)

43. T Pedersen, S Patwardham, J Michelizzi, WordNet: similarity measuring the relatedness of concepts, in *Proceedings of the nineteenth national conference on artificial intelligence (AAAI-04), July 25-29, 2004; San Jose, CA* (AAAI Press, Menlo Park, CA, 2004), pp. 1024–1025

44. V Kolhatkar, *An extended analysis of a method of all words sense disambiguation. MSc thesis* (Department of Coputer Science, University of Minnesota)

45. AJ Cowell, RS Jensen, ML Gregory, PC Ellis, K Fligg, LR McGrath, OH Kelly, E Bell, Collaborative knowledge discovery & marshalling for intelligence & security applications, in *2010 IEEE international conference on intelligence and security informatics (ISI) May 23-26, 2010; Vancouver BC Canada* (IEEE, Piscataway, NJ, 2010), pp. 233–238

46. R Riensche, LR Franklin, PR Paulson, AJ Brothers, D Niesen, LM Martucci, RS Butner, G Danielson, Development of a model-driven analytical game: Observations and lessons learned, in *The 3rd international conference on human centric computing (HumanCom 10) August 11-13, 2010; Cebu, Philippines* (IEEE, Piscataway, NJ, 2010)

47. R Riensche, PR Paulson, G Danielson, S Unwin, RS Butner, S Miller, LR Franklin, N Zuljevic, Serious gaming for predictive analytics, in *AAAI spring symposium on technosocial predictive analytics, March 23-25, 2010* (AAAI Press, Stanford, CA, 2009)

48. R Riensche, LM Martucci, JC Scholts, MA Whiting, Application and evaluation of analytic gaming, in *International conference on computational science and engineering (2009 CSE '09), August 29-31, 2009; Vancouver BC, Canada* (IEEE, Piscataway, NJ, 2009), pp. 1169–1173

49. CD Corley, RT Brigantic, M Lancaster, J Chung, C Noonan, J Schweighardt, S Brown, AJ Cowell, AK Fligg, AW Piatt et al., BioCat: Operational biosurveillance model evaluations and catalog, in *Supercomputing 2011 Computational Biosurveillance Workshop, November 12-18, 2011* (IEEE, Seattle, 2011)

50. R Anderson, A Copping, F Can Cleave, S Unwin, E Hamilton, *Conceptual model of offshore wind environmental risk evaluation system: Environmental effects of offshore wind energy fiscal year 2010. PNNL-19500* (Pacific Northwest National Laboratory, Richland, WA, 2010)

51. Pacific Northwest National Laboratory, *Signature Discovery Initiative* (Pacific Northwest National Laboratory, Richland WA, 2012). Web. 3/12/2012. http://signatures.pnnl.gov/

52. Pacific Northwest National Laboratory, *Carbon Sequestration Initiative* (Pacific Northwest National Laboratory, Richland WA, 2011). Web.3/12/2012. http://csi.pnnl.gov

53. Pacific Northwest National Laboratory, *Microbes FSFA* (Pacific Northwest National Laboratory, Richland WA, 2011). Web.3/12/2012. http://microbes.pnl.gov/wiki/

54. A Sanfilippo, L McGrath, P Whitney, Violent frames in action. Dynamics of Asymmetric Conflict: Pathways Toward Terrorism and Genocide **4**(2), 103–112 (2011)

55. W Pike, J Bruce, B Baddeley, D Best, L Franklin, R May, D Rice, R Riensche, K Younkin, The scalable reasoning system: lightweight visualization for distributed analytics. Inf Vis **8**(1), 71–84 (2009)

56. Pacific Northwest National Laboratory, *IN-SPIRE™ Visual Document Analysis* (Pacific Northwest National Laboratory, Richland WA, 2012). Web. 3/12/2012. [http://in-spire.pnnl.gov/]

57. Drupal Association, *Drupal*. Web. 3/12/2012. http://drupal.org

2

Terrorist networks and the lethality of attacks: an illustrative agent based model on evolutionary principles

Paul Ormerod

Abstract

A data base developed from the Memorial Institute for the Prevention of Terrorism's (MIPT) Terrorism Knowledge Base for the years 1998–2005 was provided to participants in the workshop. The distribution of fatalities in terrorist attacks is, like many outcomes of human social and economic processes, heavily right-skewed. We propose an agent based model to analyse this, and to enable generalisations to be made from the historical data set. The model is inspired by modelling developments in cultural evolutionary theory. We argue that a more appropriate 'null' model of behaviour in the social sciences is on based upon the principle of copying, rather than the economic assumption of rationality in the standard social science model.

Keywords: Agent based model, Terrorist fatalities, Cultural evolution, Mutations

Introduction

Asal and Rethemeyer [1] report an econometric analysis of a data base developed from the Memorial Institute for the Prevention of Terrorism's (MIPT) Terrorism Knowledge Base. The dataset is complete for the years 1998–2005. Of the 395 clearly identified terrorist organizations operating throughout the world over this period, only 68 killed 10 or more people during that period. Indeed, only 28 killed more than 100 people. The econometric study analyses the factors which can account for this dramatic difference in organizational lethality.

They conclude that "(1) large organizations, (2) organizations that address supernatural audiences through religious ideologies, (3) organizations with religious-ethnonationalist ideologies— ideologies that define an other and play to the supernatural, (4) organizations that build and maintain extensive alliance connections with peers, and (5) organizations that maintain control over territory are the primary actors in this story. Though much of the organizational and social movements literature suggest that new organizations are less effective and able, our data was unable to find evidence that newness matters. Some widely held theories about the correlates of lethality—including the belief

that state sponsorship and "homebase" regime-type would affect organizational lethality—could not be substantiated with our data. In fact, there is equivocal evidence that state sponsorship tend to restrain killing by client organizations. Size coupled with religious and ethnonationalist ideology generates the capability needed to pursue deadly ends".

This paper considers a potential generalisation of the econometric approach using the methodology of agent based modelling (ABM). Section 2 briefly considers methodological aspects of the issue, and section 3 discusses some principles of agent behaviour. Section 4 sets out the model and section 5 discusses some illustrative results.

Some methodological reflections

The Asal and Rethemeyer paper is detailed and thorough, and takes proper account of the heavily right-skewed nature of the dependent variable, the number of people killed in each incident. The dependent variable ranges from 0 to 3505 with a median of 0, a mean of 31.36 and a standard deviation of 202.04. Of the 395 organizations for which there are data, 240 of those organizations perpetrated one or more incidents that resulted in no fatalities.

However, econometric analysis of data, no matter how sophisticated, essentially involves fitting a plane through

Correspondence: pormerod@volterra.co.uk
Volterra Partners LLP, London, UK

the n dimensions of the explanatory data. Even when the regression technique is based upon the principle of maximum likelihood, the result can still be given this geometric interpretation. Helbing [2] offers a more detailed description of the potential restrictions of this approach, but one of the essential problems can be summarised as follows.

A restriction on the ability to generalise from econometric results is that a small number of data points may exercise a strong influence on the fit of the n-dimensional plane. Consider, for example, the standard linear regression model $y = X\beta + \varepsilon$, where the vector of estimated parameters is $b = (X^T X)^{-1} X^T y$ and the fitted values are $y^* = Xb = X(X^T X)^{-1} X^T y$.

The hat matrix, H, maps the vector of fitted values to the vector of observed values, and describes the influence each observed value has on each fitted value [3], where $H = X(X^T X)^{-1} X^T$. It is the orthogonal projection onto the column space of the matrix of explanatory factors, X.

This matrix can be used to identify observations which have a large influence on the results of a regression. If such observations exist, ideally we would like to have more data from this part of the observation space. So if we have a small number of observations in the tail of the distributions of both an explanatory and the dependent variable and these are correlated, such observations will inevitably exercise a strong influence on the results.

Perhaps not surprisingly, therefore, large terrorist organisations, and particularly those which maintain and build extensive alliances, are identified in econometric analysis as being two of the key factors which are linked to effective attacks leading to high levels of fatality.

However, more generally, we are interested not so much in projecting the single path of history which we actually observe into the future, but in considering the evolutionary potential of the groups. The policy message from the econometrics is to focus on large, well connected groups in the prevention of attacks. But, for example, what is the potential for small, less connected groups to acquire the ability to develop the capacity to carry out highly effective attacks?

Agent based modelling is a way of trying to examine the evolutionary potential of any given system. Helbing and Barietti [4], for example, state that 'computer simulation can be seen as experimental technique for hypothesis testing and scenario analysis'. They go on to argue that 'agent-based simulations are suited for detailed hypothesis-testing, i.e. for the study of the consequences of ex-ante hypotheses regarding the interactions of agents. One could say that they can serve as a sort of magnifying glass or telescope ("socioscope"), which may be used to understand our reality better... by modeling the

relationships on the level of individuals in a rule-based way, agent-based simulations allow one to produce characteristic features of the system as emergent phenomena without having to make a priori assumptions regarding the aggregate ("macroscopic") system properties'.

Approaches to agent behaviour
The standard socio-economic science model, SSSM [5], postulates a high level of cognitive ability on the part of agents. Agents are assumed to be able to gather all relevant information, and to process it in such a way as to arrive at an optimal decision, given their (fixed) tastes and preferences. Even with the relaxation of the assumption of complete information [6], agents are still presumed to have formidable cognitive powers. This, the core model of economics, has a certain amount of explanatory power, though as [5] goes on to state; 'Within economics there is essentially only one model to be adapted to every application: optimization subject to constraints due to resource limitations, institutional rules and/or the behavior of others, as in Cournot-Nash equilibria. The economic literature is not the best place to find new inspiration beyond these traditional technical methods of modeling'.

Perhaps the most important challenge to this approach comes when decisions do not depend not on omniscient cost-benefit analysis of isolated agents with fixed tastes and preferences, but when the decision of any given agent depends in part directly on what other actors are doing. In such situations, which are probably the norm rather than the exception in social settings, not only do choices involve many options for which costs and benefits would be impossible to calculate (e.g., what friends to keep, what job to pursue, what game to play, etc.), but the preferences of agents themselves evolve over time in the light of what others do.

Complex choices can be fundamentally different from simple two-choice scenarios, such that the problem becomes very difficult to predict, as has been demonstrated in ecological [7] and human settings [8]. Such scenarios are where so-called zero-intelligence models [9] do better at understanding emergent patterns in collective behaviour. However, despite their empirical success e.g. [10-12], they have met with resistance amongst social scientists.

The zero intelligence model is based upon the particle model of physics. Indeed, one of the fastest-rising keywords in the physics literature is 'social'. Literally thousands of papers in physics are devoted to modeling social systems, and indeed regular sections of leading journals such as *Physica A* and *Physical Review E* are devoted to this topic. The analogy between people and particles has been so consistent that a recent popular review was appropriately titled *The Social Atom* [11].

This approach has provided significant insights into modeling collective interactions in social systems, from Internet communities to pedestrian and vehicular traffic, economic markets and even prehistoric human migrations e.g. [13-15].

The idea that there are serious limits to human cognitive powers in complex systems is one which has strong empirical support. Kahneman, for example [16] argues that 'humans reason poorly and act intuitively'. Decisions may often be taken in circumstances in which the assumption that individuals have no knowledge of the situation is a better approximation to reality than is the assumption that they possess complete information and have the capacity to process this information to make optimal decisions.

An illustration of the limits to human awareness and social calculation is the well known Prisoner's Dilemma game, invented by Drescher and Flood in 1950. The optimal strategy or "Nash equilibrium" for the one period game was discovered very quickly. However, as documented in detail in [17]. Flood recruited distinguished RAND analysts John Williams and Armen Alchian, a mathematician and economist respectively, to play 100 repetitions of the game. The Nash equilibrium strategy ought to have been played by completely rational individuals 100 times. It might, of course, have taken a few plays for these high-powered academics to learn the strategy. But Alchian chose co-operation rather than the Nash strategy of defection 68 times, and Williams no fewer than 78 times. Their recorded comments are fascinating in themselves. Williams, the mathematician, began by expecting both players to co-operate, whereas Alchian the economist expected defection, but as the game progressed, co-operation became the dominant choice of both players.

Even now, after almost 60 years of analysis and literally thousands of scientific papers on the subject, when sufficient uncertainty is introduced into the game, the optimal strategy remains unknown. Certainly, some strategies do better than most in many circumstances, but no one has yet discovered the optimal strategy even for a game that is as simple to describe as the Prisoner's Dilemma.

Assumptions of optimality and rationality can be certainly be useful when payoffs are predictable from one event to the next – hunting and gathering in a consistent environment, for example, or even modern situations where the complexity of choices is low [18]. But more generally, the zero intelligence model may be more useful as the 'null'.

However, as is argued in [19], human agents are fundamentally different from particles in physics in that, however imperfectly, they can act with purpose and intent. So the basic null model of zero intelligence needs

to be modified to incorporate some aspect of this functionality [20].

Simon in his seminal paper on behavioural economics [21] argued that the fundamental issue which all sentient beings have to take into account when taking decisions is to reduce the massive dimensionality of the choice set which they face: 'Broadly stated, the task is to replace the global rationality of economic man with a kind of rational behavior that is compatible with the access to information, and the computational capacities that are actually possessed by organisms, including man, in the kinds of environments in which such organisms exist'.

An important way of coping with an evolving, complex environment is to follow a strategy of copying, or social learning as it is described in cultural evolution. In social and economic systems, decision makers often pay attention to each other either because they have limited information about the problem itself or limited ability to process even the information that is available [22].

A striking example of the power of simple copying strategies in an evolving environment is provided by the computer tournament described by [23]). As the abstract states: 'Social learning (learning through observation or interaction with other individuals) is widespread in nature and is central to the remarkable success of humanity, yet it remains unclear why copying is profitable and how to copy most effectively. To address these questions, we organized a computer tournament in which entrants submitted strategies specifying how to use social learning and its asocial alternative (for example, trial-and-error learning) to acquire adaptive behavior in a complex environment. Most current theory predicts the emergence of mixed strategies that rely on some combination of the two types of learning. In the tournament, however, strategies that relied heavily on social learning were found to be remarkably successful, even when asocial information was no more costly than social information. Social learning proved advantageous because individuals frequently demonstrated the highest-payoff behavior in their repertoire, inadvertently filtering information for copiers. The winning strategy relied nearly exclusively on social learning and weighted information according to the time since acquisition'.

In other words, in a complex environment in which the pay-off to various strategies was, by design, constantly evolving, simple copying proved a very effective strategy.

Copying, of course, is the essence of the principle of preferential attachment, initially formulated in a general way by Simon [24] and rediscovered by Barabasi and Albert [25]. In its more recent incarnation, the model has been hugely influential because it resulted in a power law (or at least long-tailed) degree distribution (connections per network node) – a kind of distribution so intriguing to many that the editor of *Wired* magazine wrote an entire book, ten years later, about its significance to modern online economies [26].

However, a key drawback of the approach is that it is ultimately static. The rankings in the distribution, in other words, gradually become fixed, and attempts to modify the basic model are rather artificial [27]. Turnover in rankings is not just a feature of modern markets of popular culture, but operates on the time scale required for cities to evolve [28].

Preferential attachment is a special case of a model developed in cultural evolutionary theory e. g, [29,30], in which it remains the basic principle of decision making, but an agent is also able (with a small probability) to make an innovative choice. The model is developed from the concept of genetic evolution, which is based on the principles of copying and mutation (innovation).

In its most recent and most general formulation [31] the model of social learning in cultural evolution is, with just two parameters, capable of replicating *any* right skewed distribution and of accounting for the turnover which is observed in relative standings in any evolutionary environment. One parameter describes the relative frequencies with which preferential attachment (copying) and innovation are used to make decisions, and the other describes the span of historical time used to observe the decisions which other agents have made. Clearly, this latter is different for a firm choosing its location to a teenager choosing which video to download from YouTube.

The model

In order to try to generalise from the data set used by Asal and Rethemeyer, we retain copying as one of the basic principles used by terrorist organisations. They can observe and copy, exactly as in the evolutionary learning computer tournament, tactics and strategies used by other organisations. In a situation in which the environment in which they operate evolves, the pay off (i.e. number of fatalities inflicted) may of course differ from previously enacted versions of the same tactic. But copying is one of the building blocks of the model.

We augment the model with further behavioural principles which seem appropriate in this context. By its very nature, the terrorist world is clandestine, and organisations will differ in their propensity to share information about tactical capabilities with other such organisations. In addition, organisations will differ in their willingness or ability to absorb and execute a tactic they have not previously used, even if it is explained to them by another organisation.

We consider these factors in the context of the ability of the organisations to acquire the capacity to carry out an innovation, or tactical mutation, developed by a terrorist group. An overview of the model is shown in

Figure 1, which is similar to the model developed to account for the diffusion of technological innovations across companies in four industries in the Greater Manchester region of the UK [32]: The model takes an initial mutation to be exogenous and it is taken up by one agent/organisation at the outset. The characteristics of the agents are governed by their willingness to innovate, their desire to keep innovation to themselves, and their willingness to communicate with others. The innovating agent will be connected to other agents via the network structure, and at the next step of the model the innovation will be passed on according to the extent agents discover the mutation and their own willingness to take it up. At further steps of the model further agents may be able to discover and take up the mutation, until eventually no further take up occurs.

We define two different methods by which tactical mutations may be passed on via the network linkages. The first is a direct relationship between two partners, while the second is a group relationship.

First, an organisation with an innovation will provide it to another only if its level of secrecy, or the propensity of a group to try to retain the benefits of its innovations, is less than the absorptive capacity, or the degree to

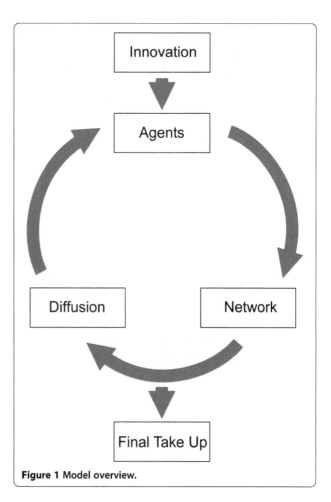

Figure 1 Model overview.

which a terrorist actively engages in activities which enable it to identify and adopt new innovations, of the organisations it is linked with. This method of adopting an mutation represents a mutual relationship or exchange between terrorist organisations and implies a degree of trust or collaboration.

The second method for spreading a mutation is based on the principle of copying. Here if a group looks at the spectrum of organisations to which it is linked and finds that the proportion that have adopted an innovation is higher than their own personal threshold, they will mimic their behaviour and adopt the mutation. In some circumstances this threshold may be very high and only when all or nearly all of the other groups an organisation has relationships with have taken up an innovation will they be persuaded to do the same. For other organisations relatively few outfits may have to have the same innovation before they adopt it. This mechanism represents a copying behaviour. This may occur even when a terrorist group may not fully understand the reasons and benefits of a mutation but relies on observing that others have adopted it. This behaviour is more likely to be a response to competitor behaviour.

Figure 2 plots the distribution of the numbers of connections between organisations in the data set.

In each separate solution of the model, a network is generated which has the same distribution as that of the data. More precisely, the null hypothesis that the model network has the same degree distribution as the data is not rejected on a Kolmogorov-Smirnov test at a p-value <0.01, far below the conventional level of statistical significance. In other words, we can regard the model networks as being identical in degree distribution to the actual data.

In this illustrative application of the model:

- Each agent is allocated at random a willingness to seek and adopt an innovation/mutation, α_i, drawn from a uniform on [0,1].

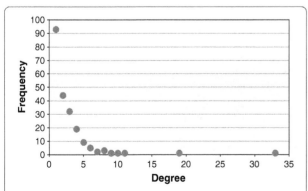

Figure 2 Degree distribution of connections between terrorist organisations.

- Each agent is allocated at random a willingness to share an innovation, σ_j, drawn from a uniform on [0,1].
- An agent adopts the innovation of another if $\alpha_i > \sigma_j$.
- Each agent has a threshold for imitating the innovations of its neighbours, τ_i drawn from uniform on [0.5,1].

This latter rule is the principle of binary choice (adopt or not adopt) with externalities [21,33].

The model proceeds in a series of steps, in each of which the following procedure is operated. First, all agents not in possession of the mutation who are not connected to any other organisation which does have the innovation are identified. These agents play no further part in this particular step of the model. Of course, in subsequent steps, agents to which they are connected may by then have acquired the mutation. So whilst they may not acquire it in this period, they are not precluded from so doing in future steps within the same solution of the model.

If the absorptive capacity, α_i of the agent without the innovation is greater than the willingness to share (or secrecy), σ_j, of the agent with the innovation, the agent is assumed to adopt the innovation. If not, the copying rule is then invoked, and the agent adopts it if its threshold is lower than the proportion of agents to which it is connected which has the innovation.

Any particular solution of the model ends when no agent adopts the mutation in a given step of the model. We measure and record the proportion of agents which have adopted the innovation.

This process is the basic building block of the illustrative approach. We can readily imagine, however, that certain capabilities are inherently harder to acquire than others. Shooting a civilian (e.g. a member of the IRA shooting a Protestant at random in Northern Ireland) requires much lower levels of skill and expertise than a co-ordinated bombing. We illustrate the effects of introducing this into the model in the following heuristic way.

We populate the model with 1000 agents and solve it 1000 times. At the end of each solution, the organisations which have acquired the innovation are deemed capable of carrying out a relatively low level attack, which we describe as Level 1 capability. The model is reinitialised, a new agent is selected at random to acquire an innovation, and the process is repeated. At the end of this, more agents will have acquired Level capability. And those which acquired it in the first solution and in addition acquire it in this new one are deemed to have acquired Level 2 capability. In other words, they have acquired sufficient technical skill to mount more serious attacks, with presumed higher levels of fatalities.

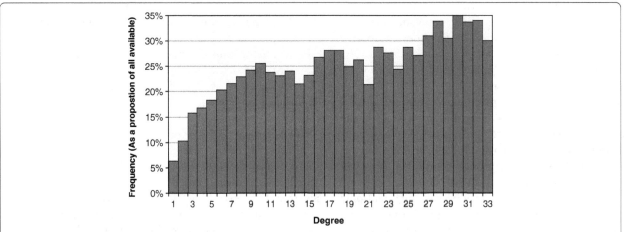

Figure 3 Proportion of terrorist organisations for each value of degree of connections which acquire the capability to carry out Level 1 attacks, average across 1,000 solutions.

Finally, we repeat the process again, and those agents which acquire the innovation on all three occasions are deemed capable of Level 3 attacks.

Discussion and results

Some properties of the model are illustrated in the three graphs below. These are the results averaged across 1,000 separate solutions of the model, and show the total percentage of organisations with a given degree (number) of links which acquire the capabilities to acquire the ability to carry out Levels 1, 2 and 3-type attacks.

First, Figure 3 shows the results for Level 1 capabilities.

Quite rapidly, the connection between the acquisition of this level of capability and the degree of an organisation's links with other terrorist groups falls away. Only a very small percentage of groups with a very low number of connections are able to acquire even this level of

capability. But the proportion of organisations which acquire it and which have, say, just 6 links is not very different from the proportion of those with 26 links which acquire. Only for those with a very high number of connections does the proportion rise.

Figures 4 and 5 show the results for the proportions which acquire Levels 2 and 3 capabilities.

The precise topology of the network and the parameters allocated to each agent differ across each of the 1,000 solutions of the model, but the same network and parameter values are retained within each solution for each of the steps of acquisition capability. So, for example, the structure may be such that an agent is connected to another which is very likely to acquire the mutation, and the parameters are such (in particular the absorption and secrecy parameters) that it, too, is therefore likely to acquire it. So the proportion of agents of any given degree acquiring Level 3 capability is not

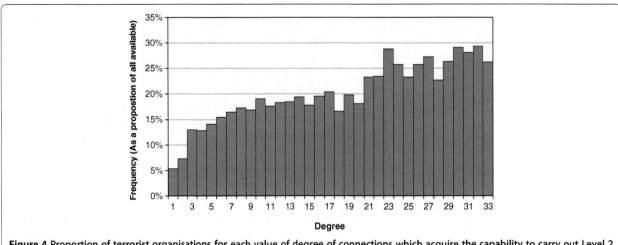

Figure 4 Proportion of terrorist organisations for each value of degree of connections which acquire the capability to carry out Level 2 attacks, average across 1,000 solutions.

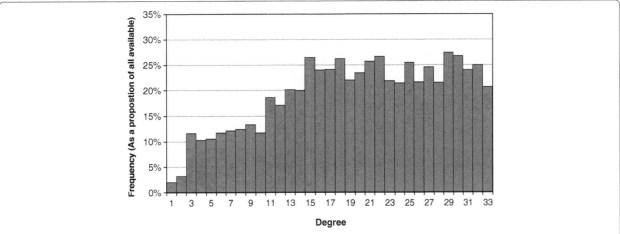

Figure 5 Proportion of terrorist organisations for each value of degree of connections which acquire the capability to carry out Level 3 attacks, average across 1,000 solutions.

simply (as an approximation) one third the value of those acquiring Level 1, but is much higher.

These results are illustrative of a principle of how to try to generalize from the data set. Indeed, we see that the proportion of organizations with only weak connections to others which acquire level 3 capabilities is, apart from those with virtually none, non-trivial. So although in the one actual history we are able to observe, organizations with low levels of connections tended not to carry out attacks involving high levels of fatalities, this does not mean that in future they will be unable to acquire such characteristics.

We are not claiming that this is a definite model with which to inform future policy, though it does offer some potential guidelines. Rather, it illustrates how an agent based model constructed on evolutionary principles in a complex environment can be used to extract more information from a data set than is possible using conventional analytical methods such as econometrics. One potential extensions is to endogenise the network, such that agents have incentives to develop new links, but also introducing extinctions of agents, which may be enhanced (made easier for the authorities) as the number of connections of an organization increase ([34] offers a general model of extinctions in an evolving network). Another is to endogenise the parameters, so that agent behavior becomes reinforced both by reference to their own previous decisions and by reference to the properties of their neighbours.

Competing interests
The author declares that he has no competing interests.
Paper presented at the Department of Homeland Security Workshop on Biologically-Inspired Approaches to Understanding and Predicting Social Dynamics, Washington DC, August 2009.

References
1. V Asal, KR Rethemeyer, The nature of the beast: organizational structure and the lethality of terrorist attacks. J. Polit. **70**, 437–449 (2008)
2. D Helbing, *Pluralistic Modeling of Complex Systems* (2010). arXiv:1007.2818v1. http://arxiv.org/, Cornell University Library
3. DC Hoaglin, RE Welsch, The hat matrix in regression and ANOVA. Am. Stat. **32**, 17–22 (1978)
4. D Helbing, S Balietti, *Agent Based Modeling,' FuturICT meeting, Zurich, June 2011* (2011). http://dl.dropbox.com/u/6002187/16June_AgentBasedModelling.pdf
5. V Smith, Constructivist and ecological rationality in economics. Am. Econ. Rev. **93**, 465–508 (2003)
6. GA Akerlof, The market for lemons: quality uncertainty and the market mechanism. Q. J. Econ. **84**, 488–500 (1970)
7. BA Melbourne, A Hastings, Highly variable spread rates in replicated biological invasions: fundamental limits to predictability. Science **325**, 1536–1539 (2009)
8. MJ Salganik, PS Dodds, DJ Watts, Experimental study of inequality and unpredictability in an artificial cultural market. Science **311**, 854–856 (2006)
9. JD Farmer, P Patelli, I Zovko, The predictive power of zero intelligence in financial markets. Proc. Natl. Acad. Sci. **102**, 2254–2259 (2005)
10. P Ball, *Critical Mass: How One Thing Leads to Another* (Heinemann, London, 2004)
11. M Buchanan, *The Social Atom* (Bloomsbury, London, 2007)
12. MJ Newman, A-L Barabási, DJ Watts, *The Structure and Dynamics of Networks* (Princeton University Press, Princeton, 2006)
13. GJ Ackland, M Signitzer, K Stratford, MH Cohen, Cultural hitchhiking on the wave of advance of beneficial technologies. Proc. Natl. Acad. Sci. **104**, 8714–8719 (2007)
14. I Farkas, D Helbing, T Vicsek, Mexican waves in an excitable medium. Nature **419**, 131–132 (2002)
15. X Gabaix, P Gopikrishnan, V Plerou, HE Stanley, Institutional investors and stock market volatility. Q. J. Econ. **121**, 461–504 (2006)
16. D Kahneman, Maps of bounded rationality: psychology for behavioral economics. Am. Econ. Rev. **93**, 1449–1475 (2003)
17. P Mirowski, *Machine Dreams: Economics Becomes a Cyborg Science* (CUP, Cambridge UK, 2002)
18. B Winterhalder, EA Smith, Analyzing adaptive trategies: human behavioral ecology at twenty-five. Evol. Anthropology **9**, 51–72 (2000)
19. RA Bentley, P Ormerod, Agents, Intelligence and Social Atoms, in *Integrating Science and the Humanities*, ed. by M. Collard, E. Slingerland (Oxford University Press, Oxford, 2011)
20. P Ormerod, M Trabbati, K Glass, R Colbaugh, Explaining Social and Economic Phenomena by Models with Low or Zero Cognition Agents, in

Complexity Hints for Economic Policy: New Economic Windows, Part IV, ed. by (Springer, Milan, 2007), pp. 201–210. doi:10.1007/978-88-470-0534-1_10

21. HA Simon, A behavioral model of rational choice. Q J Econ **69**, 99–118 (1955)

22. TC Schelling, Hockey helmets, concealed weapons, and daylight saving: a study of binary choices with externalities. J Confl. Resolut. **17**, 381–428 (1973)

23. L Rendell, R Boyd, D Cownden, M Enquist, K Eriksson, MW Feldman, L Fogarty, S Ghirlanda, T Lillicrap, KN Laland, Why copy others? Insights from the social learning strategies tournament. Science **328**, 208–213 (2010)

24. HA Simon, On a class of skew distribution functions. Biometrika **42**, 425–440 (1955)

25. R Albert, A-L Barabási, Statistical mechanics of complex networks. Rev. Mod. Phys. **74**, 47–97 (2002)

26. C Anderson, *The Long Tail: Why the Future of Business Is Selling Less of More* (Hyperion, New York, 2006)

27. SN Dorogovtsev, JFF Mendes, Evolution of networks with ageing of sites. Physical Review E. **62**, 1842 (2000)

28. M Batty, Rank Clocks. Nature **444**, 592–596 (2006)

29. SJ Shennan, JR Wilkinson, Ceramic style change and neutral evolution: a case study from Neolithic Europe. Am. Antiq. **66**, 577–594 (2001)

30. MW Hahn, RA Bentley, Drift as a mechanism for cultural change: an example from baby names. Proc. R. Soc. B **270**, S1–S4 (2003)

31. RA Bentley, P Ormerod, M Batty, Evolving social influence in large populations. Behav. Ecol. Sociobiol. **65**, 537–546 (2011)

32. P Ormerod, B Rosewell, G Wiltshire, Network Models of Innovation Processes and the Policy Implications, in *Handbook on the Economic Complexity of Technological Change*, ed. by C. Antonelli (Edward Elgar, Cheltenham UK, 2010)

33. DJ Watts, A simple model of global cascades on random networks. Proc. Natl. Acad. **99**, 5766–5771 (2002)

34. P Ormerod, R Colbaugh, Cascades of failure and extinction in evolving social networks. J. Artif. Soc. and Soc. Simul. **9**, 4 (2006)

3

Social network integration and analysis using a generalization and probabilistic approach for privacy preservation

Xuning Tang and Christopher C Yang[*]

Abstract

Social Network Analysis and Mining (SNAM) techniques have drawn significant attention in the recent years due to the popularity of online social media. With the advance of Web 2.0 and SNAM techniques, tools for aggregating, sharing, investigating, and visualizing social network data have been widely explored and developed. SNAM is effective in supporting intelligence and law enforcement force to identify suspects and extract communication patterns of terrorists or criminals. In our previous work, we have shown how social network analysis and visualization techniques are useful in discovering patterns of terrorist social networks. Attribute to the advance of SNAM techniques, relationships among social actors can be visualized through network structures explicitly and implicit patterns can be discovered automatically. Despite the advance of SNAM, the utility of a social network is highly affected by its d completeness. Missing edges or nodes in a social network will reduce the utility of the network. For example, SNAM techniques may not be able to detect groups of social actors if some of the relationships among these social actors are not available. Similarly, SNAM techniques may overestimate the distance between two social actors if some intermediate nodes or edges are missing. Unfortunately, it is common that an organization only have a partial social network due to its limited information sources. In public safety domain, each law enforcement unit has its own criminal social network constructed by the data available from the criminal intelligence and crime database but this network is only a part of the global criminal social network, which can be obtained by integrating criminal social networks from all law enforcement units. However, due to the privacy policy, law enforcement units are not allowed to share the sensitive information of their social network data. A naive and yet practical approach is anonymizing the social network data before publishing or sharing it. However, a modest privacy gains may reduce a substantial SNAM utility. It is a challenge to make a balance between privacy and utility in social network data sharing and integration. In order to share useful information among different organizations without violating the privacy policies and preserving sensitive information, we propose a generalization and probabilistic approach of social network integration in this paper. Particularly, we propose generalizing social networks to preserve privacy and integrating the probabilistic models of the shared information for SNAM. To preserve the identity of sensitive nodes in social network, a simple approach in the literature is removing all node identities. However, it only allows us to investigate of the structural properties of such anonymized social network, but the integration of multiple anonymized social networks will be impossible. To make a balance between privacy and utility, we introduce a social network integration framework which consists of three major steps: (i) constructing generalized sub-graph, (ii) creating generalized information for sharing, and (iii) social networks integration and analysis. We also propose two sub-graph generalization methods namely, edge betweenness based (EBB) and K-nearest neighbor (KNN). We evaluated the effectiveness of these algorithms on the Global Salafi Jihad terrorist social network.

* Correspondence: chris.yang@drexel.edu
College of Information Science and Technology, Drexel University,
Philadelphia, USA

Introduction

Social Network Analysis and Mining (SNAM) techniques have drawn significant attention in the recent years due to the popularity of online social media. With the advance of Web 2.0 and SNAM techniques, tools for aggregating, sharing, investigating, and visualizing social network data have been widely explored and developed. SNAM is effective in supporting intelligence and law enforcement force to identify suspects and extract communication patterns of terrorists or criminals. In our previous work [1-3], we have shown how social network analysis and visualization techniques are useful in discovering patterns of terrorist social networks. Attribute to the advance of SNAM techniques, relationships among social actors can be visualized through network structures explicitly and implicit patterns can be discovered automatically.

Despite the advance of SNAM, the utility of a social network is highly affected by its d completeness. Missing edges or nodes in a social network will reduce the utility of the network. For example, SNAM techniques may not be able to detect groups of social actors if some of the relationships among these social actors are not available. Similarly, SNAM techniques may overestimate the distance between two social actors if some intermediate nodes or edges are missing. Unfortunately, it is common that an organization only have a partial social network due to its limited information sources. In public safety domain, each law enforcement unit has its own criminal social network constructed by the data available from the criminal intelligence and crime database but this network is only a part of the global criminal social network, which can be obtained by integrating criminal social networks from all law enforcement units. However, due to the privacy policy, law enforcement units are not allowed to share the sensitive information of their social network data. A naïve and yet practical approach is anonymizing the social network data before publishing or sharing it. However, a modest privacy gains may reduce a substantial SNAM utility. It is a challenge to make a balance between privacy and utility in social network data sharing and integration.

In order to share useful information among different organizations without violating the privacy policies and preserving sensitive information, we propose a generalization and probabilistic approach of social network integration in this paper. Particularly, we propose generalizing social networks to preserve privacy and integrating the probabilistic models of the shared information for SNAM. To preserve the identity of sensitive nodes in social network, a simple approach in the literature is removing all node identities. However, it only allows us to investigate of the structural properties of such anonymized social network, but the integration of multiple anonymized social networks will be impossible. To make a balance between privacy and utility, we introduce a social network integration framework which consists of three major steps: (i) constructing generalized sub-graph, (ii) creating generalized information for sharing, and (iii) social networks integration and analysis. We also propose two sub-graph generalization methods namely, edge betweenness based (EBB) and K-nearest neighbor (KNN). We evaluated the effectiveness of these algorithms on the Global Salafi Jihad terrorist social network.

This paper is organized as follows. In the next section, we review the existing works about privacy preservation of social network. Previous techniques are classified based on their assumption of attack models the definition of sensitive information, and the privacy preservation techniques. In section 3, we introduce the researchd framework. Social network generalization and integration techniques are introduced in section 4. The experiment design, results and discussions are presented in section 5. We conclude our work and introduce future work in section 6.

Related work
Sensitive information of social network

Given a social network, the definition of sensitive information depends on the specific applications. In the literature, the social network sensitive information can be classified into node properties, neighborhood graphs, edge properties, and network properties in general.

Node properties

In a social network, identity of nodes can be an important type of sensitive property [4-7]. A node with sensitive identity means that its identity is private and should not be released. On the other hands, a node with insensitive identity means that the identity of this node can be released with no harm. Another type of sensitive property of a node can be its degree centrality [8-12]. Given a node, the degree centrality equals to the total number of edges connecting to this node, which is the number of friend in a social network. In a directed graph, edges can be further divided into in-links and out-links. Releasing the degree centrality of a given node, attacker can find out the number of nodes associated to this node which may further release its identity.

Neighborhood graphs

Node neighborhood graph is a concept highly related to degree centrality but with some differences [12]. Given a node and its neighbors, how these neighbors connect with each other can be unique. Publishing the neighborhood graph of a node may release the identify of this node.

Edge properties

Besides the properties of network nodes, Zheleva and Getoor also studied some sensitive properties related to network edges[13]. Two types of information of an edge can be potential sensitive information. One is the existence of an edge between two given nodes. The other is the label of a given edge which represents the type of relationship.

Network properties

Social network data has a set of important properties which can be considered as sensitive information in some cases, such as diameter, radius, betweenness, closeness, clustering coefficient etc.

Social network privacy attack model

To have a better protection against privacy attack, it is important to understand different types of privacy attack models. In this section, we introduce two categories of attack, active and passive attacks [11,14].

Active attacks

Backstorm et al. [14] introduced the active attack model. An adversary can actively select an arbitrary set of target actors, creates a small number of new actors with edges connecting to these targeted users, and then creates a pattern of links among the new actors. By planting new actors and connection patterns in the anonymized social network sophisticatedly, the adversary is able to identify the new actors as well as the targeted actors if the generated connection patterns are uniquely stand out in the anonymized network. Theoretically, the creation of $O(\sqrt{\log n})$ nodes in an n-node network will begin compromising the privacy of the arbitrary targeted nodes. Backstorm et al., [14] further divided the active attacks into walk-based attack and cut-based attack. Both of them employed the strategy of inserting nodes into the target network and then link these nodes with the target nodes. The difference between them is the theoretical number of nodes used in the attack.

Passive attacks

Backstorm et al. [14] also investigated the passive attack model, where adversaries do not create any new nodes or edges. Backstorm et al. pointed out that attacker with certain knowledge can easily differentiate the target nodes or edges from the others due to their unique structural information. Most current studies focus their research on preventing passive attacks, which includes: (1) node passive attack [8-11], where adversaries are supposed to take advantage of node's degree centrality information to uncover node's identity; (2) edge passive attack [13-15], where adversaries are supposed to know

the existence of certain edges, leading to the disclosure of sensitive information by tracking the identify of other edges or nodes via known edges; (3) sub-graph passive attack [9,11,12], where adversaries are supposed to make use of sub-graph information known in advanced to identify sensitive information of node, such as node identity; (4) graph metrics passive attack [16], where the adversaries have certain background knowledge of the graph metrics, for example hub fingerprint, closeness centrality or betweenness centrality. With the knowledge of these graph metrics, it's also possible that adversaries can uncover several sensitive information of the social network.

Privacy preservation models and algorithms

In the recent years, a number of approaches for preserving privacy of relational data have been studied extensively, which include k-anonymity [17,18], l-diversity[19], Personalized anonymity[20], and (α,k)-Anonymity[21]. One common objective of these algorithms is to ensure every node is indistinguishable to other (k-1) nodes after anonymization. Although these methods work well in relational table data, most of them cannot deal with social network data due to the complex structure of social network and various background and attack model employed by an adversary. In the recent years, a few research groups have investigated the privacy preservation of social network data. They preserve the data privacy mainly by three approaches: perturbation-based approach, generalization-based approach, and protocol-based approach. Different techniques correspond to different type of sensitive data as well as privacy requirement.

Perturbation-based technique

The perturbation-based technique perturbs a social network by adding, deleting or switching edges in a social network in order to increase the difficulty of identifying a node. Most of them are using greedy algorithm guided by an objective function to modify the social network step by step until the anonymized network satisfied some given conditions. Liu and Terzi proposed the K-degree Anonymous Algorithm to ensure that each network node is indistinguishable to other (K-1) nodes [10]. Starting from the original degree sequence **d** of input graph **G**, the algorithm constructs a new degree sequence $\hat{d}$ which satisfies two conditions including: $\hat{d}$ is k-anonymous and $\sum_i |d(i) - \hat{d}(i)|$ is minimized. Zhou and Pei proposed the K-neighborhood Algorithm to make sure that node identity cannot be re-identified by an adversary with a confidence larger than 1/k, even though the adversary has background knowledge of the neighborhood graph [12]. The whole process is divided into two phases. First, the algorithm extracts the neighborhoods of all nodes in the network. To facilitate the comparisons among neighborhoods of different nodes, the researchers proposed a neighborhood component coding technique to represent the neighborhoods in a concise way. In the second step, the algorithm greedily organizes nodes into groups and anonymizes the neighborhoods of nodes in the same group. The greedy algorithm is guided by an anonymization cost which is measured by the similarity between the neighborhoods of two nodes. Ying and Wu proposed the Spectrum Preserving Algorithm which preserves the privacy by randomly perturbing edges in the network [16]. The whole process can be divided into three steps: at first, the eigenvalues of the input graph is computed; and then based on some proved theorems, the boundaries of eigenvalues are given; finally the algorithm perturbs the graph by adding, deleting or switching edges of the graph. If the eigenvalues of perturbed graph is within the given boundaries, the perturbation is accepted and continued for next perturbation. The algorithm terminates until the precondition is satisfied.

Generalization-based technique
The generalization-based technique preserves a social network by grouping certain number of nodes or edges together and then only release the general information of the groups of nodes or edges. Nodes within a group cannot be differentiated because they all share exactly the same properties of the group. In most cases, a generalization-based technique divides nodes according to some predefined loss functions. Hay et al. proposed a node splitting-based technique to achieve k-anonymity of the social network [9,11]. Starting from a single partition of a social network, the algorithm keeps on splitting the selected partition into two sub-groups until all predefined criteria are satisfied. Similarly, Campan and Truta introduced a node clustering-based approach to satisfy the k-anonymity requirement and minimize the information loss [8]. In their algorithm, clusters are created one at a time. To form a new cluster, a node in V with the maximum degree but not yet be allocated to any cluster is selected as a seed for the new cluster. Then the algorithm puts nodes to this currently processed cluster until it reaches the desired cardinality k. At each step, the current cluster grows with one node. The selected node should not be assigned to any cluster yet but it should be able to minimize the growth of information loss of the current clusters. Zheleva and Getoor proposed an edge clustering-based technique to hide the sensitive information on edges [13]. Their technique is divided into two phases. In the first phase, the technique provides a clustering of the nodes into m equivalence class (C1,C2,...,CM) such that each node is indistinguishable in its quasi-identifying attributes from K-1 other nodes. In the second step, this work presents

several techniques to protect sensitive information of the social network and then compare their performance, which includes partial-edge removal, cluster-edge anonymization, and cluster-edge anonymization with constraints. Cormode and Srivastava proposed the safe groupings technique for a bipartite Graph $G = (V,W,E)$, where V and W correspond to two types of objects [15]. In their work, a safe grouping of a bipartite graph partitions nodes into groups such that two nodes of the same group of V have no common neighbors in W and vice versa. A greedy algorithm is proposed to find K safe groups of V and L safe groups of W. For each node u, the algorithm attempts to assign u to the first group with fewer than n nodes. If it makes the grouping unsafe, the algorithm will try the second available group and so forth. If there is no group that meets the requirements, a new group will be created to contain this node. After getting K safe groups of V, the algorithm move forward to find L safe groups of W following a similar same process.

Protocol-based technique
The protocol-based technique is using the encryption approach rather than anonymizing the social network data. Social network data is encrypted by following a protocol before sharing with other parties. The protocol ensures that other parties are only able to obtain the insensitive information for their applications but the sensitive information is preserved. Frikken and Golle proposed the pieces assembling approach for private social network analysis [22].

Summary
In this section, we provide a summary of the literature by comparing the privacy preservation techniques and the preserving data in social network as shown in Table 1. In general, some privacy preservation techniques are developed for preserving specific information but are not applied to other information. The choice of the privacy preservation techniques also depends on the application of social network analysis.

Research problem
The existing works focus on preserving privacy of social network data for data publishing so that the global network structure can be analyzed. However, it has not considered how to integrate social network data from different sources so that social network analysis and mining can be conducted on the integrated data and yet the privacy of the shared data can be preserved. Individual published social network data only capture parts of the complete social network. Unless we can integrate multiple social networks and conduct SNAM on the integrated social network, the utility of the anonymized data is still limited. Given multiple law enforcement

Table 1 Classification of privacy preservation techniques based on sensitive information

		Types of sensitive information						
		Node Existence	Node Properties	Link Existence	Link Properties	Subgraph Property	Aggregated Graph property	Other Graph information
Privacy preservation techniques	Perturbation Based Technique		[10]	[16]			[16]	
	Generalization Based Technique	[4,6]	[8,9,11]	[4,6,15]				[8]
	Hybrid (Perturbation & Generalization)		[12]	[13]	[13]	[12]		
	Protocol Based Technique							[22]

units and each of them has a criminal social network which captures a partial picture of a complete criminal social network, the objective of this work is preserving the privacy of the shared data from each law enforcement unit and conduct SNAM tasks on the integrated data. In this section, we first define formally the research problem, introduce what sensitive information to preserve, what insensitive information to share and what SNAM task can be conducted. Then, we proposed a research framework to address the research problem.

Problem definition

Given a set of network $\mathcal{g} = \{G_1, G_2,...,G_n\}$ in a distributed setting where each organization i owns its piece of G_i, assuming the complete network $G(G = \cup_{i=1}^{n} G_i)$ is unknown to each individual organization, the goal of this paper is to study how to anonymize each G_i into G_i' so that: 1) the sensitive identities of G_i can be protected; 2) G_i' can be shared with other organizations and the integrated anonymization graph $G'(G' = \cup_{i=1}^{n} G_i'$ can be used for SNAM task. Concretely, each network G_i' consists of both insensitive nodes and sensitive nodes. Node identities of those insensitive nodes are known to the public or the sharing parties while the node identities of those sensitive nodes are unknown to the public and needed to be protected. Our focus in this paper is to protect the node identities of those sensitive nodes. On the other hand, for SNAM purpose, some network properties, including topology, diameter and some other abstract features of the anonymized network, will be released and shared across organizations. Last but not least, it's important to note that some network features cannot be preserved in our method, such as neighborhood information. Therefore, not all SNAM tasks can be achieved

in our integrated anonymized network. In this paper, we only study how to preserve the usefulness of the integrated anonymized network regarding to distance-related analysis, such as computing the closeness of each node. To summarize, although some existing works have studied how to anonymize network for data publishing, the research problem that we study here is different. We not only anonymize a given network to protect its' node identity but also focus on integrating anonymized networks to achieve better SNAM results

Framework of social network integration with privacy preservation

To further motivate our research framework, we assume organization P (O_P) has a social network G_P and organization Q (O_Q) has another social network G_Q, both G_P and G_Q are partial networks of a complete social network which is unknown to any organization. O_P needs to conduct a Social Network Analysis and Mining (SNAM) but G_P is incomplete due to its limited sources of information. As a result, it will be difficult or even impossible for O_P to get accurate SNAM results. If there is no privacy concern between different organizations, one can integrate G_P and G_Q to generate an integrated **G** and obtain a better SNAM result. However, due to privacy concern, O_Q cannot share G_Q completely with O_P but only shares the insensitive information of G_Q with O_P according to the privacy policies. At the same time, O_P does not need all data from O_Q but only those that are critical for the SNAM tasks. For these reasons, to integrate social networks of different organizations without violating privacy policies, we only need to share information that is critical to the performance of SNAM and yet preserve the sensitive information.

Figure 1 demonstrates the general framework of social network integration for SNAM. In this framework, O_Q employs sub-graph generalization techniques to create a generalized social network, G_Q', from G_Q without violating the privacy policy. The generalized social network only contains generalized information of G_Q without releasing any sensitive information. For example, a generalized social network cannot release the exact identity of each nodes or exact shortest distance between any two nodes. On the other hand, generalized information can include diameter of a sub-graph, average number of adjacent nodes between two subgroups, degree of an insensitive node and other insensitive information. The generalized social network G_Q' will then be integrated with G_P to support a social network analysis and mining task. Given the generalized information from G_Q, it is expected to achieve better performance on SNAM task than conducting the analysis and mining on G_P alone. There are two important sub-tasks in our proposed framework which we will address in the following sections:

Task 1 Given a social network G with sensitive information, produce generalized social network G' and determine the generalized information which can be released.

Task 2 Integrate a generalized social network with the local social network, and then utilize shared generalized information to achieve better SNAM results.

Notations
In Table 2, we define a set of notations for the proposed social network integration techniques.

Methodology
Social network generalization
In task one, given a social network G with sensitive information, we employ clustering-based technique to produce a generalized social network G'. We suppose $G = (V, E)$, where V is a set of nodes, E is a set of edges and $|V| = n$, K of these nodes are insensitive nodes, and n-K of these nodes are sensitive nodes. We generate a generalized social network in two steps. In the first step, we decompose G into K sub-graphs $G_i = (V_i, E_i)$, where $V = U_{i=1 to K} V_i$ and each sub-graph contains one insensitive node. In the second step, each sub-graph will be transformed to a generalized node of the generalized graph G'. Furthermore, two generalized nodes will be connected in G' if and only if there is one or more edges connecting nodes from these two sub-graphs respectively.

In this section, we propose two graph partition algorithms, K-nearest neighbor (KNN) method and Edge betweenness based (EBB) method, to generate a generalized social network G' for sharing purpose. Both KNN and EBB methods are developed by following one common principle that the identity of insensitive nodes can be published safely while the identity of sensitive nodes cannot, so that, to produce a generalized social network, we need to divide the original network into several sub-graphs each of which represented by an insensitive nodes, and the final generalized network should be also represented by these insensitive nodes.

K-nearest neighbor (KNN) method
Given a social network G with K insensitive nodes $v_1^c, v_2^c, \ldots, v_k^c$ KNN method divides G into K sub-graphs by assigning each node v to its nearest insensitive node. Let $SP^D(v, v_i^C)$ be the distance of the shortest path between v and v_i^C. Starting from the sensitive nodes

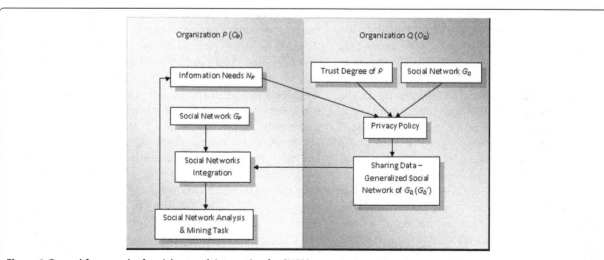

Figure 1 General framework of social network integration for SNAM.

Table 2 Notations and definitions

$G = (V, E)$	a social network G with $|V|$ nodes and $|E|$ edges
V	node set of G
E	edge set of G
$G\prime$	a generalized version of G
$G_i = (V_i, E_i)$	a sub-graph of G where $V = \cup_{i=1 \ to \ k} V_i$ and $E_i \subset E$
v_i^c	the center of a sub-graph G_i which is an insensitive node too
v_p	node p
$Num(G_i)$	The number of nodes in G_i
$Num(G_i,G_j)$	the number of nodes in G_i that are adjacent to another subgraph G_j
$SP^D(v_p,v_q,G_i)$	the distance of the shortest path between nodes v_p and v_q in G_i
$SP^D(v, v_i^C)$	the distance of the shortest path between v and v_i^C in G_i
$Prob(SP^D(.)=\beta)$	The probability of the distance that equals to β
$S\_SP^D(G_i)$	shortest length of the shortest paths between any two nodes in G_i ($S\_SP^D(G_i) = \{SP^D(v_m,v_n,G_i)| \ \forall \ v_p, v_q \in V_i, SP^D(v_m,v_n,G_i) \leq SP^D(v_p,v_q,G_i)\}$)
$L\_SP^D(G_i)$	longest length of the shortest paths between any two nodes in G_i ($L\_SP^D(G_i) = \{SP^D(v_m,v_n,G_i)| \ \forall \ v_p, v_q \in V_i, SP^D(v_m,v_n,G_i) \geq SP^D(v_p,v_q,G_i)\}$)
$S\_SP^D(v_i^C,G_i)$	shortest length of the shortest paths between v_i^C and other nodes in G_i ($S\_SP^D(v_i^C,G_i) = \{SP^D(v_m,v_i^C,G_i)| \ v_p \in V_i, SP^D(v_m,v_i^C,G_i) \leq SP^D(v_p,v_i^C,G_i)\}$)
$L\_SP^D(v_i^C,G_i)$	longest length of the shortest paths between v_i^C and other nodes in G_i ($L\_SP^D(v_i^C,G_i) = \{SP^D(v_m,v_i^C,G_i)| \ v_p \in V_i, SP^D(v_m,v_i^C,G_i) \geq SP^D(v_p,v_i^C,G_i)\}$)

adjacent to insensitive node, KNN method assign sensitive node, one node per time, to the closest sub-graph G_i where $SP^D(v, v_i^C)$ is shorter than or equal to $SP^D(v, v_j^C)$ where $j = 1, 2, .., K$ and $j \neq i$. After dividing a social network into K sub-graphs, we collapse all nodes of a sub-graph into one generalized node, and represent this node with the identity of the insensitive node of this sub-graph. Finally, for each possible pair of generalized nodes, say G_i and G_j in the generalized graph $G\prime$, an edge will be created if and only if there is one or more edges between any two nodes in G from sub-graph G_i and G_j respectively.

Figure 2 presents a simple example to illustrate the idea of KNN and show how it works to produce generalized social network. Figure 2 (a) is the given social network which has seven nodes. Among them, v_1 and v_2 are insensitive nodes while the others are all sensitive nodes. By using KNN method, the given social network will be divided into two isolated social networks as shown in Figure 2 (b). Finally, one sub-graph is represented by v_1 and another sub-graph is represented by v_2, Figure 2 (c) demonstrates the final generalized social

network where two generalized nodes are connected together because v_4 and v_5 are connected in G. The *KNN* subgraph generation algorithm is presented below:

```
length = 1;
V = V - {v₁ᶜ, v₂ᶜ, ... vₖᶜ};
While V ≠ ∅
    For each vⱼ ∈ V
    For each i = 1 to K
        IF(SPᴰ(vⱼ, vᵢᶜ) == length);
            Vᵢ = Vᵢ + vⱼ;
            V = V − vⱼ;
    End For;
    End For;
    length++;
End While
For each (vᵢ,vⱼ) ∈ E
    IF(Subgraph(vᵢ) == Subgraph(vⱼ))
    //Subgraph(vᵢ) is the subgraph such that vᵢ ∈
    Subgraph(vᵢ)
        Gₖ = Subgraph(vᵢ)
        Eₖ = Eₖ + (vᵢ,vⱼ)
```

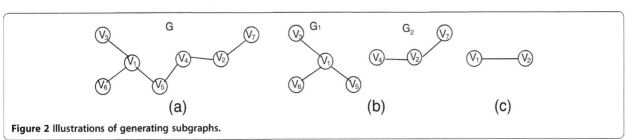

Figure 2 Illustrations of generating subgraphs.

ELSE
    Create an edge between *Subgraph*(v_i) and
    Subgraph(v_j) and add it to E'
End For

Edge betweenness based (EBB) method

Instead of assigning sensitive nodes to the closest sub-graphs represented by insensitive nodes, the EBB method progressively remove edges with the highest betweenness and it also ensure that each separated sub-graph contains exactly one insensitive node. The betweenness of an edge is defined as the number of shortest paths between pairs of nodes that pass through it. If a network consists of a few of dense communities which are only loosely connected by some inter-community edges, these inter-community edges will have high betweenness, so that removing them will naturally break the social network into multiple communities. The EBB algorithm is presented as follows:

```
//EBB(G), Edge Betweenness Based method
Initialize e = {};
While(there are more than one insensitive node in
graph G)
    Identify edge (vᵢ,vⱼ) in G which is not an element of e
    and has the highest betweenness;
    Remove (vᵢ,vⱼ) from G;
    IF(G is still connected after removing edges (vᵢ,vⱼ))
        EBB(G);
    ELSE IF (G is disconnected and split to two graph
    Gₚ and G_q)
        IF(No insensitive node in Gₚ) or (No insensitive
        node in G_q)
            Add (vᵢ,vⱼ) back to G;
            e = e + (vᵢ,vⱼ);
Go Back to Step 2;
        ELSE
            EBB(Gₚ);
            EBB(G_q);
End While;
//Add edge between generalized node to form
generalized graph
For each (vⱼ,vⱼ) ∈ E
    IF(Subgraph(vᵢ) == Subgraph(vⱼ))
        Gₖ = Subgraph(vᵢ)
        Eₖ = Eₖ + (vᵢ,vⱼ)
    ELSE
        Create an edge between Subgraph(vᵢ) and
        Subgraph(vⱼ) and add it to E'
End For
```

Figure 3 shows an example of how EBB method works to produce generalized social network. Given a social network with nine nodes, v_1 and v_2 are insensitive nodes

while all other nodes are sensitive nodes. Since edge (v_1, v_2) has the highest Betweenness and it is safe to be removed, EBB method delete this edge to form two separated sub-graphs each of them contains exactly one insensitive node, as shown in Figure 3 (b). Finally, the EBB method generalizes these two sub-graphs into two generalized nodes, and then connects them to form the generalized graph as shown in Figure 3 (c).

Generalized sub-graph information

Given a generalized social network G_i and its center v_i^C, we select shareable network properties based on the information need and the privacy policy. In this paper, we treat node identity as sensitive information that we should protect, and consider distance between nodes to be useful information for SNAM task. Let v_a and v_b be any two nodes in G_i and the length of the shortest path between v_a and v_b be $SP^D(v_p,v_q,G_i)$. We define the longest length of the shortest paths between any two nodes in G_i, denoted by $L\_SP^D(G_i)$, as

$$L\_SP^D(G_i) = \{SP^D(v_m, v_n, G_i)|\exists v_m, v_n, \forall v_a, v_b \in V_i, SP^D \times (v_m, v_n, G_i) \geq SP^D(v_a, v_b, G_i)\}$$

We also define the shortest length of the shortest paths between any two nodes in G_i, denoted by $S\_SP^D(G_i)$, as

$$S\_SP^D(G_i) = \{SP^D(v_m, v_n, G_i)|\exists v_m, v_n, \forall v_a, v_b \in V_i, SP^D \times (v_m, v_n, G_i) \leq SP^D(v_a, v_b, G_i)\}$$

To reduce the risk of releasing sensitive information, instead of sharing exact information of shortest path, we propose to share the expected length between two nodes within a generalized social network. Formally speaking, the length of any shortest paths in G_i, α, must be smaller or equal to $L\_SP^D(G_i)$ and larger or equal to $S\_SP^D(G_i)$, where $S\_SP^D(G_i) \leq \alpha \leq L\_SP^D(G_i)$. We compute and share the probability of the length of the shortest path between any two nodes in G_i, denoted as $Prob(SP^D(G_i) = \alpha)$, and $0 \leq Prob(SP^D(G_i) = \alpha) \leq 1$

Similarly, let the length of the shortest path between v_a and v_i^C, be $SP^D(v_a,v_i^C,G_i)$. We define the longest length of the shortest paths between v_i^C and other nodes within G_i, denoted by $L\_SP^D(v_i^C,G_i)$, as

$$L\_SP^D(v_i^C, G_i) = SP^D(v_m, v_i^C, G_i)|\forall v_a \in V_i, SP^D (v_m, v_i^C, G_i) \geq SP^D(v_a, v_i^C, G_i)$$

We also define the shortest length of the shortest paths between v_i^C and other nodes within G_i, denoted by and $S\_SP^D(v_i^C,G_i)$, as

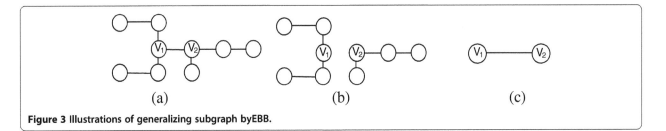

Figure 3 Illustrations of generalizing subgraph byEBB.

$$S\_SP^D\left(v_i^C, G_i\right) = \left\{ SP^D\left(v_m, v_i^C, G_i\right) \middle| \forall v_a \in V_i, SP^D\left(v_m, v_i^C, G_i\right) \leq SP^D\left(v_a, v_i^C, G_i\right) \right\}$$

Since the length of shortest paths between v_i^C and any other nodes in G_i must be smaller or equal to $L\_SP^D(v_i^C, G_i)$ and larger or equal to $S\_SP^D(v_i^C, G_i)$, denoted as $S\_SP^D(v_i^C, G_i) \leq \beta \leq L\_SP^D(v_i^C, G_i)$. We compute the probability of the length of the shortest path between any node and v_i^C, $Prob(SP^D(v_i^C,G_i) = \beta)$, where $0 \leq Prob(SP^D(G_i) = \alpha) \leq 1$.

We also denote $Num(G_i)$ as the number of nodes in G_i and $Num(G_i,G_j)$ as the number of nodes in G_i that are adjacent to another subgraph G_j.

The generalized subgraph information for sharing includes: (i) $L\_SP^D(G_i)$, (ii) $S\_SP^D(G_i)$, (iii) $Prob(SP^D(G_i) = \alpha)$, (iv) $L\_SP^D(v_i^C,G_i)$, (v) $S\_SP^D(v_i^C,G_i)$, (vi) $Prob(SP^D(v_i^C,G_i) = \beta)$, (vii) $Num(G_i)$, and (viii) $Num(G_i,G_j)$.

Generalized graph integration and social network analysis
In section 4.2 and 4.3 we introduced how to divide a social network into sub-graphs, and then generalize these sub-graphs to nodes, then finally produce a generalized social network. We also discussed what kind of information will be shared along with the generalized social network. In this section, given a generalized social network G' and the shareable information of the sub-graphs of G, we propose our own techniques to integrate social network and shared information to improve the performance of SNAM task.

Suppose organization O_p has a social network G_p and organization O_Q has another social network G_Q, O_p wants to integrate G_Q with its own G_p to compute more accurate closeness centrality. We propose to achieve this goal without violating the privacy policies in three steps: (1) produce generalized social network G'_p and G'_Q; (2) integrate G'_p and G'_Q into $G_{Integrated}$; (3) estimate the distance between any two nodes of the integrated social network. Among these three steps, step one can be achieved by our proposed techniques in section 4.2 and 4.3. In step two, although the sub-graphs represented by a common insensitive node in G'_p and G'_Q are different and the connectivity between these insensitive nodes are also different, according to our proposed techniques, G'_p

and G'_Q are represented by the same group of insensitive nodes since G_p and G_Q share same insensitive nodes. As a result, we can combine G'_p and G'_Q into $G_{Integrated}$ by taking union of their edges. In this section, we focus on the step 3 which estimate distances between any two nodes based on G_p, $G_{Integrated}$ and shared information of sub-graphs of G'_Q.

To re-estimate the distance between two nodes v_i and v_p of G_p by making use of $G_{Integrated}$ and the shared information of sub-graphs of G'_Q, we first identify the two closest insensitive nodes for v_i and v_j in G_p, and then use $G_{Integrated}$ and the generalized information of G'_Q to re-estimate their distances. Formally speaking, let the closest insensitive node to v_i in G_p be V_A^C, and the second closest insensitive node to v_i in G_p be $V_{A'}^C$. We set the weights λ_A and $\lambda_{A'}$ as

$$\lambda_A = \frac{SP^D\left(v_i, v_{A'}^c, G_P\right)}{SP^D\left(v_i, v_A^c, G_P\right) + SP^D\left(v_i, v_{A'}^c, G_P\right)},$$

$$\lambda_{A'} = \frac{SP^D\left(v_i, v_A^c, G_P\right)}{SP^D\left(v_i, v_A^c, G_P\right) + SP^D\left(v_i, v_{A'}^c, G_P\right)},$$

with $\lambda_A + \lambda_{A'} = 1$ and the weight of the closest insensitive node is higher.

Similarly, let the closest insensitive node to v_j in G_P be v_A^C, and the second closest insensitive node to v_j in G_P be v_B^C, we set the weights λ_B and $\lambda_{B'}$ as

$$\lambda_B = \frac{SP^D\left(v_j, v_{B'}^c, G_P\right)}{SP^D\left(v_j, v_B^c, G_P\right) + SP^D\left(v_j, v_{B'}^c, G_P\right)},$$

$$\lambda_{B'} = \frac{SP^D\left(v_j, v_B^c, G_B\right)}{SP^D\left(v_j, v_B^c, G_P\right) + SP^D\left(v_j, v_{B'}^c, G_P\right)},$$

with $\lambda_B + \lambda_{B'} = 1$

In $G_{Integrated}$, v_A^C, v_A^C, v_B^C, and $v_{B'}^C$ are the centers of generalized sub-graphs G_A, G_A, G_B, and G_B, respectively.

We estimate the distance between v_i and v_j, $d(v_i,v_j)$, by integrating the estimated distances of the four possible paths going through these insensitive nodes by a linear combination with weights equal to $\lambda_a \times \lambda_b$.

$$d(v_i, v_j) = \sum_{\substack{a \in \{A,A'\} \\ b \in \{B,B'\}}} \lambda_a \times \lambda_b \times D(v_i, v_j)$$

$D(v_i, v_j)$ is the estimated distance between v_i and v_j on the path going through v_a^c and v_b^c, where a can be A or A' and b can be B or B'.

$$D(v_i, v_j) = \begin{cases} D'(G_a, v_i) + 1 + \sum_{\forall G_k} (E(G_k) + 1) + D'(G_b, v_j) & a \neq b \\ D''(v_i, v_j) & a = b \end{cases}$$

where G_k is a generalized node on the shortest path between G_a and G_b in $G_{Integrated}$ If $a \neq b$ which means v_i and v_j are not in the same subgraph, then $D(v_i, v_j)$ is estimated by $D'(G_a, v_i)$, $D'(G_b, v_j)$, and $E(G_k)$. Otherwise, if v_i and v_j are in the same subgraph then $a = b$. In this case, $D(v_i, v_j)$ is estimated by $D''(v_i, v_j)$. $D'(G_a, v_i)$ corresponds to the expected length of the distance between v_i and the sub-graph gatekeeper within G_a. Similarly, $D'(G_b, v_j)$ corresponds to the expected length of the distance between v_j and the sub-graph gatekeeper within G_b. In addition, $E(G_k)$ is the expected length of the distance between any two nodes of sub-graph G_k that the shortest path between v_i and v_j is going through. If v_i is not the same as v_a^c, $D'(G_a, v_i)$ is computed by $E(G_a)$ and the percentage of nodes in G_a that is adjacent to the sub-graph that is immediately following G_a in the shortest path between v_i and v_j in $G_{Integrated}$. If v_i is the same as v_a^c, $D'(G_a, v_i)$ is equal to the expected length of the distance between the insensitive node, v_a^c, to the other nodes in G_a. Computation of $D'(G_b, v_i)$ is done similarly.

$$D'(G_a, v_i) = \begin{cases} \left(1 - \dfrac{Num(G_a, G_k)}{Num(G_a)}\right) \times E(G_a) & v_i \neq v_a^c \\ \sum_{\beta = S\_SP(v_a^c, G_a)}^{L\_SP(v_a^c, G_a)} Prob(SP^D(v_a^c, G_a) = \beta) \times \beta & v_i = v_a^c \end{cases}$$

where $\dfrac{Num(G_a, G_k)}{Num(Ga)}$ is the percentage of nodes in G_a as a gatekeeper which is adjacent to G_k and G_k is the sub-graph that immediately follows G_a in the shortest path between v_i and v_j in $G_{Integrated}$.

$E(G_k)$ represents the expected length of the distance between any two nodes of the sub-graph G_k, which is computed as:

$$E(G_k) = \sum_{\alpha = S_S P(G_k)}^{L\_SP(G_k)} (Prob(SP^D(G_k) = \alpha) \times \alpha$$

$D''(v_i, v_j)$ corresponds to the estimated distance between v_i and v_j when both v_i and v_j are nodes of the same sub-graph. In this case, if any of v_i or v_j is the same as v_a^c, $D''(v_i, v_j)$ should equal to the expected length of the distance from the insensitive node to the other nodes in, G_a. Otherwise, $D''(v_i, v_j)$ should equal to the expected length of the distance between two nodes of the sub-graph.

$$D''(v_i, v_j) = \begin{cases} \sum_{\beta = S\_SP(v_a^c, G_a)}^{L\_SP(v_a^c, G_a)} Prob(SP^D(v_a^c, G_a) = \beta) \times \beta & v_i \, or \, v_j = v_a^c \\ E(G_a) & else \end{cases}$$

Experiment and discussion

Practically, there isn't any intelligence unit has a complete terrorist social network but each of them has a partial terrorist social network. The objective of this work is to support these intelligence units to share their social networks while preserving the sensitive information. In this section, we investigated our proposed techniques on a real-world dataset of terrorists. We extracted several social networks from the terrorist dataset to simulate the real-world problem. Intensive experiment was conducted under different settings to evaluate our proposed techniques.

Dataset

In this work, we employed the Global Salafi Jihad terrorist social network, denoted as **G**, in our experiment. The Global Salafi Jihad terrorist social network consists of 366 nodes (terrorists) and 1,275 edges (connection between terrorists)[23]. These terrorists come from four major groups, including Central Staff of al Qaeda (CSQ), Core Arab (CA), Southeast Asia (SA), and Maghreb Arab (MA). We randomly sample α percent of nodes from the Global Salafi Jihad terrorist social network as insensitive nodes, that their identities are known by all organizations. Suppose there are two independent organizations O_P and O_Q, we simulate G_P for O_P by randomly removing β percent of edges from the Global Salafi Jihad terrorist social network. Similarly, we randomly remove β percent of edges from the Global Salafi Jihad terrorist social network to simulate G_Q for O_Q. As a result, both G_P and G_Q are partial graph of G. Moreover, G_P are different from G_Q in terms of their edges.

Evaluation

As discussed before, there is no generic approach for privacy preservation since sensitive information can be defined in various ways. Moreover, shareable useful information is also different in terms of different SNAM tasks. In this work, we treat node identity as sensitive information and consider distance between nodes as useful information that we want to maintain. To evaluate our proposed technique, we assume that the SNAM task conducted by G_P is to compute closeness centrality for each node. If G_P is close to G, then distances between any two nodes in G_P should be roughly equal to their distance in G, leading to similar closeness centrality for each node. Otherwise, nodes in G_P should have different closeness centrality in G. In this work, closeness centrality for a node in G_P is computed as:

$$closeness\ centrality_{G_P}(v_i) = \frac{n-1}{\sum_{j=1,i\neq j}^{n} SP(v_i, v_j, G_P)}$$

where n is the total number of nodes in G_P.

Given a complete social network G and the integrated social network $G_{Integrated}$, the performance of our proposed technique is evaluated by the error function defined as:

$$Error(G_{Integrated})$$
$$= \sum_{i=1}^{n} |closeness\ centrality_{G_{Integrated}}(v_i)$$
$$-closeness\ centrality_G(v_i)|$$

Experiment

Figure 4 demonstrates the average closeness centrality of nodes of original graph (G), integrated graph using EBB method ($G_{Integrated}$ (EBB)), integrated graph using KNN method ($G_{Integrated}$ (KNN)) and incomplete graph (G_P). In Figure 4, the blue line represents the average closeness centrality computed from G, which is a gold standard, so that the closer to this blue line the better it is.

For each α from 0.05 to 0.95, we increased β (percentage of edges randomly removed from G) from 0.2 to 0.8. We observed that the performance of G_P ($G_{Integrated}$ (KNN)) and ($G_{Integrated}$ (EBB)) decreased consistently when more edges are removed from the complete graph, no matter what the value of α is. Although our proposed technique integrates networks and estimates the average closeness centrality, the performance will not be as good as the average closeness centrality computed from the

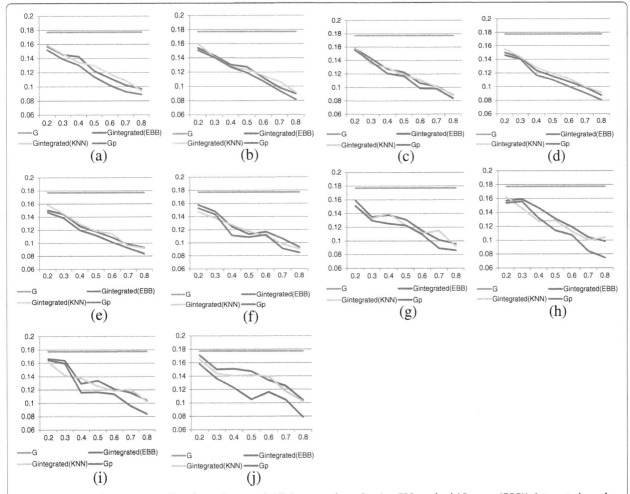

Figure 4 Average closeness centrality of complete graph (G), integrated graph using EBB method ($G_{integrated}(EBB)$), integrated graph using KNN method ($G_{integrated}(KNN)$) and incomplete graph G_P: (a) α = 0.05, (b) α = 0.15, (c) α = 0.25, (d) α = 0.35, (e) α = 0.45, (f) α = 0.55 (g) α = 0.65, (h) α = 0.75, (i) α = 0.85, (j) α = 0.95.

actual graph G. When more edges are removed before integration (β increase), the performance will degrade.

We further investigated the performance of our proposed technique by increasing the percentage of insensitive nodes from 0.05 (Figure 4(a)) to 0.95 (Figure 4(j)). Similar patterns are observed from 4(a) to 4(j). In terms of average closeness centrality, increasing or decreasing the percentage of insensitive nodes in network did not make substantial impact to the performance of our purposed technique. One plausible explanation is that: the average closeness centrality used in this experiment only reflects the performance of our approach in an abstract level. Some nodes in the integrated network may have higher closeness centrality than its original closeness centrality in the complete graph while some nodes may have lower closeness centrality in the integrated network than in the complete graph. As a result, when we consider the average closeness centrality, the differences may be offset by each other.

Figure 5 (a) presents the error ratio of ($G_{Integrated}$ (KNN)) with different α and β. Similarly, Figure 5 (b) presents the error ratio of $G_{Integrated}$ (EBB) with different α and β. We compute the errors in closeness centrality obtained from the networks with and without integration ($Error(G_{integrated})$ and $Error(G_p)$) using the error function defined in 5.2. and the error ratio is defined as:

$$\frac{Error(G_P) - Error(G_{Integrated})}{Error(G_P)}$$

Different from the average closeness centrality which we used as a measurement in Figure 4, the error function accumulates the closeness centrality difference for each

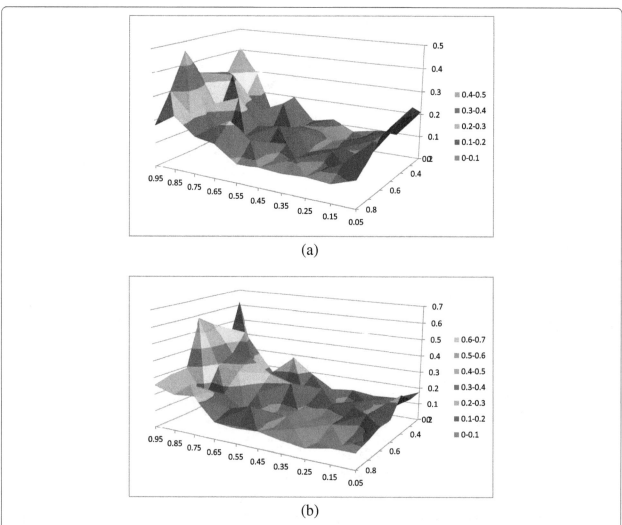

(a)

(b)

Figure 5 (a) error ratio of $G_{integrated}(KNN)$ with different settings of β and α; (b) error ratio of $G_{integrated}(EBB)$ with different settings of β and α.

individual node, so that the offset effect of average close-ness will not occur. The experiment results of Figure 5 can be used to verify our explanation to the Figure 4 in the last paragraph.

The experiment results demonstrate that when α is high (means more insensitive nodes), the improvement of our proposed technique comparing to the partial graph is also higher. The highest improvement was achieved when α equals to 0.95. The improvement decreased slowly along with the decrease of α. This observation indicated that our explanation of Figure 4 is correct. With more insensitive nodes, the integrated network will be closer to the original network so that the improvement of our technique will be higher.

Last but not least, from both Figures 4 and 5, we do not observe any significant differences of the performance between using KNN or EBB to produce generalized network. However, as it is shown in section 4.2.2, the EBB algorithm is dominated by the step of calculating the edge betweenness which has time complexity $O(N^3)$. On the other hand, KNN is much more efficient which is only $O(N)$. As a result, when the network size is huge, KNN is preferred. Moreover, in a fully connected network where several edges have the same betweenness weight, EBB will take longer to produce the generalized network. However, KNN also has its limitation. For example, KNN starts from each insensitive node to look for sensitive nodes in its neighborhood to form a sub-graph step by step. However, the search process is not fully simultaneous, but is controlled by a FOR loop. As a result, the sequence in the FOR loop is matter, especially for some nodes in the middle of two insensitive nodes. As a result, the division of sub-graph by using KNN is less natural than EBB method.

Conclusion
In this paper, we investigate the privacy preservation techniques for social network integration. We introduce a research framework which consists of three major steps. First of all, we propose the K-Nearest Neighborhood method and the Edge Betweenness Based method to decompose a social network into multiple sub-graphs. Secondly, we propose techniques to generalize a social network by sharing the probabilistic model of the generalized information. At third, we introduced the techniques of social network integration and distance estimation.

Using the Global Salafi Jihad terrorist social network as test bed, we thoroughly evaluated our proposed technique with different parameters and settings. The experiment results demonstrated that an organization can improve the accuracy of computing closeness centrality by sharing and integrating generalized information. Our proposed techniques were able to preserve the privacy as well as increase the utility of the shared social

networks. We observed that KNN performed better than EBB but did not have substantial difference. Moreover, our proposed techniques were not sensitive to the number of insensitive node but relatively sensitive to the number of removed edges.

In the future, we will continue to examine our techniques in more datasets. We will explore other graph partition models and integration techniques to improve the performance of our technique. Moreover, we will also extend our work to maintain other useful information besides distance.

Competing interests
The authors declare that they have no competing interests.

Authors' contributions
CCY proposed the research framework. CCY and XT developed the algorithms together. XT implemented the algorithms and conducted experiments. CCY and XT together drafted the manuscript. All authors read and approved the final manuscript.

References
1. Yang CC, Sageman M: Analysis of terrorist social networks with fractal views. *J Inf Sci* 2009, 35(3):299–320.
2. Yang CC, Ng T: "Terrorism and crime related weblog social network: Link, content analysis and information visualization,". *IEEE Int Conf Intell Secur Inform IEEE*, 23-24 May 2007:55–58.
3. Yang CC, Liu N, Sageman M: "Analyzing the terrorist social networks with visualization tools,". *IEEE Inte Conf Intell Secur Inform*, 23-24 May 2007:331–342.
4. Yang CC, Tang X: Social networks integration and privacy preservation using subgraph generalization. In *Proceedings of the ACM SIGKDD Workshop on CyberSecurity and Intelligence Informatics.* Edited by. : ACM; :53–61.
5. Yang CC, Tang X: Information Integration for Terrorist or Criminal Social Networks. *Ann Inform Syst* 2010, 9:41–57.
6. Tang X, Yang CC: "Generalizing terrorist social networks with K-nearest neighbor and edge betweeness for social network integration and privacy preservation,". *IEEE Int Conf Intell Secur Inform IEEE*, 23-24 May 2007:49–54.
7. Yang CC, Thuraisingham B: Privacy-Preserved Social Network Integration and Analysis for Security Informatics. *IEEE Intell Syst* 2010, 25(3):88–90.
8. Campan A, Truta T: "A clustering approach for data and structural anonymity in social networks,". In *Proceeding of the second ACM SIGKDD International Workshop on Privacy, Security, and Trust in KDD; 2008.*
9. Hay M, Miklau G, Jensen D, Weis P, Srivastava S: "Anonymizing social networks,".: University of Massachusetts Technical Report; 2007:07–19.
10. K. Liu, and E. Terzi, "Towards identity anonymization on graphs", Proceedings of the: *ACM SIGMOD international conference on Management of data.* NY, USA: ACM New York; 2008:93–106.
11. Hay M, Miklau G, Jensen D, Towsley D, Weis P: Resisting structural re-identification in anonymized social networks. *Proc VLDB Endowment Arch* 2008, 1(1):102–114.
12. Zhou B, Pei J: "Preserving privacy in social networks against neighborhood attacks,". In *IEEE 24th International Conference on Data Engineering.*: ICDE; 2008:506–515.
13. Zheleva E, Getoor L: Preserving the privacy of sensitive relationships in graph data. *Lecture Notes Comput Sci* 2008, 4980:153.
14. Backstrom L, Dwork C, Kleinberg J: "Wherefore art thou r3579x?: anonymized social networks, hidden patterns, and structural steganography,". In *Proceedings of the 16th international conference on World Wide Web.* Edited by. NY, USA: ACM New York; :181–190.
15. Cormode G, Srivastava D, Yu T, Zhang Q: Anonymizing bipartite graph data using safe groupings. *Proc VLDB Endowment Arch* 2008, 1(1):833–844.
16. Ying X, Wu X: "Randomizing social networks: a spectrum preserving approach," *SIAM Conf. on Data Mining* August 2008.
17. Sweeney L: k-anonymity: A model for protecting privacy. *Int J Uncertainty Fuzziness Knowledge Based Syst* 2002, 10(5):557–570.

18. Samarati P: **"Protecting respondents' identities in microdata release,".** *IEEE Transac Knowledge Data Eng* 2001, :1010–1027.

19. Machanavajjhala A, Kifer D, Gehrke J, Venkitasubramaniam M: **"l-diversity: Privacy beyond k-anonymity".** *ACM Trans Knowledge Discov Data (TKDD)* 2007, **1**(1):3.

20. X. Xiao, and Y. Tao, "Personalized privacy preservation", Proceedings of the: *ACM SIGMOD international conference on Management of data.* NY, USA: ACM New York; 2006:229–240.

21. Wong R, Li J, Fu A, Wang K: *"(alpha, k)-anonymity: an enhanced k-anonymity model for privacy preserving data publishing,".*: ACM Press; :754–759.

22. Frikken K, Golle P: *"Private social network analysis: How to assemble pieces of a graph privately,".* NY, USA: ACM New York; :89–98.

23. Sageman M: *Understanding Terror Networks.*: University of Pennsylvania Press; 2004.

4

Validating distance decay through agent based modeling

Arvind Verma[1]*, Ramyaa Ramyaa[2] and Suresh Marru[2]

Abstract

The objectives of this research are to display the utility of using agent based model and simulated experiments in understanding criminal behavior. In particular, this research focuses upon the distance decay function that has wide applicability in understanding ways in which offenders move about their awareness space and select their targets for committing crime. The basis for distance decay is an assumption that the offender apprehends recognition by his neighbors and so tends to commit his crime a little away but not too far from his home location. But this is an untested assumption and based upon another assumption that recognition comes from frequent interactions. There is no simple way to test these assumptions in real life. This paper argues that simulated experiments using agent based modeling are appropriate methods for difficult to test criminological concepts. In this research, two types of agents are created- one representing the offender and the other- the victim. They are assigned specific characteristics that control their action such as moving in a neighborhood, making rational choice to maximize their gain while minimizing the risk of apprehension from interaction with other residents of the neighborhood. The simulation result displays that beginning with these small principles the final model emerges as a pattern of target selection similar to the distance decay function. The importance of this technique lies in the fact that such experiments provide the means to apply agent based modeling to validate a variety of criminological concepts. While the technique has limitations of validation it can help in understanding the behavior of offenders as they commit their crimes individually as well as in groups.

Keywords: Distance decay agent based modeling movement patterns, Computational criminology

Introduction

This paper aims to develop an agent based model to test the well known concept of 'Distance Decay' [1] that forms the basis for understanding the movement pattern and target selection of offenders and for designing a variety of crime control measures. The spatial movement patterns of motivated offenders are important to study in order to understand how offenders select their targets. Indeed, spatial research is important for many criminological perspectives such as geographic profiling [2] and to understand criminal behavior and resulting crime patterns [3]. Criminological research suggests that offenders tend to travel short distances to commit their crimes. The number of crimes decreases exponentially as the distance from their home or base location increases [4]. The rational choice perspective also argues that an

offender will choose a target at shorter distance than a longer one. Furthermore, routine activity theory [5] suggests that criminal events are likely to occur around the regular paths taken by the offenders, which invariably will lie close to their home location, as these will be more common for their activities. It makes sense to believe that criminals will minimize their time and effort to commit the crime by selecting targets closer to their usual places of residence or places familiar to them.

The distance decay concept developed from the geometry of crime [1] has argued that motivated offenders select their targets within their awareness space which has been described as the places offenders know as they go about daily life [6]. Moreover, this awareness space is formed around the home, work place and areas of leisure and recreational activities of the offender. Spending more time at a place increases familiarity and suggests opportunities to the offender. Thus, within this region of awareness space lie the 'activity space' where

* Correspondence: averma@indiana.edu
[1]Department of Criminal Justice, Indiana University, Bloomington, USA
Full list of author information is available at the end of the article

offenders commit their crimes. On the other hand, another implication of this decay concept is that offenders apprehend recognition in their local neighborhood and would therefore not commit crimes in areas where they are likely to be known. This region of no crime around the home location has been dubbed as an illustration of 'buffered distance decay function' [7] implying that predatory offenders avoid committing crimes in immediate vicinity of their homes. While such buffers are absent for spontaneous or crimes of passion [8] crimes that are premeditated will involve such a buffer zone [9].

Offenders travel long distance only when they have a specific target in mind that involves planning and careful consideration. The distance between a drug dealer's home and place of transaction was seen to be less than a mile [10]. Research suggests that property crimes involve traveling greater distance [11] than crimes of predatory violence [12]. It has also been reported that most offenders commit a large number of their offenses a short distance from their residences and as the distance increases the number of offenses decreases [13]. Further, it has also been pointed out that even if the costs in time, money and energy to overcome distance reduces the probability of committing crimes with increasing distance for an individual at an aggregated level, the distance decay results hold [14]. A study of robbery found that offenders travelled further if they performed more professional robberies [15]. Robbers combined effort minimization and opportunity maximization, and that they did not travel far unless there was an incentive (usually monetary) to do so. Another study from Finland supports the distance decay model for crimes of homicide and rape [16].

Apparently, the distance to travel is determined under the condition of cost benefit rational consideration and if targets are available near by then it makes little sense to go far. However, all such research examining the spatial pattern of crime sites and inferring the distance traveled by the offender are based upon a number of assumptions. For instance, inherent in the notion of distance decay function are several conjectures about ways in which the offender forms his perceptions and engages with people around him. A major assumption is that the offender will not commit a crime in the area where he fears of being recognized by the residents [1]. The observation of buffer zone around the home location for instance would support this contention since the neighbors are likely to recognize the offender. But anyone moving into a new neighborhood soon realizes that it takes time to build acquaintance with the local residents. In western societies where privacy is a major factor in social interactions it is a common experience that familiarity and friendship with the neighbors takes time. Residents slowly become familiar with one another for interaction amongst

residents take time. But this presumption in turn is based on another belief that living in an area for certain period of time *invariably* leads to interactions with the neighbors and local residents, who would come to know the person. This assumption implies that those who would see the offender frequently are likely to recognize him. That is, the more interactions take place between the offender and the residents the greater is the possibility of being recognized.

Similar assumption governs the concept of awareness space, which comes from becoming familiar with an area. Here we may apply the routine activities approach to argue that daily activities take him to or through specific areas and where he spends large proportion of his time. Accordingly, the more time he spends in an area the greater is going to be his awareness of its layout, resident population, vulnerabilities, rhythm of activities and attractive targets. This implies greater awareness of an area will enable the offender to find out vulnerable targets that can easily be attacked. Yet, offenders have been described in various ways based upon their 'hunting' patterns [7]. The 'troller' involved in other non-predatory activities commits an offense based on opportunity. On the other hand 'trapper' creates a position that allows him to encounter victims in situations, which are under his control. Finally, there is a limit to the distance that the offender will travel as part of his routine activities and to seek out targets to commit his crimes. This implies an assumption of cost benefit analysis based upon a rational calculation of effort and benefit on part of the offender.

Therefore, based upon the above discussion the set of assumptions governing the phenomenon of distance decay are the following:

- Frequent interactions with residents implies they begin to recognize the offender
- Fear of being recognized will desist the offender from committing the crime
- Living and working for long periods increases familiarity with an area
- Familiarity is the basis of awareness space of the offender
- Predatory crimes are committed within the awareness space of the offender
- Cost benefit considerations will restrict the offender from traveling long distance to commit the crime

To this we can add one more factor, which is that successful commission of a crime will encourage the offender to commit more crimes.

It is difficult to test the validity of these assumptions in a real life situation. In criminology there are many independent variables, such as offender cognition and adaptability that cannot be manipulated, for physical, practical, or moral reasons [17]. Thus, one cannot send a motivated offender to a specific location and observe how he learns to commit his crimes and if the selection of targets reflects distance decay. Even when some information about the home location of few offenders and the burglaries that they have committed is available [3] it is impossible to judge if the above-mentioned assumptions hold true. For instance, it was seen that offenders have not committed any crime in the immediate vicinity of their home [3]. Yet, the reason for this pattern could only be speculated that this is due to the fear of being recognized. We cannot test its validity from observing the distances amongst different crime sites. One method of testing this assumption is to directly ask a large sample of offenders why their selection of targets follows a distance decay function and statistically test their responses. But how an offender begin to develop his awareness space and make his judgment about recognition by local residents is difficult to know from survey questionnaire. An offender himself may not be able to explain how his learning takes place. If at all it can be done then it has to be judged by observing the behavior of a large number of offenders over a period of time. Clearly, this is impossible in reality and has to be assessed by some other methods.

Furthermore, criminological theories themselves are relatively poor in explaining the crime phenomenon and its control mechanism due to the limitations of its data and inability to experiment with variety of variables [18]. The limits imposed by theory, data and experimentation makes it difficult to work from theory to experiment, or empirical description to theory [17]. Criminological explanations tend to be stated in broad terms that are difficult to test empirically, perhaps a reason why social sciences have difficulty making headway [19]. The problem is not limited to criminology for even in physical sciences the inability to explain uncertainties in weather patterns, the growth and effect of modern technology and communication networks, the adaptive nature of living organisms and many other complex systems from seemingly large collections of simpler components is formidable [20].

Computational criminology

A recent development in the realm of criminology has been the applications of computers and mathematical modeling to test a variety of scenarios that are difficult to judge in real life. Crime is a multidimensional, complex, and dynamic activity. In order to understand its nature one has to comprehend not only its spatio-temporal dimensions, but also the nature of crime, the victim-offender relationship; role of guardians and history of

similar incidents. Crime and its control analysis involve massive computing challenges due to the large volume of data and complexity of the human behavior. For example, a set of serious crimes for a period of 6 months in Indianapolis metropolitan area amounts to 30,000 plus data points. Rationalizing police beats based on this kind of sample crime data along with physical and resource constraints is a gigantic data analysis task. This cannot be done except by applying latest computer simulation techniques and clustering algorithms to achieve customized patrol beats for equitable workload [21]. Criminological problems like crime pattern analysis, target selection by motivated offenders, awareness space of serial criminals, offender profiling, movement patterns of victims and offenders that lead to hot spots are some areas where expertise from criminal justice, mathematics, data mining, visualization, geographic information systems, distributed computing together with applications of complex algorithms and computer simulations are required.

Computational Criminology is emerging as a new interdisciplinary field that applies computer science and mathematical methods to the study of criminological problems [22]. The complexity of human behavior, social interactions and law and society parameters present extraordinary challenges to model criminal behavior and determine the best possible means to control it. Computational Criminology is guided by the notion that crime is a rational act in which the offender weighs the risks and rewards to shape his or her behavior. Utilizing the concepts derived from Environmental Criminology [1] and Routine Activity Approach [5] growing research has focused upon ways in which individuals with motivations for criminal behavior live and move within their awareness spaces, form networks of friends and seek opportunities for crimes. The spatio-temporal dynamics of these individuals determine how they learn, encounter and sometimes exploit situations for their criminal acts. This field is bringing promising innovative techniques of analyzing criminal behavior and exploring solutions to deal with them. Computational Criminology has found applications in modeling burglaries [23], in counter-terrorism planning [24], for analyzing criminal justice system [25], to explore drug market dynamics [26] and to model street robbery [27].

Computer modeling and simulations helps to capture the complexity and diversity of human behavior in a robust and systematic way. These models can re-create and predict the appearance of complex phenomena based on the simulation of the simultaneous operations and interactions of multiple agents. Simulation and data collection can work together to advance scientific understanding [20]. Simulation provides the means whereby various characteristics of the agents, society, and the landscape can be held constant or systematically varied that are impossible using traditional social science methods [28]. These modeling techniques work on the principle whereby a computer evaluates the model numerically and produces data in order to estimate the characteristics of the model [23]. Simulated data comes from a rigorously specified set of rules rather than direct measurement of the real world [29] and this provides flexibility to the analyst to experiment with a variety of social settings. The process is one of emergences from the lower (micro) level of systems to a higher (macro) level. As such, a key notion is that simple behavioral rules generate complex behavior [24]. It is also suggested [30] that simulations function like a thought process and where 'what if' type questions under specific conditions can be examined and impact of chance can be assessed. Simulations are now becoming valuable for their capability of conducting 'virtual program evaluation' in criminology [31]. Furthermore, simulation models are able to make dynamic decisions based on changing information [32].

While the computer program could accommodate a variety of rules to simulate the process the use of simple models is suggested on grounds that these provide greater insight into the dynamics [23]. It is also noted that with simple models the subtle effects of its hypothesized mechanisms are easier to understand or discover and that the complexity should be found in the results, not in the assumptions of the model [29]. If the goal of a simulation is to attain a greater degree of understanding of some fundamental process, then it is the simplicity of the assumptions, which is important, not the accuracy of the surrounding environment [29].

Agent based modeling

A particular technique within the realm of Computational Criminology suggests that such learning scenarios can be tested through agent based modeling. In these models an independent agent is created that has the ability to take decisions based upon specific inputs and to interact with the environment and other agents. An agent can represent an individual, group, an entity or an organization. The simulation sets some rules for iteration and each step is governed by some probability that introduces variations in the system. The agent assesses the current situation and takes a decision about the next step based on the assigned probability. This mechanism incorporates a realistic human like behavior on part of the agent [33]. Thus agent based modeling provides the means to experiment with a variety of situational factors that guide human behavior. This in turn helps to model human action and judge the impact of the environment on decisions made by a human being. Agent based models can be used to create systems which mimic real scenarios and produce a dynamic history of the system under

investigation [34]. In particular, such modeling assists in experimenting with social situations that human beings confront on a daily basis that would otherwise be impossible to carry out.

Four important characteristics of the agent have been identified [23]. The agent has *autonomy* to make decisions independently without being guided by some external source once the initial conditions are set and the system is activated. Agents can be *heterogeneous* and possess different characteristics. Thus, one agent can be an offender and the other a victim. Agents are *reactive* and have the capability to respond to the environmental cues and modify their action. Thus, an offender will change his path if the residents are suspicious of his activity. Finally, the agents are programmed with *bounded rationality* by limiting their perception of their environment so that choices are not always perfectly optimal [23]. This ensures that the agent is not acting as a rational agent, which is similar to the condition of human frailty that is influenced by desires and temptations and makes them take risks. Feedback can be incorporated in agent-based models by allowing agents to change how they apply rules, based on experience [31]. Agent-based modeling in crime related situations has been applied to experiment with the effects of collective mis-belief in agent societies and illustrate how mis-beliefs can spread [35]; to outline a model that can be used to investigate civil violence [36] and to model burglary in an urban environment [23]. Computational Criminology is showing signs of gaining momentum [37].

Computational format for agent based modeling

We have prototyped a simulation tool using the techniques of agent based modeling and describe below the steps in plain terms. This simulation mimics the learning process of a motivated offender to search for suitable targets around his home location. This model is to validate one of the assumptions defined in the previous section where an agent built on machine learning concepts is trained to commit break-ins around the neighborhood. In particular, we focus upon the proposition two outlined by Brantingham and Brantingham [1] model which tests the distance decay from the home base. We see this as the first model in a series of possible models that reflect the evolving complexity of human movement in daily activities. We programmed the agent to follow a machine-learning algorithm that helps it 'learn' from environmental cues and modify its actions accordingly. The following describe the steps and logical structure of the agent modeling process:

A grid structure is created to represent the city landscape. Each cell represents a 'house' and all the grid rows and columns are the 'streets'. A motivated criminal agent [henceforth called c-agent] is designed to move randomly in this grid structure from one starting cell. For this model we focus upon the movement of the agent and align the grid so that the starting cell [home] is at the center of the grid. A characteristic assigned to the offender is 'cost consideration' based on the well known rational choice perspective. The c-agent has to expend effort to move around and select targets for break-ins to make a gain. The c-agent is given a base equity and assigned one 'mark' as the cost of moving the distance of one cell. The movement involves a 'loss' of equity based on the distance he has travelled at the rate of one unit for every cell crossed in the path. The c-agent starts from home location and randomly chooses one of the four neighboring cells to cross, as the c-agent is designed to move only on the horizontal and vertical axis. This random selection of direction is done at every stage by letting the simulation program arbitrarily choose a number from 1–4. Thus, the c-agent moves across the grid in indiscriminate manner and after traveling some distance turns back to return home.

For the return path the c-agent chooses the shortest path to return home so that the return journey 'cost' is minimal. The program is designed to ensure that the agent has the map of the grid structure and knows how to get back 'home' from any location. Depending upon the distance travelled [the number of cells traversed] the c-agent is deducted portion of 'marks' from the equity. The program is designed to ensure that the c-agent 'turns back' after expending a proportion of the equity to ensure that he is able to reach home without losing all the money. This is necessary to ensure that the c-agent does not 'decide' to continue traveling after committing the crime. A condition is required to ensure that the c-agent will not go on a crime spree, bloating his equity and continuing to add to it! The program makes the c-agent turn back immediately after break-in of a cell and puts a maximum amount that can be spent in traveling. This helps to trigger the turning back and by various experimentation we set this number to be 10% of the initial equity. Based on these parameters the computer simulates the c-agent to move around the home location and to minimize the costs. The movement pattern is a 'circle' around his home location, which is the smallest area to keep the costs down.

We 'experimented' with the behavior of the c-agent by varying these conditions one by one. If the c-agent was freely allowed to roam in a random manner without turning back the movement covered all the cells. Once a condition of 'cost' was introduced the c-agent learned to concentrate upon neighboring cells and spend not more than 90% of the base equity in his movement before turning back home. Even though the c-agent was programmed to randomly select any of the four cells [representing the four directions] surrounding his location

at every step, the final pattern emerged as a circle around the home cell. See Figure 1 below:

For the next step, in all the other cells we situated stationary agents who serve as residents [and victims] of that 'neighborhood'; we designate these as v-agent. Each cell is populated and valuable goods are provided in each home that is attractive to the c-agent. The value of goods is kept uniform across the grid to keep the program simple. The program makes the c-agent 'break-in' a cell and the value pertaining to that cell is transferred to the equity of the c-agent. The selection of cell to break-in is also done randomly after leaving the home cell. That is, the c-agent moves to a neighboring cell and the program gives an option of breaking into the cell. If the c-agent decides to break in the program stipulates the c-agent to turn back and go home after adding the goods' value to his equity. The program estimates the equity after reaching home which then becomes the initial equity to start the process again. In this experimentation we observed that the c-agent targeted the nearest cells to his home location. This was expected as it helped in keeping the 'cost' of travel low and adding value to the base equity.

Distance decay assumes that local residents know the offender and hence he will not commit the crime around his home for fear of being recognized. As mentioned above, it is unclear how one person gets to know another person. Clearly, mutual interaction is the starting point of recognition and perhaps frequent interactions cement the process of becoming acquainted. This simulation uses the memory function to remember a resident and the frequency and time elapsed in such encounters. It works on the logic that if a person is encountered a number of times the chances of remembering each other is much more. At the same time, if the person is met once and not crossed within the specified amount of time, there is a high chance of forgetting. The simulation takes these aspects into account and learns the neighborhood locations and its residents.

We use this concept in teaching the computer to set a system where by an agent gets to recognize another agent when in proximity. We instruct the computer to make the c-agent 'aware' of the resident [v-agent] whose 'house' he is crossing while traveling. We also instruct the c-agent to become aware of the identity of four other residents surrounding the cell that is being crossed [at the boundary of the grid this is suitably accounted]. In order to simplify the program we do not permit the c-agent to travel angularly and move only on the Manhattan path.

The geographical coordinates of the cells mark the identity of the v-agents. Furthermore, a time stamp is assigned to this identity when the c-agent crosses the cell. As time passes, the probability with which the c-agent can recall the identity of the v-agent is made to decrease. This is set up by letting the c-agent toss a

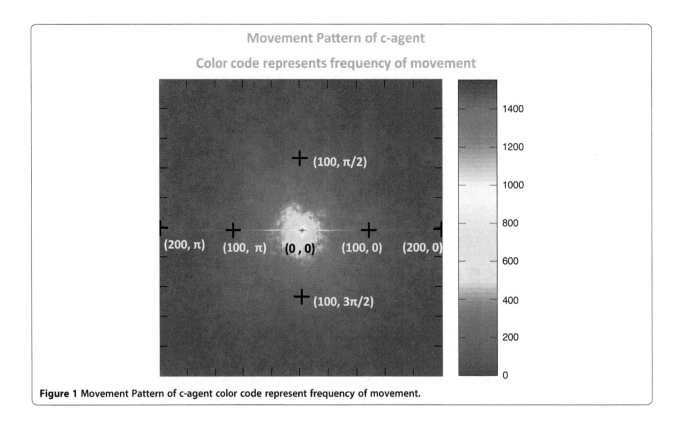

Figure 1 Movement Pattern of c-agent color code represent frequency of movement.

weighted coin to decide whether he can remember this v-agent where the weights correspond to the time period for every v-agent. This probability is assigned by a standard procedure in computer sciences- to determine an action based on probability a procedure similar to tossing a weighted coin is followed. For example, if the probability is given as a fractional number between 0–1, then the computer generates a random real number from 0 to 1. If this random number is greater than the assigned probability, the agent will do one action, like going back home and if not, the other action of roaming further. Again, some experimentation was done to fine tune the program and ensure that the c-agent does not 'jump' widely across the grid. The learning takes place by letting the c-agent build a data file of long and short-term memory of interactions with the house occupants in the space he is moving. The decision to commit crime comes from his memory- if he recognizes a house occupant he will not commit the crime. If the recognition is 'fuzzy' [the house occupant is in his short term memory] he will toss a weighted coin and take a chance of committing the crime. The c-agent 'gambles' on the house occupant not recognizing him for the recognition is mutual-the c-agent and v-agents recognize each other only through interaction when a particular cell is crossed.

For instance, if the c-agent is crossing location L_1 he will recognize resident v-agent L_1 living there. We then let the c-agent go to location L_2 at time T_0. If asked at time T_{0+n}, the probability that c-agent will recognize the resident v-agent L_1 is $1-f(n)$ where the function 'f' increases with respect to n. An example of such a function is $f(n) = 0.1*n$. So, after 1 step, the c-agent will be identified 90% of the time, but after 6 steps, only 40% of the time. We had to experiment with such functions for with this particular function, the memory is active for only 10 steps.

Further, the above memory has no way to "get to know" a person. That is we need something that says if you repeatedly see a person, you will remember him for a long time after you saw him - much longer than you will remember someone whom you have not seen repeatedly. Our requirement then is to implement a (linearly) decaying memory, i.e., if a v-agent does not see the c-agent for a while, the v-agent forgets the criminal. However, we had to incorporate familiarity (for instance, acquaintances will remember a person temporarily even when they have not been seen in a while). To capture this, we set the memory decay rate to slow down at each encounter. We remedy it by altering the above function as $f(n, x) = x*n$

As before, we start with $x = 0.1$

This will mean that memory is active for only 10 steps.

If within the 10 steps, the c-agent interacts with the v-agent we change x to $x*0.9$

This will ensure that the criminal will be remembered longer than 10 steps. This is a linear function, but it can be modified to any function as desired. A number of experiments were conducted with varying functions to finalize the program.

Moreover, recognition is mutual. Thus, the resident v-agent will remember the c-agent for a certain period of time once his cell is crossed. We set the learning by the simple idea of symmetry. The c-agent and v-agents (residents) are symmetric - i.e. the c-agent is seen by a v-agent if and only if the c-agent can see the v-agent, and this happens every time a cell is crossed by the c-agent or if the c-agent is in the neighboring cell following on the X or the Y-axis.

Some other details had to be accounted also. When a memory decayed fully, the decay rate will also be reset. There were two cases with no memory: when a v-agent has never seen the criminal [c-agent], and when a v-agent has seen the c-agent so long ago that the memory has decayed. We tried considering this to be different, in the sense that a forgotten, but refreshed memory has a slower decay than a new memory. However, in our experimentation we found that this difference was not significant for the outcome. The computer was set so that the criminal's memory of the v-agent was the same as the v-agent's memory of the c-agent.

Using this, at each grid point, the c-agent knows the probability with which he will be recognized [and hence caught]. Based on this probability, he decides whether or not to break-in there. At every stage the computer calculates the probability by the toss of a coin to determine if the c-agent should commit the crime or leave that cell alone.

The system monitors the interaction of the c-agent with these other v-agents each time a cell is crossed in random movement. That is, when the c-agent moves from point 'L_A' to point 'L_B' on the grid all the intervening cell residents get to see the c-agent and vice versa. This serves the objective of 'recognition' of the criminal agent by the particular resident whose house is crossed during the movement. The resident v-agent observes the c-agent crossing his property and keeps this recognition in a short-term memory. If the criminal c-agent returns from a different path from point 'B' to his home location then again all intervening cells that are crossed in this path also get to recognize the c-agent.

Now, each resident v-agent is given a 'memory' that is short term and long term in its design. As the c-agent crosses a cell the v-agent recognizes him for a short duration according to the in built clock of the system. If the c-agent interacts frequently with a particular resident [v-agent] by crossing through his cell repeatedly the recognition becomes embedded into long term memory. Clearly, the 'neighbors' of the c-agent will be those who will have him in their long-term memory.

Next, the c-agent is assigned the characteristic to 'break into homes' at infrequent time periods when moving randomly. In the present situation, all homes have the same attraction value so that opportunities for break-in are uniformly distributed. With this characteristic the c-agent commits break-ins randomly in the region around his home in various movement paths based upon the distance and recognition of the v-agent. This gives a scatter plot of random commission of break-ins around the home location of the offender. Each of the break-ins provides the 'profit' for the offender for committing the crime. The simulation displays the cells that are targeted more frequently in a color code.

Each v-agent is also given the characteristics of 'catching' the offender [c-agent] if the recognition is reached to the level of long-term memory and if the c-agent tries to 'break-in'. This is achieved by reducing the probability of successful break in if the probability of recognition was high. The simulation suggests that the neighboring residents catch the c-agent more often close by around his home location. Once 'caught' the c-agent loses a certain percentage of the equity and the program starts again. We experimented with the size of the grid to observe this phenomenon and decided to enlarge the size to a 200×200 cell grid for a meaningful pattern to emerge. The numbers of simulations were also enlarged to 500 with each ranging from 1000 to 2000 steps.

We combine all the characteristics to set the following scenario: the c-agent moves randomly around his home but does not travel too far due to the costs of travelling. Every time he crosses a cell he is recognized by the resident and the more often this happens the resident begins to recognize the c-agent. The cells, representing houses provide uniform opportunities and hence a 'profit' for the c-agent, which serves as the incentive to commit the crime. The c-agent 'gains marks' for every successful break-in and 'loses marks' by travelling [one mark per cell], or if he gets caught through recognition. If the resident v-agent has the c-agent in his long-term memory then the resident catches the c-agent. The c-agent will then lose a certain percentage of his equity. Every time the c-agent is caught or the base equity drops below a threshold the program resets and starts the process again. This simulation is run a large number of times and the resulting plot of distance traveled around the home location is shown below Figure 2:

The scatter displays that the c-agent has to travel far to maintain the gain for 'local' residents are going to catch him. The color code indicates the frequency of the c-agent hitting the target. Significantly, there is a small buffer zone where no crimes are committed. The blue region represents the space where the c-agent does not commit any crimes. The red and yellow regions display the regions where the crimes are committed frequently. The light blue represents the region where crimes are committed but infrequently.

The frequencies of committing a crime and the distance from the home location are then plotted in a cumulative frequency plot shown below Figure 3:

The resulting plot indicates the distribution as suggested by the distance decay function. The shape resembles the one theorized by Brantingham and Brantingham [1] though it is jagged and has a small buffer zone where the probability of committing the crime is negligible. The simulation suggests that given the above conditions the c-agent will not travel far to commit the crime and will avoid places in close proximity to his home. We believe a very large number of 'runs' could smoothen the curve and the peaks and sudden drops would coalesce. We consider the overall shape of the cumulative frequency curve and not address the jagged peaks and valleys that are embedded in it. A large number of crimes are shown to be committed since all houses are equally attractive to the c-agent. In practice, houses will have varying goods to steal and attractiveness to break-in. This will lower the frequency of break-ins and which will vary across the space around the home of the c-agent.

Discussion

The designed program found remarkable coherence with the 'distance decay' concept. The c-agent would commit the break-ins much more frequently near his home location and would not travel far to seek the targets. Even

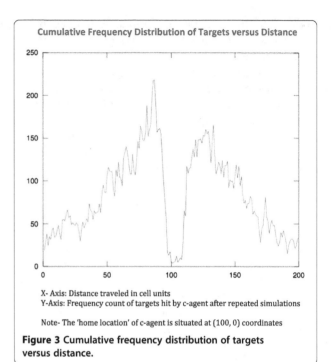

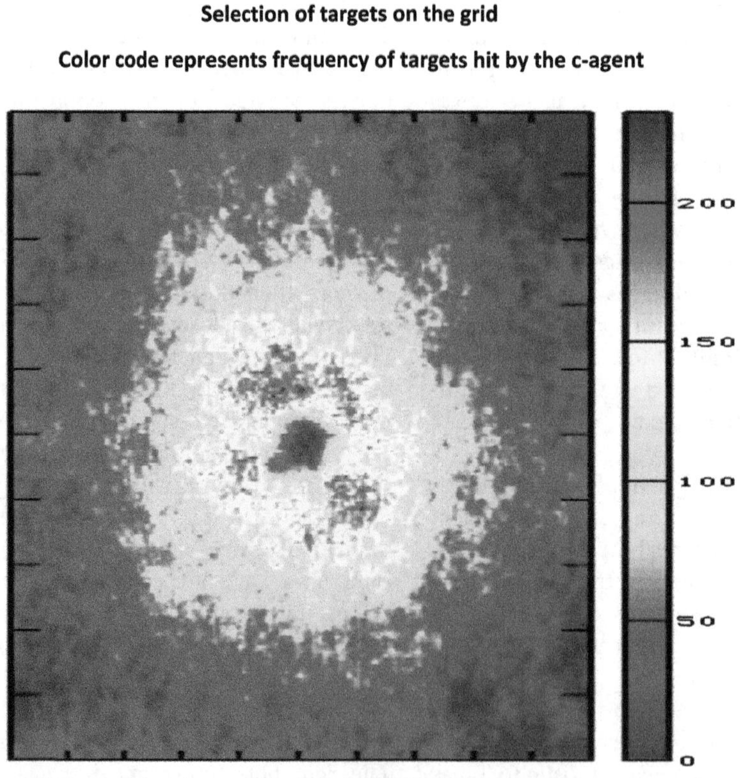

X- Axis: Distance traveled in cell units
Y-Axis: Frequency count of targets hit by c-agent after repeated simulations

Note- The 'home location' of c-agent is situated at (100, 0) coordinates

Figure 3 Cumulative frequency distribution of targets versus distance.

Selection of targets on the grid

Color code represents frequency of targets hit by the c-agent

Figure 2 Selection targets on the grid color code represents targets hit by the c-agent.

when greater opportunities were provided by way of expanding the grid and ensuring that every cell provided 'valuable' goods, the agent did not seem 'interested' in venturing far from the home location. Despite the increase in probability of being recognized through greater interaction, the probability of 'gain' would work out more than the 'loss' even though the value of goods was kept marginal. We also experimented with some modifications to the wandering of the criminal. The program was modified so that at each grid point, the c-agent was given the option of deciding to go home. This result was only to make him circle around his home more time but seek targets in close proximity.

The second modification was to let the agent decide how long the trip would be before leaving home. This helped in learning where he is caught and where he can commit the crime to gain a profit. But overall, the selection of the targets did not change much. We made one more modification to set a real life situation by introducing a probability option at every home. The c-agent was not to know if the cell is occupied and would have to take a chance to break in. The probability of occupancy was kept uniform for every cell. The results suggested that final plot still resembled the one shown in Figure 2 and supported the distance decay function.

Nevertheless, this result needs to be interpreted with caution. Simulation is still a nascent methodology in criminology and its applicability is not widely practiced. There are several questions regarding the validity of the simulated model and its implications for criminological theories. Three criteria for 'validating' computer models have been proposed [38]. The qualitative credibility is established if the model is consistent with what is expected of the result. The internal quantitative credibility is met when the model output corresponds to observations that are a part of the data used to develop and calibrate the model. Furthermore, external quantitative credibility corresponds to the situation when the model output corresponds well to observations from data not used to develop and calibrate the model [38]. It needs to be kept in mind that in social sciences good and even valid evaluation data is difficult to obtain. Indeed, in criminology not only is the data difficult to obtain but also by its very nature is likely to be deliberately misleading [31]. The offender is unlikely to provide full information about his criminal behavior and even the police data is likely to be governed by organizational policies. Accordingly, for a system based upon agent based modeling it seems 'qualitative credibility' is perhaps the main basis for accepting these results. The distance decay concept corresponds to a good extent to the theoretical model suggested by Brantingham and Brantingham [1] and its replication is a point of validation of the model.

As discussed above, there are no data sets that can be used to test the efficacy of the simulated model. The police do not record exact movement of offenders in reaching their targets. Furthermore, ways in which offenders search for their targets are perhaps unknown to them too. The offender builds his awareness space by frequent movement and interaction in a given area. But the selection of targets could be based upon some additional intelligence and observation rather than exclusively on the condition of 'recognition'. Even in cases where the police are able to apprehend the offender and obtain a full confession this information is not recorded properly and in any case such examples are too little and far between to develop into a useful data base. Agent based models do not represent an empirical test of the theory but rather the extent to which the theory is plausible [7]. Thus, validation of the model has to be accepted largely on the basis of qualitative credibility [38].

Another major limitation is that the selection of the target is unlikely to be guided only by the two conditions of cost and fear of recognition. Crime pattern theory [39] and the extant research suggest offender movement is structured by neighborhood characteristics, the target backcloth, and influenced by other locations in the offender's activity space, such as workplace or past residences [40,41]. However, it seems that these two conditions may be playing a significant role for these by themselves do replicate the distance decay function.

Moreover, we acknowledge that this is a simplistic model that begins with the first condition suggested by Brantingham and Brantingham [1]. The agent begins as if there is no awareness space and the movement is solely guided by geography and the conditions stipulated in the model. In reality, the offender commits crimes in the awareness space as suggested by the fully developed Brantingham and Brantingham model [1]. But our model is able to show how this awareness space is itself *developed* by the random movements. Every time the agent ventures out, explores the neighborhood and returns back, the information about the paths, c-agents and 'gains' made in the break-ins is registered in the memory. This is the process by which the agent builds his awareness space and which mimics the development of awareness space of human beings too. The agent learns to maximize the gain by experimenting with various paths and break-ins. This by itself an important contribution for it provides the means to test many other variations of the learning process.

Indeed, this is the significant contribution of the paper that it demonstrates a methodology whereby, simple assumptions guide the behavior of agents and this in turn helps explore and understand the complex phenomenon of crime. Agent based modeling has the further advantage of not being completely deterministic in its formulation. The system of 'gain and loss' induces a feedback into the action of the agent. The consequence is that the agent 'learns' to find suitable targets that increase his gain and minimize the loss. It is this 'learning' that corresponds to real life learning where reward and punishment operate to shape the behavior of the motivated offender.

Future work

We are now developing the simulation to add more features to the program. In the future we intend to broaden the assumptions and apply more characteristics to the c-agent and the v-agents. The grid would have one-way streets, blocked exits and non-uniform distribution of homes to target. The next version of the simulation will go beyond simple grid based structure and incorporate real-world aspects based GIS city maps. Further, to test the theory in a realistic situation we need to make each resident of the region [v-agents] also move randomly. If everyone is moving the c-agent will have the option of breaking into neighboring cells also, even when the resident have him in his long term memory. Furthermore, each cell will be differentially weighted for affluence and security features. This will set the stage for the offender to pick and choose more affluent targets even if he has to travel longer distances. Another feature is to add a characteristic of deciphering if the home is unoccupied. The c-agent will 'observe' if newspapers are piled up or there is no vehicle in the garage for every cell and if so found, the probability of committing the crime will increase accordingly. Finally, some police 'guardians' will also be made to move randomly and the c-agent will be required to commit the crime only if the police vehicle is at least a minimum distance away. We believe such a program will help understand ways in which motivated offenders construct their awareness space; develop skills in identifying vulnerable targets and finally in selecting them for crime. We have used the system of frequent interactions that leads to recognition. This will be explored further to see how the agent will build friendships with similarly motivated offenders and increase his awareness space and range of operations. The Brantingham and Brantingham model [1] describes a wider range of operations for the motivated offender. The offender first commits crimes around his home location; then adds the surrounding areas of his place of work and recreation and gradually includes the regular paths that he takes in his routine movements from home to work to shopping area and back to home. If the principles that guide this movement and establish the model are as described above- rational choice based upon cost consideration and risk of recognition, added with routine activities that takes him to other parts of the region, then we expect the simulated model to emulate this pattern.

Conclusion

Clearly, agent based modeling provides an interesting mode to experiment with various situations that can closely resemble the reality. This has significant implications for testing different criminological theories by setting up an experiment and simulating the machine to carrying out all the possibilities. The major factor is to let the machine learn by trial and error and not to define the possibilities. The logical structure has to be arranged in a manner where the experiment has unexpected situations and possibilities. Above all, the researcher should not impose the conditions to reach a pre-defined conclusion. The machine must be designed to mimic human learning by trial and error, basing preferential actions on statistical results that increase the probability of success.

Agent based modeling appears to provide a promising method to examine, explore and even test criminological theories. There is a general consensus that criminal behavior is learned through interaction and perhaps on a trial and error basis [42]. Past actions that lead to undesirable outcome are not repeated and new avenues are explored. Agent based modeling can implement this conceptualization through laboratory experiments. The rational choice perspective [43] also suggests that offenders make an assessment of risk and gain, which guides their action. Such a 'bounded rationality' lends itself for reproduction in a machine environment through an agent based modeling method similar to the one outlined above [44]. Such a learning environment could also be extended to include more than one agent [45]. A feedback system could enable the agents to learn from one another through mutual interaction. Such a program can examine theories about group behavior; formation of mob and crowd control tactics to be used by the police. Agent based models constructed on Geographic Information System platform could be developed to present real life scenario and to analyze ways of handling large group of anti-social elements such as seen during London riots recently. Furthermore, gang culture; formation of special interest groups and spread of information within extended communities through modern communication are all arenas where machine learning through agent based modeling can find applications. The ability to explore options and validate concepts is perhaps the most significant possibility coming out of this technology.

Competing interests
The authors declare that they have no competing interests.

Authors' contribution
AV conceptualized the research and designed the basic structure of the experiment. He also did the literature review and writing of the article. SM helped set up the theme for computer simulation and design of the analysis.

RR designed and carried out the simulation and the production of the figures and results. All authors read and approved the final manuscript.

Author details
[1]Department of Criminal Justice, Indiana University, Bloomington, USA.
[2]Department of Computer Science, Indiana University, Bloomington, USA.

References

1. PJ Brantingham, PL Brantingham, *Environmental Criminology* (Sage, Beverley Hills, Ca., 1981)
2. K Rossmo, Geographic Profiling, *Target Patterns Of Serial Murderers PhD Thesis* (Simon Fraser University, Burnaby, 1995)
3. GF Rengert, AR Piquero, PR Jones, Distance decay reexamined. Criminology **37**(2), 427–445 (1999)
4. DL Capone, W Woodrow Jr, Nichols, Urban Structure and Criminal Mobility. Am. Behav. Sci. **20**, 119–2213 (1976)
5. LE Cohen, M Felson, Social Change and Crime Rate Trends: A Routine Activity Approach. Am. Sociol. Rev. **44**, 588–608 (1979)
6. M Felson, *Crime and Nature* (Sage, Thousand Oaks, CA, 2006)
7. K Rossmo, *Geographic Profiling* (CRC Press, Boca Raton, FL, 2000)
8. JL LeBeau, The methods and measures of centrography and the spatial dynamics of rape. J. Quant. Criminol. **3**, 125–141 (1987)
9. D Canter, P Larkin, The environmental range of serial rapists. J. Environ. Psychol. **13**, 663–669 (1993)
10. JE Eck, Drugs Trips, *Drug Offender Mobility* (Paper presented at the 44th American Society of Criminology Annual Meetings, New Orleans, 1992)
11. P Wiles, A Costello, *The 'road to nowhere': the evidence for travelling criminals, Home Office Research Study 207* (Home Office, London, 2000)
12. R Block, A Galary, D Brice, The Journey to Crime: Victims and Offenders Converge in Violence Index Offences in Chicago. Secur. J. **20**, 123–137 (2007)
13. A Rand, *Patterns in juvenile delinquency: A spatial perspective* (University Microfilms International Ann Arbor, MI, 1984)
14. PJ Van Koppen, JW de Keijser, Desisting distance decay: On the aggregation of individual crime trips. Criminology **35**(3), 505–515 (1996)
15. PJ Van Koppen, W Robert, J Jansen, The road to the robbery: travel patterns in commercial robberies. Br. J. Criminol. **38**(2), 230–246 (1998)
16. P Santtila, A Zappala, M Laukkanen, Testing the utility of a geographic profiling approach in three rape series of a single offender: A case study. Forensic Sci. Int. **131**(1), 42–52 (2003)
17. L Liu, J Eck (eds.), *Artificial Crime Analysis Systems: Using Computer Simulations and Geographic Information Systems* (IGI Global, Pennsylvania, 2008)
18. D Weisburd, A Piquero, How Well Do Criminologists Explain Crime? Statistical Modeling in Published Studies. Crime and Justice **17**, 453–502 (2008)
19. P Hedström, *Dissecting the Social: On the Principles of Analytical Sociology* (Oxford University Press, UK, 2005)
20. JH Miller, SE Page, *Complex Adaptive Systems: An Introduction to Computational Models of Social Life* (Princeton University Press, Princeton Studies in Complexity, 2007)
21. A Verma, R Ramyaa, S Marru, Y Fan, R Singh, *Rationalizing Police Patrol Beats using Voronoi Tesellations* (Proceedings of the IEEE International Conference on Intelligence and Security Informatics, Vancouver BC, Canada, 2010)
22. PL Brantingham, PJ Brantingham, Computer simulation as a tool for environmental criminologists. Security Journal **17**(1), 21–30 (2004)
23. N Malleson, *Agent Based Modeling of Burglary PhD Thesis* (School of Geography, The University of Leeds, UK, 2010)
24. HH Tsang, AJ Park, M Sun, U Glasser, *GENIUS: A Computational Modeling Framework for Counter-Terrorism Planning and Response* (Proc. IEEE Intelligence and Security Informatics Vancouver BC, Canada, 2010)
25. A Alimadad, P Borwein, PL Brantingham, PJ Brantingham, V Dabbaghian-Abdoly, R Ferguson, E Fowler, AH Ghaseminejad, C Giles, J Li, N Pollard, A Rutherford, A Waal, Utilizing Simulation Modeling for Criminal Justice System Analysis, in *Artificial Crime Analysis*, ed. by L Liu, J Eck (Idea Group Publishing, Hershey, PA, 2009), pp. 372–411
26. A Dray, L Mazerolle, P Perez, A Ritter, Policing Australia's heroin drought: using an agent-based model to simulate alternative outcomes. J. Exp. Criminol. **4**(3), 267–287 (2008)
27. L Liu, X Wang, J Eck, J Liang, Simulating crime events and crime patterns in a RA/CA models, in *Geographic Information Systems and Crime Analysis*, ed. by F Wang (Idea Publishing, Reading, PA, 2005), pp. 197–213
28. ER Groff, Simulation for Theory Testing and Experimentation: An Example Using Routine Activity Theory and Street Robbery. J. Quanti. Criminol. **23**, 75–103 (2007)
29. R Axelrod, Advancing the art of simulation in the social sciences, in *Simulating Social Phenomena*, ed. by R Conte, R Hegselmann, P Terna (Springer, Berlin, 1997), pp. 21–40
30. SD Johnson, Repeat Burglary Victimization: A tale of two theories. J. Exp. Criminol. **4**, 215–240 (2008)
31. J Eck, L Liu, Contrasting simulated and empirical experiments in crime prevention. J. Exp. Criminol. **4**, 195–213 (2008)
32. E Bonabeau, Agent-based modeling: Methods and techniques for simulating human systems. Proc. Natl. Acad. Sci. **99**, 7280–7287 (2002)
33. S Moss, B Edmonds, Towards good social science. J. Artif. Soc. Soc. Simul. **8**(4), 13 (2005). http://jasss.soc.surrey.ac.uk/8/4/13.html
34. M Joshua, *Epstein, Robert Axtell, Growing Artificial Societies Social Science From the Bottom Up* (Brookings Institution Press and MIT Press, Cambridge, MA, 1996)
35. J Doran, Simulating collective mis-belief. J. Artif. Soc. Soc. Simul. **1**(1) (1998). http://jasss.soc.surrey.ac.uk/1/1/3.html
36. JM Epstein, Modeling civil violence: An agent-based computational approach. Proc. Natl. Acad. Sci. **99**(3), 7243–7250 (2002)
37. PL Brantingham, PJ Brantingham, M Vajihollahi, K Wuschke, Crime analysis at multiple scales of aggregation: A topological approach, in *Putting Crime in its Place: Units of Analysis in Geographic Criminology*, ed. by D Weisburd, W Bernasco, G Bruinsma (Springer, New York, 2009)
38. R Berk, How you can tell if the simulations in computational criminology are any good? J. Exp. Criminol. **4**, 289–308 (2008)
39. PL Brantingham, PJ Brantingham, *Patterns in Crime* (Macmillan, New York, 1984)
40. W Bernasco, P Nieuwbeerta, How do residential burglars select target areas? Br. J. Criminol. **45**(3), 296–315 (2005)
41. W Bernasco, A sentimental journey to crime: Effects of residential history on crime location choice. Criminology **48**, 389–416 (2010)
42. RL Akers, *Social Learning and Social Structure: A General Theory of Crime and Deviance* (Northeastern University Press, Boston, 1998)
43. RV Clarke, DB Cornish, Rational Choice, in *Explaining Criminals and Crime*, ed. by R Paternoster, R Bachman (Roxbury, Los Angeles, 2001), pp. 23–42
44. D O'Sullivan, M Haklay, Agent-based models and individualism: Is the world agent-based? Environ. Plann. **32**(8), 1409–1425 (2000)
45. PL Brantingham, U Glasser, B Kinney, K Singh, M Vajihollahi, Modeling Urban Crime Patterns, in *Viewing Multi-Agent Systems as Abstract State Machines*, ed. by D Beauquier, E Börger, A Slissenko (Proc. 12th International Workshop on Abstract State Machines, Paris, 2005)

5

An agent-based model and computational framework for counter-terrorism and public safety based on swarm intelligence[a]

Andrew J Park[1][*], Herbert H Tsang[2], Mengting Sun[3] and Uwe Glässer[3]

Abstract

Public safety has been a great concern in recent years as terrorism occurs everywhere. When a public event is held in an urban environment like Olympic games or soccer games, it is important to keep the public safe and at the same time, to have a specific plan to control and rescue the public in the case of a terrorist attack. In order to better position public safety in communities against potential threats, it is of utmost importance to identify existing gaps, define priorities and focus on developing approaches to address those.

In this paper, we present a system which aims at providing a decision support, threats response planning and risk assessment. Threats can be in the form of Chemical, Biological, Radiological, Nuclear and Explosive (CBRNE) weapons and technologies. In order to assess and manage possible risks of such attacks, we have developed a computational framework of simulating terrorist attacks, crowd behaviors, and police or safety guards' rescue missions. The characteristics of crowd behaviors are modeled based on social science research findings and our own virtual environment experiments with real human participants. Based on gender and age, a person has a different behavioral characteristic. Our framework is based on swarm intelligence and agent-based modeling, which allows us to create a large number of people with specific behavioral characteristics. Different test scenarios can be created by importing or creating 3D urban environments and putting certain terrorist attacks (such as bombs or toxic gas) on specific locations and time-lines.

Introduction

Since September 11, 2001, counter-terrorism and national security have become the main focus of defense and security authorities around the globe. Counter-terrorism initiatives aim at developing effective and efficient strategies and tools in order to prepare against, prevent and respond to a wide variety of terrorist threats, including Chemical, Biological, Radiological, Nuclear and Explosive (CBRNE) threats [1]. As such, governments and security agencies have been actively trying to improve their capabilities by funding and supporting innovative science and technology approaches that address national public safety and security needs and provide tools for CBRNE response and preparedness.

In order to better position communities against potential threats, it is of utmost importance to identify existing gaps, define priorities and focus on developing approaches to address those. In Canada, national security agencies have identified different priority areas to improve CBRNE response capabilities and to organize counter-terrorism activities. One major area is Risk Assessment and Priority Setting; i.e. to develop advanced tools and techniques that allow for a reliable understanding of threats, consolidated risk assessment, and rating of threat scenarios. A well-defined risk assessment approach leads to a systematic analysis of capability gaps and provides guidelines for setting of investment priorities in order to address the most critical gaps [1].

As such, computational and mathematical methods arguably have an enormous potential for serving practical needs in counter-terrorism initiatives by offering new approaches and tools for preparing initial assess-

*Correspondence: apark@tru.ca
[1]Institute for Canadian Urban Research Studies (ICURS), Simon Fraser University, Burnaby, BC, Canada and Thompson Rivers University, Kamploops, BC, Canada
Full list of author information is available at the end of the article

ments of the risk of various scenarios involving CBRNE terrorist attacks and recommendations for appropriate responses.

In our previous work on the Mastermind project [2-4], we explored the use of computational modeling in crime analysis, investigation and prevention. Simulation models provide effective experimental platforms for decision support in evidence-based policy making. Our focus in the Mastermind project was on spatial-temporal aspects of a wide range of criminal activities in urban environments. In [3], we discussed the potential of enhancing the framework to be used in the analysis of terrorism and counter-terrorism. This paper introduces such an enhanced framework that builds on top of our previous research (Mastermind) and makes an extension to allow the simulation of larger number of agents.

The work presented here aims at providing a decision support, CBRNE response planning and risk assessment system, called *GENIUS*. (In Roman Mythology, *Genius* is a tutelary deity or guardian spirit of a person or place [5]). We use spatial-temporal features of the environment and CBRNE threat indicators for risk analysis through studying different potential scenarios and for real-time situation analysis. The proposed system can be applied in different application contexts including critical infrastructure protection, dangerous hazard emergency response, and special event security planning (e.g. the 2010 Winter Olympics in Vancouver).

The remainder of this paper is structured as follows. Section "The GENIUS system" provides an overview of the *GENIUS* project and discusses the main building blocks of *GENIUS* in more detail including technical details of the system. Section "Experiments and preliminary results" provides some preliminary results, and Section "Conclusions" concludes the paper. Furthermore, the objectives of this paper are as follows:

- To develop a model to support the analysis and modeling of complex, large-scale agent systems.
- To assess the effectiveness of different evacuation strategies in high occupancy building.
- To compare and examine different evacuation scenarios.

The GENIUS system
A Computational Framework
In the project *GENIUS*, the framework provides some standardized components and possibly a basic design for the modeling and simulation tools to investigate human behavior in urban environments. The goal is to capture the complexity and diversity of human behavior in a robust and systematic way. In the course of this project, using the Agent-Based Modeling (ABM) techniques, we developed a methodological framework and tool environment to address the needs and challenges of modeling complex behaviors.

ABM is a class of computational models for simulating the actions and interactions of autonomous agents with each other and the environment. This approach is based on the idea that a system is composed of decentralized individual agents and that each agent interacts with other agents and the environment according to localized knowledge and rules. The goal of the model is to re-create and predict the appearance of complex phenomena based on the simulation of the simultaneous operations and interactions of multiple agents. The process is one of emergence from the lower (micro) level of systems to a higher (macro) level. As such, a key notion is that simple behavioral rules generate complex behavior.

The *GENIUS* framework is divided into five components: 1) the Agent Module (AM) model for decision making process and different behaviors of the agents, 2) the Spatial and Environmental Module (SEM) that models the navigation space, 3) the Visualization Module (VM) to allow the visualization of the results during and after the simulation, 4) the Target Selection Module (TSM) models specific agent behaviors while making decision and accomplishing a specific goal, and 5) the Event Generation Module (EGM) that generates threats in a timed fashion. This is a flexible architecture which allows the modification of each module easily.

The goal of this research is to develop a framework to support the analysis and modeling of complex, large-scale agent systems. Moreover, instead of the current approach of using input-output behavior of individual agents, the model allows the behavior to be parametrized in terms of variables that represent aggregated behavior of large numbers of agents. In the subsequent sections, we explain each module in detail.

Agent-Based Modeling
Agent-based modeling is a computational method that enables researchers to create, analyze, and experiment with models composed of decentralized agents that interact with each other and within an environment according to localized knowledge [6]. This modeling technique is using a bottom-up approach in contrast to a top-down approach where the system is breaking down into compositional sub-systems and each sub-systems are refined in greater detail. The bottom-up approach allows the agents to make local decisions for themselves and we can observe the emergent behavior in the global level. In the past decade, the concept of agent-based modeling has been successfully developed and applied to problems that exhibit complex behavioral patterns [7].

The agent behavior engine in *GENIUS* is constructed using the *Swarm Intelligence* (SI) paradigm [8]. The expression *Swarm Intelligence* was first introduced by

Beni and Wang in the context of cellular robotic systems [9]. Since then, SI has been successfully applied in many areas, including forecasting pedestrian evacuation times [10], diagnosis of human tremor [11] and a variety of optimization applications. SI is a decentralized and self-organized system where the collective behaviors of agents interacting locally with their environment cause coherent functional global behaviors. Typically these agents are unsophisticated and global patterns emerge from their collective behavior. SI relies upon countless interactions between individual agents, each of which is following simple rules of thumb.

Agents

The central component of the *GENIUS* is an agent-based modeling tool that utilize *swarm intelligence* (SI). Agents provide a natural abstraction for using geographically distributed computational and memory resources. Typically, agents are autonomous mobile actors that may be invoked to satisfy specific goals, possibly requiring travel within an environment. In our model, each agent represents an individual moving around in an urban environment. Agents navigate within the environment and may assume different roles such as citizens, visitors, or police. Depending on their roles, they exhibit different behaviors [6].

The approach that *GENIUS* uses in defining an agent's behavior is based on a hierarchical parametric approach which is a part of the Agent Module (AM) module. The essence of defining a different type of an agent is a set of numerical parameters, each of which controls some aspect of the agent's behaviors. Parameters are typically unitized vectors, each representing a sub-routine which performs some low level complex transformations on the part of the behavior it controls. Because parameters are abstracted from their low level numerical parameters, they have mathematically rigorous properties such as the ability to be combined, subtracted, and/or added together while still maintaining controllable and repeatable effects to the agent model.

Using a parametric model to model human behaviors is not new in the literature. Wakita et. al [12] modeled the driving behavior when following another vehicle. Parameters can be varied independently to modify a specific agent's behavior (e.g. walking speed, memory, decision rules etc.) This authoring paradigm is highly flexible, allowing a wide range of applications. The entire set of parameters can be exposed individually for full low level authoring control or a sub-set of these parameters with constraints can be presented to a novice user for customization and personalization. In general, agents can be described by the following characteristics [6]:

- **Perception**: the agents can perceive their environment and other agents in their vicinity.

- **Performance**: the agents have a set of behaviors that they can perform, often include the following: motion, communication, and action.
- **Memory**: the agents can record their perceptions of the previous states and actions.
- **Policy**: the agents operate using a set of rules, heuristics, or strategies.

Higher-level constructs can be imposed on the basic parameter scheme by combining low-level parameters to create application specific descriptive elements. In this way we have begun to build up a hierarchical library of behaviors and agent types which all can be combined and changed in any number of ways. In the highest level of the hierarchy of the *GENIUS* system, there are three types of agents profile in our model: 1) police, 2) citizen, and 3) visitor and they all behave differently. Furthermore, the second level of the agent's profile hierarchy can be refined using the following parametric qualities: age (small children, adult, seniors), gender (male and female), and personalities (bold or fearful).

Users can define a number of agents with the same characteristics or create an agent with an individual profile separately. The characteristics of crowd behaviors are modeled based on our previous research studies in examining pedestrians in an urban environment [13]. These experiments were performed in our own virtual environment. Through the experiments, we found that people had different behavioral characteristics based on their gender and age. Our framework incorporates these findings to create a large number of people with specific behavioral characteristics.

Figure 1 shows the visualization of a group of agents while the simulation is running. Note that in order to simulate a large number of agents, we have introduced the idea of the *cluster agent*. From a distance, the cluster of many agents will be presented by a single agent (cluster agent) with an area surrounding him/her. However, when the cluster is zoomed in, the individual agents can be seen in a finer details. This is part of the *GENIUS*'s Visualization Module (VM).

Environment

The environment is a simulated surrounding in which an agent is located. Typically the environment also includes simulated physical elements and other agents. This is part of the Spatial and Environmental Module (SEM).

Currently, in SEM there are two types of threats: gas and bombs. Bomb explosion is onmidirectional, where gas explosion can be affected by the wind and hence the affected area will be an ellipse in shape in comparison to a circular shape.

Different test scenarios can be created by importing or creating 3D urban environments and putting certain

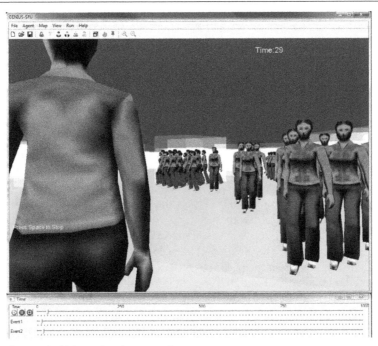

Figure 1 The visualization of a crowd which consist of a group of agents.

terrorist attacks (such as bombs or toxic gas) on specific locations and timeline. There are two methods to create virtual environments which represent urban environments where the agents are able to move around. To create a virtual environment one can 1) import an existing black and white map or 2) select the building blocks in real time.

Events

We have modeled a real-time situation analysis in *GENIUS*, which is a part of the Event Generation Module (EGM). Users can either create multiple real-time events while the simulation is in progress or create multiple timed events as well.

Technical Details

GENIUS has been developed using the 3D game engine called Darkbasic Professional. This game engine provides all the basic features for crowd simulations such as 3D modeling, lighting, cameras, animation, graphical user interface, collision detection, keyboard and mouse control, etc. This affordable game engine also uses a simple BASIC-like language, so that the learning curve is relatively short. Rapid prototyping can be done easily with this engine. MATLAB® was used to convert a map image to a binary table which can be imported to *GENIUS* to visualize the environment.

In summary, *GENIUS* provides a framework for decision support, threats response planning and risk assess-

ment framework. Users can define an agent's profiles by using high-level constructs (roles) or by defining low-level parameters to create application specific descriptive elements. *GENIUS* allows the user to define different environments, agents' profiles (walking speed, perception, memory, role and policy), different types of threats (gas and bombs), and rescue strategies. As a result, the user can study different scenarios and make appropriate planning strategies. The following section describes a couple of experiments that we used to verify and validate our model.

Experiments and preliminary results

To examine our model and show its applicability to real problems, we performed a set of simulations. Through these simulations, we examined different evacuation strategies and demonstrated the effectiveness of *GENIUS* as a tool for studying such behaviors. *GENIUS* was designed and executed in an open and dynamic framework that consists of thousands of agents. The main goal of the following testing scenarios is to validate the simulation and analyze results of the simulator.

Scenario A: Rescue personnel affecting evacuation time

The first experiment is an evacuation scenario. Thirty citizen agents are placed in a confined building where there are only four exits available. A bomb goes off inside the building and we expect our citizen agents to find evacuation routes.

The explosion of a bomb was simulated with realistic visualization and the behaviors of the people were animated in real-time. Figure 2 shows the setup for the building and the agents. When the bomb went off, people became panic and tried to escape from the building. However, many of them could not find exits, so that they could not escape. After 100 cycles, there were still 10 people inside the building. Figure 2b shows the number of people that have escaped over the time. At the end of 100 time steps, only 66.6% of the agents were escaped.

For the second experiment, four rescue personnel were added with the same scenario. As shown in Figure 2c, they were placed at each of the exits. After the explosion of the bomb, these rescuers went into the building and led the people to get out of the building.

Figure 2d shows that 50 time steps after the bomb exploded, about 93% of the agents escaped. Eventually all citizen agents escaped from the building after about 100 time steps in contrast to the last scenario where only 66.6% of the agents escaped.

These two experiments show that placing rescue personnel for an emergency case makes a big difference in evacuating people from the dangerous zone. One would expect these rescue personnel to have complex knowledge of the environment, and therefore be able to provide more reliable information to the other agents in the crowd. However, the rules that these rescue personnel operate are very simple. In terms of perception, they have better sight distance and angle than normal agents. Their walking speed is faster and in terms of personality, they are bolder than normal agents. The operation rules are also very simple as well. In the case of emergency, when a rescue agent walks into the hot zone, their duty is to find people and lead them out of the hot zone. Then they go back to the zone and try to find more people.

We observed that with rescue personnel in placed, they could help others to reach their destinations faster and more efficiently. This observation agreed with our intuition and also research by Pelechano and Badler [14].

Scenario B: Rescue personnel in BC Place

The second simulation scenario was more realistic. The scenario took place at the Vancouver downtown environment during the 2010 Winter Olympic games. There were 50 people gathered around inside the BC Place, where the Opening and Closing Ceremonies of the Vancouver 2010 Olympic Games were going to be held. Then the terrorists placed a timed toxic gas bomb at the north side of the venue. The toxic gas was in the air, moving to the south since the wind was simulated, blowing form the north to the south. People began to run to the south exits of the venue. Then suddenly the bomb went off at those exits. People became panic and some of them were killed.

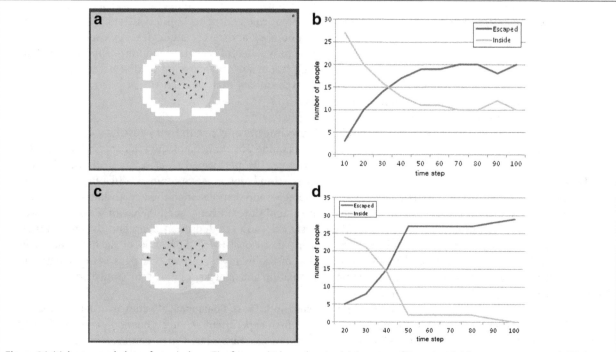

Figure 2 Initial setup and plots of a typical run. The figures which are showing (**a**) the setup of Scenario A (without rescue personnel), (**b**) the graph which plots the number of escapees over time in Scenario A (without rescue personnel), (**c**) the setup of Scenario B (with rescue personnel), (**d**) the graph which plots the number of escapees over time in Scenario B (with rescue personnel).

An agent-based model and computational framework for counter-terrorism and public safety based on...

57

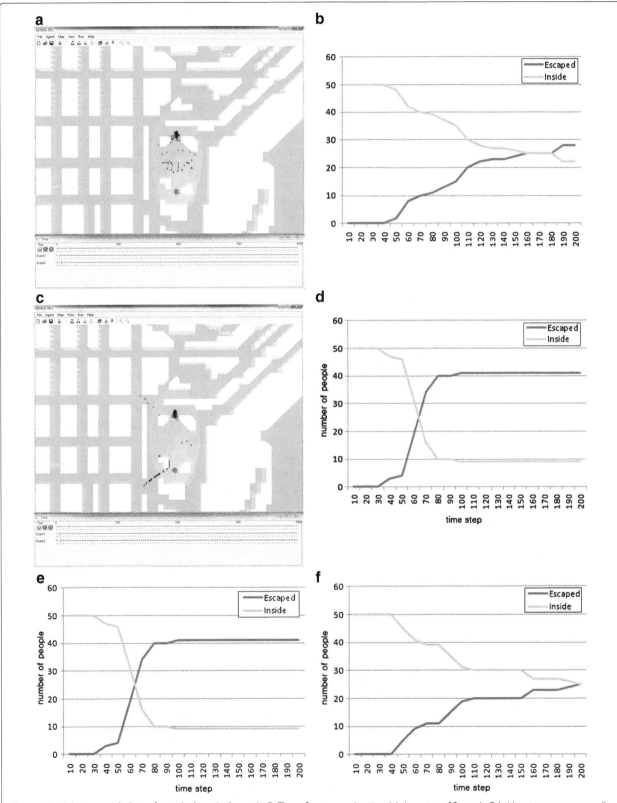

Figure 3 Initial setup and plots of a typical run in Scenario B. These figures are showing (**a**) the setup of Scenario B (without rescue personnel), (**b**) the graph which plots the number of escapees over time in Scenario B (without rescue personnel), (**c**) the setup of Scenario B (with rescue personnel), (**d**) the graph which plots the number of escapees over time in Scenario B (with rescue personnel), (**e**) the graph of Scenario B (with 6 rescue personnel), (**f**) the graph of Scenario B (with 2 rescue personnel).

The first experiment had the basic setup in Figure 3a showing the top down view of the area and fifty agents were placed inside the BC Place. After 150 time steps, there were still half of the people could not escape from the dangerous zone.

For the second experiment, six rescue personnel were placed at strategical locations in preparation for terrorist's attacks. When the toxic gas was detected, these personnel quickly went into the venue and began to lead the people out (Figure 3c). Although another bomb exploded, the rescuers collectedly helped the people get out of the dangerous area.

When Figure 3b is compared with Figure 3d, there is a noticeable difference in the escape rate. Almost 80% of the people could be rescued during the initial critical time period when there were rescue personnel present at strategic locations. However, only 56% were able to escaped in the absence of rescue personnel.

The third experiment investigates the effect of the number of rescue personnel. Figure 3e and Figure 3f compare the situations where there were 6 rescue personnel vs. 2 rescue personnel respectively. After 200 time steps, only 25% of the agents were able to escape when only 2 rescue personnel were present, in comparison to 40% in the case of 6 rescue personnel. It shows that the number of rescue personnel has an effect on the effectiveness in rescuing people from danger.

As part of the Visualization Module, another notable feature of *GENIUS* is its integration to the geographic coordinate system. The latitude and longitude of the agent's location was stored during the simulation. Note that when the simulation is concluded, each agent's movement was recorded and can be played again using GoogleEarth™. Figure 4 shows an example of displaying the agent's movement after the simulation using GoogleEarth™. The round structure is the BC Place and the green human figures represent the agents moving around in the area. In addition, note that the 3D building structure can also be observed in GoogleEarth™. The integration of GoogleEarth™ allows the addition of data from a variety sources, such as satellite imagery, aerial photography and Geographic Information System (GIS).

Scenario C: Evacuation Simulation from High-Rise Buildings

The third simulation scenario was the scenario of an evacuation from the high-rise buildings. This scenario is relevant to counter-terrorism and response since the terrorists attacked on the Twin Towers of the World Trade Center on September 11, 2001. According to the World Trade Center evacuation study [15,16], one of the factors that affected evacuation was preparedness planning. Thus, the effect of fire drills was explored in this particular scenario.

The extension of the *GENIUS* framework provides an ability to construct multiple-story high-rise buildings and place stairs (fire escape) and elevators at any location of the floor. Exits can be located on the ground floor. Different kinds of agents can be placed on each floor and a scheduled event (fire or gas) can be set on any spot of the floor.

In the experiments, a 10-story building was used and 6 people were placed on each floor. The scheduled fire was set on the 10th floor. The same number of stairs, elevators, and exits with the same locations were used for each experiment. Two different age groups were tested: young adults vs. older adults. Older adults had more physical limitations than young adults in terms of walking speed and sight distance. For each age group, two experiments were conducted: one with the agents who had fire drills and the other with the agents who had no fire drills. Those

Figure 4 The replay of the agent's movement using GoogleEarth.

who had fire drills could find stairs and exits more quickly than those who had not.

Figure 5b shows the difference between a previous fire drill experience and no experience for young adults. After 34 cycles, about 88% of the young adults who had had fire drills escaped from the building whereas 73% of those who had not had fire drills escaped. The difference is much bigger for the case of older adults (Figure 5c). 23% of the older adults who had had fire drills escaped after

34 cycles where as only 8% of those who had not had fire drills escaped. Figure 5d and Figure 5e show the difference between young adults and older adults for both cases of fire drills and no fire drills, which is about 65%.

Conclusions

We have presented a novel decision support, threats response planning and risk assessment framework. The preliminary results of *GENIUS* have been discussed and

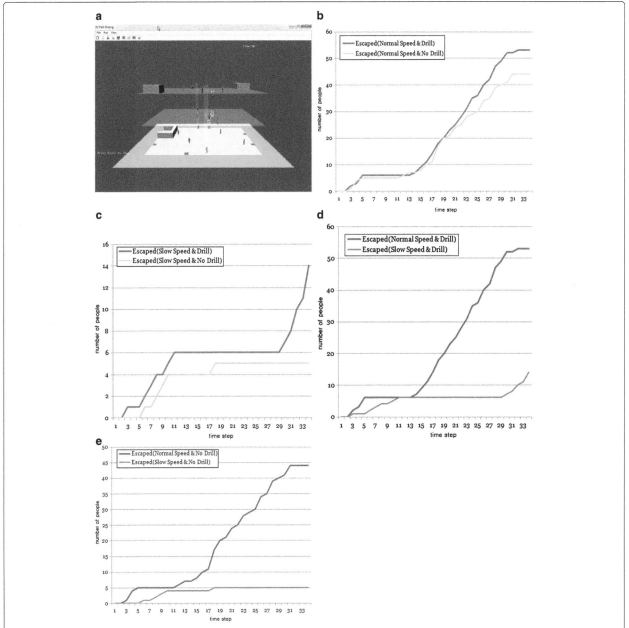

Figure 5 Initial setup and plots of a typical run in Scenario C. These figures are showing (**a**) the setup of Scenario C, (**b**) the graphs which plot the number of escapees of young adults over time in Scenario C (drills vs. no drills), (**c**) the graphs which plot the number of escapees of older adults over time in Scenario C (drills vs. no drills), (**d**) the graphs which plot the number of escapees of both young and older adults over time in Scenario C (drills), (**e**) the graphs which plot the number of escapees of both young and older adults over time in Scenario C (no drills).

reviewed. The results from three scenarios and nine experiments have provided promising outcome. We have examined the relationship between rescue personnel and evacuation rate. It is noted that the presence of rescue personnel helps to reduce casualty rate. In our experiments, it is also shown that the small number of rescue personnel has less effect on evacuation rate than the larger number of rescue personnel. We have also tested the effect of fire drills in the case of the evacuation from high-rise buildings. It is observed that a fire drill exercise helps people find fire stairs and escape quickly. The difference between young adults and older adults in escaping from high-rise buildings is relatively big. This suggests that people who have physical limitations need better ways of escaping from high-rise buildings.

In future work, it will be important to consider incorporating other types of personality profiles in *GENIUS*. For example, threatening individuals (e.g., terrorists) can be added and simulated for hostage situations. Simulation of natural disasters such as storms and floods in *GENIUS* can be a good addition. For the case of escaping from the high-rise buildings, the effects of other factors (leadership, communication, building structures, etc) can be explored. Currently, *GENIUS* is being ported to Unity which is a more advanced game engine that supports various platforms including Windows, OS X, Android and iOS. This game engine provides a more flexible and robust development environment and enables more realistic visualization in *GENIUS*.

Endnotes
[a]Parts of this study have been presented previously at the IEEE International Conference on Intelligence and Security Informatics 2010 (ISI 2010) in Vancouver, Canada.

Competing interests
The authors declare that they have no competing interests.

Authors' contributions
The work presented here was carried out in collaboration among all authors. AJP, HHT, and UG defined the research theme. AJP and MS modeled and developed the framework. HHT and AJP designed methods and experiments, carried out the simulation experiments, analyzed the data, interpreted the results, and wrote the paper. All authors read and approved the final manuscript.

Acknowledgements
The authors would like to thank the anonymous referees whose comments and suggestions have significantly improved this article. This research was partially supported by the MoCSSy Program, Simon Fraser University under the CTEF grant. Research was also supported in part by the Natural Sciences and Engineering Research Council of Canada's (NSERC) Postdoctoral Fellowship.

Author details
[1]Institute for Canadian Urban Research Studies (ICURS), Simon Fraser University, Burnaby, BC, Canada and Thompson Rivers University, Kamploops, BC, Canada. [2]Trinity Western University, Langley, BC, Canada. [3]Interdisciplinary Research in the Mathematical and Computational Sciences (IRMACS) Centre, Simon Fraser University, Burnaby, BC, Canada.

References

1. Defence R&D Canada—Centre for Security Science, CRTI—Call for Proposals: Guidebook for Fiscal Year 2008-2009 (2008)
2. PL Brantingham, B Kinney, U Glässer, P Jackson, M Vajihollahi, in *Artificial Crime Analysis Systems: Using Computer Simulations and Geographic Information Systems*, ed. by L Liu, J Eck. Mastermind: Computational Modeling and Simulation of Spatiotemporal Aspects of Crime in Urban Environments (Information Science Reference, Hershey, PA, 2008), pp. 252–280
3. PL Brantingham, U Glässer, P Jackson, M Vajihollahi, in *To appear in Mathematical Methods in Counterterrorism*. Modeling Criminal Activity in Urban Landscapes (Springer, Vienna, 2009), pp. 9–31
4. U Glässer, M Vajihollahi, in *Intelligence and Security Informatics: Proceedings of the EuroISI 2008*. Computational Modeling of Criminal Activity (Springer, Berlin/Heidelberg, 2008), pp. 39–50
5. W Smith, *Dictionary of Greek and Roman Biography and Mythology*. (Little, Brown and Company, Boston, 1870). [http://www.ancientlibrary.com/smith-bio/1349.html]
6. N Gilbert, *Agent-Based Models (Quantitative Applications in the Social Sciences)*. (Sage Publications Inc, Thousand Oaks, annotated edition, 2007)
7. D Teodorovic, Swarm intelligence systems for transportation engineering: Principles and applications. Transportation Res Part C: Emerging Technol. **16**(6), 651–667 (2008)
8. J Kennedy, R Eberhart, in *Neural Networks, 1995. Proceedings., IEEE International Conference on*, 4. Particle swarm optimization, (2002), pp. 1942–1948
9. G Beni, J Wang, in *Proceedings of the NATO Advanced Workshop on Robots and Biological Systems*. Swarm Intelligence in Cellular Robotic Systems, Tuscany, Italy, 1989)
10. J Izquierdo, I Montalvo, R Plrez, V Fuertes, Forecasting pedestrian evacuation times by using swarm intelligence. Physica A: Stat Mech and its Appl. **388**(7), 1213–1220 (2009)
11. RC Eberhart, X Hu, in *Proceedings of the Congress on Evolutionary Computation*. Human Tremor Analysis Using Particle Swarm Optimization, Washington D.C., 1999), pp. 1927–1930
12. T Wakita, K Ozawa, C Miyajima, K Takeda, in *Proceedings of AVBPA*. Parametric Versus Non-parametric Models of Driving Behavior Signals for Driver Identification, Hilton Rye Town, 2005), pp. 739–747
13. A Park, Modeling the Role of Fear of Crime in Pedestrian Navigation. PhD thesis. (Simon Fraser University, Burnaby, BC, Canada 2008)
14. N Pelechano, NI Badler, Modeling Crowd and Trained Leader Behavior during Building Evacuation. IEEE Comput. Graph. Appl. **26**(6), 80–86 (2006)
15. RRM Gershon, KA Qureshi, MS Rubin, VH Raveis, Factors associated with high-rise evacuation: qualitative results from the World Trade Center Evacuation Study. Prehospital and disaster med : the official j Nat Assoc. EMS Physicians and the World Assoc. Emergency and Disaster Med. assoc. Acute Care Found. **22**(3), 165–73 (2007)
16. RRM Gershon, LA Magda, HEM Riley, MF Sherman, The World Trade Center evacuation study: Factors associated with initiation and length of time for evacuation. Fire and Mater. **35**(5-6), 481–500 (2011)

6

Diversity and resistance in a model network with adaptive software

Neal Holtschulte[*] and Melanie Moses

Abstract

Attacks on computers are increasingly sophisticated, automated and damaging. We take inspiration from the diversity and adaptation of the immune system to design a new kind of computer security system utilizing automated repair techniques. We call the principles of effective immune system design Scalable RADAR: Robust Adaptive Decentralized Search and Automated Response. This paper explores how node diversity is maintained on a network that can generate software variants at individual nodes and make local decisions about sharing variants between nodes. We explore the effects of different network topologies on software diversity and resource trade-offs. We examine how the architecture of the lymphatic network balances trade-offs between local and global search for pathogens in order to improve our design. Experiments are performed on model networks of connected computers able to automatically generate repairs to their own software in response to an attack, bug, or vulnerability. We find that increased connectivity leads to increased overhead, but decreased time to repair, and that small world networks more efficiently distribute repairs. Diversity is diminished by increased connectivity, but has a more complex relationship with network structure, for example, a highly connected network may exhibit low overall diversity but maintain high diversity in a small number of low degree nodes in the periphery of the network.

Introduction

In the realm of cyber security the attacker currently has the advantage. Defenders face a wide variety of constantly adapting threats, but a great deal of software and many operating systems are identical. Due to this monoculture, an attack that works against one computer will work against many. Software monoculture also encourages attackers by increasing attack scalability at no cost to the attacker, e.g. Microsoft Windows is not necessarily more vulnerable than other operating systems, but its large market share makes it a preferred target.

Animal immune systems also face an onslaught of diverse and adaptable attackers, yet effectively defend against disease and infection. Immune systems do so by being adaptable, robust, scalable, and diverse. Diversity is a valuable asset to a defender. Diversity prevents any one attack from compromising a large portion of the defender's systems. The system of automated software repair that we describe makes it possible to synthesize

diversity and deploy software variants that will not be vulnerable to the same attacks, increasing difficulty and cost for attackers.

We call the principles of effective immune system design Scalable RADAR: Robust Adaptive Decentralized Search and Automated Response [1]. We seek to adapt these principles to the realm of computer security and tilt the balance of power in favor of the defender. Our goal is to automatically identify security vulnerabilities and attacks in software and repair them in real time at the very large scales required by real computing systems.

In this paper we simulate the detection of malicious inputs, repair of underlying bugs, and distribution of repairs on a variety of network topologies. This is not a model of how malware spreads, but rather we model how computers on a network can distribute patches or repaired variants of software in a fashion that does not require top down control or manual intervention. In the current implementation, the faults that need repaired are generic and represent bugs, vulnerabilities, exploits, or any other undesirable behavior, but the faults do not spread as computer worms do.

We build our model to investigate several key questions: What is the relationship between network topology and

---
*Correspondence: neal.holts@cs.unm.edu
Department of Computer Science, University of New Mexico, Albuquerque, USA

the speed with which nodes acquire immunity to attack? How is network overhead, in terms of the amount of software shared, related to the time to resist attack? Do some networks balance the tradeoff between software sharing and time to resistance better than others? Does the diversity of software in a network increase or decrease the time for nodes to acquire resistance to new attacks? What is the optimal level of diversity and how can it be maintained without sacrificing local response times?

We model different network topologies including rings, small world networks, a community structure network, and a binary tree, and subject each network to the same series of simulated "attacks". We measure the time between the start of each attack and the incorporation of a repair (either generated locally or shared by a neighboring node). We also measure the amount of overhead in terms of the number of software variants shared between nodes, and we measure the diversity of software on each network.

We hypothesize that networks with greater connectivity and shorter mean path length will more rapidly distribute repairs, but will decrease diversity in the process. This may prove short-sighted if decreased diversity makes it more difficult to find repairs to later attacks.

Small world networks are found widely in nature [2,3], but we hypothesize that networks with more isolated components (such as a binary trees or rings) will likely promote greater diversity in the same way that speciation can occur when a subset of a population becomes isolated from the rest of the population and is subjected to different fitness criteria [4]. The binary tree and ring networks, however, will take longer to acquire resistance as the limited information flow will force nodes to spend more time generating repairs locally.

Background and literature review
Principles from immunology
When faced with a deadly infection, the immune system must rapidly find and neutralize a small number of pathogens hiding among trillions of healthy host cells or the host dies. In [1] we propose a set of design principles used by immune systems, ant colonies and other complex biological systems. We identify mechanisms that have evolved for Scalable Robust, Adaptive, Decentralized Search and Automated Response (Scalable RADAR). These properties are relevant to computer security, where distributed, autonomous, rapid, robust and adaptive control networks are required to defend against increasingly sophisticated attacks. The immune system has evolved lymphocytes (B and T cells) to adaptively recognize and neutralize pathogens. Other immune cells carry pathogens to lymph nodes where lymphocytes can find them. The architecture of the lymphatic network that connects lymph nodes to each other and to tissue facilitates the search for pathogens and production of antibodies that neutralize them.

Immune system inspired approaches have been particularly successful in computer security (reviewed in [5]) where immune inspired intrusion detection are distributed, scalable and sometimes robust to small failures, but there has been little success in scalable automated response. We identify design principles that lead to scalable RADAR in the immune system as a foundation for developing architectures for computer security systems that mimic the principles of scalable RADAR.

Immune systems are **robust**. Degeneracy (partial overlap in the functionality of multi-functional components) and proportional response to threats both contribute to robustness. Components are degenerate such that if one cell dies, there are multiple similar cells to perform its task with some degree of competency. Immune systems are **adaptive** because populations of individuals change in response to environmental signals. For example, activated B cells produce a large and variable population of daughter B cells. Those that bind to pathogens most effectively reproduce faster, so the population of cells improves its ability to neutralize the pathogen.

Search in the immune system is **decentralized**. No cell tells the other cells what their task is, or when or where they should do it. Cells sense chemical signals, environmental stimuli, and rates of interaction with other immune cells to determine how, when and where to search. While control of the search for pathogens is completely decentralized, communication between individuals is aggregated spatially in lymph nodes that concentrate interactions between immune cells and pathogens to improve the search process. Immune cells **respond** to attacks by integrating local signals from their environment to determine their behavior. Some local responses may be 'errors', but the response of the whole system is governed by collective agreement.

Immune systems **scale** up to trillions of cells. Because cells respond only to local signals, each can act in parallel without need for information signals to travel to every individual for a search to be effective or a response to be initiated. However, our analysis suggests that scalable response requires more communication between individuals as the system grows. We hypothesize that scalable communication patterns are promoted by the physical architecture of lymphatic networks. The immune system balances the need for local detection of pathogens with a systemic response to attack by distributing immune cells across a semi-modular hierarchical system of lymph nodes connected by the circulatory and lymphatic networks. When we compare across animals from mice to horses, the average size of a lymph node and the number of lymph nodes both increase with animal size, but the increase is sub-linear, so that a horse has more and larger lymph nodes than a mouse, but neither the increase in lymph node size nor the increase in number are as great as the increase in body size.

In this paper we draw from our understanding of these scalable RADAR principles, and we focus on testing which computer network architectures balance the need to maintain diversity while rapidly responding to systemic threats.

Patch distribution

Traditionally, patch distribution has been centralized and hierarchical. System administrators are responsible for pushing out patches to a network, or individuals are prompted to begin the update process by notifications which direct them to a site where the patch can be downloaded. These distribution methods naturally lead to problems as computer systems grow more complex. According to [6], "manually applied patches are not effective in countering worms because they require human reactions and they are usually slow and do not scale well."

Systems of any significant size have automatic patching and updating processes, but these systems still download software from a central source. Additionally, diversity in the code base is seen as a problem to be overcome rather than a resource to be utilized. In [7], a system administrator laments "We have over 100 UNIX systems running more than half a dozen UNIX based OSes (more than a dozen when counting different OS versions). ... all configured slightly differently to suit their particular users' needs. ... the majority of our days were spent merely fighting fires."

Most patch distribution and management research focuses on timeliness, orderliness, and control. But all these systems rely on manually generated repairs and centralized distribution of patches overseen by a system administrator. The ability to automatically generate and evaluate repairs allows us to take a fresh perspective.

Automatically evolving software that resists attack

Genetic programming (GP) is a biologically-inspired method of automatically creating or modifying software. GP uses operations such as mutation and crossover to evolve a population of software based on a user-defined fitness function.

Forrest and Weimer use GP to evolve variants of programs that are resistant to security vulnerabilities [8-11]. Their design uses swap, copy, and delete operators on program instructions in order to repair bugs while retaining the original program's required functionality. Both the fitness function and 'required functionality' are defined using test suites. Test suites are a common tool of software engineers. Test suites consist of correct input/output pairs that a program is expected to satisfy and are designed to test software correctness.

Forrest and Weimer have recently investigated the benefits of "synthesizing diversity" by generating neutral software variants. A software variant is said to be neutral with respect to a suite of test cases if it passes all the same test cases as the original program. Neutral software variants have been shown to repair bugs experimentally seeded into test programs [12]. When program variants evolved by GP were evaluated on the tests that had been removed from the original test suite, an average of 19 out of 5000 variants passed one or more of the tests. In other words, the variants had repaired some of the seeded bugs by chance. Based on these results, they introduce the idea of mutational robustness, that lightweight random changes to program code is relatively unlikely to discernibly change program behavior.

Unspecified behavior may not be exercised by test cases so mutations that affect such behavior may still be considered neutral by the above definition of neutral. Such mutations will only affect "fringe" behavior that is commonly exploited by malware. Neutral mutations can then be used to synthesize diversity and proactively protect against unknown bugs and novel attacks. "Normal" users may not even know that the software they are using is different from the software used by the person in the neighboring cubicle because the mutations are neutral with respect to the standard program behavior. Rather than viewing neutral mutants as an overhead to be avoided or an indication of test suite inadequacy (e.g. [13,14]), we propose that they enhance the evolutionary process and are useful in their own right as a source of proactive diversity.

Given that GP can be used to automatically generate software diversity, how should software be distributed so as to maintain diversity? In this paper we investigate the effect on diversity of distributing variants on different network topologies.

We seek to replicate the scalability, robustness, and adaptiveness of the natural immune system by mimicking scalable RADAR principles. By analogy with the lymphatic network, we focus on the design of the network that computers use to share repairs. In our model, repairs are shared locally among neighboring nodes instead of being managed by a centralized, global controller. We investigate network topologies that are conducive to RADAR properties. Our goal is to determine which network topologies have the fastest response to newly discovered bugs or exploits with the lowest overhead. To this end, we run experiments on each network topology for a large and a small network. Each experiment is run many times, simulating consecutive, increasingly problematic attacks, and we measure overhead, time to resistance, and diversity.

Research design and methodology

We ran two sets of six experiments on seven different network topologies. Networks were initialized with 1024 nodes in one set of experiments and 64 nodes in the other. Each experiment was run 100 times with different random seeds.

Each experiment consists of nine phases corresponding to the nine increasingly severe attacks used (see Table 1). At the beginning of each phase, every node is simultaneously subjected to the same attack. Each node that is not resistant to the attack sends requests for software variants to all its neighbors. Vulnerable nodes also attempt to generate their own repairs.

Nodes continue to generate software variants until a resistant variant is found or is received from a neighbor. Additional requests for variants are sent at regular intervals (see Table 2 for the specific number of time steps for intervals and actions).

Nodes respond to requests for variant software by transmitting a copy of their own software to the requesting node. Nodes always respond to requests for software variants regardless of whether or not they themselves are vulnerable to the current attack. This is wasteful since vulnerable software will be useless to the receiver, but it is only obviously wasteful because every node is subjected to the same attack at the same time. In future work this contrived attack pattern will be modified and nodes will not know a priori whether or not their neighbors' software will be effective.

The effectiveness of received software variants is not checked immediately upon receipt. Effectiveness is checked after the node has completed its current activity, such as generating its own repair. When a node that is not yet resistant to the current attack identifies a resistant software variant, the node replaces its own software with the variant. Incorporating a neighbor's software decreases diversity in the network, but the individual node no longer needs to spend its own resources attempting to generate a repair. This illustrates a tradeoff between local resources and global diversity.

Table 1 Attacks

Attack	Vulnerable space
0.9	79.5%
0.95	85.6%
0.98	91.0%
0.99	93.6%
0.995	95.5%
0.999	98.0%
0.9999	99.4%
0.99999	99.8%
0.999999	99.9%

Attacks are values in the range zero to one. Any software with a resistance less than the attack is considered vulnerable to the attack. The percentage of the entire resistance space vulnerable to each attack is given below.

Table 2 Constants

Constant name	Value	Unit
Attack interval	50000	time steps
Software edge traversal time	100	time steps
Software request edge traversal time	100	time steps
Software incorporation time	1	time step
Repair attempt time	100	time steps
Random variants tested per repair attempt	10	software variants
Software request interval	300	time steps
Node count	1024	nodes

The model simulates parallelism by associating an update time with all objects and incrementing update times by a specified amount when different actions are performed. Table 2 shows the time step penalties and other constants used in the simulation. Any actions not listed, such as a node checking its own vulnerability, incurs no delay. Attack interval is the number of time steps before the next attack occurs. There was never a case of a node being vulnerable to the previous attack when the next attack occurred.

Figure 1 shows a small ring network with three software variants (represented by small envelopes) enroute to neighboring nodes.

Each node on the network stores a 20-bit binary number used to represent the software that is attacked and, in response, repaired and distributed by the nodes. The nodes are initialized with identical, low-quality binary numbers. We will refer to these binary numbers simply as software or software variants.

The initial software is low-quality in the sense that it is vulnerable to almost any attack. These "attacks" represent either external attacks (infiltration by a malicious or unauthorized user), or bugs or vulnerabilities. They represent any sort of flaw discovered in the software that can, in principle be fixed using the GP techniques of Forrest and Weimer [11]. Each attack is a number in the range zero to one, with zero being the least severe and one being the most severe. In each experiment, the network is subjected to increasingly severe attacks. As the attack gets closer to one, fewer software variants exist that are resistant. Table 1 shows the nine attack values used for all experiments and the corresponding percentage of all possible values of 20-bit binary numbers that are vulnerable to these attacks. Any software with a resistance less than the attack is considered vulnerable.

A software variant (20-bit binary number), s, is converted to a floating point value, v, in the range zero to one as follows:

$$v = \frac{s}{(2^{20}) - 1}$$

where $(2^{20}) - 1$ is the maximum value that can be represented in a 20-bit binary string.

Software is initialized to the binary string most closely representing the value 0.547, which has one of the lowest

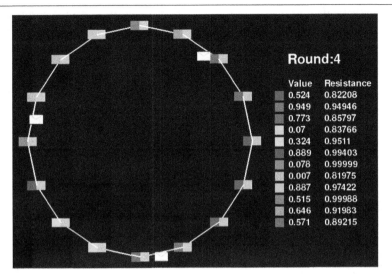

Figure 1 A screenshot of the visualization of software variant sharing on a small ring network with each node connected to its nearest neighbors. Software variants are represented by small envelopes. Three variants can be seen enroute. Nodes themselves are represented by bisected rectangles. The salmon color represents the attack and becomes increasingly red as the experiment moves through the attack progression. The other color in each rectangle is a unique color associated with each software variant. Values, colors, and resistances of these variants can be seen in the table on the right side of the image.

possible resistances in the middle of the range zero to one.

$$init = ((2^{20}) - 1) \cdot 0.547)$$

Resistance, r, for software with value, v, is calculated as follows:

$$r = \frac{sin(16 \cdot 2\pi \cdot v) + 1}{2}$$

This sine function has 16 optima in the range zero to one, a minimum y-value of zero, and a maximum y-value of one.

Figure 2 shows a snapshot of an experiment using a small number of nodes. The horizontal red line represents the value of the current attack. Green dots are representations of software on different nodes. The x coordinate of the nodes is the software value, the y coordinate is the resistance. The blue sine curve shows the resistance for values in the range. The five green dots beneath the red line show that five nodes are vulnerable to the current attack.

"Repairs" are automatically generated by naively testing random binary numbers for resistance against the current attack. If software is generated which resists the attack, then the node replaces its software with this new variant. Each attempted repair consists of testing ten randomly generated binary numbers.

The model simulates parallelism by associating an update time with all objects. At each time step, every object is checked to see if its update time is less than or equal to the global time. If so, the object is updated. For example, if node n has update time 100 and the current

time is greater than or equal to 100, then n will check to see if it is vulnerable, check if any variants have been delivered from its neighbors, and, if enough time has passed since its last request for software variants, send another request. It takes one time step for a node to incorporate a software variant, but 100 time steps to make ten repair attempts. When a node makes these repair attempts, its time will be incremented by 100. Nodes respond to requests to share software without incurring any delay,

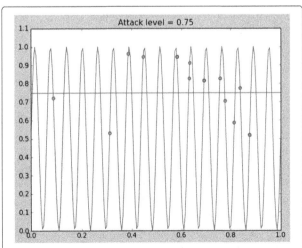

Figure 2 A snapshot of a dynamic graph showing nodes (green dots) and where their "software" falls on the resistance landscape (blue sine curve). As the attack (horizontal red line) rises, nodes must keep their software above the red line in order to resist the attack.

but both requests and software variants take time to traverse edges on the network. For more details, see Table 2. Any actions not listed, such as a node checking its own vulnerability incurs no delay.

Experiments were run on the following network topologies. All of these topologies were generated using the NetworkX module for python [15]:

- Ring k=1 (R1): A ring in which each node is connected to its two nearest neighbors (one on each side). The 1024 node R1 network has 1024 edges. The 64 node network has 64 edges. The 1024 node network was generated with the following call to the NetworkX module:

```
networkx.connected_watts_strogatz_
graph(1024, 2, 0.0)
```

The connected Watts-Strogatz network forms a ring and holds this form when the rewiring probability is set to zero.

- Ring k=5 (R5): A ring in which each node is connected to its ten nearest neighbors (five on each side). The 1024 node R5 network has 5120 edges. The 64 node network has 320 edges.

```
networkx.connected_watts_strogatz_
graph(1024, 10, 0.0)
```

- Small World Ring (SWR) aka Newman Watts Strogatz network: A ring where each node, u, has three edges, one connected to each neighbor and one random long range connection. Addition of the long range edges turns the ring into a small world network in which every node is connected to every other node by a relatively short path. The 1024 node SWR network has 2048 edges. The 64 node network has 128 edges.

```
networkx.newman_watts_strogatz_
graph(1024, 2, 1.0)
```

- Small World Ring Rewired k=5 (RR): A ring in which nodes are connected to all their neighbors within a radius of five nodes just like the R5 network. However, RR is then 'rewired' such that edges are randomly chosen to be removed and replaced with edges that connects two nodes chosen uniformly at random. This mirrors the approach taken by [2] to investigate small world networks. Rewiring takes place as follows: With 5% probability an arbitrary endpoint of each edge is replaced with a node selected uniformly at random. Rewiring probabilities in the range 1% to 10% produce networks with the lowest mean shortest path with a minimum of long range connections [2].

```
networkx.connected_watts_strogatz_
graph(1024, 10, 0.05)
```

Mean shortest path is calculated by taking the sum of the lengths of the shortest paths between all pairs of nodes in a network and dividing by the number of pairs. It is a common measure of small world networks, which are characterized by the small number of edges in the path between any two nodes. Small world networks have been popularized by the "Six Degrees of Kevin Bacon" game in which players try to connect an actor to Kevin Bacon through six or fewer co-star connections.

- Small World Preferential Attachment (PA): A random graph incrementally built up by preferential attachment. New nodes connect to existing nodes probabilistically, with greater weight given to existing nodes that already have many connections. The 1024 node PA network has 1023 edges. It does not have 1024 edges because the network is initialized with two nodes with one edge between them then 1022 nodes are added and one edge is added to connect each of the 1022 nodes. The 64 node network has 63 edges.

```
networkx.barabasi_albert_graph
(1024, 1023)
```

- Binary Tree (Bin): A hierarchical network, in the form of a complete binary tree. The 1023 node Bin network has 1022 edges. The 63 node network has 62 edges.

```
branching_factor = 2
height = int(math.log(1024, 2))-1
networkx.balanced_tree(branching_
factor, height)
```

- Caveman Graph (Cave): A modular network generated by making n cliques of size k. Then one node in each clique is rewired to connect to an adjacent clique. We generated caveman graphs with 16 cliques. Code for the caveman graph cannot be found in the current version of NetworkX, but can be accessed here [16].

```
cliques = 16
clique_size = 1024 / cliques
networkx.connected_caveman_graph
(cliques, clique_size)
```

For each experiment we measure the following:

- Prior Immunity: The chance that a node's current software is already resistant to a new attack. We count the times a node is immediately resistant to a new attack divided by the total number of new attacks against all nodes.

- Effective Shared: The chance that a software variant that node v receives from its neighbor resists the attack against v. We count the number of effective variants received divided by the total number of variants received. Only variants received while v is vulnerable are counted. Variants received after acquiring resistance are not counted towards the numerator or denominator. By ignoring late variants we will elevate the percentage of effective shared variants, but for this metric we are only interested in variants shared during the vulnerable phase.
- Total Software Sharing: a count of instances of software sharing between nodes over the course of the entire experiment. For this metric, unlike 'effective shared', we include software shared after the destination node has already achieved resistance. This metric measures network overhead.
- Average Time to Resistance: The average number of time steps between the start of an attack on a node and the node achieving resistance. This time could be zero if a node has prior immunity. Since nodes continually attempt to automatically generate repairs, average time to resistance is also a measure of the CPU overhead, the amount of CPU cycles a node spends generating variants.
- Diversity: We measure diversity using the Shannon Index

$$H' = -\sum_{i=1}^{S} p_i ln(p_i)$$

where S is the total number of distinct software variants and p_i is the probability that a node has variant i. That is, p_i equals the number of instances of variant i divided by the total number of nodes.

Results and discussion

All figures and data reported below are for 1024 node networks. The 64 node networks exhibited comparable results.

Prior Immunity: The chance that a node will be resistant to a novel attack is approximately 48% and was essentially constant across all network topologies. This value was the same whether there were 1024 or 64 nodes on the network. This is not surprising since the quality of a software variant is not evaluated along a continuum. It either is vulnerable to the current attack or it isn't. Even nodes on networks with greater diversity had the same chance of resisting novel attacks.

Total Software Sharing: The number of shared software variants is greater in networks with more edges. Figure 3 shows the total number of software variants shared between nodes. R5, the five-neighborhood ring, and RR, the rewired ring, have five times as many edges

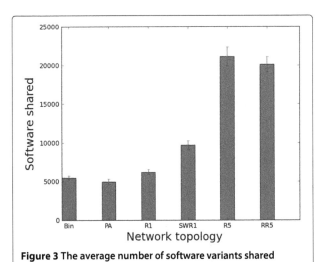

Figure 3 The average number of software variants shared during 100 iterations of each experiment for each network topology. This is a measure of the network overhead, which we wish to minimize. Software is shared when a neighboring node requests a variant in response to an attack. Network topologies are ordered from left to right by increasing number of edges. The data shown is for 1024 node networks. The caveman network is not shown because it dwarfs the other columns. The caveman network shares about 250,000 software variants.

as the other networks (see Table 3). Consequently, they share between four and five times as many variants over the course of an experiment. The caveman network is not shown because it dwarfs the other columns. The caveman network has far more edges than any other network and consequently shares around 250,000 software variants.

Figure 3 also indicates that over the course of the nine attacks, on average eight to ten software variants are shared across each edge on each network, hence the network with 1024 edges shares about 10,000 variants and the RSW network with 5120 edges shares about 45,000.

Average Time to Resistance: The software sharing overhead should be viewed in the context of the time it takes nodes on these networks to acquire resistance to new attacks. Figure 4 shows that the network with the largest amount of software sharing is also the quickest to resist new attacks with Cave taking 6 steps on average. However, both PA and SWR buck the trend with low network overhead and modest average time steps to resistance.

Effective Shared: Figure 5 shows that the chance of receiving an effective variant depends on the network topology. More effective software variants are delivered on the random preferential attachment network than on any other, followed by the small world ring. One possible explanation for this effect for the random preferential attachment network is that few nodes in such networks contain the majority of the edges. Such nodes would be expected to quickly receive resistant software which they could then rapidly distribute to their neighbors.

Table 3 Network topologies

Topology	Edges	Nodes	Considered "small world"	Mean shortest path
Ring k=1	1024, 64	1024, 64	No	256.25, 16.25
Ring k=5	5120, 320	1024, 64	No	51.65, 3.66
Small World Ring	2048, 128	1024, 64	Yes	5.48, 3.11 *
Rewired Ring	5120, 320	1024, 64	Yes	5.27, 2.57 *
Preferential Attachment	1023, 63	1024, 64	Yes	2.00, 1.97 *
Binary Tree	1022, 62	1023, 63	No	14.07, 6.59
Caveman	32256, 96	1024, 64	No	9.00, 8.87 *

Two sets of experiments were run on six network topologies.
*denotes average values.

Diversity: Figure 6 shows the Shannon Index for each topology after each attack. The index after initialization is zero (not shown) because every node has the same software. The distance-one neighbor ring (R1) maintains the most diversity, which is easily explained by the relative difficulty with which any software variant would spread across this network. After R1, the binary tree (Bin) maintains the next highest diversity, suggesting that high mean shortest path corresponds to high diversity, which makes sense since longer path lengths limit the spread of software variants.

The 64 node networks exhibited comparable results to those reported above, not withstanding the dramatic difference in degree of the 64 node caveman network relative to the other networks. The chance of prior immunity, average time to resistance, and percentage of effective shared software was not significantly different between 64 and 1024 node networks with the same topologies.

Future work will look at more intelligent software sharing paradigms. For example, nodes may simply ignore a percentage of requests or we may use an economic model such as the one for reducing the bandwidth overhead on P2P networks introduced by [17]. Though far from the only pertinent feature of peer-2-peer networks, the preferential attachment network does have the same degree distribution (power law). Likewise, the caveman graph has a modular structure. Community structure is characteristic of many networks found in the real world such as P2P networks [18]. In future work, we will examine more realistic topologies with both community structure and power law degree distributions.

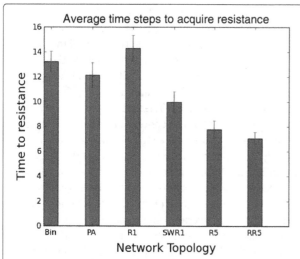

Figure 4 Average number of time steps between novel attacks and individual nodes' resistance to these attacks. These numbers are averaged over 100 iterations of each experiment for each network topology. Since one set of attempted repairs takes 100 time steps, this shows that on average no more than two sets of attempted repairs are made before a repair is generated locally or a resistant variant is received from a neighboring node. Network topologies are ordered from left to right by increasing number of edges. The data shown is for 1024 node networks.

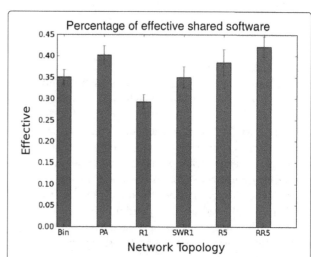

Figure 5 Percentage of shared software variants that effectively resist the receiving node's current attack. Only variants received while the node was vulnerable were counted. Variants received too late were not counted. Network topologies are ordered from left to right by increasing number of edges. The data shown is for 1024 node networks.

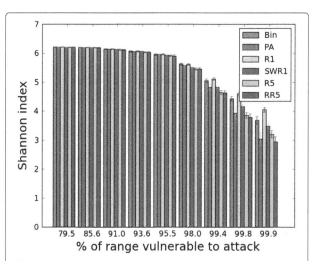

Figure 6 Average Shannon Index (a measure of diversity) over 100 iterations of each experiment for each network topology. Topologies are ordered from left to right by increasing number of edges. R1 stands for the ring network in which each node is connected to its nearest neighbors. R5 stands for the ring network in which each node is connected to its five nearest neighbors. SWR stands for the small world ring with one random long-range connection. RR stands for the rewired ring. PA stands for random preferential attachment. Bin stands for binary tree. The data shown is for 1024 node networks.

We will also add realism by replacing simulated bug fixes with actual repairs of bugs in open source C code. By performing real repairs we can increase the realism in a variety of ways, for example, the timing of variant sharing can be based on the number of clock cycles elapsed while generating the repair.

Conclusions

In this paper we simulate the detection of malicious inputs, repair of underlying bugs, and distribution of repairs on a variety of network topologies. We measure the speed with which nodes acquired immunity to attack, the overhead in terms of amount of software shared, and the diversity of variants that emerge on the network without any central control or distribution. We modeled the following network topologies: rings, a Watts-Strogatz small world network, a network formed by preferential attachment, a binary tree, and a so-called caveman network.

The total number of software variants shared over the course of an experiment directly corresponds to the number of edges in each network with eight to ten variants shared over each edge. The networks with more edges (R5, RR, Cave) show less sharing per edge. This may be due to the fact that more software sharing speeds up the acquisition of resistant variants, which stops nodes from requesting additional variants and therefore reduces software sharing. In short there is a negative feedback

mechanism involved in software sharing in response to an attack.

The number of shared software variants for a given network topology is inversely proportional to the average time steps between a novel attack on a node and the node's resistance to the attack. In fact, Figure 3 is nearly the mirror image of Figure 5. It's interesting to note that the random preferential attachment network's average time to resistance is slightly lower than that of R1 and Bin, despite the fact that these graphs have the same number of edges and similar amounts of software shared. This can perhaps be explained by Figure 5, which shows that the chance that a shared software variant resists the current attack is highest on the preferential attachment network.

The fact that there is a difference in shared software quality on the different networks at all is surprising since there was no difference in prior immunity. The structure of these networks makes it possible for them to distribute resistant software more effectively without ever comparing software variants directly.

In the rings, R1 and R5, all nodes are created equally, with the same degree and all positions in the networks being equivalent. In all the other networks, except for the binary tree, there is a wide range in node degree. Nodes with higher degree will receive a larger number of software variants in response to any request. These high degree nodes may then distribute this software to all of their neighbors, resulting in the increased effectiveness seen. Recall that 'effectiveness' refers to the proportion of shared variants that resist the current attack level.

Small world networks generated by preferential attachment are characterized by robustness to the removal of random nodes, but quickly become disconnected if high degree nodes are removed. In other words, PA networks possess nodes with high "betweenness" through which the majority of the information traffic must pass. Betweenness is a measure of the probability of a node lying on a randomly chosen shortest path between nodes. In future work, we will investigate whether these high-betweenness nodes are responsible for the increased percentage of effective software sharing. Future experiments will address this question by examining the relationship between time to resistance and degree, distance to a highly connected node, and distance to the root in the binary tree. We will also look at the number of effective variants traveling up the binary tree (towards the root) versus the number traveling down towards the leaves.

Diversity as measured by the Shannon Index is largely a function of the mean shortest path of a network, but there is more to it than that. The random preferential attachment networks maintain high diversity as measured by a raw count of distinct software variants (see Figure 7), but have relatively low Shannon diversity, which also takes into account the number of each variant present on the

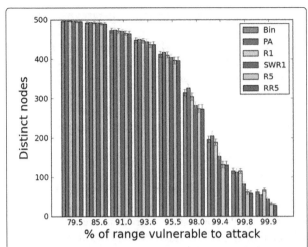

Figure 7 Diversity measured as a count of unique software variants on the network. These counts were averaged over 100 iterations of each experiment for each network topology. The preferential attachment (PA) network has a higher count of distinct nodes relative to the other networks than would be expected based on Figure 6.

network. This suggests that while PA networks are dominated by relatively few variants, corners of the networks maintain many unique variants. This is encouraging since we believe that diversity can be leveraged for increased robustness. It may be possible to implement different software sharing policies to encourage greater diversity on this and other networks. We leave this for future work.

In the immune system, the structure of the lymphatic network through which immune cells communicate is critically important for scalable RADAR. The precise topology of the lymphatic network is not known, but it is known that the network enables both local and global communication between lymph nodes, and as the number of lymph nodes increases, each lymph node communicates more [1]. This is thought to balance the needs for fast local search and systemic response. In this paper we have analyzed network topologies to determine which topologies promote diversity and rapid patch distribution with minimal overhead. In summary, overhead is proportional to the number of edges, but inversely proportional to time to resistance.

We find encouraging evidence that some network topologies allow effective patches to be widely deployed while still maintaining patch diversity. For example, effective patches are easily shared among nodes in small world networks. Furthermore, networks formed by random preferential attachment have low software diversity, but a high number of distinct software variants compared to the other topologies. In other words, there is low diversity in the majority of nodes, but high diversity in a minority of nodes. We believe this to be due to the ability of preferential attachment networks to distribute

variants rapidly through their high degree nodes, reducing Shannon diversity of the overall network, while diverse nodes maintain a foothold in the low degree nodes at the periphery of the network. This is a desirable feature because if the majority of nodes are vulnerable to a new attack, it is likely that these nodes can be "recolonized" by a variant waiting in the wings. These results hold across multiple orders of magnitude difference in network size from 64 to 1024 nodes. Identifying the role of network topology in maintaining diversity and rapid response is a step toward developing more robust distributed computer security systems that mimic the adaptive qualities of the natural immune system.

Competing interests
The authors declare that they have no competing interests.

Authors' contributions
NH and MM contributed to the writing and analysis that went in to this paper. Both authors read and approved the final manuscript.

Acknowledgements
We thank Soumya Banerjee for helpful discussions and insights. This work is supported by grants from the National Institute of Health (NIH RR018754), DARPA (P-1070-113237) and National Science Foundation (NSF EF 1038682).

References
1. Moses M, Banerjee S: **Biologically Inspired Design Principles for Scalable, Robust, Adaptive, Decentralized Search and Automated Response (RADAR).** In *IEEE Symposium Series in Computational Intelligence 2011 (SSCI 2011)*. Paris, France:2011.
2. Watts DJ, Strogatz SH: **Collective dynamics of 'small-world' networks.** *Nature* 1998, **393:**440–442.
3. Kleinberg JM: **Navigation in a small world.** *Nature* 2000, **406:**845.
4. Rundle HD, Schluter D: **Natural Selection and Ecological Speciation in Sticklebacks.** *Adaptive Speciation* 2004, **19**(3):192–209. http://citeseerx. ist.psu.edu/viewdoc/download?doi=10.1.1.127.3225&rep= rep1&type=pdf.
5. Forrest S, Beauchemin C: **Computer immunology.** *Immunological Rev* 2007, **216:**176–197. http://dx.doi.org/10.1111/j.1600-065X.2007.00499.x.
6. Castaneda F, Sezer EC, Xu J: **WORM vs. WORM: preliminary study of an active counter-attack mechanism.** In *Proceedings of the 2004 ACM workshop on Rapid malcode, WORM '04*. (ACM, New York, NY, USA; 2004:83–93. http://doi.acm.org/10.1145/1029618.1029631.
7. Ressman D, Valdes J: **Use of CFengine for automated, multi-platform software and patch distribution.** In *In USENIX 14th System Administration Conf. (LISA)*. USENIX Association, Los Angeles; 2000. pp. 207–218.
8. Fast E, Le Goues C, Forrest S, Weimer W: **Designing better fitness functions for automated program repair.** In *Proceedings of the 12th annual conference on Genetic and evolutionary computation GECCO '10*. ACM, New York, NY, USA; 2010. pp. 965–972. http://doi.acm.org/10.1145/ 1830483.1830654.
9. Forrest S, Nguyen T, Weimer W, Le Goues C: **A genetic programming approach to automated software repair.** In *Proceedings of the 11th Annual conference on Genetic and evolutionary computation, GECCO '09*. ACM, New York, NY, USA; 2009. pp. 947–954. http://doi.acm.org/10.1145/ 1569901.1570031.
10. Nguyen T, Weimer W, Le Goues C, Forrest S: **Using Execution Paths to Evolve Software Patches.** In *Proceedings of the IEEE International Conference on Software Testing, Verification, and Validation Workshops,ICSTW '09*. IEEE Computer Society, Washington, DC, USA; 2009. pp. 152–153. http://dx.doi.org/10.1109/ICSTW.2009.35.
11. Weimer W, Nguyen T, Le Goues C, Forrest S: **Automatically finding patches using genetic programming.** In *Proceedings of the 31st*

International Conference on Software Engineering, ICSE '09. IEEE Computer Society, Washington, DC, USA; 2009. pp. 364–374. http://dx.doi.org/10.1109/ICSE.2009.5070536.

12. Schulte E, Fry ZP, Fast E, Forrest S, Weimer W: **Software Mutational Robustness Bridging The Gap Between Mutation Testing and Evolutionary Biology.** 2012. http://arxiv.org/abs/1204.4224.

13. Offutt AJ, Untch RH: Mutation 2000: Uniting the Orthogonal. *Mutation Testing for the New Century.* Kluwer Academic Publishers, Norwell, MA USA; 2001. http://books.google.com/books?hl=en&lr=&id=LFvgCktM0sYC&oi=fnd&pg=PA34&dq=mutation+2000:+uniting+the+orthogonal&ots=pzA3SMn_EF&sig=1fo1swiEoFCvi5otlEk5zkRkalw.

14. Siami Namin A, Andrews JH, Murdoch DJ: **Sufficient mutation operators for measuring test effectiveness.** In *Proceedings of the 30th International Conference on Software Engineering*, ICSE '08: (ACM Press; 2008. pp. 351–360. http://doi.acm.org/10.1145/1368088.1368136.

15. **NetworkX: High productivity software for complex networks,** http://networkx.lanl.gov/. Accessed 20 April 2012.

16. **NetworkX, Network generators: Community,** https://bitbucket.org/bedwards/networkx-community/raw/370bd69fc02f/networkx/generators/community.py. Accessed 20 April 2012.

17. Roussopoulos M, Baker M: **CUP: Controlled Update Propagation in Peer-to-Peer Networks.** USENIX 2003 Annual Technical Conference 2002. p. 15 http://arxiv.org/abs/cs/0202008.

18. Porter MA, Onnela JP, Mucha PJ: **Communities in Networks. World Wide Web Internet And Web.** *Inf. Syst.* 2009, **56**(9):1082–1097. http://arxiv.org/abs/0902.3788.

7

Forecasting the locational dynamics of transnational terrorism: a network analytic approach

Bruce A Desmarais[1]* and Skyler J Cranmer[2]

Abstract

Efforts to combat and prevent transnational terrorism rely, to a great extent, on the effective allocation of security resources. Critical to the success of this allocation process is the identification of the likely geopolitical sources and targets of terrorism. We construct the network of transnational terrorist attacks, in which source (sender) and target (receiver) countries share a directed edge, and we evaluate a network analytic approach to forecasting the geopolitical sources and targets of terrorism. We integrate a deterministic, similarity-based, link prediction framework into a probabilistic modeling approach in order to develop an edge-forecasting method. Using a database of over 12,000 transnational terrorist attacks occurring between 1968 and 2002, we show that probabilistic link prediction is not only capable of accurate forecasting during a terrorist campaign, but is a promising approach to forecasting the onset of terrorist hostilities between a source and a target.

Introduction

The accurate forecasting of transnational terrorism is among the most pressing problems of contemporary security policy. Counter-terrorism efforts may be greatly aided if resources, ranging from analytic focus to prevention capabilities, can effectively target the source of terrorist threats before terrorists can launch attacks. Traditional efforts to statistically forecast terrorism are complicated by the fact that most forecasting models perform best when there is a long series of data to study, thus rendering them impotent for identifying new sources of threat and forecasting attacks from sources that have not attacked before. For example, a protracted terrorist campaign may provide enough data for accurate time-series forecasting, but, from a policy perspective, may not be useful because the target government already understands that it is under attack from that source. The major challenge in forecasting transnational terrorism, as we see it, is identifying sources of threat (countries who's nationals conduct terrorist attacks against a given target state)

before any attacks from that source have been observed and quantifying the extent of the threat.

We approach the problem of forecasting transnational terrorism from a network analytic perspective with the supposition that the structure of the transnational terrorist network may be the best predictor of its own evolution. We construct the global transnational terrorism network, in which a directed edge exists from the state that produces a transnational terrorist to the state attacked by that terrorist, using the ITERATE dataset [1]. The data cover more than 12,000 transnational terrorist attacks between 1968 and 2002. We create an edge forecasting framework for the transnational terrorist network by integrating a deterministic similarity-based edge prediction method developed by Liben-Nowell and Kleinberg [2] with a model-based probabilistic approach developed by Hanneke, Fu, and Xing [3]. The result is a likelihood-based forecasting model capable of quantifying the transnational terrorist threat one state poses to another, even before any attacks have occurred between the two states. Specifically, we predict edges in the transnational terror network by substituting the network structure embedded in the recent patterns of transnational terrorism into the model that best predicted the network up to time $t-1$. Thus, the predictive models for t are not based on the data

---

*Correspondence: desmarais@polsci.umass.edu
[1] Department of Political Science, University of Massachusetts at Amherst, Amherst, Massachusetts 01003, USA
Full list of author information is available at the end of the article

from t. The result is a forecasting model that predicts edges that occur in the next time period (year) with probabilities orders of magnitude greater than those that do not occur. As such, our model provides forecasts of the locational dynamics of terrorist threats both before and after the first attacks have been realized. Our model lifts a major limitation of traditional approaches to forecasting transnational terrorist events and can provide early warnings of emerging threats.

Background

Though transnational terrorism has been a highly visible policy problem for the United States since the terrorist attacks of September 11, 2001, transnational terrorism is an older phenomena that, in many ways, came into its heyday with skyjacking, hostage taking, and bombing campaigns in the 1960's and 1970's. Quantitative research on transnational terrorist violence[a] has focused largely on two related themes: the predictors of terrorist violence and trend analysis of the violence itself. The first thread of literature, developed largely in the field of political science, has linked higher probabilities of transnational terrorist violence to target states that have democratic governments [4], politically left governments [5], more veto-players in their governments [6], are perceived to be more likely to grant concessions to terrorists [7], and have further economic reach [8]. While this literature does much to shed light on the factors that may make a state more likely to suffer transnational terrorist attacks, it does little to provide forecasts of terrorist violence with any degree of precision. A second thread of literature has focused on trends in transnational terrorist violence itself. This literature, based at the intersection of political science and economics, has established that terrorist attacks exhibit cycling behavior [9], the number of terrorist attacks is decreasing but their lethality is increasing [10], substantial increases in levels of violence are usually unsustainable for the terrorist group [11], terrorist attacks are persistent following shocks in states suffering from low levels of terrorism (not for states suffering high levels of terrorism) [12], and terrorists tend to substitute targets when one type of target is hardened [13].

The literature that might help forecast terrorist events, however, has a major limitation: existent findings are either overly broad (i.e. democracies are more likely to be attacked by terrorists) or rely on voluminous attack data before trends can be identified and forecasts made. The lack of specificity from most statistical models of terrorist attacks is problematic from a policy perspective because, while it may warn a government that it is at elevated risk of terrorist attacks based on its attributes, it does little to inform the government about the source or timing of the threat. The trend analyses, while useful for predicting the ebb and flow of terrorist campaigns, are limited

by not being able to make accurate predictions about the onset of hostilities. Furthermore, the literature on why discontented groups resort to terrorism [14,15] is dedicated more to *explaining* the onset of terrorist campaigns than *predicting* such onset.

To date, the literature is moot in terms of statistical models designed not only to forecast attacks during terrorist campaigns, but to forecast emerging terrorist threats, *and* do so with a high degree of locational specificity: predicting not only when but from which country transnational terrorist attacks will emanate. Such a tool would provide insight from an academic perspective and prove useful from a policy perspective. It is with this aim that we develop a hybrid methodology from both deterministic and stochastic edge prediction techniques to predict the timing and locational dynamics of transnational terrorism.

Data

The data for our study are drawn from the "International Terrorism: Attributes of Terrorist Events" (ITERATE) dataset [1]. These data are well suited to our aims as they cover all transnational terrorist attacks over a 34 year period (1968–2002). The operational definition of transnational terrorism used for data collection is "the use, or threat of use, of anxiety-inducing, extra-normal violence for political purposes by any individual or group, whether acting for or in opposition to established governmental authority, when such action is intended to influence the attitudes and behavior of a target group wider than the immediate victims and when, through the nationality or foreign ties of its perpetrators, its location, the nature of its institutional or human victims, or the mechanics of its resolution, its ramifications transcend national boundaries." ([1], p. 2) The ITERATE data are one of the most comprehensive and commonly used data sets on transnational terrorism (for example, see [4,5,8,10-12,16]).

The ITERATE data, among other variables, codes the known nationalities of the terrorists who participate in a given transnational attack and the location of the attack. From these variables, we create the network of transnational terrorist attacks by year. We code a directed edge as existing from country i to country j if a national of country i participates in a terrorist attack on location j; we call these *terrorist edges*. Note that many attacks, such as the September 11, 2001 attacks on the United States, are perpetrated by non-state actors (e.g., al-Qaeda). In such instances, we code a directed edge from every known nationality of the attackers involved in the attack implementation to the target vertex. One may object that transnational terrorists sometimes emigrate from their homelands, developing doctrine, training, and establishing support networks in states that are neither their home nor their target. However, when we consider the process of radicalization, this is less concerning. When a terrorist emigrates to develop their plans and capabilities, the process of radicalization proceeded the emigration and, thus, will typically take place in their home country. It is the case that some of the better-known terrorist masterminds spend substantial portions of their lives abroad, hopping from place to place, but this is more typical of senior group leadership and less typical of those who actually execute the attacks. As such, many of the globe-hoppers would not be included in the dataset anyway (if they did not participate in an identifiable way in the attack). Second, attempting to consider where a terrorist has spend their "important years" would introduce substantial coding problems. For example, many of the 9/11 hijackers received critical training (i.e. flight training) in the United States, but drawing a looping edge from the U.S. to the U.S. makes little substantive sense. Furthermore, data on where terrorists have spent their time prior to their attacks is not generally available and is prone to error and uncertainty; terrorists typically try to conceal their training camps and hideouts. As it stands, no information is available in our dataset beyond the known nationalities of attackers, and so we use that as a criteria for constructing the network.

To construct the network, we must also define the universe of possible terrorist edges in a given year, which requires a definition of membership in the international system. We rely principally on the definition of the state system provided by the Correlates of War Project, which keeps a database of all countries that belong to the international community in a given year.[b] We augment membership in the international community by adding a few non-state actors that have been either the source or the target of transnational terrorism (e.g. Palestine and the United Nations). Though such entities are not technically countries, including them in the network is preferable to excluding them because contested territories are important producers of transnational terrorism and not including international governmental organizations would misclassify the target of the attack (i.e. where it occurred rather than who was targeted).

All together, we produce a network with a median of 175 vertices over the time span that we study. A feature of these data that is somewhat atypical in network analysis is that self-ties are present. It is common for terrorists from state i to commit an attack in state i. While we include these "loops" in our analysis, it is important to point out that all of these loops are affiliated in some way with a *transnational* terrorist incident. The ITER-ATE data do not code domestic terrorist attacks and, as such, loops represent acts in which a native of the target country collaborates with foreign terrorists to launch an attack.

Two empirical features of this network are particularly relevant to our forecasting approach: edge innovation and transitivity. By edge "innovation," we refer to terrorist edges that did not exist in the previous time period or periods. Substantively, edge innovation means that a terrorist from country i attacked a target in country j, where there had not been an attack from i to j for some time. The number of new and recurrent edges in the network over time is depicted in Figure 1. The shading indicates the degree to which the current edges also occurred in the past. What we see here is that, over the period 1980 – 2002, edges in the current network are just as likely to be innovations in the network (i.e., those that have not formed in the previous 10 years), as they are to be recurrent edges from the previous year. The relatively low degree of recurrence in the network implies that forecasting based on the dynamics of edge stability/memory will fail to capture a substantial portion of the year-to-year activity in the network. We can also see the importance of forecasting models designed to predict edge innovations; traditional time-series approaches to forecasting these innovations would prove fruitless.

The second feature we focus on, transitivity, is a measure of how important the network proximity of two vertices is to the likelihood of terrorist edge forming between those vertices (i.e., if the network is highly transitive, then configurations in which $a \rightarrow b \cap a \rightarrow c \Rightarrow b \rightarrow c$ will be common). The foundational work on edge prediction in networks uses measures of network proximity to forecast future ties [2]. If transitivity is a persistent feature in a network, then proximity-based forecasts should be relatively successful. However, if, in the terrorism network, the neighbor of a neighbor is not a neighbor, then another approach to link forecasting would be necessary.

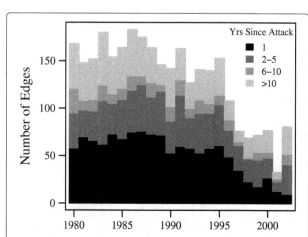

Figure 1 Number of country-country edges in the transnational terrorism network by year. Shading indicates the number of edges that are recurrent from previous years and how many are new edges, or *innovations* in the network.

We measure the degree of transitivity in the transnational terrorism network over time using a conditional uniform graph (CUG) test. The CUG test for transitivity [17,18] evaluates the observed degree of transitivity (the proportion of potential transitive triads that are actually closed) against a null distribution computed on a random sample of networks without transitivity. The null distribution of networks places a uniform probability on the possible networks, which have the same number of mutual and asymmetric dyads as the observed networks (i.e., the null distribution of networks is a uniform distribution conditional upon having the same dyad census as the observed network). The results of the CUG tests are depicted in Figure 2. In 21 of the 23 years depicted, the observed value of transitivity is larger than any of the 1,000 simulated null values. This indicates that there is a substantial degree of transitivity in the terrorism network. The exceptions are 1999 and 2001. It is not clear why the network would not be noticeably transitive in this period. The lower overall density of the network may make it more difficult to identify this feature.

These two results, (1) that many edges represent innovations with respect to the recent past and (2) the network exhibits significant transitivity, indicate that proximity-based link prediction should be a fruitful exercise on the transnational terrorism network. The persistence of innovation means that any information that can be leveraged about the indirect ties in the network will be quite valuable. The transitivity indicates that indirect ties will have predictive power with respect to edge formation.

Why is transnational terrorism transitive?

It is not immediately intuitive why the network of transnational terrorist attacks would exhibit the high degree of transitivity we observe with the CUG test. Conflictual international networks, such as international war [19], exhibit substantial intransitivity; whereas transitivity is commonly a feature of cooperative international networks (e.g. military alliances) [20,21].

When approaching this question theoretically, it is useful to distinguish between two common types of terrorist groups by motivation: ethno-nationalist groups and religious/ideological groups. Ethno-nationalist groups have specific goals of creating a state for their ethnic group or liberating their nation from occupation (real or perceived) and, as such, their attacks tend to be confined to only one target. Examples of such groups include the Provisional Irish Republican Army (PIRA) and the Kurdistan Workers' Party (PKK). For ethno-nationalist groups, terrorist violence is tied directly to the attainment of their nationalistic goals. Conversely, religious/ideological groups are organized around a religious or political/ideological ideal and tend to lack a clear policy objective.[c] However, such groups tend to have broader, multinational, support bases

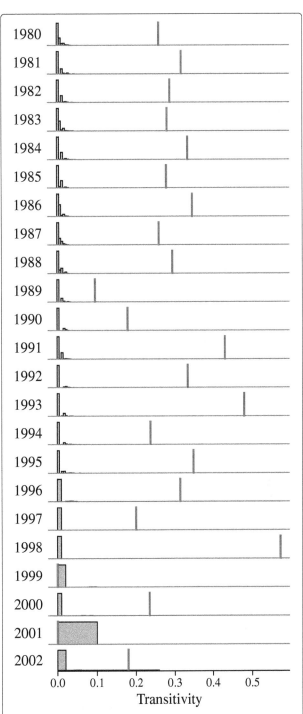

Figure 2 Conditional uniform graph tests for transitivity in the transnational terrorism network. For each year, the histogram of the null distribution of transitivity is depicted in gray, and the observed value of transitivity is located at the red line. The null distribution is constructed by measuring the transitivity of 1,000 networks simulated from a uniform graph distribution conditional on the dyad census.

and to attack targets in a number of countries. They tend to target countries that exhibit religious/ideological cultures that are counter to the groups' ideals. Groups such as al-Qaeda and the Red Army Faction fall into this category.

We offer two theoretical explanations for the transitivity of the transnational terrorist network, the first of which applies more to religious/ideological groups than to ethno-nationalist groups. These explanations are not mutually exclusive and both may be occurring simultaneously. First, consider a religious/ideological terrorist group X headquartered in state A. Suppose group X's ideology makes states B and C targets for attacks or campaigns. Assuming the group has a support base in state A, it is likely to recruit and train heavily there. During the course of its campaigns against B and C, group X continues to recruit from A, but also recruits from B and C. This pattern is both feasible and reasonably common for religious/ideological groups who may be headquartered in one country, but whose support base spans several. After some time, group X will have operational units in each of the three countries. Early (and continued) recruiting in A for attacks in B and C result in an out-2-star from A (i.e., two edges that form the start of a transitive triad). However, when recruits from B participate in attacks on C (or recruits from C participating in attacks on B), a transitive triad is formed. This process, through which ideological/religious groups garner multinational support bases, is illustrated in the left column of Figure 3.

A second situation that can give rise to transitivity in the network, for either ethno-nationalist or religious/ideological groups, is an environment with multiple terrorist groups. For example, extreme right and extreme left groups may be active in the same region and their overlapping attacks may form transitive patters. This two-group process is illustrated in the right column of Figure 3. Furthermore, a multi-group region need not be populated with groups of opposing ideals in order to form transitive triads. Bapat [22] provides an explanation for why infighting between groups with a common opponent is common, especially as peace processes progress. When a target state makes a move towards peace with its attackers, that move will usually involve active negotiations with one or several groups. In order to get their desired concessions, the negotiating group must moderate its behavior. This, however, is often not welcome by other groups or by radicals within the negotiating group. If the negotiating group is successful, it will, at best, seize power away from rival groups or, at worst, seize power away from rivals while negotiating a settlement that is unacceptable to a broad swath of rivals and radicals; either way, rival groups have an incentive to resist the change and radicals within the negotiating group have an incentive to form splinter groups. Resisting groups have been known to launch

spoiler campaigns agains the target state (attacks designed to provoke the target state and make peace less likely) or launch attacks directly on the negotiating group. At the same time, the negotiating group needs a monopoly on terrorist violence in order to be a reliable negotiating partner for the government, so it has an incentive to crack down on dissidents and rivals.

Method

Our method of forecasting is based on a probabilistic modeling framework, and incorporates proximity measures from a deterministic edge prediction method. For the probabilistic base of our method, we use the temporal exponential random graph modeling (TERGM) framework developed by Hanneke, Fu, and Xing [3]. To define the specific TERGMs, we incorporate vertex-similarity measures drawn from Liben-Nowell and Kleinberg [2], who originally used those measures in a deterministic manner. We first review the TERGM approach to modeling networks, then we describe the vertex-similarity measures and how we incorporate them into the TERGM modeling framework.

The exponential random graph model (ERGM) [23,24] is defined by a flexible discrete, exponential family joint distribution for a network N. The likelihood function is

$$\mathcal{P}(N, \theta) = \frac{\exp\{\theta'\mathbf{\Gamma}(N)\}}{\sum_{\text{all } N^* \in \mathcal{N}} \exp\{\theta'\mathbf{\Gamma}(N^*)\}}, \quad (1)$$

where $\theta \in \mathbb{R}^p$ is the parameter vector, $\mathbf{\Gamma}:N \to \mathbb{R}^p$ is a vector of statistics that are computed on the network, and the summation in the denominator is a normalizing constant computed on the support of N (denoted $\mathcal{N}$). This model is flexible in that $\mathbf{\Gamma}$ can be specified to capture virtually any form of interdependence among the edges in the networks, as well as dependence of the edges on exogenous features.

Hanneke, Fu, and Xing [3] extended the ERGM to model a network observed at numerous discrete time points, which extends the first-order dependence of the original model formulation [25]. This is accomplished mathematically by including past realizations of N in the $\mathbf{\Gamma}$ that defines the ERG distribution for the current network. The network is observed in T discrete time periods. Let N^t be the observed network at time t. Temporal interdependence of the networks can be built into the model by conditioning N^t on K previous realizations of the network.

The probability of observing N^t in the temporally interdependent ERGM (TERGM) of order K is written as

$$\mathcal{P}(N^t|K, \theta) = \frac{\exp\{\theta'\mathbf{\Gamma}(N^t, N^{t-1}, \ldots, N^{t-K})\}}{C(\theta, N^{t-K}, \ldots, N^{t-1})}. \quad (2)$$

Recall that the denominator in Equation 1 is a normalizing constant (i.e., a partition function). We update the

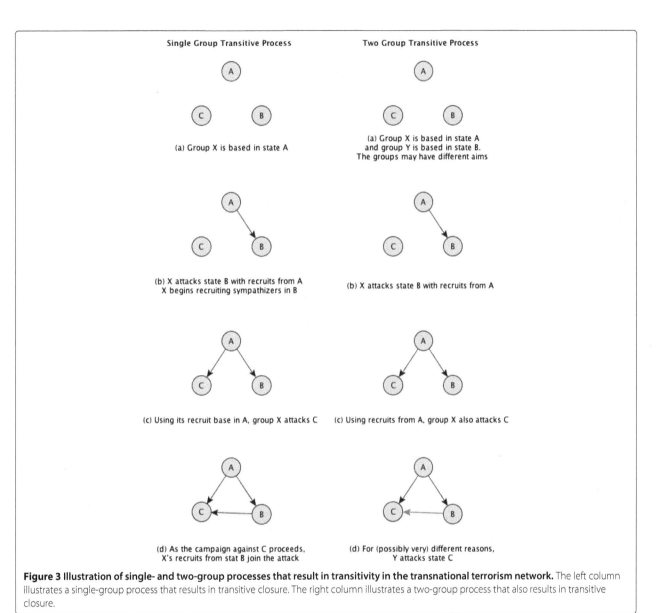

Figure 3 Illustration of single- and two-group processes that result in transitivity in the transnational terrorism network. The left column illustrates a single-group process that results in transitive closure. The right column illustrates a two-group process that also results in transitive closure.

notation in 2 to reflect this property. The likelihood function is defined as $\prod_{t=K+1}^{T} \mathcal{P}(N^t|K, \boldsymbol{\theta})$.[d] In our implementation, a new $\boldsymbol{\theta}$ is estimated for each t (i.e., $\boldsymbol{\theta}^t$). We allow parameters to vary by period due to temporal heterogeneity in the network structure, which is indicated by the considerable decrease in the density of the network over time and is visible in Figure 1.

In what can safely be called the foundational work on edge prediction in complex networks, Liben-Nowell and Kleinberg [2] capitalize the insight that vertices close or similar to each other in a network are likely to link in the future. They describe multiple measures of "proximity" in a network. Each measure of proximity results in a score $\delta(i,j)$ for each dyad of vertices ij in the network. These scores are then computed on a training network defined over an interval of the past. Dyads are then ranked with

respect to these scores. For prediction, the potential new edges are constrained to be those meeting a certain degree threshold in the training network. The subset of dyads defined on this network are then ranked with respect to their proximity scores and dyads that have high δ are predicted to be edges in the next time interval. Each proximity measure is evaluated with respect to its predictive performance.

We build upon this work by integrating proximity measures into the Γ of the TERGM. In our approach, the individual proximity measures are combined into a single model using the estimated weights ($\boldsymbol{\theta}$). A single best performing proximity measure need not be selected, a feature which provides considerable flexibility in the proximity terms to include. Also, the TERGM estimates permit us to forecast the probability of edges in the future. Each proximity measure δ is integrated into the TERGM by adding

$$\Gamma(N^t, N^{t_0, t-1}) = \sum_{ij} N_{ij}^t \delta(i,j)^{t_0, t-1}.$$

If states i or j were not in the international system during the period taken as the training network interval $[t_0, t-1]$, then we set $\delta(i,j)^{t_0, t-1} = 0$. Considering Figure 1, there appears to be significant dependence of the current network on the network from $t-1$ and that in $[t-5, t-2]$. We therefore perform our analyses setting t_0 at $t-1$ and $t-5$.

We consider 7 measures of the proximity of vertices. Figure 4 provides illustration of the sub-graph configurations that constitute 4 of the proximity measures.

1. **Flow**. This measure generalizes preferential attachment [2] to the directed case. Preferential attachment is implemented as a measure of proximity by Liben-Nowell [2] as $\delta(i,j) = k_i k_j$, where k is the degree (i.e., the number of edges) of a given vertex. To take advantage of the direction of the ties, we conceive of a process whereby an attack from i to j is likely if i sends many attacks and/or j receives many attacks. In other words, we posit that frequent attackers are close to regular targets in the network. The measure of flow is $\delta(i,j) = k_i^o k_j^i$, where k^o and k^i are the out and in-degrees respectively.
2. **CTarget**. The number of common targets shared by two countries: $\delta(i,j) = \sum_h N_{ih} N_{jh}$.
3. **CAttacker**. The number of common attackers shared by two countries: $\delta(i,j) = \sum_h N_{hi} N_{hj}$
4. **JacSim**. The Jaccard similarity between two countries is $\delta(i,j) = [\mathbf{CTarget} + \mathbf{CAttacker}]/[k_i + k_j]$, which normalizes the measure of common neighbors by the total number of neighbors of the vertices in the dyad.
5. **AASim**. The Adamic/Adar similarity adjusts the measure of common neighbors for the rarity of the neighbors to which the two countries tie. This measure is defined as $\delta(i,j) = \sum_h [\ln(k_h)]^{-1} (N_{ih} N_{jh} + N_{hi} N_{ji})$.
6. **SameCom**. Common community membership. We partition the countries into communities using the random walk modularity optimization algorithm "Walktrap" [26] and create an indicator, $\delta(i,j) = \mathbf{1}(c_i == c_j)$, of whether i and j are members of the same community.
7. **Distance**. Lastly, we include the minimum path length between i and j. We set $\delta(i,j)$ equal to the number of countries in the network plus one if there is no path from i to j.

In each model we include a count of the number of edges in the network to model the network's density. In addition to the proximity measures, and following Hanneke, Fu, and Xing [3], we include a memory term (**PrevAttack**) to capture persistence in the ties between the training network and the current network. The memory term at time t is specified as $\sum_{ij} N_{ij}^t N_{ij}^{t_0, t-1} + (1 - N_{ij}^t)(1 - N_{ij}^{t_0, t-1})$. We try each statistic computed on the networks over the interval $[t-1, t-1]$ and $[t-5, t-1]$. In the interest of comparing the performance of models on edges that did not occur in the past 10 years, we start our analysis at 1980 and go through the end of the dataset in 2002. Each model contains the edges term and some subset, including the empty set, of the memory and proximity terms, at both the one and five year intervals. The memory term and each of the proximity terms is (a) included computed on the one year training interval, (b) included computed on the five year training interval, and (c) excluded from the model. This leads to a total of $3^8 = 6,561$ models estimated at each t

The forecast model for t is selected as the best performing model up to $t-1$. Performance is judged based on the predictive log score (i.e., the forecast log-likelihood) [27]. By using the predictive log score, in expectation, we use the model with the minimum Kullback-Leibler divergence from the actual model that generated the data [27]. We use θ^{t-1} to perform the forecast of N^t, which was estimated to fit N^{t-1} based on $N^{t_0 - 1, t-2}$. Thus, it is a true forecast in that the TERGM used to predict N^t has only been trained on the series of networks up to $t-1$.

The forecasting algorithm we employ is summarized as:

1. Estimate each of the 6,561 forecasting models for each time point from 1980 up to the previous year. Denote the structural measures in model M as $\mathbf{\Gamma}_M$. Let $\boldsymbol{\theta}_M^t$ be the parameters estimated on N^t using $\mathbf{\Gamma}_M$.
2. Select as the forecasting model (M^*) for time t to be that model maximizing

$$\sum_{i=1981}^{t-1} \ln \left[\mathcal{P}(N^i | \boldsymbol{\theta}_M^{i-1}, \mathbf{\Gamma}_M) \right].$$

3. Forecast the next network from the distribution

$$\frac{\exp\{[\boldsymbol{\theta}_{M^*}^{t-1}]' \, \mathbf{\Gamma}_{M^*}(N, N^{t_0, t-1})\}}{C\left(\boldsymbol{\theta}_{M^*}^{t-1}\right)}.$$

4. Draw many forecast networks from the distribution in item 3 and compute the mean edge value in order to estimate the probability of any particular edge.

We apply this algorithm to all 23 years of the transnational terrorist network under consideration.

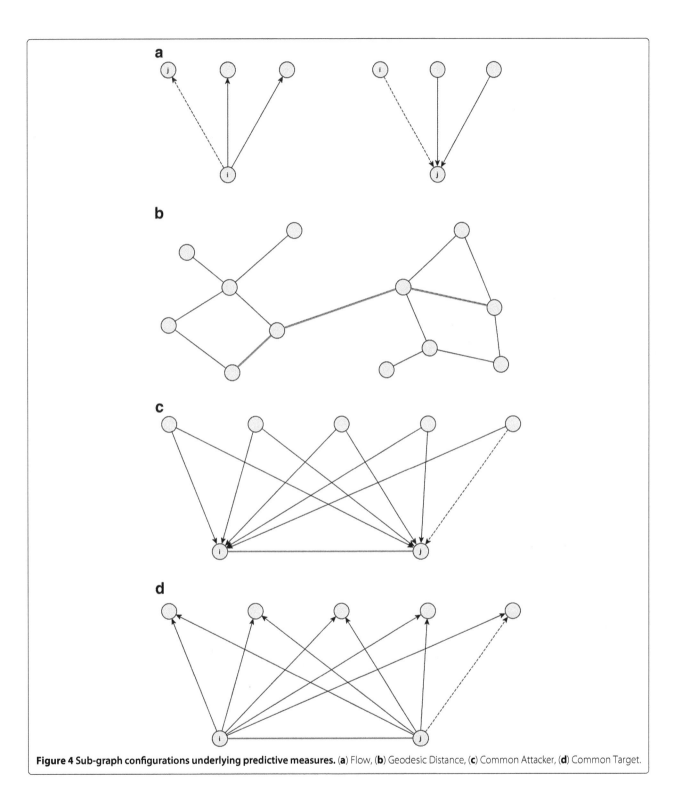

Figure 4 Sub-graph configurations underlying predictive measures. (a) Flow, (b) Geodesic Distance, (c) Common Attacker, (d) Common Target.

Results

There are a number of questions to be asked of our results. First, what is the overall performance of our approach to forecasting transnational terrorism? Second, does our approach offer leverage in predicting innovations in transnational terrorist relationships? Third, can

we see any patterns in the proximity and memory features that predict transnational terrorism? We address these questions in turn.

We begin by considering the overall performance of our forecasting method. The overall predictive performance is evaluated using the area under the receiver operating characteristic curve (AUC) [28]. The receiver operating characteristic (ROC) curve gives the relationship between the false positive and true positive rates in predicting the value of a dichotomous outcome (e.g., the presence or absence of an edge in a network). A perfect classifier has an AUC of 1 and the closer to 1 an AUC is, the better the model is predicting. In Figure 5, we contrast the AUCs for the one-year-ahead forecasts of the best-predicting specification and two specifications that include only memory terms of 1 and 5 years respectively. Comparing to the "just memory" models allows us to identify the contribution of adding the indirect network proximity terms to the forecasting model. The proximity model with the highest log score up to $t - 1$ performs much better than the memory models. The AUC is approximately 0.95 on average, which compares to 0.83 and 0.72 for the five and one year memory models respectively. The implication is that future edges in the transnational terrorism network can be forecast based on network proximity in the recent past.

Above, we make the claim that network proximity based forecasting will allow us to leverage the considerable transitivity in transnational terrorism and forecast edge innovations: to predict a terrorist edge from one state to another where no such edge existed within a given window of time. Here, we evaluate the performance of our method on edges that did not occur in the recent past. A straightforward way to evaluate the predictive performance of our forecasting method is to consider the difference between the probability of edge formation assigned to those dyads that do form edges versus the probability of edge formation among those that do not form edges. Figure 6 shows forecasted probabilities assigned to edges that experience attacks and those that do not experience

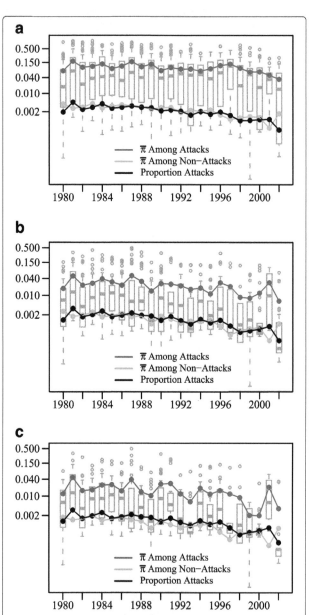

Figure 6 Forecasted probabilities for edges that experience attacks and those that do not experience attacks. Forecasted probabilities for edges that experience attacks and those that do not experience attacks. $\bar{\pi}$ is the mean forecast probability in the respective year. The probability of an attack from one location to another in year t is computed with the TERGM estimates from the model that, in terms of predictive log score, most accurately predicted N^{t-1} from $N^{t_0-1,t-2}$. In the interest of clarity, the y-axis is depicted on the log scale. Box plots depict the distribution of π among those directed dyads that experienced an attack in t.

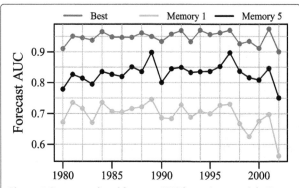

Figure 5 One-year-ahead forecast AUC for various models. To compute the forecast AUC, we use the parameters estimated by modeling N^{t-1} based on $N^{t_0-1,t-2}$ to forecast N^t based on $N^{t_0,t-1}$. The "Best" model is the one that has had the highest average predictive log score up to t. "Memory 1" only has a memory effect from the previous year and an edges term. The "Memory 5" model only has a memory effect from the previous 5 years and an edges effect.

attacks (potential edges that are not realized). We consider innovations of edges that have not occurred in the previous 1, 5 and 10 years, respectively. The results are similar for each of the three innovation intervals. The model assigns consistently low probabilities (in the range of 0.002) to potential edges that result in non-attacks.

More importantly, the edges that do form are, on average, forecast to do so with one to two *orders of magnitude* higher probability than are non-edges. The strong performance of our forecasting model in predicting edge innovations is a major contribution to the policy problem of identifying and addressing threats from the myriad of potential sources of transnational terrorism.

Lastly, we consider the contributions of the individual proximity and memory measures to the fit of the model. Figure 7 displays the ratio of the mean one-year-ahead forecast areas under the ROC curve with and without the given measure. A value greater than unity indicates that the average forecast AUC is higher when the respective term is included in the model. The plots show results from one (red) and five (blue) year memory models and all results are shown over time. Those statistics that consistently produce ratios greater than one can be said to make consistent contributions to the predictive performance of the model. Consistently highly performing measures include **PrevAttack, Flow, CAttacker** and **AASim**. The **SameCom** and **Distance** measures contribute substantial predictive performance in some years, but their effects are more volatile. For all of the measures that consistently add to the predictive performance of the model, the measure is computed on the five year interval. The superior performance of the measures computed with five year memories reinforces the result from Figure 5 that the transnational terrorism network exhibits long memory.

Case test: The Saudi link to the U.S. in 2001

The terror attacks of September 11, 2001 are the most spectacular and terrible the world has yet seen. They were also unexpected by policy and intelligence analysts. Among the surprises of the 9/11 attacks was the fact that 15 of the 19 hijackers were Saudi; indeed, it was the first time a Saudi citizen had committed any sort of attack on U.S. soil in almost three decades. As a test case, we examine what information our forecasting model provides about that 9/11 link from Saudi Arabia to the U.S.

To begin the case analysis, consider the ranked list, reported in Table 1, of the ten most highly predicted

Table 1 Top ten predicted sources of terrorism against targets inside the U.S., 2001

Rank	Country	P(Attack)
1	Algeria	0.126
2	Pakistan	0.055
3	Iraq	0.044
4	Jordan	0.037
5	Cuba	0.037
6	Canada	0.029
7	Romania	0.024
8	**Saudi Arabia**	0.012
9	**Egypt**	0.011
10	Iran	0.011

The rank-ordered sources of transnational terrorist threat most highly predicted by our forecasting model for the year 2001.

sources of attacks on the U.S. in 2001. Saudi Arabia is the 8th highest predicted source of attack and the list generally suggests a high risk posed by Middle Eastern countries; with Algeria, Pakistan, Iraq, Jordan, Egypt, and Iran also making the top 10. Canada may seem like an odd country to make the top 10 threat list, but attacks on the US from Canada have occurred, the most recent attack by a Canadian citizen preceding 9/11 occurred in 1999. This list, we believe, would be a useful guide for intelligence analysts and law enforcement officials attempting to efficiently divide their counter-terrorism resources between a larger number of possible threats.

The comparatively high probability assigned to attacks by Saudi citizens bodes well for our model, but how does the prediction for 2001 compare to other years and which statistics in our model produce the prediction? Figure 8 shows the percentile rank of Saudi Arabian citizens among those from all other countries in the world in a given year, with respect to the predicted probability of an attack on the U.S. We can see from the Figure that, at the time of the 9/11 attacks, the probability of attack on U.S. soil by Saudi citizens was the highest it had ever been (and the second

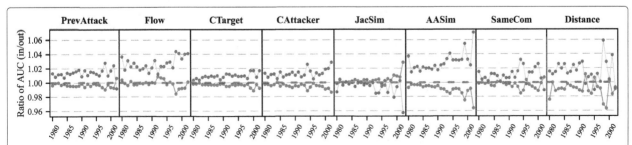

Figure 7 Relative forecasting performance of models with and without respective effects. Depicted is the ratio of the average one-year-ahead forecast areas under the ROC curves with and without the particular term. Terms computed on the one (five) previous year(s) are in red (blue).

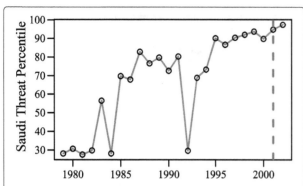

Figure 8 Relative threat of an attack on the U.S. posed by Saudi nationals. The y-axis gives the percentile rank of Saudi Arabia among all other countries in the world at the time, with respect to the predicted probability of an attack on the U.S. The red bar is placed at 2001, which is the one and only recorded instance of a Saudi attacking on U.S. soil.

Table 2 Predictive model for 2001

δ	t_0	θ	δ %tile*
PrevAttack	1996	1.64	0
Flow	1996	0.027	99.99
CAttacker	1996	0.24	98.46
AASim	2000	0.5	0
SameComm	2000	0.441	0
Distance	1996	4.07	98.89

*δ %tile is the Percentile rank of $\delta(SA, US)$. The model used to predict the network in 2001. This is the model that best predicted the network in 2000 based on the θ estimated on the 1999 network. The θ in this table were estimated on the 2000 network. The percentile rank is based on a comparison with all of the other predictive scores (i.e., δ) of the other directed pairs of countries for which 2001 predictive scores are computed. The t_0 denote the beginning of the interval on which the predicting network is defined for that statistic, with all predictive network intervals ending in 2000.

highest achieved during the timeframe of our dataset). Interestingly, we also see that, based on the connectivity of the network, the Saudi threat begins mounting seriously in the late 1980's; during this time, attackers from Saudi Arabia strike in Israel. The drop noticed in 1992 occurs because, for that year, Saudi Arabia has no outgoing edges during the five year training period and the U.S. and Saudi Arabia have no common attackers. We see the probability of an attack jump back up again, elevate, and stay high following 1992. During this time, Iran becomes a common attacker for the U.S. and Saudi Arabia and a surge of international attacks by Saudi citizens begins: Saudis participate in attacks in Egypt, Jordan, the Philippines, Kenya and Tanzania, Pakistan, Uruguay, Albania, and Cambodia. Note, while not edges to the U.S. territorially, and therefore not recorded as edges to the U.S. in our networks, the 1998 Kenyan and Tanzanian attacks were orchestrated by al-Qaida and targeted U.S. embassies in those countries. This is also the time during which Osama bin Laden turned his resources against the U.S.; a response to his outrage over U.S. military forces being allowed in Saudi Arabia during the Gulf War.

We can see in Table 2, that flow, common attacker, and distance are producing the prediction for 2001, since these statistics comprised the model that best predicted the network in 2000. Flow and distance are both intuitive. Flow captures the fact that simultaneously Saudi Arabia is a (increasingly) large sender of attacks and the U.S. is (increasingly) a large receiver of attacks. Distance simply indicates that the geodesic distance between the U.S. and Saudi Arabia is large. The common attacker tie, as recorded in the ITERATE data, is a bit less intuitive, because the states are tied by Canada. This is not as odd as it might initially seem and actually reinforces our theoretical query into the transitivity of the network:

Islamic extremists, and bin Laden in particular, were taking advantage of geographic proximity and soft borders by using Canada as a base for attacks on the U.S. [29]. In the meantime, a Canadian citizen was recruited by bin Laden, and participated in an attack on westerners (British and Irish) in Saudi Arabia [30]. This activity in Canada also explains the fact that Canada appears on our 2001 top-threat list for the U.S.

Conclusion

Our study of the transnational terrorist network makes at least three major contributions. First, we contribute to the literature on edge forecasting in complex networks. We integrate deterministic proximity-based forecasting into the probabilistic TERGM modeling of the evolution of a network based on its own topography. This approach can be applied to the edge prediction problem in many areas. This general method may prove useful for predicting the occurrence of edges in any variety of other networks such as international conflict (war), scientific collaboration and friendship.

We contributed to the state of knowledge about transnational terrorism by identifying that (1) there is an even mix of memory and innovation in the transnational terrorism network and (2) the network exhibits substantial transitivity. The transitivity we observe is likely due to to economic, political, linguistic, and religious clustering that are subsumed under country labels. In other words, the way in which we define the vertices in the networks acts as a catch-all for the features likely to drive terrorism. Future research should address what specific features of countries predict terrorist link formation.

Lastly, but perhaps most importantly, we have advanced terrorism forecasting models in two critical directions. Our approach provides the necessary source-target specificity required to be useful for protecting the target *and* addressing the source. Second, by leveraging the information on indirect ties in the network, our method is able to predict the occurrence of new terrorist edges. The ability to predict edge innovation is critical from a policy perspective because early warning is essential for the allocation of security resources that can, potentially, save lives.

Endnotes

[a]It is worth noting that there is a deep literature on psychological traits that make an individual more likely to become a terrorist and on the psychological group dynamics that affect a group's cohesion, but we do not consider this literature extensively here because its focus relates to individual behaviors rather than the amount of violence states suffer at the hands of terrorists. See [14,31] for reviews of this literature.

[b]These data are freely available at http://www.correlatesofwar.org/.

[c]They tend to at least lack realistic policy objectives, though they may have stated objectives such as the imposition of global Islamic law or communism.

[d]Note that the computation of the likelihood requires the omission of the first K networks. Hanneke, Fu, and Xing [3] point out that one could also specify a separate probability model for these networks, but it is unclear what benefit would come of such an exercise, since this convenience model would, by construction, be misspecified.

Competing interests
The authors declare that they have no competing interests.

Authors' contributions
BAD developed the models in this article and drafted the manuscript. SJC developed the models and drafted the manuscript. Both authors read and approved the final manuscript.

Acknowledgements
This work was supported, in part, by a research grant from the College of Social and Behavioral Sciences, University of Massachusetts Amherst and by a grant from the University of North Carolina at Chapel Hill's University Research Council.

Author details
[1]Department of Political Science, University of Massachusetts at Amherst, Amherst, Massachusetts 01003, USA. [2]Department of Political Science, University of North Carolina at Chapel Hill, Chapel Hill, North Carolina 27599, USA.

References
1. EF Mickolus, T Sandler, JM Murdock, PA Flemming, International Terrorism: Attributes of Terrorist Events (ITERATE), 1968-2007. Vinyard Software. (Dunn Loring, 2008)
2. D Liben-Nowell, J Kleinberg, in *Proceedings of the Twelfth International Conference on Information and Knowledge Management*. The link prediction problem for social networks, (2003), pp. 556–559
3. S Hanneke, W Fu, EP Xing, Discrete Temporal Models of Social Networks. Electron. J. Stat. **4**, 585–605 (2010)
4. Q Li, Does democracy promote or reduce transnational terrorist incidents? J. Confl. Resolution. **49**(2), 278–297 (2005)
5. MT Koch, SJ Cranmer, Testing the "Dick Cheney" hypothesis: do governments of the left attract more terrorism than governments of the right? Confl. Manag. Peace Sci. **24**(4), 311–326 (2007)
6. JK Young, L Dugan, Veto players and terror. J. Peace Res. **48**, 19–33 (2011)
7. AH Kydd, BF Walter, The strategies of terrorism. Int. Secur. **31**, 49–80 (2006)
8. Q Li, D Schaub, Economic globalization and transnational terrorism. A pooled time-series analysis. J. Confl. Resolution. **48**(2), 230–258 (2004)
9. W Enders, GF Parise, T Sandler, A time-series analysis of transnational terrorism: trends and cycles. Defense Peace Econ. **3**(4), 305–320 (1992)
10. W Enders, T Sandler, Is transnational terrorism becoming more threatening? A time-series investigation. J. Confl. Resolution. **44**(3), 307–332 (2000)
11. W Enders, T Sandler, Patterns of transnational terrorism, 1970-1999: alternative time-Series estimates. Int. Stud. Q. **46**(2), 145–165 (2002)
12. W Enders, T Sandler, Transnational terrorism 1968-2000: thresholds, persistence, and forecasts. South Econ. J. **71**(3), 467–482 (2005)
13. PT Brandt, T Sandler, What do transnational terrorists target? Has it changed? Are we safer? J. Confl. Resolution. **54**(2), 214–236 (2010)
14. M Crenshaw, *Explaining Terrorism: Causes, Processes, and Consequences* (Routledge, London, 2010)
15. M Crenshaw, The causes of terrorism. Comp. Polit. **13**(4), 379–399 (1981)
16. AB Krueger, Malečková, Education, poverty and terrorism: Is there a causal connection? J. Econ. Perspect. **17**(4), 119–144 (2003)
17. BS Anderson, CT Butts, KM Carley, The interaction of size and density with graph-level indices. Soc. Netw. **21**(3), 239–267 (1999)
18. CT Butts, Social networks: a methodological introduction. Asian J. Soc. Psychol. **11**, 13–41 (2008)
19. SJ Cranmer, BA Desmarais, Inferential network analysis with exponential random graph models. Pol. Anal. **19**(1), 66–86 (2011)
20. SJ Cranmer, BA Desmarais, EJ Menninga, Complex dependencies in the alliance network. Confl. Manage. Peace Sci. **29**(3), 279–313 (2012)
21. SJ Cranmer, BA Desmarais, JH Kirkland, Toward a network theory of alliance formation. Int. Interact. **38**(3), 295–324 (2012)
22. NA Bapat, State bargaining with transnational terrorist groups. Int. Stud. Q. **50**(2), 215–232 (2006)
23. S Wasserman, P Pattison, Logit models for social networks: I. an introduction to Markov graphs andp. Psychometrika. **61**(3), 401–425 (1996)
24. J Park, M Newman, Statistical mechanics of networks. Phys. Rev. E. **70**(6), 66117–66130 (2004)
25. G Robins, P Pattison, Random graph models for temporal processes in social networks. J. Math. Sociol. **25**, 5–41 (2001)
26. P Pons, M Latapy, in *Computer and Information Sciences - ISCIS 2005, Volume 3733 of Lecture Notes in Computer Science*. Computing communities in large networks using random walks, (2005), pp. 284–293
27. J Geweke, G Amisano, Optimal prediction pools. J. Econometrics. **164**(1), 130–141 (2011)
28. ZC Qin, in *Proceedings of 2005 International Conference on Machine Learning and Cybernetics, Volume 5*. ROC analysis for predictions made by probabilistic classifiers, (2005), pp. 3119–3124
29. BBC News, Bin Laden 'using Canada as base' (2000). http://news.bbc.co.uk/2/hi/americas/793178.stm
30. L Gordon, Briton Admits Blasts. (The Guardian 4 February, 2001). http://www.guardian.co.uk/world/2001/feb/05/saudiarabia
31. M Crenshaw, in *Terrorism: Roots, Impact, Responses*, ed. by L Howard. How Terrorists think: psychological contributions to understanding terrorism, (1992), pp. 71–80

8

Through a computational lens: using dual computer-criminology degree programs to advance the study of criminology and criminal justice practice

Colby L Valentine[1*], Carter Hay[2], Kevin M Beaver[2] and Thomas G Blomberg[2]

Abstract

Computational criminology seeks to address criminological and criminal justice problems through the use of applied mathematics, computer science, and criminology. The development of mathematical and computational methods along with the emergence of cyberspace demonstrates the need for innovative degree programs that focus on computational criminology. The purpose of this article is to highlight the significance of dual computer-criminology degree programs. The article first discuses two major shifts in the study of criminology: the facilitation of new methodologies and data techniques; and, the development of new types of crime and delinquency through advancements in computer technology. Next, the article describes the need for dual computer-criminology degree programs and employs Florida State University's program as an example of what these programs offer aspiring criminologists. Finally, the article concludes with discussion of future plans for the Florida State University dual computer-criminology degree program that are applicable to other criminology programs both within the United States and also internationally.

Keywords: Computer criminology, Degree program, Cyber crime, Florida State University

Introduction

Beginning Fall 2007, Florida State University (FSU) offered an interdisciplinary undergraduate degree program in Computer Criminology and in Fall 2011, FSU began offering students the opportunity to pursue a Master's of Science in Computer Criminology. The FSU Department of Computer Science and the College of Criminology and Criminal Justice jointly developed these new degree programs in response to the technological and computational shifts that have emerged in the field of criminology and criminal justice. Specifically, these degree programs relate to the specialization of computational criminology, which seeks to address criminological problems through the use of applied mathematics, computer science, and criminology. Degrees that focus on mathematical and computation science are crucial to

prepare new students and future scholars for the changing subject matter in the field as research is advancing and new areas of focus are unraveling every day as well as preparing criminal justice practitioners in their efforts to effectively confront the emerging cyber aspects of crime.

Computational criminology is an emerging field that has developed primarily from two areas over the past 30 years. First, the development of crime simulation models and related computer methodologies has emerged as a new way to study crime. Computational criminology has been pioneered in the field of environmental criminology. Liu and Eck (2008) describe artificial crime analyses and simulation as methods to reveal hidden processes of urban crimes by combining criminology, computer simulation, and geographic information systems [1]. Two other prominent researchers in this area, Patricia and Paul Brantingham, have focused their research on environmental or contextual factors that can influence criminal activity. Their research initiated the development of the Computational Criminology Initiative (CCI), which

* Correspondence: colby.valentine@dc.edu
[1]Dominican College, 470 Western Highway, Orangeburg, New York 10962, USA
Full list of author information is available at the end of the article

allows for new visualization techniques for understanding crime patterns.

Another area of computational criminology that has emerged in criminological and computer science research is the development of computer crimes and related criminal activity in cyberspace [2]. However, the development of research in computer and cyber crime within the field of criminology has just begun to develop over the past few years. The first conference devoted to cyber and computer criminology was the "Cyber Criminology and Digital Forensics Initiative Conference" which was held in Spokane Valley, Washington in October 2006. Then in 2007, the *International Journal of Cyber Criminology* (IJCC) began publication as a peer reviewed online (open access) interdisciplinary journal dedicated to the study of cyber crime, cyber criminal behavior, cyber victims, cyber laws, and cyber investigations [3].

The development of mathematical and computational methods along with the emergence of cyberspace as a new locus for criminal activity demonstrates the need for innovative degree programs that focus on computational criminology. The two purposes of this article are: first, to describe from a criminological perspective the techno-logical and computational shift in the study of criminology and criminal justice, and second, to highlight how dual computer-criminology degree programs advance the study of crime in ways that address needs for both researchers and practitioners in the field of criminal justice.

The article begins with a discussion of two major shifts in the study of criminology: the facilitation of new methodologies and data techniques; and, the development of new types of crime and delinquency through advancements in computer technology. Next, the article describes the need for dual computer-criminology degree programs and employs FSU's program as an example of what these programs offer aspiring criminologists. Finally, the article concludes with discussion of future plans for the FSU dual computer-criminology degree program that are applicable to other criminology programs.

The technological shift in the study of criminology and criminal justice

Computational criminology is an emerging field that is generating new and innovative methodologies. These include new criminological models, calculated algorithms, spatial and temporal dynamics of crime and terrorism, co-offending network analysis, data structures and soft-ware development, and the mining of crime, offender and criminal justice systems data. For example, advancements in computational power and the availability of new data have allowed new types of methodologies to evolve within the study of criminology. Brantingham and colleagues (2009) describes one niche computational criminology

addresses regarding crime analyses and data for studying crime patterns:

The recent emergence of computational criminology, grounded on improvement in the computational power available to researchers, provides, potentially, a way to link theory and research at a micro level with theory and reassert at the meso levels of analysis (p.90).

The authors further expand on this concept by presenting an algorithm based on analysis of land unit to unit similarity to demonstrate how crimes patterns develop in and around certain neighborhoods [4]. The findings offer an innovated data technique that may aid in the computational expansion of crime pattern research that can guide more effective geographic targeting of crime control efforts. Additional work pioneered by Brantingham and collegues (2005; 2009) demonstrate how mathematical and computational methods, such as those based on the abstract state machine (ASM) paradigm, allow for the modeling and simulation of crime patterns. These methods aim to advance criminological approaches toward crime reduction and prevention. For example, some of the purposes of mathematical computation models include helping predict the likelihood of criminal activity occurring in certain places, creating scenarios in crime analysis and simulating prevention techniques to provide a basis for experimental research that is difficult to produce in real-work settings, and designing critical infrastructure protection [5,6].

Artificial crime analysis and crime simulation is an emerging area that highlights the advancement in computation criminology. Liu and Eck's (2008) edited book that addresses a number of issues relating to crime analyses using computer simulations and geographical information systems. Their book is focused around four sections exploring such topics as using simulation to understand crime patterns and criminal justice processes, an analysis of conditions that might influence crime patterns, crime event and pattern simulation, and criminal justice operation simulations. Several chapters provide examples that demonstrate how simulations are used as a tool to understand crime patterns [1]. The book also summarizes four purposes of artificial crime analysis: theorizing, estimating, testing, and planning [7].

Some of the research on crime analysis and simulation specifically illustrate the purposes for using crime simulations. For instance, agent-based models for crime simulations can be particularly useful for theorizing. Specifically, spatial adaptive crime event simulations (SPACES) can be used to explore theory. Theoretical experiments or scenarios can determine how elements of a theory work together and whether the theory can help produce crime patterns. If so, then SPACES may be able to produce hypotheses that can be tested using empirical data [8]. Further, simulations can be implemented to test policies. Szakas, Trefftz, Ramirez, and Jefferis (2008) use simulations to test various police patrols methods. These methods, for example, can assist with geographical profiles of suspects or parolees at home and/or at work [9]. Simulations can also be used in predicting and understanding the effect of changes within the criminal justice system [10]. These examples demonstrate how advancements in computation and simulation models yield new methods and techniques, which can advance insights on a variety of issues relating to crime and justice practices.

The rapid growth in computational simulations in the field of criminology and criminal justice is further demonstrated by research that focuses on a variety of issues and complexities related to applying these mathematical models. The *Journal of Experimental Criminology* published a special issue relating to simulated experiments in criminology and criminal justice. The special issue focused on simulation models and their contributions to criminology regarding unique techniques used to test intervention practices and model outcomes. For example, Auerhahn (2008) used data-validated dynamic systems simulation modeling to examine the effect of California's Three Strikes law on the state's prison population. The simulation model allowed for a prospective analysis of the future effects of the legislation. Therefore, when evaluating policy, the simulation model has an advantage for criminologists by looking both retrospectively at the legislation and also formulating future effects and foreseeing the consequences of those outcomes [11]. Another innovative study developed an agent-based model to test the effects of three different police strategies (i.e., random patrol, hot-spot policing, and problem-orientated policing) on a street-level drug market. The authors simulated a disruption in the heroin supply chain to attempt to better understand the various police interventions [12]. Both of the above computational models illustrate how the use of such methods further develops criminological thought and practice related to providing useful simulations capable of generating comprehensible empirical description from which grounded explanations and predictions can be derived.

Computational methods have the ability to enhance the study of criminology but they also can pose a number of challenges for researchers. Berk (2008) examines the complexities of model validation, specifically degrees of credibility, for computational models and further concludes that simulation models can benefit the development and refinement of theory. However, criminologists must continue to test computer models against data [13]. Further, Townsley and Birks (2008) discuss the need for replication of computational model to enhance their validity [14]. Despite these challenges, simulations have great promise

in the field of criminology and are yet another tool for criminologists to use that can complement traditional data-driven methods.

New types of crime and delinquency

Beyond mathematical and computational methods, the development of cyber and computer crime has also transformed the way criminologists study crime and delinquency. Historically, criminologists have focused on traditional forms of crime (e.g., murder, assaults, kidnapping, etc.); however, during the past few decades, crime has moved to the Internet, opening the door to new types of crime and delinquency, as well as, new methods of engaging in crime. This section briefly describes how the study of criminology has shifted to include the Internet through advancements in technology and the use of computers. Although cyber crime research is relatively new to criminology, this area of research is gaining momentum [15]. As a result, the literature on this topic is extensive and summarizing it is beyond the scope of this article. As a result, we provide only a snapshot of the research, taken from the journal that pioneered the field, to demonstrate this new avenue of research emerging from the development and growth of computer and cyber crime. Thus, the purpose of this section is to clarify the way in which computers have become central to the commission of many categories of crime. Specifically we review and discuss three categories of computer crimes that illustrate this emerging pattern and point to the need to prioritize the intersection of computer science and the traditional study of criminology and criminal justice.

Cyber and computer crime have emerged as new areas of research for criminologists and in doing so have provided new opportunities to apply theory to help explain such crime. Crimes that are associated with the prevalence of computers target the technological industry, its customers, and others [16]. Some of the crimes that are incorporated into this category include counterfeiting, identity theft, corporate theft, component theft, and piracy. Digital piracy is the act of copying digital goods (i.e., software, documents, audio, and video) without permission from and compensation to the copyright holder using computer technology [17-19]. Digital piracy is one area of research that has emerged within cyber criminology and covers topics such as music, gaming, and other computer programs.

Empirical research on piracy has focused on some of the correlates that may be associated with digital piracy, in addition to, examining criminological theories in the context of digital piracy. For example, Moore and McMullan (2009) conducted qualitative interviews with university students to determine whether neutralization techniques were employed by file sharers and found that each participant indicated support for at least one technique of neutralization in justifying their piracy activities [20]. Also focusing on neutralization theory, Higgins, Wolfe, and Marcum (2008) examined the trajectories of digital piracy among college students and found that the level of neutralization utilized by a potential music pirate affects the piracy that actually occurs [21]. In addition, Higgins (2007) examined other criminological theories, self-control and rational choice, to explain digital piracy and found that low self-control and situational factors had direct and indirect effects with intentions to engage in digital piracy [22].

The above research demonstrates how the merging of computer technology and criminology has created a new research area for scholars. Advancements in technology have created new types of crime, such as digital piracy, for researchers to examine using criminological theories. In addition, a computational understanding of piracy can give scholars a unique understanding of the crime. Dual computer-criminology degree programs, thus, facilitate the merging of two disciplines that can aid future research on piracy and other computer related crimes and, also, aid in the prevention and control of further illegal digital transmissions.

Other forms of cyber crimes, that use the computer as an instrument of the crime or are incidental to the crime, have illustrated the shift in crimes from society to cyberspace. For example, crimes that use the computer as an instrument of the crime include offenses when the computer is used to gain something. Therefore, the criminal uses the computer or the network to perform crimes such as theft, fraud, exploitation, threats, or harassment [16]. Cyber bulling and cyber stalking has become a hot topic among schools, parents, the media, political forums and, more recently, among criminologists. The empirical research on cyber bullying is extensive and reveals the high prevalence among adolescents of internet-based harassment that includes abusive e-mails, insulting messages or pictures posted on online message boards, and Web-sites that disseminate disparaging information about an individual [23-25]. One special concern about cyber bullying is its potentially relentless nature. Because many adolescents—for legitimate reasons—frequently use the Internet, they can be exposed to cyber bullying even when physically removed from bullies. Thus, as Mason (2008:324) notes, with cyber bullying, "home may no longer be a place of refuge" [26]. With these issues in mind, cyber bullying has attracted significantly attention in many disciplines, and the *International Journal of Cyber Criminology* has published numerous articles on this topic, which include an international study of bullying in web forums [27], an examination of polices and legal obligations associated with cyber bullying [28], and the effectiveness of cyber bullying prevention strategies [29].

Compared to cyber bullying, less research has been conducted on cyber stalking. Pitarro (2007) conducted an analysis on cyber stalking and examined the deviant behaviors and tactics associated with cyber stalking crimes, legislative intervention measures, and preventative initiatives [30]. Another descriptive article appeared in the *International Journal of Cyber Criminology* providing an overview of the current state of knowledge on cyber-stalking and examined the difficulties in investigating and prosecuting cyber-stalkers. Roberts (2008:281) concludes her article by arguing for the "...continued training of law enforcement and legal officers to increase their techno-logical sophistication and understanding of cyber-stalking behaviours" [31]. A dual computer-criminology degree tackles both the understanding and technological elements of this crime.

Prior research on cyber bullying and cyber stalking, demonstrate how specific types of crimes have evolved through advancements in the Internet; thereby, providing new ways to engage in deviant behaviors. Cyber bullying, threats, harassment, and stalking have developed as new research areas focusing on the way some individuals misuse technology. Consequently, the increasing prevalence of this type of crime should be further integrated into the study of criminology and dual computer-criminology degree program are a necessary medium to advance such research and subsequently guide polices aimed at preventing and reducing these particular crimes.

Further, crimes that focus on computers as a target exemplify the need for an understanding in computation technology and mathematical methodologies to employ effective investigation and prevention strategies. For example, crimes that focus on the computer as a target include such acts as, denying the user or owner access to their computer or data, alteration of data on the computer, network intruding, and computer vandalism [16]. A common example of such a crime is hacking. *Hacking* is commonly described as "act of re-designing the configuration of hardware or software systems to alter their intended function" [32]. Bachmann (2010) examined the risk propensity and rationality of computer hackers. The author used a number of criminological theories to explain the findings of the study including rational choice, self-control, and, related specifically to cyber crime, space transition theory [32]. This type of computer related deviance is an example of how criminologists can benefit from individuals with an educational background in both criminology and computer science. Scholars with a degree in computer criminology have an understanding of how computers facilitate the study of crime and how crimes are accomplished through the use of computers. Further, to aid in the prevention and intervention of such crimes, individuals need to understand the methods of such crimes and the elements of computer systems that an education in computer criminology can provide through the teaching of criminological research, theory, computer systems, and procedures.

Dual computer-criminology degree programs

Given these developments in computational models, computer technology, and cyber crime, it is not surprising that there is a growing recognition of the need and usefulness of studying crime at the computational level through dual computer-criminology degree programs. Computer criminology is a relatively new field, and departments are beginning to add computer criminology as a major for current and incoming students. In particular, the FSU dual computer-criminology degree program presents what could become a standard in the future to keep up with the rapidly growing areas of cybercrime and its control. The FSU program focuses on areas such as information-related crime, cyber-forensics, and computer/network security. Computer criminology includes both how to use computers to facilitate the study of crime and the study of how crimes are accomplished through the use of computers. Students graduating from FSU will be prepared to do graduate work and research in this area, or have the opportunity to become effective employees of government, law enforcement, or other related public and private agencies.

FSU's dual computer-criminology degree program is presented as a case example to illustrate how a computer criminology degree can prepare students for future graduate work and/or employment. To this end, the next section provides examples of courses from both criminology and computer sciences that are available to students at both the undergraduate and graduate level.

Undergraduate degree program

In 2007, Florida State University first offered an undergraduate degree program in computer criminology for current and incoming students. The degree program is a four-year program that focuses on a combination of general education requirements based on University standards, computer science courses, and criminology courses. Students may elect to pursue the major by either graduating through the Department of Computer Sciences within the College of Arts and Sciences or through the College of Criminology and Criminal Justice. One of the key hallmarks of the program is the close connection between the computer science program and the criminology program. In short, students pursuing a degree in computer criminology get the "best of both worlds" by learning from world-class researchers in computer science as well as world-class researchers in criminology.

Students majoring in computer criminology are required to take courses that focus on computer science, criminology, and mathematics. Some of the required courses for computer science include courses that focus on the fundamentals of computer organization, computer operating systems, and computer programming. The capstone course offered in the computer science department for the major is cybercrime detection and forensics. The courses focus on learning tools, techniques, and procedures for detecting cybercrime and analyzing collected data related to past and ongoing cybercrime offenses. The course also concentrates on forensic approaches that preserve the legal value of the collected evidence.

In addition to the required computer science courses, students are also required to complete a number of criminology courses. The criminology curriculum includes courses that focus on criminological theories, crime investigation techniques, and research methodologies in criminology. The capstone course offered in the criminology department for the major is criminal justice system responses to cybercrime. This course explores the various types of criminal conduct associated with computers and the World Wide Web. Additionally, it covers digital forensics, theories of digital crime and terrorism, and policy implications and laws related to cybercrime. Furthermore, the criminology capstone course covers in detail the prominent forms of computer crime and the legal issues that emerge in confronting those crimes. That class has been organized in part around Taylor et al.'s (2011) Digital Crime and Digital Terrorism, and one appealing feature of that text is its attention to the global and international nature of much computer crime [16]. Many computer crimes involve actions that cross international boundaries and this text meticulously describes the legal issues that surround both computer and cyber crimes. For example, the text dedicates an entire section to controlling digital crime through legislation, law enforcement, and investigation.

Further, students can choose to take additional courses, in both majors, to focus their studies to their personal interests within the field. In computer science, some the courses focus on issues related specifically to computer structures such as ethical aspects of computer security, fundamental theories in computer security, and computer operating systems. Within criminology and criminal justice, some of the specialized courses concentrate on the criminal justice system, theories of criminal justice, the court system, corrections, and law enforcement. The wide range of courses offered by both programs allows the student to focus on their particular interests within the field of computation criminology. Students are also required to complete a mathematics course, which is offered by the Department of Mathematics in the College of Arts and Sciences. The purpose of the course is to develop knowledge and skills in fundamental mathematics' topics that are relevant to the computer specialization part of the degree, particularly to the systematic development of software.

Students obtaining a bachelor's degree in computer criminology are also given the opportunity to complete an internship before graduation. This internship, if the student decides to enroll in the course, can provide the student with work experience that will help in obtaining a job after graduation.

Graduate degree program

In 2011, FSU extended the undergraduate degree program with the addition of a graduate degree in computer criminology. Students pursuing a Masters of Science in computer criminology are admitted to and graduate from the Department of Computer Science; however, the graduate degree focuses on courses from both criminology and computer sciences. The degree program is a coursework-only track and provides a large number of courses at the graduate level. For example, courses in criminology cover topics such as crimes of the powerful, theoretical issues and research on the law and legal control of deviance in society, criminological theory, historical reviews of thought about crime and punishment, and comparative criminology and criminal justice. In addition, a variety of computer sciences courses are also offered and include topics such as computer security, network security, active, and passive defenses, data and computer communications, computer and network administration, advanced operating systems, and database systems.

Employment and research opportunities

Computer crime, as previously described, can be broadly defined as any criminal activity that involves the use of information technology, including illegally accessing information, intercepting data, damaging or deleting data, interfering with the functioning of a computer system, identity theft, etc. Information-related crime and computer/network security issues are already major concerns. These issues affect all levels of business, government, and academia and have grown in importance as most organizations link their networked computer environments to the Internet. A computer criminology student will learn both how to use computers to facilitate the study of crime and will study how crimes are accomplished through the use of computers.

Based on current trends, we anticipate there will be a significant demand for graduates of both the undergraduate and graduate computer criminology program. It is well known that there is a shortage of information technology experts. Similarly, there is a pressing need for information technology specialists to handle issues related to information crime, cyber-forensics, and computer/network security. However, there is also a need for computer skills for the prevention, detection, and study of all types of crime, whether or not they involve

the use of information technology. Graduates of the program will be prepared to work either for law enforcement agencies as information crime specialists, within companies or organizations as network security specialists, or within academia and government to study the causes of crime and the best methods for its prevention and control.

Conclusion

The purpose of this article was to describe the technological and computational shifts in the study of criminology and criminal justice as well as highlight the significances of dual computer-criminology degree programs. The FSU program description was used to provide an example of an ongoing dual computer-criminology program at both the undergraduate and graduate level. It is anticipated that some of the master's students in computer-criminology will decide to continue their studies for a Ph.D., given the growing discipline and policy importance of cyber-crime. FSU is currently involved in discussions on the structure, content, and requirements for a Ph.D. in computer criminology. The expansion of the program would push for the advancement of research that informs public policy. For instance, compared to a master's degree that trains students to be informed, knowledgeable users of scientific research, the Ph.D. prepares students to conduct their own original research to generate new insights on issues of scientific and public policy importance. This necessarily emphasizes comprehensive training in theory, research methods, and statistics that would be specific to the study of cyber-crime. Thus, the goal of a Ph.D. program in computer criminology would be to produce Ph.D. graduates who could generate the new research needed to inform policymakers and the scientific community on the causes and consequences of cyber crime and the appropriate legal and extra-legal responses to it. In addition to the Ph.D. program, FSU is also currently involved is discussions on including the dual computer-criminology degree program with the FSU distance learning program to expand the number of students who are able to learn from the best researchers and instructors in the fields of criminology and computer science. The anticipated implementation of both the Ph.D. program and the online program will continue to enhance the computer-criminology degree program and further benefit the expanding field of computational criminology.

Competing interests
The authors declare that they have no competing interests.

Authors' contributions
CV made substantial contributions to the conception and design of the article, drafted the manuscript, and formatted the manuscript. CH provided information about the degree programs, offered important intellectual

content, revised earlier drafts, and offered suggestions on earlier drafts. KB provided information about the degree programs, revised earlier drafts, and offered important intellectual content. TB revised earlier drafts and offered important intellectual content. All authors read and approved the final manuscript. All authors reviewed and made edits to the revised manuscript.

Authors' information

Colby Valentine, PhD, is an assistant professor of Criminal Justice in the Social Sciences Division of Dominican College. Her current research focuses on inmate misconduct, officer-involved domestic violence, and neighborhood predictors of intimate partner violence. She has recent publications in *Journal of Family Violence, Family Court Review,* and *Journal of Human Behavior in the Social Environment.*

Carter Hay, PhD, is an associate professor in the College of Criminology and Criminal Justice at Florida State University. His research examines the causes and prevention of individual involvement in crime and delinquency, with recent or forthcoming publications appearing in such journals as *Crime & Delinquency* and *Youth Violence and Juvenile Justice.*

Kevin M. Beaver, PhD, is an associate professor in the College of Criminology and Criminal Justice at Florida State University. He is past recipient of the American Society of Criminology's Ruth Shone Cavan Young Scholar Award and his research focuses on the genetic and biosocial foundations to antisocial behaviors. His research has produced more than 150 articles and book chapters which appear in a variety of interdisciplinary publication outlets.

Thomas G. Blomberg is Dean and Sheldon L. Messinger Professor of Criminology at Florida State University's College of Criminology and Criminal Justice and Editor of *Criminology and Public Policy.* He had published extensively in the areas of penology, social control, and education and recidivism. His recent books include *Punishment and Social Control: Enlarged Second Edition* (2003*)* and *American Penology: Enlarged Second Edition* (2010).

Author details

[1]Dominican College, 470 Western Highway, Orangeburg, New York 10962, USA. [2]Florida State University, College of Criminology and Criminal Justice, 634 W. Call Street, Tallahassee, Florida 32306-1127, USA.

References

1. L Liu, J Eck, An overview of crime simulation, in *Artificial crime analysis systems: using computer simulations and geographical information systems*, ed. by L Liu, J Eck (Information Science References, Hersey PA, 2008), pp. xiv–xxi
2. D Thomas, B Loader, Introduction – cyber crime: law enforcement, security and surveillance in the information age, in *Cyber crime: Law enforcement, security and surveillance in the information Age*, ed. by D Thomas, B Loader (Routledge, London, 2000), pp. 1–13
3. K Jaishankar, Cyber criminology: evolving a novel discipline with a new journal. Int. J. Cyber. Criminol. 1, 1–6 (2007)
4. PL Brantingham, PJ Brantingham, M Vajihollahi, K Wuschke, Crime analysis at multiple scales of aggregation: a topological approach, in *Putting crime in its place: units of analysis in geographic criminology*, ed. by D Weisburg, W Bernasco, GJN Bruinsma (Springer, New York, 2009), pp. 87–107
5. PL Brantingham, U Glasser, B Kinney, K Singh, M Vajihollahi, A computational model for simulating spatial aspects of crime in urban environments, in *Proceedings of the 2005 IEEE international conference on systems, Man and cybernetics*, ed. by M Jamshidi, 2005, pp. 3667–3674
6. PL Brantingham, U Glasser, P Jackson, M Vajihollahi, Modeling criminal activity in urban landscapes, in *Mathematical methods in counterterrorism*, ed. by N Memon (Springer, Berlin, 2009), pp. 9–31
7. J Eck, L Liu, Varieties of artificial crime analysis: purpose, structure, and evidence in crime simulations, in *Artificial crime analysis systems: using computer simulations and geographical information systems*, ed. by L Liu, J Eck (Information Science References, Hersey PA, 2008), pp. 413–432
8. X Wang, L Liu, J Eck, Crime simulation using GIS and artificial intelligent agents, in *Artificial crime analysis systems: using computer simulations and geographical information systems*, ed. by L Liu, J Eck (Information Science References, Hersey PA, 2008), pp. 209–225
9. J Szakas, C Trefftz, R Ramirez, E Jefferis, Development of an itelligent partol routing system using GIS and computer simulations, in *Artificial crime analysis systems: using computer simulations and geographical information systems*, ed. by L Liu, J Eck (Information Science References, Hersey PA, 2008), pp. 339–351
10. A Alimadad, P Borwein, P Brantinham, P Brantinham, V Dabbaghian-Abdoly, R Ferguson, E Fowler, AH Ghaseminejad, C Giles, J Li, N Pollard, A Rutherford, A van der Waall, Using varieties of simulation modeling for criminal justice analysis, in *Artificial crime analysis systems: using computer simulations and geographical information systems*, ed. by L Liu, J Eck (Information Science References, Hersey PA, 2008), pp. 372–409
11. K Auerhahn, Using simulation modeling to evaluate sentencing reform in California: choosing the future. J. Exp. Criminol. 4, 241–266 (2008)
12. A Dray, L Mazerolle, P Perez, A Ritter, Policing Australia's 'heroin drought': using an agent-based model to stimulate alternative outcomes. J. Exp. Criminol. 4, 267–287 (2008)
13. R Berk, How you can tell if the simulations in computational criminology any good. J. Exp. Criminol. 4, 289–308 (2008)
14. M Townsley, DJ Birks, Building better crime simulations: systematic replication and the introduction of incremental complexity. J. Exp. Criminol. 4, 309–333 (2008)
15. K Jaishankar, *Cyber criminology: exploring internet crimes and criminal behavior* (Taylor and Francis Group, Boca Raton, 2011)
16. RW Taylor, EJ Fritsch, J Liederbach, TJ Holt, *Digital crime and digital terrorism*, 2nd edn. (Prentice Hall, Upper Saddle River NJ, 2011)
17. RD Gopal, GL Sanders, S Bhattacharjee, M Agrawal, SC Wagner, A behavioral model of digital music piracy. J. Organ. Comput. Electron. Commer. 14, 89–105 (2004)
18. WD Gunter, GE Higgins, RE Gealt, Pirating youth: examining the correlates of digital music piracy among adolescents. Int. J. Cyber. Criminol. 4, 657–671 (2010)
19. GE Higgins, BD Fell, AL Wilson, Digital piracy: assessing the contributions of an integrated self-control theory and social learning theory using structural equation modeling. Criminal. Justice. Studies. 19, 3–22 (2006)
20. R Moore, EC McMullan, Neutralizations and rationalizations of digital piracy: a qualitative analysis of university students. Int. J. Cyber. Criminol. 3, 441–451 (2009)
21. GE Higgins, SE Wolfe, CD Marcum, Music piracy and neutralization: a preliminary trajectory analysis from short-term longitudinal data. Int. J. Cyber. Criminol. 2, 324–336 (2008)
22. GE Higgins, Digital piracy, self-control theory, and rational choice: an examination of the role of value. Int. J. Cyber. Criminol. 1, 33–55 (2007)
23. S. Hinduja, JW Patchin, *Bullying beyond the schoolyard: preventing and responding to cyberbullying* (Corwin Press, Thousand Oaks CA, 2009)
24. J Wang, RJ Iannotti, TR Nansel, School bullying among adolescents in the united states: physical, verbal, relational, and cyber. J. Adolesc. Heal. 45, 368–375 (2009)
25. M Ybarra, K Mitchell, Online aggressor/targets, aggressors, and targets: a comparison of associated youth characteristics. J. Child. Psychol. Psychiatry. 45, 1308–1316 (2004)
26. KL Mason, Cyber bullying: a preliminary assessment for school personnel. Psychol. Sch. 45, 323–348 (2008)
27. C Su, TJ Holt, Cyber bulling in Chinese Web forums: an examination of nature and extent. Int. J. Cyber. Criminol. 4, 672–684 (2010)
28. S Shariff, DL Hoff, Cyber bullying: clarifying legal boundaries for school supervision in cyberspace. Int. J. Cyber. Criminol. 1, 76–118 (2007)
29. EM Kraft, J Wang, Effectiveness of cyber bullying prevention strategies: a study on Students' perspectives. Int. J. Cyber. Criminol. 3, 513–535 (2009)
30. ML Pittaro, Cyber stalking: an analysis of online harassment and intimidation. Int. J. Cyber. Criminol. 1, 180–197 (2007)
31. L Roberts, Jurisdictional and definitional concerns with computer-mediated interpersonal crimes: an analysis on cyber stalking. Int. J. Cyber. Criminol. 2, 271–285 (2008)
32. M Bachmann, The risk propensity and rationality of computer hackers. Int. J. Cyber. Criminol. 4, 643–656 (2010)

9

Distribution of event complexity in the British Columbia court system an analysis based on the CourBC analytical system

Amir H Ghaseminejad[*], Paul Brantingham and Patricia Brantingham

Abstract

This paper reports an exploratory research on the distribution of event complexity in the British Columbia court system. Analysis of event distribution shows that the frequency of events sharply decreases with the increase in the number of persons and counts. The most frequently observed type of event is the event that has one person involved with one count. The number of events observed sharply declines when we query for events with a larger number of people involved or more counts charged. It is found that the number of events observed exponentially decreases when more complex events comprising more counts are analyzed. The same exponential decrease is observed for events with two or more people. This means that, in general, the least complex events are the most frequently observed ones. The events with more than one person involved have a mode of two counts. A first approximation model for the distribution of the load on the system based on different levels of complexity is proposed. The proposed model can be used for and be evaluated by predicting the load distribution in the BC criminal court system.

Keywords: Event complexity, Counts, Courts, Persons, Distribution, Data mining, Entity relationships, Charge, Event

Introduction

Common law criminal justice systems have experienced a series of major problems in recent years including declining rates of case clearances and prosecutions, rising rates of remand in custody, increasing delays between charge and trial dates, and increasing rates of case collapse at trial [1] [2] [3] [4]. Sources of these problems may reside at many points in the system with important operational feedbacks between decisions and events occurring in the investigative, prosecutorial, judicial and correctional elements of the system [5]. Case complexity is thought to be a major contributor to justice system problems, but little systemic science addresses the issue at any agency level [6] [4].

Interoperable justice agency databases could be used to identify systemic trouble points relate them to case complexity and perhaps develop improvements. For a variety of good reasons ranging from issues of privacy to the requirements of fair trials judicial data systems are

rarely made available to researchers interested in understanding system problems.

The Institute for Canadian Urban Research Studies (ICURS) has collected information about all crimes handled in the British Columbia criminal court system during a 3-year period encompassing 2008 through 2010 using publically available court data published by the courts from a judicial Records Management System named JUSTIN. These published data have been reverse engineered into a research data warehouse called CourBC. A research tool called the CourBC Analytical System has been developed to facilitate repetitive queries and data mining in this database.

A file, in a British Columbian criminal court, represents all linked courtroom actions. This would involve crimes committed by one or more individuals, that is, all crimes associated with co-accused. The crimes may be divided into informations or indictments when the crimes are linked by occurrence time or place, called folders in CourBC. A file is processed in a specific court and has a folder number, one or more associated documents, one or more persons involved, one or more crime codes involved,

* Correspondence: ahghasem@sfu.ca
Institute for Canadian Urban Research Studies, Simon Fraser University, Vancouver, Canada

and one or more counts arising from those crime codes [7]. Figure 1 is an Entity Relationship Diagram showing the structure of the relationship between entities in the court system. A unique folder in a court can contain many documents, a document in a court-folder can be associated to many persons and a person can be associated to many documents in a folder in a court. In this paper, we refer to a unique folder in a court as an event. A document associated to a person can be related to many crime codes. Moreover, one or more counts can be assigned to the same crime related to a person and a document.

One of the capabilities of the CourBC Analytical System is to find the number of unique court events based on the attributes of the file in court system.

Event complexity

The data in the CourBC Analytical System includes court name and location, hearing date, file number, folder number which uniquely identifies an event in a court, document number, number of counts; as well as bail and custody status, crime statute, section, subsection, next appearance detail, findings, results and convictions. It also includes the scheduling information which enables the researchers to track an event as it goes through hearings and identify the result for each count. Scheduling data includes reason for appearance, hearing time in the day, information about plea, age of the file in the court system measured in number of days. This enables the researchers to analyze the events in terms of the number of people involved, the severity of crime, and the type of the verdict. On the one hand, the CourBC dataset enables the researchers to conduct descriptive studies on the distribution of crime types and to analyze the differences in varying court locations; on the other hand, this data makes it possible to study the impact of crime complexity and other determinants on the number of hearings for each event in the court system. Moreover, the data has the potential to be used for modeling the central tendencies and the distribution of outcomes as a dependent variable influenced by variables such as crime severity, number of people involved, and location.

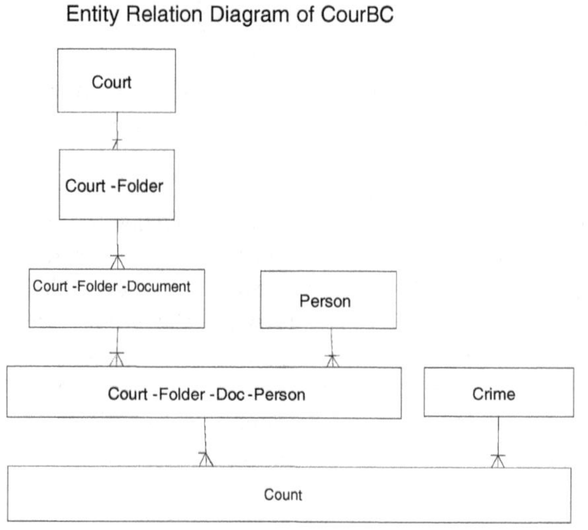

Events are handled in one or more court appearances. An event may be simple, that is, have clear evidence and present no difficult legal issues. An event, on the other hand, may involve many accused with multiple defence counsel, include a large number of charges for specific crimes, involve multiple witnesses, and involve legally untested issues or any combination of these complicating attributes. Complexity is the term used to describe the differences between the simple and straightforward case and one with many distinct and inter-related components.

The complexity of an event is a determinant of the police, legal system and correctional resources that the event will probably consume. Event complexity is a complicated construct and is a predictor for the overall load imposed by an event on the overall criminal justice system [5].

The essential qualities of event complexity are the type of the crime, the number of people involved in the crime, the number of persons involved, the evidence collected, and the event's legal and moral severity [6] [8] [9]. The court system can be modeled as a relational database that identifies criminal events as folders in each court. Each folder in a court may include one or many documents. One document can be related to many persons and a person can be charged for many counts of the same crime.

We can theorize that event complexity has a positive correlation with number of persons, number of documents in the folder, number of counts charged and the type of crime [1] [6] [8].

$$EC = f(p, d, c, ct) \qquad (1)$$

Where:

EC is event complexity
p is number persons
d is number of documents
c is number of counts charged and
ct is crime type.

All criminal cases, and therefore all events tracked in COURBC, are marked by various legal issues having varying levels of legal uncertainty. This level of legal uncertainty is a determinant of event complexity but can only be assessed through a review of the facts of the case. The likelihood of legal uncertainty increases with the number and novelty of legal issues presented. The number of legal issues presented is likely to increase

Entity Relation Diagram of CourBC

Court

Court -Folder

Court -Folder -Document

Person

Court -Folder -Doc -Person

Crime

Count

Figure 1 The ERD for Court System.

with the number of persons charged, the number and severity of crimes charged, and the severity of potential penalties upon conviction. In addition, the human agents involved in the event, (lawyers, judges, prosecutors) and their backgrounds and history can influence the complexity of the case. This may lead to events that, from "person, document, and count" point of view, are simplistic but still have a certain internal complexity [6]. CourBC cannot, at present, address these components of complexity, but such legal and agent based complexity is relatively rare as indicated by the limited number of cases appealed to higher courts.

In this paper we present a first approximation model for the complexity of events that cover a great majority of events.

Findings

In this section we present our analysis of the characteristics of the data, and will highlight the distribution of event as it was observed. As is shown in Figure 2, Figure 3, and Figure 4, the conditional probability of having more counts with a chosen number of docs has a positive correlation with the number of documents in the file.

$$P(c|d) \propto d \quad (2)$$

Where:

i is the maximum counts charged in the folder
d is the number of documents in the folder.

In Figure 2, it is shown that the chance of observing a single count is higher in events that have a single document and declines steadily as the number of documents in the event increases.

On the other hand, in Figure 3, the chance of having three counts is greater for the events with a higher number of documents. Similarly, the chance of comprising five counts is greater for events with six docs than the events with one document.

Figure 4 shows that the chance of an event with 14 counts is higher for events with six docs than events with only one document. Therefore, we can conclude that the number of documents and the number of counts are not independent variables. Counts in the folder are known to be a good predictor of complexity of the events because of the decisions that must be made about all of them during the course of prosecution. In this paper, we will assume that counts are a good proxy variable for the influence of the number of docs on complexity.

In this paper, consistent with past studies of case complexity and case processing [8], complexity is considered as a combination of two variables: counts and persons. The frequency distribution of events in terms of these two variables is analyzed. We study a cross section of the events being processed in the court system over a 3 year period. Each event in our dataset is analyzed to identify the number of persons involved in the case, the maximum doc number associated to the event, and maximum number of counts assigned to the events.

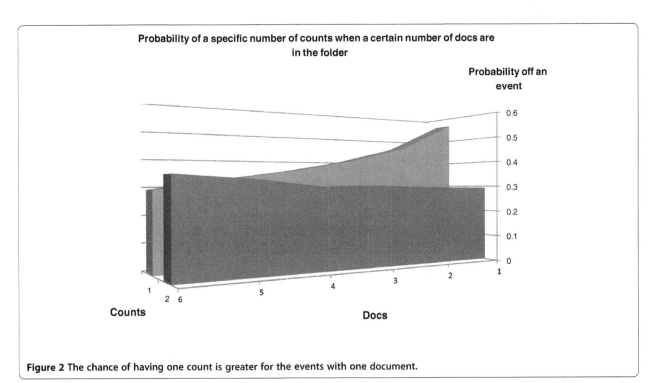

Figure 2 The chance of having one count is greater for the events with one document.

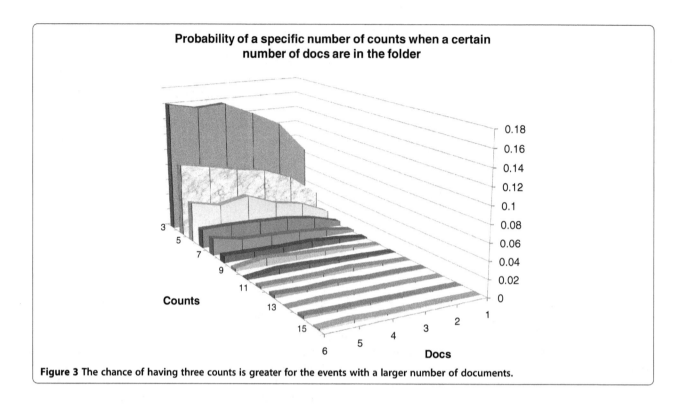

Figure 3 The chance of having three counts is greater for the events with a larger number of documents.

There are events that are processed within the time interval of our cross section but have been brought to court before our time interval. For some of these, events had hearing(s) before our time window and some of the docs or persons or counts may have been eliminated (legally concluded) from further hearings. Therefore, we expect the complexity of these events may have been more than what we observe and overall complexity of the events being processed in the system may be slightly greater than what we observe. All that

considered, the limitations do not impede the significance of our finding about the distribution of complexity in our cross section time window. In other words, our observation is a plausible description of the complexity of the events as they were being processed in the time window.

Our study shows that the distribution of events is such that, regardless of number of docs in the folder, the frequency of events sharply decreases with the increase in the number of persons and counts. As shown in Figure 5, the most frequently observed type of event has one person involved with one count. The number of events observed sharply declines when we query for events with a larger number of people involved or more counts charged.

Figure 6. Shows how even for events with two people involved the number of events observed exponentially decreases when the event complexity increases.

This means that in general the least complex events are the most frequently observed ones. However, we found that the cases with more than one person involved have a mode that is at two counts. We turn in the next section to development of a model of case complexity and court workloads derived from these findings that we think could be used to help identify and address both existing and potential case handling trouble point. Linking this model to models derived from a compatibly defined police information database may allow us to begin to identify dysfunctional feedbacks between these two components of the criminal justice system.

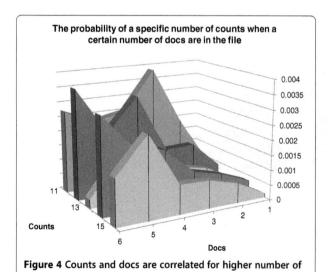

Figure 4 Counts and docs are correlated for higher number of counts.

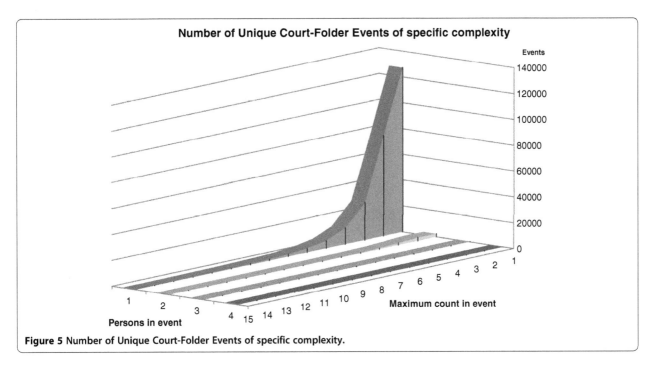

Figure 5 Number of Unique Court-Folder Events of specific complexity.

Abstraction from findings

In this section, we propose a first approximation linear model for the distribution of case complexity and claim that the distribution of the load on the justice system can be predicted based on this model. In this model, event complexity has a positive correlation with counts and a positive correlation with persons in the file.

$$EC \propto k * p * c \qquad (3)$$

Where:

EC is event complexity

p is the number of persons in the folder

c is the maximum counts charged in the folder.

k is a coefficient that presents the sensitivity of event complexity to number of persons and maximum counts in the folder.

As shown in the relationship shown above, event complexity grows proportional to the number of persons in the folder and the maximum counts charged in the folder.

We can operationalize event complexity by measuring the load on the justice system. One probable approach to measuring the load on the system is analyzing the number

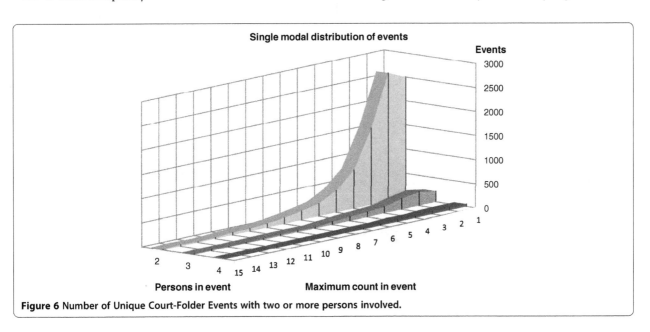

Figure 6 Number of Unique Court-Folder Events with two or more persons involved.

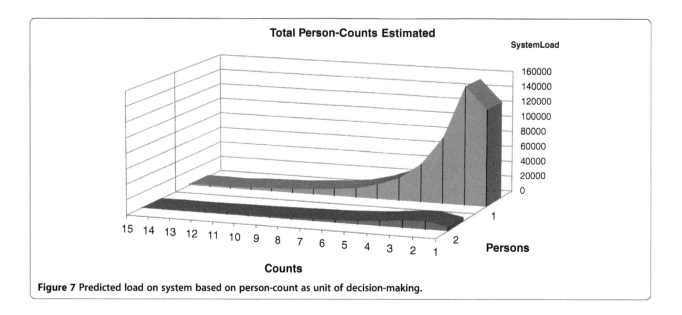

Figure 7 Predicted load on system based on person-count as unit of decision-making.

of hearings occurring in different types of events. Our Hypothesis is that the number of hearings related to different events is proportional to the number of persons and counts in the event. The following formula shows the first approximation linear model of this relationship.

$$LS \propto k * f * p * c \qquad (4)$$

Where:

LS is load on the justice system
f is the frequency of a folder with a specific person-count being observed
p is the number of persons in the folder
c is the maximum counts charged in the folder

k is a coefficient that presents the sensitivity of the load on the system to the complexity

In the relationship shown above, load on the justice system grows proportional to frequency of observing a folder with a specific person-count being observed and the number of persons in the folder and the maximum counts charged in the folder.

Based on this model, as shown in Figure 7, we have calculated the estimated load on the system measured with the number of person-counts that should be decided by the court system. We can hypothesize that the load on the system for the most frequently observed events involving one person should have a mode on events with two counts. Also, the load related to events with two persons involved, has a mode of two counts. However, as shown in Figure 8, events with three persons involved have a mode at three counts. Similarly, the mode for four persons involved is observed at a higher number of counts.

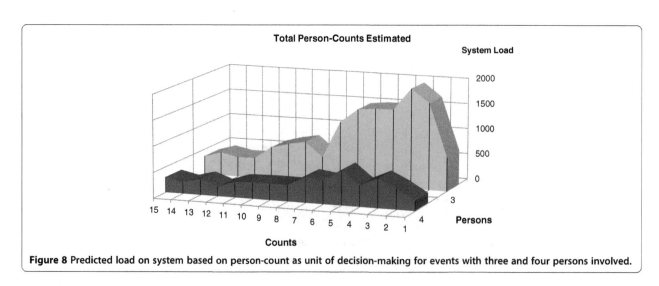

Figure 8 Predicted load on system based on person-count as unit of decision-making for events with three and four persons involved.

As it is clear from these figures, we expect the share of complex events in the load on the system grow nonlinearly. The reason why our proposed multi variable linear models have produced the non-linear results is in the distribution of the real events. The frequency of the events with higher complexity is non-linearly less than the frequency of simpler events. According to our data the number of people and counts in complex cases do not compensate to bring the overall load of complex events the prominence of the share of simpler cases in system's load. We are going to evaluate this model by comparing the number of hearings of the events with the predictions of our model and verify if the assumption of linear relationship will survive, or we may need to add a function to account for the relationship of the number hearing and event attributes to our model.

Conclusion and future research

The observations reported in this study set the foundations for modeling the distribution of event complexity. This distribution can be used in both process modeling, and agent based modeling of the criminal justice system where there is a need to test the model with cases of different complexities.

We are planning to find the best-fit distribution to our crime complexity data in a parsimonious way. Such a distribution must be plausible from the theoretical perspective and must be evaluated with a reasonable goodness of fit. The possible variables should be analyzed for co-linearity and only the important independent ones should be included. We expect that such analysis will be confirmatory and consisting with the proposed model in this paper.

To test the hypothesis proposed in this paper predicting the load on the system, we will analyze the number of court hearings/appearances for all events under the classification used in this paper. If the predictions of this paper are true we expect to observe more hearings for cases with more people and more counts involved but we expect that most number of hearings involve events with one person and two counts. Similarly, among events with two persons events with two counts are expected to dominate court workloads. While the modal point may be two, it will be important to see how rapidly the number of court hearings/appearances increases as complexity increases for higher numbers of persons and counts. It is possible to observe that the load on the system from more complex events is more than their proportional frequency. If such thing is observed it means that complex events' share of the load on the system grows nonlinearly. We will attempt to develop a multi variable linear (if necessary non-linear) model of the relationship between load on the system and the dimensions of crime complexity. Such a model will enable the

decision makers to predict the expected load on the system as result of events based on their complexity. Moreover, we are planning to add crime type and crime severity into our complexity model in the next round of analysis. There is good reason to think that different types of crime present different levels of complexity in court. In addition, a large number of legal system and law enforcement analyses could be performed if we could have access to court documents and law enforcement records in database form and for a wider time frame. We think that we will be able to link this database to police databases so that we will be able to test the proposition that the complexity of cases in court is grounded in the complexity of cases as they present to police.

Once COURBC is linked to police databases, we plan to explore the overall extent to which case complexity at different points in the criminal justice system drives the overall use of resources by the system.

Competing interests

The authors declare that they have no competing interests.

Authors' contributions

PLB conceived and developed the original project. AHG developed the original data collection tool. AHG, PLB and PJB supervised data collection and collaborated in development of the underlying database. AHG developed the analytic system and conducted the analysis. PLB and PJB consulted on analysis and interpretation of results. AHG, PJB, PLB co-wrote the manuscript. All authors read and approved the final manuscript.

References

1. M Gannon, M Karen, B Karen, T-B Andrea, K Rebecca, *Criminal Justice Indicators* (Statistics Canada, Ottawa, 2005). Catalogue No. 85-227-XIE
2. Statistics New Zealand, *Crime in New Zealand: 1996–2005* (Statistics New Zealand, Wellington, 2006)
3. J Thomas, *Adult Criminal Court Statistics 2008–2009. Juristat 2010,* **30***, No. 2* (Canadian Centre for Justice Statistics, Ottawa, 2010). Statistics Canada Catalogue Number 85-002-X
4. W Michael, Inmate Perspectives on the Remand Crisis in Canada. Canadian Journal of Criminology and Criminal Justice **51**, 355–379 (2009)
5. A Azadeh, B Patricia, B Paul, D-A Vahid, F Ron, F Ellen, H Ghaseminejad Amir, G Christopher, L Jenny, P Nahanni, R Alexander, A van der Waall, Utilizing Simulation Modeling for Criminal Justice System Analysis, in *Artificial Crime Analysis*, ed. by L Lin, E John (Idea Group Publishing, Hershey, PA, 2008)
6. M Heise, Criminal Case Complexity: An Empirical Assessment. J Empir Leg Stud 1, 331–369 (2004)
7. J Jordan, *The Administrative and Information Technology Environment of the Superior Courts Judiciary in British Columbia* (AIJA Law and Technology Conference, Sydney, Australia, 2008)
8. Dg Horne, *Case complexity and case processing time* (unpublished ma thesis 1981, Simon Fraser University, Burnaby, b.c, 1981)
9. M Schlanger, *Comment on Measuring Case Complexity,* Empirical Legal Studies Blog posted September 25, 2006 www.elsblog.org. Accessed March 12, 2011

10

Fluency of visualizations: linking spatiotemporal visualizations to improve cybersecurity visual analytics

Zhenyu Cheryl Qian[1][*][†] and Yingjie Victor Chen[2][†]

Abstract

This paper adopts the metaphor of representational fluency and proposes an auto linking approach to help analysts investigate details of suspicious sections across different cybersecurity visualizations. Analysis of spatiotemporal network security data takes place both conditionally and in sequence. Many visual analytics systems use time series curves to visualize the data from the temporal perspective and maps to show the spatial information. To identify anomalies, the analysts frequently shift across different visualizations and the original data view. We consider them as various representations of the same data and aim to enhance the fluency of navigation across these representations. With the auto linking mechanism, after the analyst selects a segment of a curve, the system can automatically highlight the related area on the map for further investigation, and the selections on the map or the data views can also trigger the related time series curves. This approach adopts the slicing operation of the Online Analytical Process (OLAP) to find the basic granularities that contribute to the overall value change. We implemented this approach in an award-winning visual analytics system, SemanticPrism, and demonstrate the functions through two use cases.

Keywords: Representational fluency; Cybersecurity analysis; Spatiotemporal visualization; Interaction design

Introduction

One of the biggest challenges the information security society faces is analyzing large-scale spatiotemporal datasets. In most organizations and companies, their computer networks are routinely capturing huge volumes of historical data describing the network events. Most of these events are recorded as spatiotemporal data because every event takes place at a certain time and in a certain location. The location could be either a physical location (e.g., an office) or a virtual space (e.g., an Internet IP address) [1]. Different kinds of events have more detailed information, such as operations, products, targets, and human involvement, which can add more dimensions to the spatiotemporal database. As a result, such a dataset is usually both high-dimensional and very large.

Peuquet [2] identified three components in spatiotemporal data: space (where), time (when), and objects (what).

*Correspondence: qianz@purdue.edu
†Equal contributors
[1]Interaction Design, Purdue University, 552 W. Wood Street, 47907 West Lafayette IN, USA
Full list of author information is available at the end of the article

Foresti et al. [3] also labeled when, where, and what (W3) as the three attributes of cybersecurity alerts and events because of their very nature. According to their definitions, when refers to the point in time where the event happened, where to the location of the event that happened, and what to the type of the event. The space of what and where are finite, and the when space is semi-infinite [3]. Finding the relations among these components and answering related questions are essential to analysis [4].

The two most popular methods to visualize and analyze the cybersecurity spatiotemporal data are geospatial visualization and time series curves. (1) The geospatial visualization is usually integrated with a time slider to adjust the time frame. The high-dimensional data are often displayed on the geospatial map with multiple views and layers overlaid with numerous data points, connections, and details. The visualization can easily overwhelm the display space on a single monitor. These types of visualizations challenge human cognition to remember what was seen previously, where it was, and its potential relationship to current information [5]. (2) The time series curves focus on providing the analyst an overview of how the data change over time. Significant value changes can be clearly reflected on the curve as peaks or valleys, which hint for the analyst to pay attention to these significant situations. This type of visualization is clean and easy to read, but it skips the context of spatial information.

In a survey of cybersecurity visualization techniques, Shiravi et al. [6] argued that user experience should be one of the key issues a successful visual analytics system should consider. The user experience is not only about elegant appearance or powerful functions, but also, and more importantly, about a smooth and fluent analysis process. Heer and Shneiderman also stressed that "visual analytics tools must support the fluent and flexible use of visualizations at rates resonant with the pace of human thought" [7]. However, in most cases the complex data and multiple visualizations lead to poor user experience.

This paper aims to promote the fluency of navigating in the spatiotemporal visualizations and to enhance the user experience of cybersecurity analysis. It demonstrates a solution to link the time series curves, geospatial visualizations, and data views together and to help the user achieve situational awareness through comprehension of the what, where, and when attributes of cybersecurity issues. This paper was originated from our previous work [8] that attempted to link the user from the temporal time series curve to geospatial visualizations. At this paper, we were able to extend the approach and its application to link the user in multiple directions among temporal visualization, geospatial visualization, and data view. We borrow the term "representational fluency" [9] from psychology and pedagogical literature to describe our efforts of enabling the user to fluently switch among different types of spatiotemporal visualizations and to more efficiently solve analysis tasks. The extensions in this paper include:

- A detailed explanation of the mechanism that selects portions from the time series curves and links to spatial visualizations. This mechanism was revised and extended.
- A new mechanism that reversely selects and links spatial visualizations and data views to time series curves.
- New use cases to demonstrate these two mechanisms.
- Redesigned interaction operations that allow the user to access information more smoothly.

To achieve smooth transitions across interactive visualizations, techniques such as brush and linking have been widely used in VA systems. This paper provides a practical technical mechanisms to link multiple visualizations and aims to help users gain better experience and improve performance when analyzing the big network security data visually.

Related work

To enhance the user experience of cybersecurity visual analytics, we suggest adopting representational fluency in designing the structure of spatiotemporal visualizations because "users of this information will need fluency in the tools of digital access, exploration, visualization, analysis, and collaboration [10]". The literature review inspects two main components: representational fluency and spatiotemporal data visualization methods.

Representational fluency of visualizations

The concept of fluency is originally associated with the ability to express oneself in both spoken and written language and to move effortlessly between the two representations. Although fluency is often associated with language, researchers have extended fluency to other fields such as physics, chemistry, engineering, and mathematics. In these fields, fluency is the ability to understand and translate among commonly used modes of representation, such as verbal, mathematical, graphical, and manipulatable. In the context of information systems, fluency is the ability to access, make sense of, and use information to build new understandings [11]. Defined by Irving Sigel [9], representational fluency is the ability to (1) comprehend equivalence in different modes of expression; (2) comprehend information presented in different representations; (3) transform information from one representation to another: and (4) learn in one representation and apply that learning to another.

Representational fluency is an important aspect of deep conceptual understanding. It was mainly discussed in pedagogical literature about promoting the transfer between learning and the development of "expertise". In our context of visual analytics, we borrowed this concept to describe how to let the analyst better comprehending the multiple visualizations of "when, where, and what" for cybersecurity situational awareness. Representational fluency is more skillfulness than skill [12]. Skillfulness connotes continuous adaptation and dynamism along with the ability to perform with facility, adeptness, and expertise. Skillfulness of representational fluency in visual analytics includes several capabilities, such as abstractly visualizing and conceptualizing transformation processes, qualifying quantitative data, working with patterns, and working with continuously changing qualities and trends. To achieve these goals, analysts should be supported with proper tools to interpret visualizations more efficiently.

Visualization methods of W3 attributes

Much previous research has been devoted to exploring different methods to visualize the large-scale high-dimensional datasets. Keim et al. [13] reviewed and summarized recent visualization techniques to deal with large multivariate datasets. One of their own techniques is a hybrid approach that is scalable with "big-data" visualization [14]. Guo et al. [15] proposed to use multiple-linked views to visualize the multivariate data. Andrienko et al. [4] created a structured inventory of existing exploratory spatiotemporal visualization techniques related to the types of data and tasks they are appropriate for. Based on the W3 attributes, Foresti et al. [3,16] developed a novel visualization paradigm, VizAlert, to visualize network intrusion from all three "when", "where", and "what" perspectives. Con-centric rings were used to represent different time periods, from inside to outside. Because of the limited screen space, the VizAlert system may be unable to display the history for a long period. The user needs to rely on interaction to pan and zoom for shifting between different periods.

Some significant approaches were to analyze spatiotemporal patterns by making separate use of multiple maps and statistical graphs. Alan M. MacEachren's GeoVISTA Center [9] uses highlighting, brushing, and linking, and filtered and linked selections to help users analyze geo-referenced time-varying multivariate data. IEEE VAST 2012 Mini-Challenge 1 (MC1) asked researchers to analyze a high-dimensional spatiotemporal dataset [17]. Most of the challenge entries used maps and statistical graphs. For example, Chen et al. [18] and Choudury et al. [19] used one 2-D map to visualize the overall computer statuses in a given time and a slider to adjust the time. Dudas et al. [20] used time series curves to show the aggregate trend of certain qualities.

Analysis process for spatiotemporal cybersecurity data sets
The analysis process on a spatiotemporal dataset often happens conditionally and in sequence [21]. At first the temporal aspect is analyzed, and then the spatial aspect, or vice versa. It is difficult to have a joint integral modeling approach. We have observed such sequential analysis processes in our own practice [22] while solving the VAST 2012 challenge MC2 [17], and in other winning entries [23,24] when they tried to solve the VAST 2013 challenge MC3 [25]. Many times when looking for issues, the user first examined the temporal aspect by looking at the time series curves to find out the anomalies (e.g., huge peak in the curve), then checked out other detailed visualizations to allocate the affecting hosts (IP addresses). Sometimes the analysis starts with a detailed visualization, e.g., an IP address showing abnormal behavior. To understand the overall picture of the affected computers, the user will then need to examine the time series curves. Sometimes this process happens iteratively. The user starts from one visualization, then goes to others, returns to the first visualization with a different parameter (e.g. time or place), and goes on to gain comprehensive cybersecurity awareness. To investigate the detail, the analyst usually need to

narrow down and even to read the raw data such as the log file.

Context - data and system
Our implementation of representational fluency was developed on a visual analytics system SemanticPrism [18]. It won the award of "outstanding integrated analysis and visualization" in the VAST 2012 MC1. From 2011 to 2013, the IEEE VAST challenges committee created three cyber-network visual analytics tasks [25] to simulate the complex nature of cyber security. VAST 2011 MC2 data contain 3-day logs of a small computer network. VAST 2012 MC1 data record 2-day logs of a huge global network. VAST 2013 MC3 data include 2-week logs of a 1200-computer network. All the datasets provided are spatiotemporal.

The high-dimensional spatiotemporal dataset we used in this paper was from the VAST 2012 MC1. It simulates a large enterprise network named the BankWorld, which contains approximately a million computers in about 4000 offices. Offices have latitude and longitude information that can be marked on the map. Computers are divided into three classes, server, workstation, and ATM (Automated teller machine). By their functions, Servers are further divided as web, email, file server, compute, or multiple, and Workstations are further divided into teller, loan, or office. Every 15 minutes each computer generates a status log. Within the 48 hour period, the network accumulated approximately 160 million logs. Each log contains a time stamp, IP address, activity flag, policy status, and number of connections (NOC). Policy status has a value range from 1 to 5 to represent healthy status from normal to severe condition. Value 1 means the machine is healthy. 2 means the machine is suffering from mild policy deviation. 3 means the machine has non-critical patches failing and is suffering from serious policy deviations. 4 means critical policy deviations and many patches are failing. 5 means the machine may be infected by virus or unknown files are found. Activity flags also have 5 possible values range from 1 to 5. Value 1 means normal activities have been detected on the machine. 2 means the machine is going down for maintenance. It may appear offline for the next couple time slots. 3 means there were more than 5 invalid login attempts. 4 means the machine's CPU is running at 100% capacity. 5 means a device (e.g. an USB drive or a DVD) has been added to the machine.

The spatial part of this VAST 2012 MC1 dataset contains two layers, the physical geographic location and virtual IP addresses. Its IP space ranges from 172.1.1.2 to 172.56.39.254. The information of both has a hierarchical structure enabling the top-level larger range to be divided into several lower-level smaller ranges. In a real computer network, the geographic locations may range from a continent, a country, a state, or a province to a specific office in a building. For IP addresses, the network can be divided into multiple levels of subnetworks that are connected through gateways. Each subnetwork occupies a partial IP address space.

With the system SemanticPrism, the analyst is able to see and compare data of different dimensions at multiple granularities. We chose visualization methods and designed interactions based on the nature of the data and the problems faced. SemanticPrism uses a multilinked-view approach to explore the data from different perspectives. Using different transformation methods, data are visualized by using the geospatial map, time series curves, and pixel-oriented visualizations. The technique of semantic zooming [26] was used as the basic interaction technique to navigate through these visualizations. Each visualization has multiple zoom levels to present different levels of details. The analyst can scan to quickly understand the overall situation of the enterprise network and navigate further to read more details of regions, offices, and even the level of individual computers.

Geospatial visualization with a time slider

The default view in SemanticPrism is a geospatial visualization with a time slider that helps to aware the network status at a given time (Figure 1). Offices of the BankWorld are marked as square dots on the analogous world map. Their different color shades indicate the maximum policy violation statuses of the computers within the offices at that time. The analyst can slide the pointer on the time slider to update the geospatial visualization to a different time frame. Different dimensions of the information (e.g. policy status and activity flags) were stacked on the map as different layers. To let the analyst see the global status, SemanticPrism provides a time-zone layer to indicate the local times of different regions in this global organization.

Besides zooming in on and out of the map, the analyst can focus and investigate the data at different levels of details through semantic zooming. Depending on the size of available space, an office can be dynamically visualized at four levels: (1) an individual dot when using the default full-map view or when the space is still quite dense after zooming; (2) a horizontal color bar to show the percentage of computers with different policy statuses in the office; (3) a series of growth curves of all policies in the office where the X axis presents the temporal direction and the Y axis the number of computers; (4) history diagrams of each computer within the office.

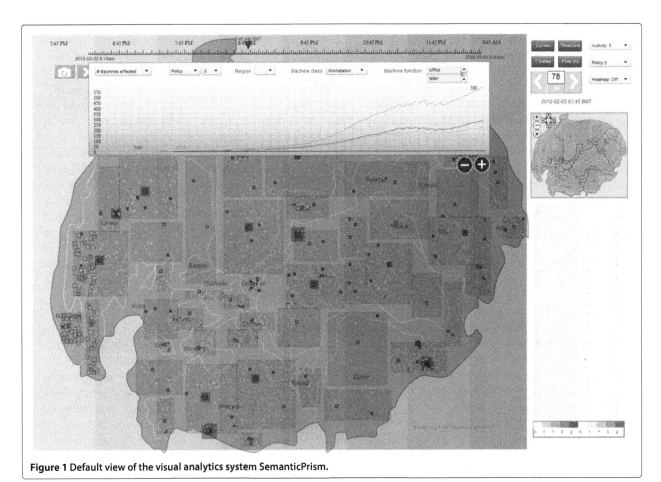

Figure 1 Default view of the visual analytics system SemanticPrism.

Time series curves

We adopted Ben Shneiderman's visual information-seeking mantra to guide the design of the SemanticPrism's information query process, "overview first, then zoom and filter, and lastly details on demand" [27]. The time series curves (the curve graph in Figure 1) can be configured to provide an overview of the growth trends of policy statuses, activities, server populations, and NOC (number of connections) over the given period. Figures 2 and 3 curves show the total number of workstations in different policies (2 5) and activities (2 5) over the 2-day period. With the support of time series curves, the analyst can easily identify the overall trend of policy violation growth and patterns of activities. By relying solely on the curves, however, the analyst cannot see the cause, details, and effects of an event. Usually he/she must manually switch to other views to investigate, such as what causes the curve to change, and where the change takes place. This significant user-experience problem motivates our new development of extending user interactions from semantic zooming to marking interesting segments on the curve.

Pixel-based visualizations

IP addresses indicate the virtual locations of network computers. For cybersecurity issues, they provide a different perspective of spatial information than physical locations. The classification of IP addresses also partially reflect the organization's network structure. SemanticPrism incorporated a pixel-based visualization to show many IP blocks. In the default zoom level, five rectangular panels show the number of computers within an IP block that are affected by each activity and policy. In the panels, each pixel represents a group of computers in a particular class-C block. The X axis consists of the IP's class-B block, and the Y axis consists of the values of class-C blocks. The colors of the pixels encode the number of computers that carry the selected policy status or activity flags in the C-level blocks. Through semantic zooming, the analyst is able to overview time series curves of all C-level blocks within one B-level block and all individual computers within a C-level bock.

Mechanism and implementation

SemanticPrism's comprehensive visualizations and interactions show multiple visualizations of where, when, and what data components (Figure 4). With it, we were able to discover all anomalies hidden within the large dataset in the competition. In this paper, we implement the representational fluency concept by extending the interaction design in this system. We consider three important representations for the user to be truly aware of the situation – raw data, spatial visualization, and temporal visualization. We seek to allow the user to shift fluently back and forth

among these three representations of the cybersecurity information without losing the analysis context.

Dimension Hierarchy in SemanticPrism

To enhance the efficiency while analyzing a large multidimensional dataset, we adopt the OLAP (online analytical processing) [21] approach to execute analytical queries. OLAP's slicing operation enables the user to take out one specific part of data. SemanticPrism [23] pre-computed the aggregation values along necessary dimensions and storing them into several database tables. The dimension hierarchy is essential for these computations. Precomputing all possible aggregations on all different granularities, however, will use too many resources. We selected several dimensions to compute in certain granularities.

SemanticPrism maintains a set of dimension hierarchies so that the analyst can have multiple navigation paths to narrow down and examine computers with a certain status (e.g., policy or activity) at a certain time slot and in a certain region. Spatially on a map, a computer is located at the following hierarchy:

Company $\Rightarrow$ Region $\Rightarrow$ Office $\Rightarrow$ Computer class

As virtual IP space, an IP address is located at

Whole IP space $\Rightarrow$ B-level IP blocks $\Rightarrow$ C-level IP Blocks

In this dataset, computers within one C-level block belong to the same office and are in the same class of server or workstation. But one office may contain many C-level blocks. Therefore the basic aggregation of computers we choose is the number of computers in one C-level IP block with a given policy/activity status at a given time. From such basic units, we can compute the number of computers of on-policy status at one office at one time, then the policy status at the region level, then to the whole company level. Thus we can have different levels of time series curves of different activity/policy statuses, from the basic level of computer classes, to regions, and lastly the entire company. The number of connections (NOC) are more related to IP-related attacks (e.g., port scan); thus we can simply use the IP address hierarchy to divide it.

With the spatial hierarchy and policy/activity status, the system has multiple paths to aggregate the basic units based on the user's analysis needs.

Link data query to visualizations

For visual analysis systems, the raw data are the resource of everything. The more details the dataset contains, the more insights and discoveries can be found. For solving cybersecurity issues, the datasets are usually very large and comprehensive. It is impossible for human beings to read through, compare, and identify issues in the large-scale datasets. Visualization becomes the only feasible way to allow the analyst to make sense of the large amount of data. However, visualizations cannot show all

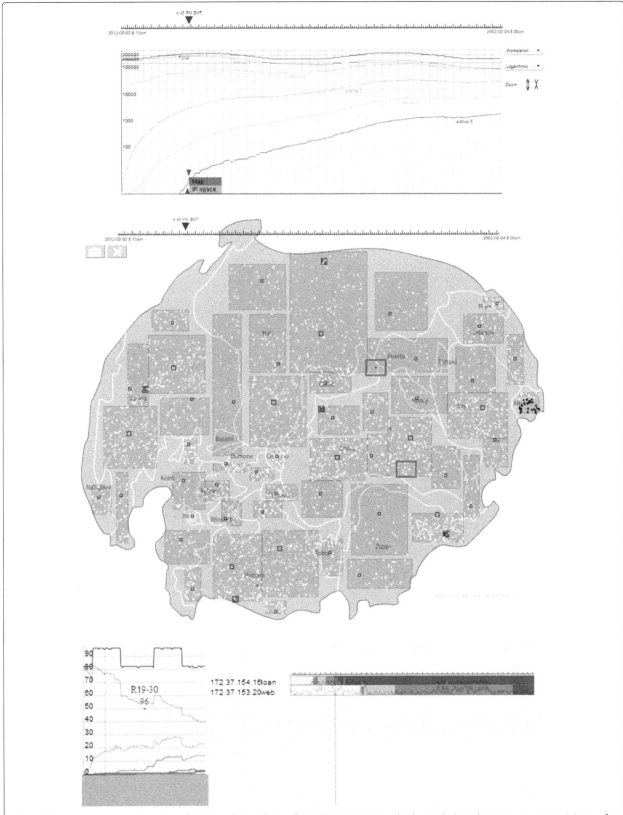

Figure 2 Investigate the number of workstations that violate policy 5. Top: We want to check out which workstations are new to violation of policy 5 at 2012-02002 4:45 p.m. by clicking on the segment in the curve. Middle: The map marks by red squares the two new offices with policy 5 violations. Bottom: Clicking on the top marked square to see the details.

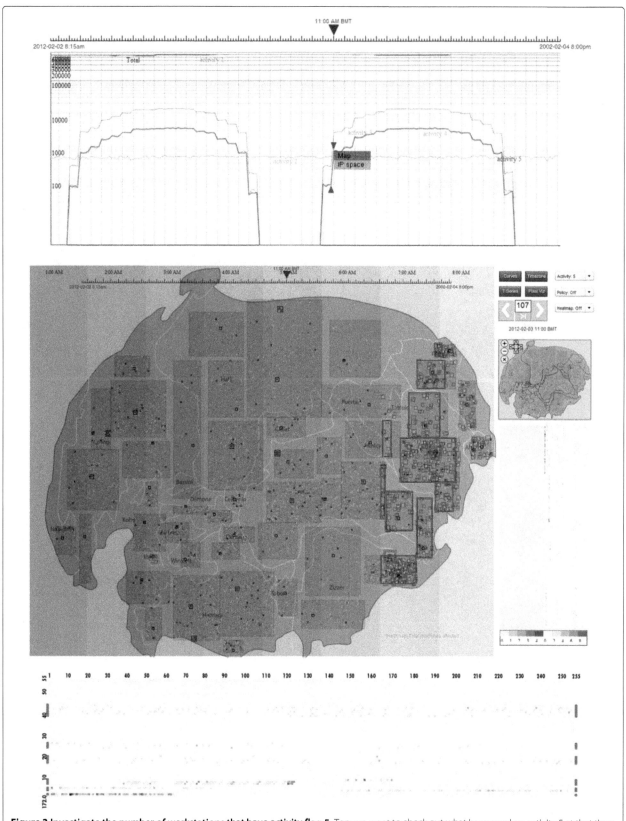

Figure 3 Investigate the number of workstations that have activity flag 5. Top: we want to check out what happened on activity 5 at that time. Middle: The map marks offices by regions. Bottom: These computers are also marked by their IP addresses.

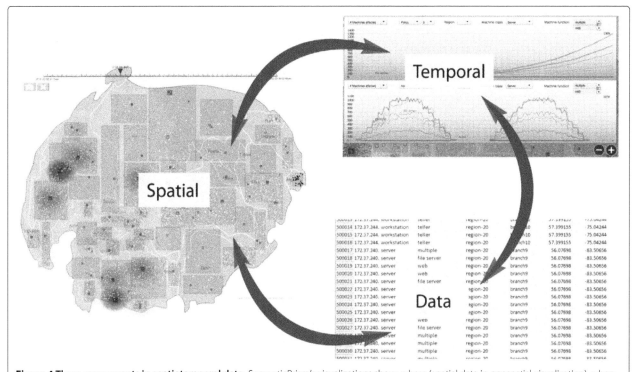

Figure 4 Three components in spatiotemporal data. SemanticPrism's visualizations show: where (spatial data in geospatial visualization), when (temporal data in time curves), and what (data objects in data tables).

the information in the dataset. Through categorization, aggregation, and visualization, only part of the information has been presented in graphs. An analyst still needs to frequently examine the original raw data (e.g., a recorded log or an event report) to determine the exact issue. Thus we should provide a direct-query interface for the user to search the raw data. Based on the searched criteria, the user can pop up visualizations, for example, to display the locations of the computers under investigation in the geographic visualization. Also from the visualizations, the analyst should be able to open, allocate, and read the piece of the raw data of an interesting point.

Link from time series curves to spatial visualization

The time series curve is the visualization to show the plot of the data narration. The data are measured at successive points in the temporal direction at uniform time intervals. In computer networks, it is a common strategy to aggregate (or count) certain network incidents at a given time interval (e.g., 15 minutes in the VAST 2012 data). Thus a series of data points along the time will be generated and can be visualized as time series curves. In our implementation, the curves are plotted on a 2-D Cartesian system with line segments connecting a series of points. X axis is the time direction and Y axis is the value of data. Thus such data have a natural temporal ordering. The user should be able to see the overall trend of the network status through the temporal curve. For a running

system, its temporal curve can present certain kinds of patterns (e.g., fixed frequency and amplitude, or various grow rates). For a complex system, such patterns are sometimes hard to define by mathematic equations, and therefore hard to be detected solely by machines. Temporal visualizations rely on a human's visual perception and pattern recognition to help the analyst to detect such potential attacks through recognizing abnormal patterns in time series curves.

Figure 5 lists six popular abnormal situations, including a sudden jump, dive, peak, valley, slop gradient change, and frequency or amplitude change in oscillating curves. In the figure, blue squares mark the data points, and red line segments label the abnormal sections. Such abnormal segments on a curve imply that there are some computers behaved abnormally during that time period. This paper only focuses on the abnormal segments as the four scenarios on the top image of Figure 5. After detecting an abnormal segment on the curve, the analyst needs to investigate what caused the change. He/she should switch from the overview curve to more detailed curves or other visualizations to investigate its when, where, and what details. Although sometimes the abnormal behavior may happen globally, in our observation such behaviors most of the time happen on computers within a small region. Again, such a region could be a physical location or in the virtual space of IP addresses. It is essential for the analyst to find out which region(s) causes these problems in detail.

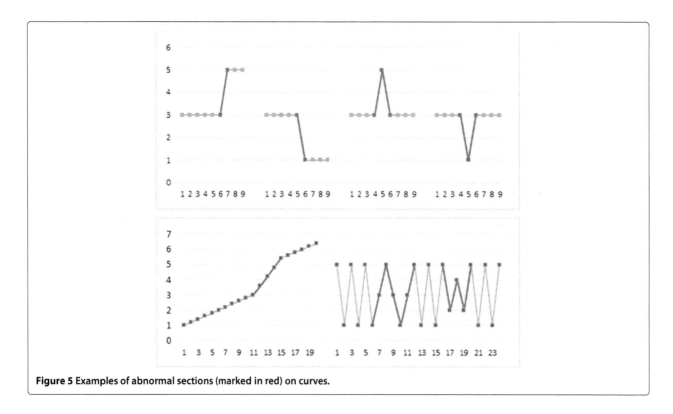

Figure 5 Examples of abnormal sections (marked in red) on curves.

While working on a large-scale complex dataset, an analyst will find it tedious and exhausting to examine each individual curve section to learn the related spatial information. This VAST 2012 Challenge dataset includes 4,000 offices and 13,000 C-level blocks. Manually examining each office or C-level block is simply impossible.

A time series curve of higher level granularity (e.g., a region) can be divided into several curves of its subgranularities (e.g., all sub-regions). Spatial data have hierarchy and can be divided into many levels of sub-regions. The aggregated value of the upper-level region is the total of all its sub-regions. For example, the total number of computers in one company must be equal to adding up all computers in its regional offices. Thus an anomaly (e.g., a jump) on a higher level curve must appear on some of its sub-curves. According to our observation, usually only a few sub-curves contribute most of the change in the higher-level curve. Thus it is essential for us to find these sub-curves and allocate the spatial information from them. In reality, curves will fluctuate slightly even in normal conditions. While finding the cause for the anomalies in the curve, we must filter out these small fluctuations.

We store the time series data according to the dimension hierarchies we discussed in the previous section. Using the OLAP slicing operation, we are able to divide an aggregated value into different granularity levels. The overall process of detecting anomaly from aggregated time series curves to geospatial details can be described as follows:

- The system maintains the hierarchies and relations of different levels of subdimensions in different directions. This information enables the system to iteratively check all subdimensions until it reaches the grounded basic granularity.
- The analyst anchors a suspicious segment on the curve. In this operation, the user defines the following parameters: start-and-end times, start-and-end data values, and value difference at this dimension.
- The detailed spatiotemporal data of the suspicious segment can be shown in two ways: locations on the geospatial map at the current time, or many curves "sliced" from the original curve. Based on the nature of the sliced curve, the system may automatically select one direction to show the details, or prompt to ask the user to select a direction to show the captured segment in detail.
- The system checks all of its subdimensions to learn which contribute the most to the overall value difference. This is done by sorting them by their percentages of value changes in the given period. If the percentages are within the same range, the system will rank the subdimensions by their absolute values. The higher the percentage of value change, the more contribution we must consider it will be giving to the overall value change. In some scenarios, some subdimensions may have much smaller values than others. The absolute value change in one smaller region might be too small to contribute to the overall,

although it is still significant enough locally. Thus we consider the relative change of numbers instead of the absolute change.

- The value changes might be caused by one or several subdimensions, or by most (or all) subdimensions. In the evenly distributed scenario, the relative percentage value of each subdimension should be very close.

- The system sums up the absolute number of changes from the highest-ranked subdimension to the lower-ranked subdimensions and tracks all subdimensions until the summary value reaches a certain user-defined threshold (e.g., 95%) of the original value. If we consider threshold as 100%, all small fluctuations will be counted and may blur the focus of the problem.

- If these subdimensions can be divided further to the next level of subdimensions, the system will iterate back to step 4 until the subdimensions are the most-grounded basic granularity.

- Group these basic granularities into a cluster if necessary. Based on the nature of these granularities, some spatial-clustering algorithms, such as DBSCAN (Density-Based Spatial Clustering of Application with Noise) [28], can be used.

- Mark these clusters on the map if these basic granularities are geographic based, or display them as a collection of time series curves if they are still time based.

Link from spatial visualization to time series curves

From a spatial visualization back to a time series curve is relatively straightforward. The spatial visualization normally presents the geographic distribution of different types of data. In the SemanticPrism (and many other spatial visualization systems), which type of data to be visualized can be controlled by menus that turn the data layers on and off. Also with zooming technology, the analyst can zoom in a smaller area on the visualization to open the view of a region or a subnetwork. Therefore from one spatial visualization we can capture a list of parameters, including the type of data items being visualized, current time, and current display area/region/subnetwork. Based on these parameters, popping up the related time series curve is simple.

Interaction design to support the fluency

An analyst may start the investigation by analyzing the curves. The abnormal segments in a curve, like sudden jumps, dives, peaks, or valleys, reflect the value change and therefore present us with a hint that something worthwhile is waiting to be investigated further. As discussed earlier, the time series curve can be seen as a series of vertices with connecting line segments. Thus the analyst can interact with two types of objects on the curve, the vertices and line segments, and can mark the suspicious segments in two ways. The first way is to mark a suspicious one-time-unit segment by simply clicking on the segment. To mark a segment across several time-unit periods, the user clicks on the starting point and end point on the curve and leaves two red triangle marks (top screen shot in Figure 2). After selecting one segment or two vertices, the system will present a pop-up menu for the analyst to select from if there are several possible subdimensions. In the example shown by Figure 3, further details can be shown in either the map or the IP pixel-based visualization. If there is only one subdimension, the system will automatically jump to the detailed view and display the marked area. Because the data are discrete with time intervals, selecting a partial segment is unnecessary. The minimal selectable range should be one segment (or the two neighboring data vertices).

The area of interest on the map is indicated by a red rectangle. Although the offices are spatially spread across the map, they are hierarchically grouped by regions. Therefore we did not use particular spatial clustering algorithms, but rather cluster offices by regions. If two or more offices are in one region, they will be marked together within one block. The boundary of the rectangle is defined by the spatial elements (offices in the middle screen shot, Figures 2 and 3). Sometimes the affected area will be tiny, for example, containing only one office. Marking the tiny area may not be visually significant enough to be noticed. Thus we define the minimum size of a marking as a rectangle measuring 45×35 pixels (Figure 2). The analyst can click on the rectangle to zoom in. The semantic zoom mechanism will automatically display details of the affected offices (middle and bottom screen shots).

Use cases

We use some examples below to show how we implement visual fluency in SemanticPrism, which tries to provide the user a smooth and efficient method to link information from different visualizations.

From time series curve to spatial visualization

In Figure 2, from the time series curve, the analyst saw the increasing number of computers are falling into high policy statuses. To accommodate multiple curves in one graph, we used thin lines in SemanticPrism to draw the curves. To identify how the policy violence spread spatially, the analyst needs to examine the locations of the computers. The user can inspect each segment on the policy-5 curve to check new computers that violate the policy. After clicking on the segment between 4:30 to 4:45 p.m., the user chooses the map from the pop-up menu to see which offices have new computers are new in policy status 5 starting at 4:45 p.m. The spatial view highlights the two new offices as the middle image in Figure 2. It is possible for the user to highlight all computers by selecting one time point. The user can simply click on the vertex in the curve to highlight all computers having the problem at that time.

In our current implementation, we simply use regions to cluster offices. Thus the two offices are marked separately. Clicking on the red marked boundary will lead the spatial view to zoom to that area. But because only one office is in that region, the system automatically zooms to the maximum level, which shows the detailed information of the office, including time series curves about policies in this office, and shows all computers with that policy 5 violation. We can see the IP 172.37.154.15 just started in policy 5 status at the given time (marked by the gray vertical line to indicate the current time).

Figure 3 demonstrated how the same curve jumps can be marked on either maps or IP addresses. The top image has 6 curves about the number of computers at different activities status (including total number of online computers) along the two days. At each hour there is a step (up or down) on the curves of activity 3 and 4. To find out what causes these steps, the analyst selects and examines one of the jumping segments (top image). By checking out the affected area on the map, he/she can see that they are actually caused by time zones – Offices open at 7 a.m. and close at 5 p.m. As time passes, offices open to turn on computers and close to shut off computers, which causes the sudden steps on the curve. The red squares mark the offices with computers that are newly emerging in activity 5. However, in here the marks are not 100% accurately aligned with the time zone because of the threshold we used (defined in step 6 the previous mechanism section). Small fluctuations happen all the time everywhere, especially for these computer activities, such as log-in errors. We assume that within a large area (e.g., a region), these small fluctuations that happened in small sub regions (e.g., in an office) will be counteracted with each other and make the regional number relatively stable in a normal situation. Therefore smaller areas might sometimes be neglected, or mismarked, as shown in the middle image of Figure 3. But the areas that contributed much to the change will be clearly marked out.

The bottom image of Figure 3 shows the distribution of new computers in the IP space. Each small square in the image represents a C-level IP block. Rows from bottom to top are the 2nd byte of the IP address (from 172.0.xx.xx to 172.55.xx.xx). Columns from left to right are the 3rd byte of the IP address (0 to 255). Besides marking each C-level block with blue squares, we also mark the B-blocks on both the left and right sides with red indicators (Figure 3 bottom).

From spatial visualization to time series curves

SemanticPrism provides a semantic zooming mechanism to change the details of display while the user is zooming in [22]. Offices on the map can change into 4 levels of details, depending on the available on-screen space. When zoomed in enough, the user is able to see the time series curves for individual offices (Figure 6).

Besides using semantic zooming to check out time series curves of different offices, the user can also click on a region or an office to see the temporal summary. Region 25 (the right-most region Alta at the top image of Figure 6) has many blacked-out offices, which means that these offices are disconnected from the Internet, possibly because of a power outage in the area. We can see that the distribution of blacked-out offices changes as time passes. To get to the affected computers over time, we can click on the region to bring out a regional time series curve (top image of Figure 7). The black curve shows that the overall computers sent out status reports during the period. A big valley on the curve shows that more and more computers lost connections in the middle of the first day. The worst time was at 11 p.m. BMT (Bankworld Mean Time). The situation recovered in the next 4 hours. The analyst can also choose to turn on the layers to highlight one activity status or one policy status. The green squares surrounding offices on the top image show offices with computers at activity 2 (going down for maintenance). Since the activity 2 layer is currently turned on, the time series curve of activity 2 is also included in the curves. However, the number of computers with activity 2 is so small, at the pixel level it is at the baseline and hides behind the policy 5 curve. The middle image in Figure 7 uses a logarithmic scale to boost these curves with extremely small values on the screen. Zooming in on this curve will break down the time series data of the region into individual offices. These curves for all offices are displayed in a grid as the bottom image of Figure 7.

Discussions

Visual analytics is the process for an analyst to learn the facts from the large volume of raw data through different forms of visualization. Representational fluency is the ability to comprehend equivalence in different modes of expression [9]. We borrow this term from psychology and pedagogical literature to describe our efforts to enable the analyst to fluently switch among different types of visualizations and data views to build up the understanding of facts. Cybersecurity issues can be visualized in temporal, in geospatial, in structural, or in raw data as logs. Visual analytics fluency allows the ability (1) to transform information from one representation to another; (2) to comprehend the equivalence in different modes of representations, including data and visualizations; and

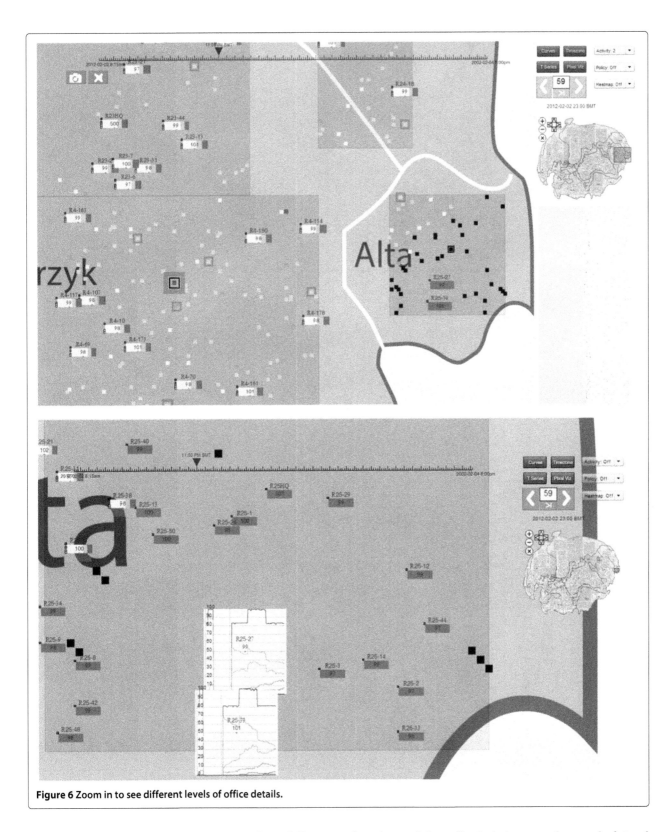

Figure 6 Zoom in to see different levels of office details.

(3) to comprehend information presented in different representations.

In this paper, we propose an auto linking mechanism that can smoothly transfer the analyst from one view to the other and thus effectively improve the speed of visual data analysis. Cognitively, a person can pay attention to only 3 or 4 things at one time. Our fluency metaphor may also reduce the cognitive load, helping the analyst to focus

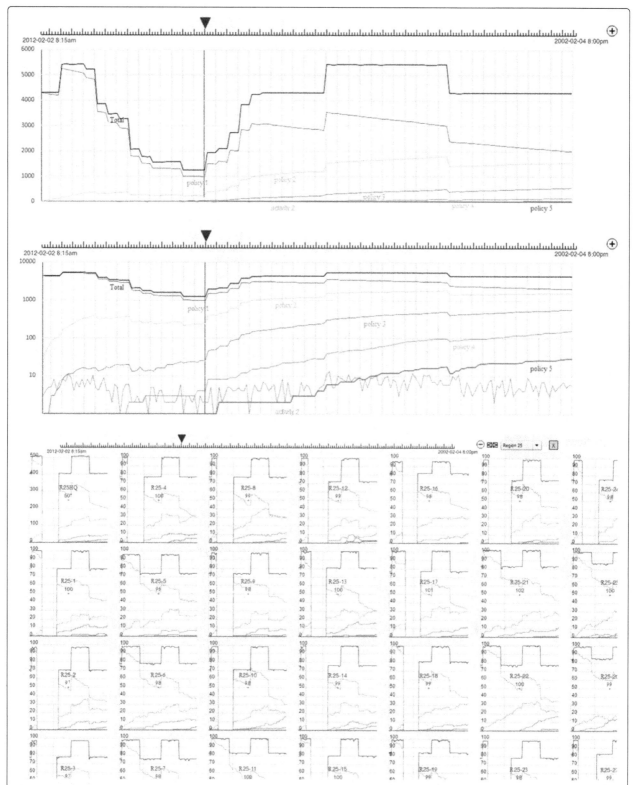

Figure 7 Time series curves corresponding to the region 25 in Figure 6. Top: Overall number of computers in different policy flags in region 25. Middle: The logarithmic scale version of the top visualization. Bottom: Zoom in on the curve to break down the regional time series curves into offices.

on some important incidents. At the stage of submitting SemanticPrism to the VAST 2012 challenge (July 2012), the four team members needed several days to identify all the anomalies by manually going over suspicious areas on all the curves and jumping across different views to examine and filter information. Most of the energy and time was exhausted during the back-and-forth navigation. With this newly developed linking mechanism, on one hand an analyst can mark suspicious segments on the time series curves and go directly to its related spatial visualization and data view. On the other hand, the analyst can simply right-click on the map, opening the menu to show one or several related time series curves.

We plan to improve this mechanism and its direct interaction design in the following directions.

First, we should extend our approach to other types of data and visualizations. The VAST 2012 MC1 dataset contains no data about computer network connectivity. In some cybersecurity analysis scenarios, visualizing such connections as the network intrusions from external IPs to internal hosts is crucial. Most often, connection data of these kinds can be visualized as a tree, or a network graph, with different layout variations (e.g., layout nodes in radial fashion). How to anchor parts of such spatial visualizations and link them to their related time series curves, geographic visualizations, or data views comprise the new domain we want to explore.

Second, we should find a method to automatically detect anomalies on the curves. A curve must be displayed at a certain resolution to allow the analyst to identify problematic areas. However, because the curves are mostly based on aggregation, the user sometimes cannot visually detect the problem when the number is too small to cause a significant visual change on the curve. Some literature on data mining and statistics [29,30] shows that allowing the system to detect anomalies on the curves by itself is possible. We will consider integrating this effective approach.

This approach can also be easily extended to handle streaming data such as real time analysis. In such case, the time series curve will become dynamic by updating itself in regular time intervals. Visually the curve will grow, extend, and slide from right to left (if the new data starts from the right end) just like the electrocardiography. Old part of curve will disappear on the left end. The user still be able to notice the anomaly happened during the recent past time intervals. For the just past time interval, the aggregations should be computed across the hierarchy of the spatial structure from top to bottom. The computing resource needed for pre-compute the aggregation depends on the length of the time interval and the complexity of the spatial structure. For this VAST 2012 MC1 data, since the time interval is pretty long as 15 minutes and there are only several thousands of spatial units,

computing aggregations for one time interval is very fast. For existing computed aggregations of each time interval, there is no need to re-compute them. The only aggregations need to be updated are the aggregations about recent past history (e.g. recent two days). But normally there is no urgent need to get the aggregation for the past history in real-time.

The inspiration and implementation of this fluency mechanism were based on the visual analytics system SemanticPrism and the VAST 2012 challenge dataset. To understand its generalizability and limits, we will use other datasets to test the possibility of linking the W3 structure visualizations. Furthermore, we aim to study the possibility of representational fluency being a suitable and valid design goal in the context of visual analytics and how to promote it to different platforms and systems.

Competing interests
The authors declare that they have no competing interests.

Author details
[1]Interaction Design, Purdue University, 552 W. Wood Street, 47907 West Lafayette IN, USA. [2]Computer Graphics Technology, Purdue University, 402 S. Grant Street, 47907 West Lafayette IN, USA.

References
1. G Jiang, G Cybenko, Temporal and spatial distributed event correlation for network security, in *American Control Conference, 2004, Proceedings of the 2004*, vol. 2 (IEEE Boston, MA, USA, 2004), pp. 996–1001
2. DJ Peuquet, It's about time: A conceptual framework for the representation of temporal dynamics in geographic information systems. Ann. Assoc. Am. Geographers. **84**(3), 441–461 (1994)
3. S Foresti, J Agutter, Y Livnat, Moon S, R Erbacher, Visual correlation of network alerts. IEEE Comput. Graphics Appl. **26**(2), 48–59 (2006)
4. N Andrienko, G Andrienko, P Gatalsky, Exploratory spatio-temporal visualization: an analytical review. J. Visual Languages & Comput. **14**(6), 503–541 (2003)
5. J Booker, T Buennemeyer, A Sabri, C North, High-resolution displays enhancing geo-temporal data visualizations, in *Proceedings of the 45th Annual Southeast Regional Conference* (ACM New York, NY, USA, 2007), pp. 443–448
6. H Shiravi, A Shiravi, AA Ghorbani, A survey of visualization systems for network security. IEEE Trans. Visualization Comput. Graphics. **18**(8), 1313–1329 (2012)
7. J Heer, B Shneiderman, Interactive dynamics for visual analysis. Mag. Queue - Microprocessors. **55**(4), 45–54 (2012)
8. YV Chen, ZC Qian, From when and what to where: Linking spatio-temporal visualizations in visual analytics, in *IEEE International Conference on Intelligence and Security Informatics* (IEEE Seattle, WA, USA, 2013), pp. 39–45
9. IE Sigel, Approaches to representation as a psychological construct: a treatise in diversity, in *Development of Mental Representation: Theories and Applications* (Psychology Press East Sussex, UK, 1999), pp. 3–12
10. M Stone, Challenge for the humanities, in *Working Together or Apart: Promoting the Next Generation of Digital Scholarship* (Washington, DC, USA, 2009). The Council on Library and Information Resources and The National Endowment for the Humanities
11. B Stripling, Assessing information fluency: gathering evidence of student learning. School Library Media Activities Monthly. **23**(8), 25–29 (2007)
12. (R Lesh, H Doerr, eds.), *Beyond constructivism: a models and modeling perspective on mathematics teaching, learning, and problem solving.* (Lawrence Erlbaum Associates, Hillsdale, NJ). ISBN 0-8058-3822-8

13. D Keim, C Panse, M Sips, ed. by Dykes J, Maceachren A, and Kraak M,
     Information visualization: Scope, techniques and opportunities for
     geovisualization, in *Exploring Geovisualization* (Elsevier Ltd Oxford, UK,
     2005), pp. 23–52
14. DA Keim, C Panse, M Sips, SC North, Pixelmaps: a new visual data mining
     approach for analyzing large spatial data sets, in *Proceedings of the Third
     IEEE International Conference on Data Mining* (IEEE Los Alamitos, CA, USA,
     2003), pp. 565–568
15. D Guo, J Chen, Eachren MacAM, K Liao, A visualization system for
     space-time and multivariate patterns (vis-stamp). IEEE Trans. Visualization
     Comput. Graphics. **12**(6), 1461–1474 (2006)
16. Y Livnat, J Agutter, S Moon, S Foresti, Visual correlation for situational
     awareness, in *Information Visualization, 2005. INFOVIS 2005. IEEE
     Symposium on* (IEEE Minneapolis, MN, USA, 2005), pp. 95–102
17. KA Cook, G Grinstein, M Whiting, M Cooper, M Havig, K Liggett, B Nebesh,
     CL Paul, VAST challenge 2012, visual analytics for big data, in *Visual
     Analytics Science and Technology, 2012 IEEE Conference on* (IEEE Seattle,
     WA, USA, 2012), pp. 151–155
18. VY Chen, AM Razip, S Ko, CZ Qian, DS Ebert, SemanticPrism: a
     multi-aspect view of large high-dimensional data: VAST 2012 mini
     challenge 1 award: Outstanding integrated analysis and visualization, in
     Visual Analytics Science and Technology, 2013 IEEE Conference on
     (IEEE Seattle, WA, USA, 2012), pp. 259–260
19. S Choudury, N Kodagoda, P Nguyen, C Rooney, S Attfield, K Xu, Y Zheng,
     BLW Wong, R Chen, G Mapp, L Slabbert, M Aiash, A Lasebae, M-sieve: a
     visualisation tool for supporting network security analysts, in *VisWeek
     2012*, 165–166 (2012)
20. L Dudas, Z Fekete, J Gobolos-Szabo, A Radnai, A Salanki, A Szabo, G Szucs,
     OWLAP - using OLAP approach in anomaly detection, in *Visual Analytics
     Science and Technology, 2012 IEEE Conference on* (IEEE Seattle, WA, USA,
     2012), pp. 167–168
21. O Schabenberger, CA Gotway, *Statistical Methods for Spatial Data Analysis*.
     (CRC Press, Boca Raton, FL, USA, 2004)
22. VY Chen, AM Razip, S Ko, ZC Qian, DS Ebert, Multi-aspect visual analytics
     on large-scale high-dimensional cyber security data, in *Information
     Visualization 2013* (Sage Publications Thousand Oaks, CA, 2013)
23. Y Zhao, X Liang, Y Wang, M Yang, F Zhou, X Fan, MVSec: a novel
     multi-view visualization system for network security, in *VisWeek* (2013)
24. S Chen, F Merkle, H Schaefer, C Guo, H Ai, X Yuan, T Ertl, Annette -
     collaboration oriented visualization of network data, in *VisWeek* (2013)
25. M Whiting, KA Cook, CL Paul, K Whitley, G Grinstein, B Nebesh, K Liggett,
     M Cooper, J Fallon, VAST challeng 2013: Situation awareness and
     prospective analysis, in *Visual Analytics Science and Technology, 2013 IEEE
     Conference on* (IEEE Atlanta, GA, USA, 2013)
26. K Perlin, D Fox, Pad: an alternative approach to the computer interface, in
     *Proceedings of the 20th Annual Conference on Computer Graphics and
     Interactive Techniques* (ACM New York, NY, USA, 1993), pp. 57–64
27. B Shneiderman, The eyes have it: A task by data type taxonomy for
     information visualizations, in *Proceedings of 1996 IEEE Symposium on Visual
     Languages* (IEEE Boulder, CO, USA, 1996), pp. 336–343
28. M Ester, H-P Kriegel, J Sander, X Xu, A density-based algorithm for
     discovering clusters in large spatial databases with noise, in *KDD, vol. 96
     1996* (AAAI Portland, OR, USA), pp. 226–231
29. RS Tsay, Outliers, level shifts, and variance changes in time series.
     J. Forecasting. **7**(1), 1–20 (1988)
30. JD Hamilton, *Time series analysis*, vol. 2. (Cambridge University Press,
     Cambridge, UK, 1994)

11

Modelling the spatial and social dynamics of insurgency

Philippe J Giabbanelli

Abstract

Insurgency emerges from many interactions between numerous social, economical, and geographical factors. Adequately accounting for the large number of potentially relevant interactions, and the complex ways in which they operate, is key to creating valuable models of insurgency. However, this has long been a challenging endeavour, as insurgency imposes specific limitations on the data that could speak to these interactions: quantitative data is limited by the difficulties of systematic collection in war, while qualitative data may include vague or conflicting insights from direct observers. In this paper, we designed a computational framework based on Fuzzy Cognitive Maps and Complex Networks to face these limitations. A software solution fully implements this framework and allows analysts to conduct simulations, in order to better understand the current dynamics of insurgency or test 'what-if' scenarios. Two approaches are presented to guide analysts in developing models based on our framework, either through a nuanced reading of the literature, or by aggregating the knowledge of domain experts.

Keywords: Civil war; Complex networks; Fuzzy Cognitive Maps; Terrorism informatics

Introduction

Initially of interest primarily to soldier-scholars seeking to systematise their experiences as counter-insurgents in wars of decolonisation [1,2], insurgency (and its cognates) increasingly became the subject of several landmark studies by political scientists [3-5], historians [6], and economists [7]. Together with this considerable renaissance in the study of insurgency, computational research into the dynamics of terrorism and rebellion has grown in prominence [8]. One of the drivers of this growth is the ability of computational approaches to account for the many complex interactions between the factors that shape a conflict, which makes such approaches a valuable complement to the associational analyses stemming from economics and seeking to identify 'root causes'. Computational models have indeed been able to systematise and articulate many of the key processes which define insurgency as a particular type of conflict. For example, a recent model used 19 factors and over 80 parameters, accounting for processes such as the consequences of intelligence gathering on the insurgent's organization or the impact of

outside support on the insurgents' actions [9]. The task of populating the model's parameters with real-world data is often left to the analysts [9] but this task can be particularly challenging as models require specific numerical values despite sources mostly providing qualitative data from empirical evidence. While the challenge of creating quantitative models of insurgency when given qualitative data has already been thoroughly addressed in the political methodology from a statistical perspective [10], this challenge remains relatively unexplored from a computational perspective.

In this paper, we develop a novel computational method that can be used to model how an array of interacting factors come together to determine loyalty or rebelliousness. This method involves two computational techniques whose synergies are essential to address the specific needs of modelling in insurgency. The artificial intelligence technique of *Fuzzy Cognitive Maps* (FCMs) has a proven track record in allowing for the development of models when supporting data is vague or conflicting. Using this technique will allow us to address one of the main shortcomings of current models as aforementioned. While FCMs have been used to model complex political phenomena, such as crises in the Republic of Macedonia [11] or Cyprus [12], this technique is not designed to

Correspondence: giabba@sfu.ca
Interdisciplinary Research in the Mathematical and Computational Sciences (IRMACS) Centre, Simon Fraser University, 8888 University Drive, V5A 1S6 Burnaby, Canada

capture the spatial dynamics that play a very important role in conflicts (*c.f.*, [13] for the role that urban geography plays in terrorism). For example, not adequately capturing the diffusion of civil wars over space [14] or the localized nature of attacks [15] would significantly lower the relevance of models to analysts. We previously demonstrated that FCMs could be used to model social processes but that they would have to be combined with another technique for local dynamics [16]. Our early work combined FCMs with *Cellular Automaton* [17], which have a long history of being used to model spatial dynamics [18] but suffer from having to rigidly divide the space into equal square cells. Therefore, we propose to represent the space as a *Complex Network* (CN), which offers several advantages over the early version of this framework: the space can be arbitrarily divided, standard generators can be used to test how a strategy would unfold in different types of space, and the analyses tools developed for complex networks can be used to explore the relationship between the structure of that space and the dynamics of insurgency.

Contribution of the paper

The principal contributions of the present work can be summarized as follows:

- We propose a computational framework to support researchers in mathematically expressing the important but often hard-to-formalise relationships spanning social and physical geography.
- We present a novel software solution that guides modellers and analysts in designing a model of insurgency in an interactive manner and then simulate it.
- We show two different approaches for the practical development of a model of insurgency based on our framework. One approach relies on a nuanced reading of a large corpus by a domain expert, while the other focuses on synthesizing the knowledge of an international group of experts.

Organization of the paper

We start by providing the technical background to our computational framework, and we formally specify it. Then, we detail the first and key step in building a model based on this framework: how to design a conceptual map articulating the interactions between several factors contributing to insurgency. We further highlight the functioning of the framework through our software implementation, with a focus on how it enables experts to interactively and efficiently set up computer models of insurgency tailored for the context they are interested in. Finally, we discuss the strengths and limitations of this framework.

Computational framework
Background

Insurgents can be mobile and difficult to identify, which limits the potential of terrain-centric and enemy-centric approaches for counterinsurgency (COIN) operations. In contrast, the population is easy to identify and often less mobile. Unlike conventional warfare, opposing forces in counterinsurgency warfare thus do not only seek to reduce each other's military capability but are also competing for the support of the population [1]. In societies with tribal power structures such as Iraq, winning the 'hearts and minds' of local opinion leaders is critical to secure support. Once opinion leaders are clearly identified (*e.g.*, using the Tactical Conflict Assessment Framework in Iraq) the question becomes: *who* among them should be targeted [19]? This question can also be approached from a geographical standpoint. Leaders must not only be persuaded that their interests are in line with counterinsurgents, but also that their interests will be protected. Given that forces cannot be deployed everywhere, the question becomes: *where* can protection be guaranteed in return for political support? Whether it is approached from a social-network perspective (*who*) or a geographical-network perspective (*where*), this is often studied as a variation of an influence maximization problem. The *influence maximization* problem posed by Domingos and Richardson [20] and modelled by Kempe and colleagues [21] asks, for a parameter k, to find the set of k nodes that provide the maximum influence. This needs to be extended in the case of insurgencies, since both insurgents and counterinsurgents want to spread their influence while blocking that of their opponent. This leads to an *influence blocking maximization* problem, which is different from the *competitive influence maximization* problem where forces are solely interested in maximimizing their influence instead of limiting others'. In the context of insurgency, these problems have often been modelled using complex networks (which account for the great variation in ties between people or places) and agent-based systems (which highlight the reasoning behind a switch in allegiance).

In [19,22], each node of the network represents a person. The attitude of a person with respect to the competing forces is represented by a value ranging from -0.5 (favourable to Taliban) to +0.5 (favourable to the US). Individuals are also categorized by their level of influence, which includes head of household or village leader. Individuals change attitude solely based on pairwise interactions between them. The outcome of interactions depend on set probabilities, and can lead to both individuals changing to their average attitude, retaining the original attitudes, or having one change to become more like the other based on a parameter. The model in [23] also propagates opinions through social links using probabilistic rules. One noteworthy simplification in these models was the absence of the context, that is, the set of political, economical, and social aspects that shape leaders' attitudes. For example, a village leader's loyalty to the government may wither as a larger number of young men in the village become unemployed. These aspects also mitigate the influence exerted during COIN operations or by the insurgent. While tribal relationships have been taken into account in some models [24], aspects such as the trustworthiness of institutions or the discrimination of counter-insurgent violence would impact the outcome of interactions with forces supportive of the government.

Taking into account the broader context in which individuals make decisions can be very challenging due to the complexity of this context and the difficulty of collecting data about it. Focusing on the counterinsurgency environment, Upshur and colleagues wrote that "researchers are not impartial but rather armed actors in a conflict; thus there is a 'combatant observer effect'. The interviewer's obvious association with a combatant organization affects the openness and honesty of respondents, as does the power disparity between a member of an occupying military force and an unarmed local population" [25]. Consequently, data corruption results in uncertainty and bias. Furthermore, disagreements on the mechanisms are not only found between the reports of direct observers but also in the analyses of scholars. For example, Fearon and Laitin reported that "the effect of primary commodity exports is considerable: [...] a country with no natural resource export only has a probability of warstart of 1%" compared to 22% when exporting" [7], but Ross considered that "the claim that primary commodity exports are linked to civil war appears fragile and should be treated with caution" [26]. Therefore, there is a need for computational models that can use the qualitative data provided by process-tracking and ethnographical studies, and have specific mathematical ways to address the uncertainty and conflicts found in the data.

Many frameworks have been proposed to model diffusion in networks [27], and they account for uncertainty in different ways. In the Weighted Generalized Annotated Program (wGAP) framework, changes are expressed by rules whose probability reflects the certainty [28]. For example, the rule $supportInsurgents(A) \overset{0.75}{\leftarrow} supportInsurgents(B) \land leader(B,A)$ states that if the village leader B for inhabitant A supports insurgents, then A will support the insurgents with 75% certainty. Similarly, the Linear Threshold Model (LTM) and the Independent Cascade Model (ICM) have rules for changes in the nodes' attitudes, and random thresholds are associated with these rules to model uncertainty [21]. The Multi-Attribute Networks and Cascades (MANCaLog)

framework provides more flexibility, the properties of nodes and edges have a weight whose uncertainty is represented by an interval that can be open or closed [27]. However, a key distinction is that these frameworks are designed to operate once the values for the uncertainty have been specified: they are not made to take in (possibly contradictory) qualitative assessments and turn them into values based on the uncertainty.

Fuzzy Cognitive Maps

Fuzzy Logic Theory is a valuable mathematical technique to deal with the conflicting and uncertain evidence found in the wealth of testimonies, media reports, and other forms of 'thick description'. As described by Li, Fuzzy Logic Theory [29]

> resembles human reasoning under approximate information and inaccurate data to generate decisions under uncertain environments. It is designed to mathematically represent uncertainty and vagueness, and to provide formalized tools for dealing with imprecision in real-world problems.

When trying to evaluate the strength (and thus the existence of) a mechanism, straightforwardly assigning a score to each source and simply computing the average or the mode would address neither vagueness nor conflicts. Instead, Fuzzy Logic Theory allows us to summarize opinions via linguistic terms (*e.g.*, a mechanism may have a "weak" or "medium" effect) and consider that each term is associated to a range of values. A *membership function* represents the range of each term, and ranges can overlap to account for the possibility that an expert judges a relationship to be "strong" while actually thinking the same as the expert who calls the relationship "very strong". The choice of a membership function depends on the problem. Triangular membership functions (Figure 1) are often used [30,31], and a plethora of alternatives exists (*e.g.*, Z-shape, Gaussian, and S-shaped membership functions [32]).

Once the evidence is summarized via a linguistic term, a set of IF-THEN rules is produced. For example, we asked experts to evaluate the extent to which an inhospitable terrain would contribute to the government's institutional weakness. Two experts judged the effect to be 'medium' while two saw it as 'high' and one called it 'very high'. The IF-THEN rules associate a crisp antecedent (*e.g.*, whether the terrain is inhospitable) to a fuzzy consequent (*e.g.*, a 'medium' or 'high' impact on the government's institutional weakness) and a confidence factor (*e.g.*, number of experts who produced that rule). In this example, we obtain:

R_1: IF (*Inhospitable terrain* is PRESENT) THEN the impact on the (*Government's institutional weakness*) is *medium* (2/5)

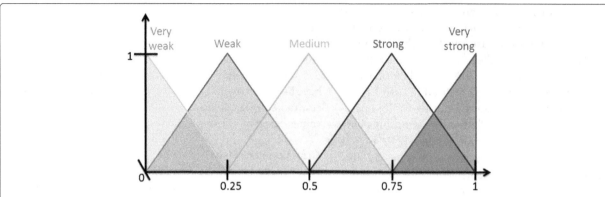

Figure 1 Triangular membership functions. Perceptions for concepts of strength correspond to membership functions, which can overlap. This particular shape is known as a *triangular* membership function.

R_2: IF (*Inhospitable terrain* is PRESENT) THEN the impact on the (*Government's institutional weakness*) is *high* (2/5)

R_3: IF (*Inhospitable terrain* is PRESENT) THEN the impact on the (*Government's institutional weakness*) is *very high* (1/5)

These rules are combined to formulate a Fuzzy Inference Systems that yields one quantitative value. Fuzzy Set Theory is repeatedly applied to obtain one crisp value from the evidence supporting each relationship in the model. These relationships are connected: for example, an inhospitable terrain can impact the ability of insurgents to control the population which in turns affects the socio-economic advantage to insurgency. Therefore, these connections can be viewed as a network named a *Fuzzy Cognitive Map* (FCM). The *nodes* of the network represent fuzzy domain concepts (*e.g.*, trustworthiness of institutions, baseline tension). The *edges* stand for causal connections, and their values are obtained via Fuzzy Set Theory. Edges are either positive or negative to indicate that the target concept respectively increases or decreases with the source concept. Since the introduction of FCM by Kosko in 1986 [33] and its initial application as an artificial intelligence tool to public policy [34], FCMs have been used successfully in critical situations where accuracy has to be obtained despite vagueness [35], such as evaluating the vulnerability of facilities to terrorism [36].

Formally, the number of concepts in the FCM is denoted by n and the matrix $S_{i,j}, i = 1\ldots n, j = 1\ldots n$ denotes the strength of the relationships from concepts i to concept j. The vector $C_i(t)$ stores the values of all concepts at time t. For example, if *inhospitable terrain* is the third concept and the *government's institutional weakness* is the fifth one, then $S_{3,5}$ represents the link from the latter to the former, and their initial values are stored in $C_3(0)$ and $C_5(0)$ respectively. The simulation of the FCM consists of updating the values stored in V until a subset of them stabilizes (*c.f.*, algorithm in [30]). For example, if the analyst is interested in knowing how the rise in unemployment

and household poverty will ultimately impact the socio-economic advantage to insurgency, then the FCM will be updated until the socio-economic stops fluctuating. The following equation is used to perform one update:

$$C_i(t+1) = f\left(C_i(t) + \sum_{j=1, j\neq i} C_j(t) \times S_{j,i}\right) \quad (1)$$

where f is a threshold function (also known as *transfer* function) that bounds the output in the interval [0, 1]. It is common practice to use such function in order to keep concepts within a specific range [37]. This function can be, for instance, a sigmoid function such as the hyperbolic tangent $f(x) = \tanh x = \frac{e^x - e^{-x}}{e^x + e^{-x}}$ [31].

Complex networks

In our framework, the geographical space over which an insurgency takes place needs to be discretized. A straightforward approach would be to map the space to a grid, that is, to partition it into squares [17]. However, this approach raises several issues. If the squares are too large, then important local differences are ignored; for example, two districts may end up merged under one cell despite tremendous discrepancies in terms of socio-economic status and, ultimately, propensity to support an insurgency. Squares could be made smaller to ensure that different contexts are represented by different cells, but the larger number of squares would negatively impact the performances of a simulation, and redundancy could occur frequently as taking too small a resolution can lead to subdividing a space that has a homogeneous context. Thus, the difficulty is to avoid redundancy in order to keep performances satisfactory, while adequately representing local differences. Using networks provides the flexibility required for this situation. In a network approach, each region deemed homogeneous with respect to factors of interest to the analyst (*e.g.*, unemployment, use of explosive device, daily murder rate) is represented as one vertex, and this vertex is connected to all adjacent regions by an edge (Figure 2). Networks have long been used to understand the properties of various phenomena in space. A recent review of research results on this approach is provided in [38], while several complete study cases can be found in [39]. Formally, locations are expressed by the set of vertices $\mathbb{V}$ while adjacency is given by the edges $\mathbb{E}$.

As our framework aims to support analysts, the space must be represented in a way that is not only efficient for calculations: analysts should also be able to navigate this space in an intuitive way. The primary reason to use cellular automata in our previous work was that their straightforward mapping of space onto a grid could easily be navigated [17]. However, this came at the expense of the aforementioned issues in efficiency. Using networks addresses the issue of efficiency, but questions are then raised regarding the ease of use by analysts. While navigating a *general* network can be a challenge, this task is simple in our case since a geographical division of space into neighbourhoods or regions produces *planar* networks. Indeed, the sub-spaces represented as vertices are linked by edges only when they are adjacent, and thus edges do not need to cross in order to display the network. A wealth of research has been conducted to display planar graphs, initially motivated by the need to display electrical schemes of large circuits for engineering purposes. Therefore, a number of algorithms such as surveyed in [41] offer convenient displays that can support analysts in exploring the geographical dynamics of insurgency. Furthermore, additional support is provided through ongoing research in natural interaction techniques for networks (*c.f.*, the work of Nathalie Henry Riche).

Coupling

Each location contains an FCM that expresses the social dynamics within that location. The FCMs all have the same structure, as the concepts and mechanisms contributing to insurgency are selected for the entire event

(*e.g.*, war in Baghdad, insurgency in Syria) rather than for a specific neighbourhood. However, the values of these concepts depend on the location. For example, we might consider that a lack of political representation contributes to both the weakness of a government and the exclusion of an ethnic group, which in turn favour insurgency. However, the level of political representation might differ across neighbourhood; in the case of Iraq and Baghdad (Figure 2), the Sunni neighbourhoods of Azamiyah and Doura would have a different level of political representation compared to the Shia neighbourhoods of New Baghdad and Kazimiyah. Some of the concepts are influenced by the values of concepts in surrounding locations, as defined by the network in the previous section. Figure 3 illustrates this influence: all locations (circles) have the same concepts linked in the same way, but one concept is influenced by neighbours. Focusing on the dotted orange circle, the ability of insurgents to control population movements at that location is influenced by the control that is exerted in the surrounding four locations. Network influences are applied first, and then the FCMs are updated to reflect how such influences would turn out based on the local context. It is possible for such influences to be cancelled out because of opposing forces (*e.g.*, inhabitants in the target neighbourhood are politically well-represented and have a high level of trust in institutions), or they could be reinforced due to the presence of factors fuelling insurgency (*e.g.*, household poverty and number of unemployed young men). This coupling allows to accurately represent local dynamics through FCMs, and asssess the spread of influences over larger areas using a network.

Formally, we extend the notation of FCMs to express the value of a concept i at time t in a location $v \in \mathbb{V}$ by $C_{i,t,v}$. The extent to which a concept a of the FCM is influenced by a (not necessarily distinct) concept b is given by $W_{a,b}$. The influence function f takes in two concepts, where the first is under the influence of the second, and computes

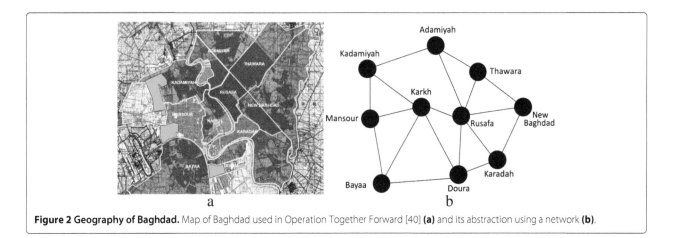

Figure 2 Geography of Baghdad. Map of Baghdad used in Operation Together Forward [40] **(a)** and its abstraction using a network **(b)**.

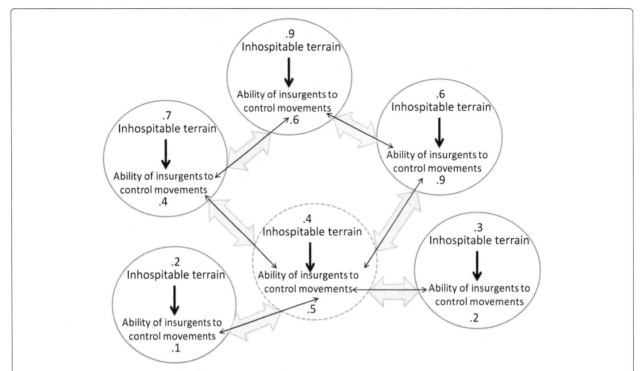

Figure 3 Impact of neighbouring influences mediated by local context. All locations (circles) have the same concepts and mechanisms (large black arrows), but neighbouring influences (blue arrows) will impact some concepts (thin black arrows). In this situation, the hostility of the terrain follows a North-South gradient, while the insurgency has a stronghold in the North-East.

the the impact of the influence. One time step of the simulation is given in Algorithm 1. The Algorithm has two parts. First, it applies the influence of neighbouring locations: for each location $i \in \mathbb{V}$ and each neighbour $j \in \mathbb{V}$, all concepts of i will be influenced by the concepts of j. While we previously used dedicated functions to specify which concepts were either influenced or influencing [16], this new formalism simply encodes such roles in $W_{a,b}$ since $W_{a,b} > 0$ states that b is an influencing concept and a the concept under influence. The second part uses the local context to mediate the influences that were received, by independently updating each FCM using the standard procedure in the literature [30].

Creating conceptual maps

The first step in designing models based on our framework is to create a conceptual map that uses expert knowledge to assess which factors are relevant to insurgency in a specific context and how these factors can be articulated. The product of this step is a network consisting of representative factors (*i.e.*, vertices) whose interactions (*i.e.*, edges) are either positive (*i.e.*, the presence of a factor increases another) or negative and are given a strength. Two broad approaches support the elicitation of knowledge from an expert in order to construct maps [42]: *direct* approaches assist the experts in constructing maps

---

Algorithm 1 Updates the simulation for one time step

Require: The FCMs at each location have initial values, time $t > 0$

1: *//Applies the geographical dynamics in parallel*
2: **for** $i \in \mathbb{V}$ **do**
3:    **for** $j \in \mathbb{V} | (j, i) \in \mathbb{E}$ **do**
4:       *//for each location j influencing a location i*
5:       **for** $a = 1 \ldots n$ **do**
6:          **for** $b = 1 \ldots n$ **do**
7:             *//for each combination of concepts in the FCMs*
8:             $C_{a,t+1,i} \leftarrow C_{a,t,i} + W_{a,b} \times f(C_{a,t,i}, C_{b,t,i})$ *//updates the value of concept a*
9: *//Standard procedure to update each FCM until stabilization [30]*
10: **for** $i \in \mathbb{V}$ **do**
11:    update(i)

(*e.g.*, Novak's concept mapping [43]) for example by asking them which concepts are important and how they are related, while *indirect* approaches infer the maps from written documents or interviews (*e.g.*, Trochim's concept mapping [44]). Both approaches can be used to create the conceptual map used by our framework, and the choice depends on the availability of experts on the different aspects of the insurgency. A direct approach may be taken when modellers and experts can meet several times to iteratively construct maps, while an indirect approach may be necessary when experts on the field communicate by sending intelligence reports. This section illustrates both approaches for a typical example of a "revolutionary war" [1] or of a terrorist campaign [45], in which insurgents are engaged in a population-centric war by shattering the confidence of the local communities in their government.

Indirect approach

Two steps were used for this approach, which was previously reported in [17]. First, a scholar in insurgency assessed which factors and interactions were deemed most important in a body of literature relevant to the example of revolutionary war. Then, each interaction was weighted by using a nuanced reading to extract the overall opinion of each peer-reviewed articles speaking to that interaction, and then combining the opinions using Fuzzy Logic. This process was resulted in Figure 4. In this section, we first report on the three groups of factors and relationships that compose the map. Then, we detail the technical choices that allowed Fuzzy Logic to be applied on each edge.

The **rebelliousness** of a community indicates the level of its participation in insurgent activities. It is thus the most closely monitored factor for this scenario. It is determined by two factors: *motive* and *opportunity*. The motive is determined by the socio-economic advantage to insurgency, which collectively incorporates the social, political,

and economic reasons for which an individual or community would want to rebel. Opportunities consist of the mechanisms and material conditions that make rebellious acts possible on an incidental basis. This model also accounts for the self-reinforcing effect of rebellion, in which existing rebelliousness facilitates further rebelliousness though mechanisms such as insurgent recruitment networks and the solidification of ascribed political loyalties [3].

The **socio-economic advantage to insurgency** depends on several factors. The ability of insurgents to control the population and to use discriminating violence determines the extent to which they can offer enticements and coercion to the local community, as does the power of the government to employ discriminate violence. Indeed, "control - regardless of the 'true' preferences of the population - precludes options other than collaboration by creating credible benefits for collaborators and, more importantly, sanctions for defectors" [3]. Community economic factors also play a powerful role. The rate or level of economic development determines the opportunity costs of participation, where economic recession makes participation in rebellion less risky or costly in comparison to times of economic boom [46]. Natural resources vulnerable to looting or military capture present a tantalising incentive to join armed groups [47]. For example, in the developing world, "conflict diamonds" or the drug trade influenced the development and proliferation of militias [48] described as a class of 'feral' insurgent [49], since their activism is a means of survival instead of an institutional mechanism to secure popular support. High unemployment among young men produces a likely

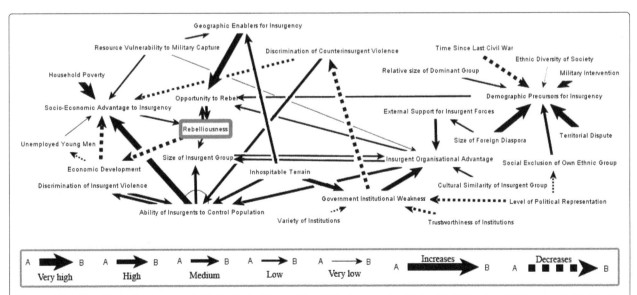

Figure 4 Map from the indirect approach. Each edge is either positive (full line) or negative (dashed line). Edges' weights have been discretized as "very high" (0.9 and above), "high" (0.76 and above), "medium" (0.7 and above), "low" (0.5 and above), or "very low" (less than 0.5).

pool for insurgent recruitment, as it provides them with opportunities to advance economically and socially [7]. On a more micro level, a household so poor that its members have little means to sustain themselves is particularly likely to join whichever group happens to offer the best immediate chance of survival [50]. For example, while Pakistani rebels often had better education than their Afghani counterparts, both came from large, impoverished households [51].

The **opportunity to rebel** is strongly linked to the strength of the insurgent organisation, which affects whether recruitment mechanisms, arms [52], information [3], and logistical capacity make it possible to rebel in an organised or meaningful way. The strength of an insurgent organisation increases in the presence of weak government institutions, limited in their ability to identify and neutralise insurgent agents [2,3,49,53]. Demographic precursors for insurgency establish conditions of instability that can be exploited by insurgent groups to provide political justifications and normative space for rebellion. An existing territorial dispute can evolve into an enduring ethnic or sectarian rivalry, providing the fault-lines for civil conflict and increased fractionalisation [54]. The presence of foreign military forces staging an intervention can inhibit the power of any party to achieve significant political progress through force of arms, paradoxically often making conflict longer-lasting and more intractable [55]. A recent previous civil war can ensure that the population has both lurking hostilities and access to weapons. The Balkan wars are one example of the facilitating effect that weapons-saturation has upon making participation in civil wars feasible [56]. A supportive foreign diaspora can make funding insurgent activities easier, while the social exclusion of certain groups makes conflict increasingly easier to justify and prosecute as the excluded group grows in size.

We capture the precise strength of the 44 discrete relationships between factors by giving each edge a weight (Figure 4). To determine the weight of a given edge, evidence was gathered from nuanced readings of peer-reviewed articles. Following a standard procedure (e.g., see word bank in [30]), the parts of selected articles that spoke to the relationship under study were examined by a field expert and categorized using a fuzzy linguistic term from the set {Very Weak (VW), Weak (W), Medium (M), Strong (S), Very Strong (VS)}. For example, the selected parts quoted in the Section on the Fuzzy Cognitive Map were used to estimate the relationship from Resource Vulnerability to Military Capture to Geographic Enabler for Insurgency; Fearon and Laitin were categorized as strong as they saw the effect of commodity exports as "considerable" [7], while Ross was categorized under weak since he sees the link as "fragile" [26]. The different categories assigned to the evidence constitute a knowledge

base which is combined using Fuzzy Logic Theory. The membership functions used in this process (Figure 1) are described by the following standard equations [57]:

$$\mu_{VW}(x) = max(min(0, \frac{0.25 - x}{0.25}), 0) \tag{2}$$

$$\mu_{W}(x) = max(min(\frac{x}{0.25}, \frac{0.5 - x}{0.5 - 0.25}), 0) \tag{3}$$

$$\mu_{M}(x) = max(min(\frac{x - 0.25}{0.5 - 0.25}, \frac{0.75 - x}{0.75 - 0.5}), 0) \tag{4}$$

$$\mu_{S}(x) = max(min(\frac{x - 0.5}{0.75 - 0.5}, \frac{1 - x}{1 - 0.75}), 0) \tag{5}$$

$$\mu_{VS}(x) = max(min(\frac{x - 0.75}{1 - 0.75}, 1), 0) \tag{6}$$

The process was carried out for each edge, using the Mamdani algorithm, the *sum* method of aggregation, and the *centroid* method for defuzzification. These technical choices are common practice, and we refer the interested reader to [37] for the technical aspects.

Direct approach

In a direct approach, a purposeful sample of experts is assembled and guided through a three step process. First, experts are given a question that will prompt them to iteratively identify concepts (*e.g.*, writing them on sticky notes), arrange them (*e.g.*, creating clusters or hierarchies by moving the notes), link them and re-arrange them to facilitate the display of links [43]. This step results in the map's structure. While that step can be carried on straightforwardly for simple problems when experts are all available in one place, it can be challenging for complex problems where a panel of international experts is needed in order to account for each part of the problem [31]. Thus, the map's structure may be set based on a subcommittee of experts. The second step is to ask all experts about the strength of each relationship, and the final step combines their knowledge using Fuzzy Logic Theory as in the previous section.

To illustrate these steps, we asked international experts about the contributors to rebelliousness. Due to the complexity of the problem and the wide range of expertise required to achieve a comprehensive understanding of insurgency, we structured the map as a set of 24 concepts and 44 relationships based on the feedback obtained about Figure 4. Experts were then asked to evaluate the strength of each relationship, by categorizing it as 'nonexistent', 'very low', 'low', 'medium', 'high', or 'very high'; experts were also given the possibility of choosing 'unsure' in order to skip evaluating relationships about which they did not feel confident. Finally, expert opinions were combined using Fuzzy Logic Theory for each relationship using the standard procedure aforementioned (*i.e.*, membership functions specified by equations 1 to 5, Mamdani algorithm, *sum* method of aggregation, and *centroid* for defuzzification). The result is shown in Figure 5.

Software solution

Three steps process

Software was built to support the development of models of insurgency via our framework. While our framework is first and foremost mathematical, it can be mostly used via a graphical user interface that aims at making the modelling process as intuitive as possible so that modellers can focus on the few equations that require a fine tuning. The modelling process is divided into three steps (Figure 6), and each step has a dedicated software component that supports both design and analysis.

A Fuzzy Cognitive Map (FCM) can be created via either the direct or indirect approaches outlined in the previous section. Then, it is provided to our software using the *Concept Map editor* (Figure 7) which guides modellers in creating their FCM via a series of steps. In our experience, some structures typically arise when experts are asked to think about what contributes to an insurgency. One such structure is the star, where all factors point to one; this arises when experts list all the contributors to insurgency but do not yet zoom out to consider second-order contributors as well as interactions. Another structure

is the cycle, which typically represents how insurgencies either grow or are sustained despite interventions. Therefore, such a structure can directly be built as the first step (Figure 7-1); alternatively, modellers can create or alter structures by directly interacting with the workspace (Figure 7-2). Then, the map is operationalized (Figure 7-3) by weighting the links, designating the factors that must stabilize for the FCM to stop evolving, designating the factors that can influence or be influenced by others (for integration with the second software component), and providing initial values. Since an FCM is assigned to one geographical area, initial values can either depend on the area, be randomly generated based on either probability distributions (*e.g.*, normal, inverse gaussian) or conditional distributions (*e.g.*, the value of a concept may depend on the value of another concept), or be populated from real-world data. As data is entered on the map, modellers can use different layouts to automatically rearrange the display (Figure 7-4). Once the map is ready, its structure can be analyzed (Figure 7-5) to find out influential factors, which was can lead to insight in how the model was conceived [30]. Finally, the map can be simulated (Figure 7-6) to show what would happen independently of spatial factors or which trajectories could be obtained based on different initial values.

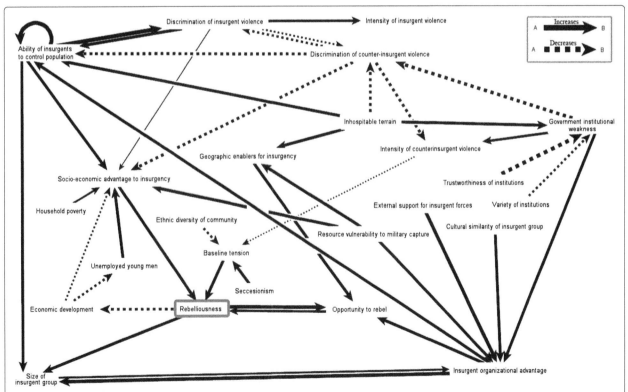

Figure 5 Map from the direct approach. Each edge is either positive (full line) or negative (dashed line). Edges' weights are proportional to their value on a scale from 0 to 1.

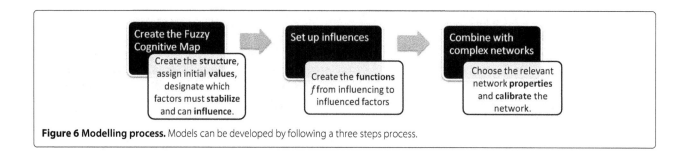

Figure 6 Modelling process. Models can be developed by following a three steps process.

Once the Fuzzy Cognitive Map has been finalized, the Coupling Editor is used to provide the mathematical equations governing influences between FCMs. This is achieved by first connecting influencing factors (in white on Figure 8a) to influenced factors (in black on Figure 8a), and assigning a function to each connection. Such functions can be designed from scratch in Java, or they can be selected from a set of templates which then only need to be parameterized. For example, modellers can consider that a slight difference in the level of economic developments in neighbouring locations is not important, but when that difference goes over a given *threshold* then it will *impact* local economic development. To input this into the model, modellers would select the 'threshold and impact' template (Figure 8a) and provide the values of both threshold and impact. Similarly, modellers may notice that a relationships is stronger at the beginning of the conflict (*e.g.*, demographic precursors) so they would use the 'decaying impact' template and specify both the impact and rate of decay. Offering access to functions commonly used in modelling complex social problems (*e.g.*, threshold and impact [58], fractional and majority votes [59]) also simplifies the process of modelling development, thereby making it accessible to participants with limited mathematical background.

The final step is to generate the spatial network. During the early phases of model development, an exact mapping might not be available to modellers. Consequently,

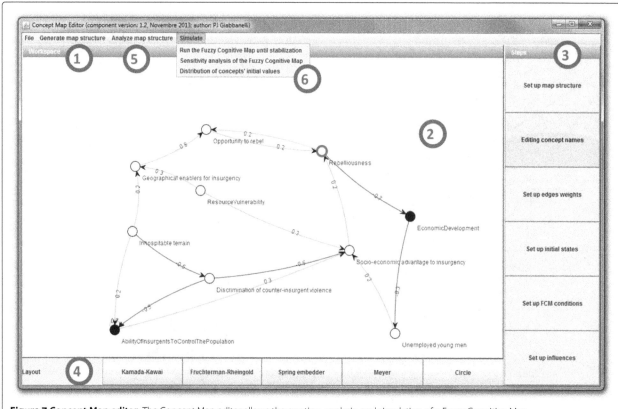

Figure 7 Concept Map editor. The Concept Map editor allows the creation, analysis, and simulation of a Fuzzy Cognitive Map.

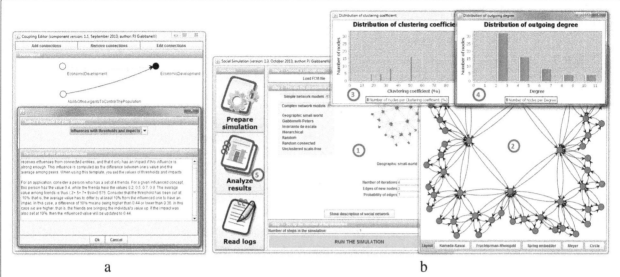

Figure 8 Coupling editor and simulation tool. The Coupling Editor allows modellers to apply commonly used functions for the influence of the surroundings **(a)**. The simulation tool provides a set of network generators that can be analyzed and tuned to match the desired topology **(b)**.

the model might have to operate on assumptions regarding the broad characteristics of the space, and only if the model proves useful then partnerships can support the acquisition of accurate data. Our software provides extensive support for the early phase by allowing modellers to choose network generators with a desired set of properties (Figure 8b-1), such as creating planar power-law networks (Figure 8b) which represent a densely connected urban centre linked to increasingly isolated settlements. Since such generators require a fine tuning, analysis tools are provided both for visual inspection (Figure 8b-2) as well as for the quantification of key metrics (*e.g.*, clustering coefficient in Figure 8b-3 or degree distribution in Figure 8b-4). Once the right network has been generated, the simulation can be performed and analyzed to see how factors of the FCM changed over time (Figure 8b-5).

Sample scenario

The simple model used in this section does not aim to make accurate recommendations regarding counterinsurgency strategies. Rather, the experiments focus on demonstrating the ability of our framework to easily represent complex dynamics and handle 'what-if' scenarios. We use the model represented in Figure 7, which articulates how geographical (*e.g.*, inhospitable terrain), economical (*e.g.*, economic development and unemployment of young men), and political factors come together in shaping rebelliousness. The values were obtained by aggregating expert knowledge using Fuzzy Logic, as in Figure 5. In this sample scenario, an insurgency has begun in a resource-based economy. Consequently, the

following assumptions were made on the initial values of concepts:

- the presence of *resources* is drawn from a normal distribution with mean 0.7 and standard deviation 0.4. That is, regions are resource-rich on average but significant inequalities are present. Given that the scenario abstracts a resource-based economy, the level of *economic development* is set to match the presence of resources, whereas the level of *unemployment* is inversely proportional to the presence of resources.
- since recently started, the level of *rebelliousness* is still very low (set to 0.1). It is fueled partly by a slight *socio-economic advantage to insurgency* (set to 0.1) and the presence of some *opportunities to rebel* (set to 0.2). As the insurgency is only nascent, insurgents have a limited *ability to control the population* (set to 0.2).
- clear ethnic differences are present and occasional skirmishes are followed by a large *discrimination of counter-insurgent violence* (set to 0.7).
- the country has a wide variety of terrains with a minority deemed inhospitable. Consequently, the extent to which is *terrain is inhospitable* is drawn from a normal distribution with mean 0.3 and standard deviation 0.5.

Once these hypotheses have been implemented using the Concept Map Editor, the dynamics of the Fuzzy Cognitive Map can be simulated to see how events would unfold independently of geographical influences between regions (Figure 9). The simulation of this toy model of insurgency confirms the expectations of experts, as insurgency gradually arises (Figure 9a) and impairs economic development (Figure 9b), thereby providing further ground for insurgency. Given that the values of some concepts are drawn from probability distributions, the outcome of several runs of the simulation can be different. To explore the range of possible outcomes, Figures 9 (c-d) provide histograms of the final values. Two equally probable outcomes appear for insurgency, either by sustaining it at an intermediate level or by having a high level of conflict. Geographical enablers are high in most cases.

Two factors are involved in influences across regions: the economic development, and the ability of insurgents to control the population (black in Figure 7). The Coupling Editor is used to formaly specify these influences (Figure 8a). A region's level of economic development is impacted by the level of economical development of neighbouring regions, as they are potential trade partners. The relationship is modelled using the 'threshold and impact' template (Figure 8a), such that a (positive or negative) difference of at least 5% between the level of economical development of a region and its trading partners will lead to a difference of 5% in that region (c.f., [58] for the equations). The control exerted by insurgents can hinder trades, which is accounted for by decreasing the level of economical development based on the insurgents' control at a rate of 0.1. Finally, the geography was

abstracted using a planar small-world graph generated using the method proposed by Zhang et al. [60]; parameter values and properties of the networks are displayed in Figure 8b.

In the absence of any intervention, the system stabilizes with high values of insurgency as would be expected from the aforementioned dynamics. To illustrate the framework's ability in handling 'what-if' scenarios, three possible counterinsurgent interventions were modelled: direct support for *economic* development (*e.g.*, by restoring the infrastructure and building local economic capacity), direct support for *security* (*e.g.*, by holding areas and training governmental security forces), and a *combination* of the two. In each case, the intervention was modelled by adding a concept in the Fuzzy Cognitive Map via the Concept Map editor, and linking that concept to the ones that are directly impacted. Consequently, the economic intervention increases the level of economic development (with weight 0.5) whereas the security interventions decreases the ability of insurgents to control the population (with weight 0.5), and the combination does both. The impact of these three possible interventions is summarized in Table 1 by showing the improvements in terms of increase in economic development and decrease in rebelliousness, unemployment, and insurgent control. Results highlight that, in isolation, economic or security interventions have little impact on rebelliousness. However, combining them can achieve a reduction of almost 10%. This is in line with recent military strategies such

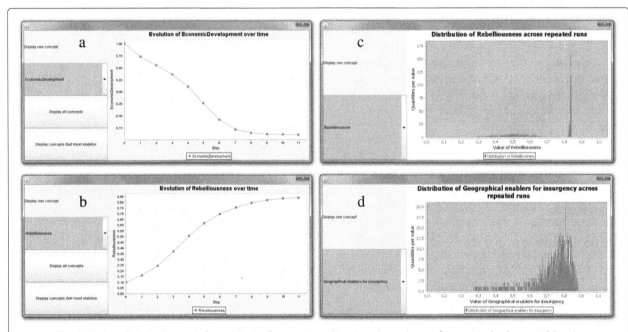

Figure 9 Simulation results. Simulations performed via the Concept Map editor show the evolution of economic development **(a)** and rebelliousness **(b)** over time. The final values of rebelliousness **(c)** and geographical enablers for insurgency **(d)** are displayed based on 10,000 runs of the simulation.

Table 1 Improvements (%) via different interventions

Intervention	Rebelliousness	Economic development	Unemployment	Ability of insurgents to control the population
Economic	2.05	56.57	29.91	None
Security	0.84	99.56	0.76	271.48
Combined	9.87	148.29	181.50	270.74

as the "US National Strategy for Victory in Iraq", which pointed out the importance of intervening simultaneously on political, economical, and security aspects [61]. Our results confirm that a combined strategy is far more powerful than the sum of its parts.

Discussion

In order to develop accurate models of conflicts that can support military analysis, computational techniques need to utilize vasts amounts of data to the best of its potential. However, uncertainty and conflicts abound in data collected by observers or synthesized by experts, making it challenging to effectively incorporate it into quantitative models. Furthermore, adequately capturing the spatial and social dynamics of insurgency tends to require different computational techniques. Our previous work proposed a novel approach to create models of insurgency from imperfect data while accounting for both spatial and social dynamics [17]. While this early framework addressed some of the needs for modelling insurgency, it also came with three limitations. First, the space had to be divided into a set of square cells, which could lead to either an over-simplification of key spatial features (*e.g.*, when cells are too large and cover very distinct neighbourhoods) or a computational burden (*e.g.*, when small cells unnecessarily partition a homogeneous space). Second, the process of model building was centred on the nuanced reading of scholarly articles, which could not be straightforwardly applied to gathering first-hand observations. Finally, the initial development of software highlighted the need for a more intuitive approach to model design, such that modellers could focus on key aspects while the modelling process would be transparent for stakeholders. This paper extends our previous work and addresses all three shortcomings aforementioned. The space is now represented using complex networks, and generators are also provided to create space when detailed maps are not available. We detail how models can be built directly from participants' experience, and provide a proof-of-concept that synthesizes the expertise of five scholars in insurgency. Finally, our focus on usability during software development has resulted in a set of tools that can effectively guide modellers and stakeholders through the process of building a computational model of insurgency.

Our framework supports the integration of data from different sources so that analysts can understand conflicts and run 'what-if' scenarios for counterinsurgency scenarios. It also provides methodological support for scholars of insurgency in two ways. First, it allows for military theories, individually or synthetically, to be tested for consistency by exploring the implications of their suppositions. Second, it allows for intriguing empirical phenomena to be encountered and explored as the disjuncture between the actual world and the world contained within the model. We expect that the use of our framework for these different endeavours will further drive its evolution, both through changes in software and refinement of its mathematical structure.

Our framework currently represents the space using an unweighted planar graph, such that influences either totally flow between two adjacent locations or do not. In practice, adjacency is dynamic: for example, a wall built for security purposes around the district of Adamiyah would virtually cut it off from neighbouring districts (Figure 2) once completed. Adjacency is also a social construct, as members of one ethnic group may rarely move to places populated by another ethnic group during a conflict. Our framework could be augmented to take these aspects into consideration, by having a dynamic network and weighting its edges depending on social factors. Furthermore, the assumption of a planar graph can be challenged due to the spread of violence in non-contiguous areas via tribal ties. This effect is particularly salient in Iraq, which has an estimated 150 tribes and 2,000 clans. While the Ba'athist ideology under Saddam Hussein emphasized the state over ethnic/sectarian divisions, tribal loyalties were nonetheless essential to maintain military support and continue to play a key role in Iraq [62]. Consequently, models often focus on tribal relationships and road network accessibility to link locations [24]. Capturing such relationships can be achieved in two stages. First, the requirement for planarity could be waived, as generating non-planar graphs is straightforward due to the availability of numerous graph generators [63]. Second, the requirement for a single edge between two nodes can also be waived. Frameworks such as wGAP already use multiple labelled edges between nodes [28], which would allow to connect places based on multiple criteria such as geographical and ethnic proximity. Such additions are virtually endless in a modelling endeavour, which highlights the need for a trade-off between the accuracy of the models and the additional complexity brought into the modelling process. Therefore, applications of our framework will prove instrumental in gradually establishing the guidelines for computational methods of insurgency and continuing to meet them via innovative frameworks.

Competing interests
The author declares he has no competing interests.

Acknowledgements
This work benefited from earlier collaborations with Piper Jackson (Simon Fraser University) on cellular automata, Vijay K. Mago (Troy University) on Fuzzy Cognitive Maps, and Simon Frankel Pratt (University of Toronto) on insurgency. The author is indebted to the scholars' whose expertise informed the design of the expert system under a direct approach: Bruce Bueno de Mesquita (New York University), Isabelle Duyvesteyn (Universiteit Utrecht), Samuel S. Stanton, Jr (Groove City College), Ethan Bueno de Mesquita (University of Chicago), and James Morrow (University of Michigan).

References

1. D Galula, *Counterinsurgency Warfare: Theory and Practice* (Praeger Security International, Westerport, Connecticut - London, 1964)
2. F Kitson, *Low Intensity Operations* (Faber and Faber, 1971)
3. S Kalyvas, Warfare in Civil Wars, in *Rethinking the Nature of War* ed. by I Duyvesteyn, J Angstrom (Frank Cass, London, 2005)
4. JM Weinstein, *Inside Rebellion: The Politics of Insurgent Violence* (Cambridge University Press, 2007)
5. SG Tarrow, *The new transnational activism* (Cambridge University Press, 2005)
6. JA Nagl, *Learning to Eat Soup with a Knife: Counterinsurgency Lessons from Malaya and Vietnam* (Praeger Publishers, Westerport, Connecticut - London, 2002)
7. JD Fearon, DD Laitin, American political science review. Ethn. Insurgency Civil War. **97**, 75–90 (2003)
8. S Blouin, Is your world complex? An overview of complexity science and its potential for military applications. Can. Mil. J. **13**(2), 26–36 (2013)
9. DC Arney, K Arney, Modeling insurgency, counter-insurgency, and coalition strategies and operations. J. Defense Modeling Simul. Appl. Methodol. Technol. **10**, 57–73 (2013)
10. JD Fearon, DD Laitin, Integrating qualitative and quantitative methods, in *Janet Box-Steffensmeier* ed. by H Brady, D Collier Oxford Handbook of Political Methodology (Oxford University Press, New York, 2008) pp. 756–76
11. AK Tsadiras, I Kouskouvelis, KG Margaritis, Using Fuzzy Cognitive Maps as a decision support system for political decisions. Lect. Notes Comput. Sci. **2563**, 291–301 (2003)
12. CC Neocleous, CN Schizas, Application of Fuzzy Cognitive Maps to the Political-Economic Problem of Cyprus, in *Proceedings of the International Conference on Fuzzy Sets and Soft Computing in Economics and Finance 2004* (St Petersburg, June 17-20, 2004), pp. 340–349
13. S Graham (ed.), *Cities, War, and Terrorism: Towards an Urban Geopolitics* (John Wiley & Sons, 2008)
14. S Schutte, NB Weidmann, Diffusion patterns of violence in civil wars. Pol. Geogr. **30**(3), 143–152 (2011)
15. M Townsley, SD Johnson, JH Ratcliffe, Space time dynamics of insurgent activity in Iraq. Secur. J. **21**, 139–146 (2008)
16. PJ Giabbanelli, A novel framework for complex networks and chronic diseases. Stud. Comput. Intell. **424**, 207–215 (2012)
17. SF Pratt, PJ Giabbanelli, P Jackson, VK Mago, Rebel with many causes: A computational model of insurgency, in *Proceedings of the 2012 IEEE International Conference on Intelligence and Security Informatics (ISI)* (IEEE, 2012), pp. 90–95

18. M Batty, *Cities and Complexity: Understanding Cities with Cellular Automata, Agent-Based Models, and Fractals* (MIT Press, 2007)
19. NJ Howard, Finding optimal strategies for influencing social networks in two player games. Masters Thesis, Massachusetts Institute of Technology, 2011
20. P Domingos, M Richardson, Mining the Network Value of Customers, in *Proceedings of the Seventh International Conference on Knowledge Discovery and Data Mining* (ACM Press, 2002), pp. 57–66
21. D Kempe, J Kleinberg, E Tardos, Maximizing the spread of influence through a social network, in *Proceedings of the ninth ACM SIGKDD international conference on Knowledge discovery and data mining* (ACM New York, NY, USA, 2003), pp. 137–146
22. BW Hung, SE Kolitz, A Ozdaglar, Optimization-based influencing of village social networks in a counterinsurgency. Lect. Notes Comput. Sci. **6589**, 10–17 (2011)
23. J Tsai, TN Nguyen, M Tambe, Security games for controlling contagion. Proc. Assoc. Adv. Artif. Intell. (AAAI) (2012)
24. S Eyre, R Rotte, T Taggart, C Chewar, A Johnson, P Roos, P Shakarian, Using RASCAL to find key villages in Afghanistan . Small Wars J. **8**(7) (2012)
25. WP Upshur, JW Roginski, DJ Kilcullen, Recognizing systems in Afghanistan. Prism. **3**(3), 87–104 (2012)
26. M Ross, What do we know about natural resources and civil war? J. Peace Res. **41**(3), 337–356 (2004)
27. P Shakarian, GI Simari, D Callahan, Reasoning about complex networks: a logic programming approach. Theory Pract. Logic Programming. **13**(4–5) (2013)
28. M Broecheler, P Shakarian, V Subrahmanian, A scalable framework for modeling competitive diffusion in social networks, in *Proceedings of the IEEE International Conference on Social Computing/Privacy, Security, Risk and Trust* (IEEE, 2010), pp. 295–301
29. Z Li, *Fuzzy Chaotic Systems* (Springer, 2006), pp. 1–11
30. VK Mago, HK Morden, C Friz, T Wu, S Namazi, P Geranmayeh, R Chattopadhyay, V Dabbaghian, Analyzing the impact of social factors on homelessness: a Fuzzy Cognitive Map approach. BMC Med. Inform. Decis. Making. **13**(94) (2013)
31. PJ Giabbanelli, T Torsney-Weir, VK Mago, A fuzzy cognitive map of the psychosocial determinants of obesity. Appl. Soft Syst. **12**(12), 3711–3724 (2012)
32. VK Mago, A Mago, P Sharma, J Mago, Fuzzy logic based expert system for the treatment of mobile tooth. Adv. Exp. Med. Biol. **696**, 607–614 (2011)
33. B Kosko, Fuzzy Cognitive Maps. Int. J. Man Mach. Stud. **24**, 65–75 (1986)
34. B Kosko, Adaptive inference in fuzzy knowledge networks, in *Proceedings of the first IEEE International Conference on Neural Networks (ICNN)* (IEEE, 1987), pp. 261–268
35. CD Stylios, VC Georgopoulos, GA Malandraki, S Chouliara, Fuzzy Cognitive Map architectures for medical decision support systems. Appl. Soft Comput. **8**, 1243–1251 (2008)
36. I Akgun, A Kandakoglu, AF Ozok, Fuzzy integrated vulnerability assessment model for critical facilities in combating the terrorism. Expert Syst. Appl. **37**(5), 3561–3573 (2010)
37. W Stach, L Kurgan, W Pedrycz, M Reformat, Genetic learning of fuzzy cognitive maps. Fuzzy Sets Syst. **153**(3), 371–401 (2005)
38. M Barthelememy, Spatial networks. Phys. Rep. **499**, 1–101 (2011)
39. A Reggiani, P Nijkamp, *Complexity and Spatial Networks* (Springer, 2009)
40. WB Caldwell, Situational update (August 28). Multinational Force-Iraq (2006)
41. T Nishizeki, MS Rahman, *Planar Graph Drawing, Volume 12 of Lecture Notes Series on Computing* (World Scientific, 2004)
42. N Jones, H Ross, T Lynam, P Perez, A Leitch, Mental models: an interdisciplinary synthesis of theory and methods. Ecol. Soc. **16**, 46 (2011)
43. B Moon, R Hoffman, J Novak, A Canas, *Applied Concept Mapping: capturing, analyzing and organizing knowledge* (CRC Press, Boca Raton, Florida, 2011)
44. K Jackson, W Trochim, Concept mapping as an alternative approach for the analysis of open-ended survey responses. Organ. Res. Methods. **5**, 307–332 (2002)
45. PR Neumann, M Smith, *The Strategy of Terrorism: How it Works, and Why It Fails* (Routledge, London and New York, 2008)
46. P Collier, A Hoeffler, Greed and Grievance in civil war. World Bank Policy Res. Working Paper (No. 2355), (2000)
47. I Duyvesteyn, The concept of conventional war and armed conflict, in *Rethinking the Nature of War* ed. by I Duyvesteyn, J Angstrom (Frank Cass, 2005)

48. M Kett, M Rowson, Drivers of violent conflict. J. R. Soc. Med. **100**(9), 403–406 (2007)

49. J Mackinlay, *The Insurgent Archipelago: From Mao to bin Laden* (Hurst, London, 2009)

50. P Justino, Poverty and violent conflict: a micro-level perspective on the causes and duration of warfare. J. Peace Res. **46**(3), 315–333 (2009)

51. CC Fair, Who are Pakistan's militants and their families? Terrorism Pol. Violence. **20**, 49–65 (2008)

52. D Byman, P Chalk, B Hoffman, W Rosenau, D Brannan, *Trends in Outside Support for Insurgent Movements* (RAND, 2001)

53. H Fjelde, I de Soysa, Coercion, co-optation, or cooperation? State capacity and the risk of civil war, 1961–2004. Confl. Manag. Peace Sci. **26**, 5–25 (2009)

54. M Fuhrmann, J Tir, Territorial dimensions of enduring internal rivalries. Confl. Manag. Peace Sci. **26**(4), 307–329 (2009)

55. PM Regan, Third-party interventions and the duration of intrastate conflicts' journal of conflict resolution. J. Confl. Resolution. **46**, 55–73 (2002)

56. B de Graaf, The wars in former Yugoslavia in the 1990s: bringing the state back in', in *Rethinking the Nature of War* ed. by I Duyvesteyn, J Angstrom (Frank Cass, 2005)

57. J Yen, R Langari, *Fuzzy logic: intelligence, control, and information* (Prentice-Hall, Inc., 1998)

58. PJ Giabbanelli, A Alimadad, V Dabbaghian, DT Finegood, Modeling the influence of social networks and environment on energy balance and obesity. J. Comput. Sci. **3**, 17–27 (2012)

59. PJ Giabbanelli, R Crutzen, An agent-based social network model of binge drinking among Dutch adults. J. Artif. Soc. Soc. Simul. **16**(2) (2013)

60. Z Zhang, L Rong, F Comellas, Evolving small-world networks with geographical attachment preference. J. Phys.ics A. **39**(13), 3253–3261 (2006)

61. National Security Council, National strategy for victory in Iraq. (2005)

62. CN Myers, Tribalism and democratic transition in Lybia: lessons from Iraq. Global Tides. **7**, 5 (2013)

63. P Giabbanelli, The small-world property in networks growing by active edges. Adv. Complex Syst. **14**(6), 853–869 (2011)

Harvesting and analysis of weak signals for detecting lone wolf terrorists

Joel Brynielsson, Andreas Horndahl, Fredrik Johansson, Lisa Kaati*, Christian Mårtenson and Pontus Svenson

Abstract

Lone wolf terrorists pose a large threat to modern society. The current ability to identify and stop these kinds of terrorists before they commit a terror act is limited since they are hard to detect using traditional methods. However, these individuals often make use of Internet to spread their beliefs and opinions, and to obtain information and knowledge to plan an attack. Therefore there is a good possibility that they leave digital traces in the form of weak signals that can be gathered, fused, and analyzed.

In this article we present an analysis method that can be used to analyze extremist forums to detect digital traces of possible lone wolf terrorists. This method is conceptually demonstrated using the FOI Impactorium fusion platform. We also present a number of different technologies which can be used to harvest and analyze pieces of information from Internet that may serve as weak digital traces that can be fused using the suggested analysis method in order to discover possible lone wolf terrorists.

Introduction

Today, one of the most challenging and unpredictable forms of terrorism is violent terror acts committed by single individuals, often referred to as lone wolf terrorists or lone actor terrorists. These kinds of terror attacks are hard to detect and defend against by traditional police means such as infiltration or wiretapping, since the lone wolves are planning and carrying out the attacks on their own. The problem of lone wolf terrorism is according to many officials presently on the rise and viewed as a greater threat towards society than organized groups. Even though available statistics suggest that lone wolf terrorists account for a rather small proportion of all terror incidents [1], they can often have a large impact on society [2]. Moreover, many of the major terrorist attacks in the United States (with exception for the 2001 attacks against World Trade Center, the Pentagon, and the White House) were executed by single individuals who were sympathetic to a larger cause—from the Oklahoma City bomber Timothy McVeigh to the Washington area sniper John Allen Muhammad. A similar development can be seen in Europe, where several terrorist attacks have been executed by lone wolf terrorists during the last years. One of the most terrifying acts was the two 2011 terror attacks in

Norway committed by Anders Behring Breivik, killing 77 persons in total.

Even though lone wolf terrorists cannot in general be captured by traditional intelligence techniques, this does not imply that there is nothing counterterrorist organizations can do to prevent them. In fact, despite the popular use of the term "lone wolf terrorist," many of the perpetrators are only loners in their offline life, but are often very active in communicating their views and radical opinions in various discussion groups or other kinds of social media. According to Sageman [3], most lone wolves are part of online forums, especially those who go on to actually carry out terrorist attacks. This makes the Internet an incredibly important source for finding potential lone wolf terrorists.

There are several communities that encourage and influence individuals to act alone (one example being the English language online magazine Inspire, published by the militant Islamist organization al-Qaeda in the Arabian Peninsula). Moreover, individuals that act alone are also often active on and influencing these kinds of communities. Online extremist forums and web sites allow for aberrant beliefs or attitudes to be exchanged and reinforced, and create environments in which otherwise unacceptable views become normalized [4]. In addition to give a possibility of becoming part of a community, the Internet is

*Correspondence: lisa.kaati@foi.se
FOI Swedish Defence Research Agency, SE-164 90 Stockholm, Sweden

also a platform where lone wolves can express their views. The 2010 suicide bomber in Stockholm, Taimour Abdulwahab al-Abdaly, was for example active on Internet and had a YouTube account, a Facebook account, and searched for a second wife on Islamic web pages. Anders Behring Breivik used several different social networking sites such as Facebook and Twitter, and posted his manifesto "2083—A European Declaration of Independence" on the Internet before committing the two terror attacks in Norway. The possession of several social media accounts is obviously perfectly normal, but the actual social media content can indicate that someone is planning a terror attack.

One of the major problems with analyzing information from the Internet is that it is huge, making it impossible for analysts to manually search for information and analyze all data concerning radicalization processes and terror plans of possible lone wolf terrorists. In addition to all material that the analysts can find through the use of various search engines, there are also enormous amounts of information in the so called hidden or Deep Web, i.e., the part of Internet that is not indexed by the search engines' web spiders (e.g., due to password protection or dynamically generated content). To produce fully automatic computer tools for finding terror plans is not possible, both due to the large amounts of data and the deep knowledge that is needed to really understand what is discussed or expressed in written text (or other kinds of data available on the Internet, such as videos or images). However, computer-based support tools that aid the analysts in their investigation could enable them to process more data and give better possibilities to analyze and detect the digital traces [5]. In this article, we suggest the use of techniques such as hyperlink analysis and natural language processing to map the existing dark web forums and to find out which forums and users that can be of interest for human analysts to take a closer look at. In order to combine the outputs from the various suggested methods, we propose using information fusion techniques implemented in FOI's Impactorium fusion platform [6-8].

It is important to understand what can and cannot be done by the type of tools that we present in this article. Our aim is not to produce tools for completely automatic analysis of web information. Rather, the goal is to do research on support tools and methods that help law enforcement officers in ongoing investigations of web extremism. The research presented in this article is part of the fusion framework that we are building, and should be seen as suggestions for how components of a full system could be implemented. Some of the components have already been implemented and evaluated (e.g., the suggested alias matching algorithms, see [9]), while other components are not yet implemented and evaluated (e.g.,

algorithms for discovering warning behaviors such as fixation in postings). A full system for investigation of web extremism must be scalable and also account for privacy and integrity issues as well as what is legally possible and not. An important output of this kind of research is to make legislators aware of the possibilities and limitations of web analysis, in particular concerning opportunities for abuse that might arise if they are implemented operationally.

What is an extreme opinion will of course depend on the viewpoint of the user. This is yet another reason for being careful before implementing systems such as the one described in this article. There must be clear legal guidelines that respect the privacy and integrity of citizens before law enforcement officers can be allowed to do semi-automatic analysis of web content. Controls must be built into the systems, to limit as much as possible the possibilities of abuse.

The rest of this article is outlined as follows. In the section "Lone wolf terrorists," we give a short background to lone wolf terrorism, and the challenge of finding and identifying such individuals before it is too late. In the section "Analysis model" we propose an analysis method for breaking down the problem of analyzing whether a person is a lone wolf terrorist or not into smaller subproblems, such as identifying motives (intent), capabilities, and opportunities. These are broken down further, until more concrete indicators are identified that can be fused in order to make an estimate of how probable it is that an individual is a lone wolf terrorist. This is followed by a short section entitled "Users" containing a description of the potential users of the system and the requirements on their training. The section "Seed identification and topic-filtered web harvesting" describes how topic-filtered web harvesting can be used to collect relevant information, and the section "Techniques for analyzing data" presents techniques that can be used to detect indicators supporting that someone has intent to commit a terror attack. The section "Ranking and assessment of aliases" describes how the gathered indicators can be assessed, and the section "Alias matching" describes how Internet users with multiple aliases can be detected. The section entitled "The FOI Impactorium fusion platform" describes how the Impactorium tool can be used to fuse weak signals for detecting lone wolf terrorists. A discussion about the future potential of this kind of techniques and privacy aspects related to automatic monitoring and analysis tools is provided in the section "Discussion." Finally, some concluding remarks are presented in the section "Conclusions."

Lone wolf terrorists

The definition of a lone wolf terrorist to be used throughout this article is the one used in [10]:

A lone wolf terrorist is a person who acts on his or her own without orders from or connections to an organization.

Lone wolves come from a variety of backgrounds and can have a wide range of motives for their actions. It is observed by [1] that lone wolf terrorists are often creating their own ideologies, combining aversion with religion, society, or politics with a personal frustration. Hence, a lone wolf terrorist can in theory come in any size, any shape, and any ethnicity, as well as representing any ideology [11].

To conduct a successful terror attack, it is necessary to have a number of skills and/or capabilities. For a lone wolf, obtaining the necessary capabilities for an attack might be a problem since they can not in general receive the same kind of systematic training such as, e.g., al-Qaeda terrorists. This may be one of the reasons why lone wolves are rarely suicide bombers, i.e., since such an attack may be too complicated and involves too much preparation [11]. However, the Internet contains much material that potential lone wolf terrorists can use to acquire the knowledge they need to succeed with more simple kinds of attacks. For example, resources such as "the Anarchist Cookbook," "Training with a handgun," "Remote Control Detonation," and "How to make a bomb in the kitchen of your mom" are known to be widespread on the Internet and have been used by lone wolf terrorists for acquiring knowledge on how to build simple pipe bombs, etc.

It is not unusual that lone wolf terrorists are sympathizing with extremist movements, but by definition they are not part of or actively supported by these movements. This makes it very hard to discover and capture lone wolf terrorists before they strike, as traditional methods such as wiretapping and infiltration of the organization are not applicable (since there are no networks or organizations to infiltrate). Moreover, it can be very hard to differentiate between those individuals who are really intending to commit an actual terrorism act, and those who have radical beliefs but stay within the law. In fact, there are very many people that have extremism opinions, but only a minority of those cross the line into taking violent action based on such beliefs.

Digital traces on the Internet

Even though lone wolf terrorists are in general extremely hard to detect by traditional means, there are often many weak signals available that, if detected and fused, can be used as markers of potentially interesting behavior that have to be analyzed deeper and investigated further. As has been mentioned by Fredholm [12], nearly all radicalization of lone wolf terrorists take place on the Internet. One example of a well-known online resource inspiring homegrown terrorism is the online magazine Inspire, published by the Yemen-based organization al-Qaeda in

the Arabian Peninsula (AQAP). Internet based recruitment to terrorist groups is also likely to grow in significance, although recruitment to terror organizations are more often dependent also on offline networks [3,4,13]. These kinds of Internet based radicalization processes often result in various digital traces, created when visiting extremist forums, making postings with offensive content, etc. There are also many other examples where Internet has been used by lone wolves to spread their views and opinions before committing an actual attack. One such example is the anti-abortion activist Scott Roeder who killed the physician George Tiller in Kansas in 2009 [14]. Tiller was one of the few doctors in the United States that performed late abortions, and before the attack Scott Roeder wrote a column on an abortion critical web page where he expressed his views against abortion and Tiller's work. Another example of a lone wolf that was using Internet to express his views is James von Brunn, also known as the Holocaust Museum shooter [15]. Von Brunn was an anti-Semitic white supremacist who was in charge of an anti-Semitic website where he was able to express his views long before the attack.

Once a terror activity has taken place, it is not unusual that, e.g., media collect various digital traces in retrospect, and make complaints about the police's or intelligence service's ineffectiveness or lack of competence. However, although it can be quite easy to find the related evidence once the terror activity already has taken place, it is much more difficult to find out what the relevant clues (weak signals) are before an actual attack has been carried out. There are some signs that can be identified, though. One such sign is activity on radical forums or other forms of social media. Another sign is radical or hateful expressions in written text.

In [16], a number of suggestions of behavioral markers for radical violence that can be identified in written text are presented. These behavioral markers are derived from a list of warning behaviors described in [17]. The behavioral markers considered in [16] are:

Leakage, i.e., the communication to a third party of an intent to do harm to a target, such as the postings made by many school shooters before their attacks.

Fixation, i.e., an increasingly pathological preoccupation with a person or a cause, such as Clayton Waagner's gathering of target information on abortion doctors.

Identification, i.e., the desire to be like an influential role-model, "warrior identification," or identification with a group or larger cause. One example of warrior identification would be the images of Anders Behring Breivik pointing an automatic weapon against the camera.

These behavioral markers can be used as indicators supporting that someone intends to commit a terror attack.

Harvesting and analysis of weak signals for detecting lone wolf terrorists 131

To find relevant digital traces for the behavioral markers, semi-automated analysis is needed since it is impossible for human analysts to manually monitor all the activities of interest on Internet. Such analysis is described in more detail in the section "Techniques for analyzing data." In the next section, an analysis model that can be used to analyze digital traces that a possible lone wolf terrorist might leave on the Internet is presented.

While there is much research on markers for extremist behavior, it is important to realize that the possibility for human biases when defining them always exists. The users who operate the analysis tools must be aware of this and measures must be taken to ensure that, as much as possible, the chosen markers are objective. One way of ensuring this is through extensive training for the analysts. In addition, it must be possible to continuously update and adapt the chosen markers if, for instance, a person has been wrongly identified as an extremist and the reason for the mistake can be identified as a single marker. This highlights the need for always explicitly storing the chain of evidence or markers that have been used for reaching a certain conclusion.

Analysis model

A classical approach to address complex problems is to break them down into more manageable sub-problems, solve these separately and then aggregate the results into a solution for the overarching problem. This approach is well suited for the analysis of weak signals. For each potential threat actor, which in most cases will be represented by one or many aliases (user names), a model is created through the successive decomposition of the threat hypothesis into a number of indicators, corresponding to the weak signals that we want to capture. Figure 1 shows a (simplified) model of how the decomposition of the hypothesis "Actor X is a potential lone wolf terrorist" could look like. At the first level, the hypothesis is separated in three general threat assessment criteria:

Intent (or *motive*), *Capability*, and *Opportunity*. If all these are met there is a potential risk for an attack. The next level of decomposition shows a number of indicators that can possibly be detected through reconnaissance on the Internet, and the indicator "Materiel procurement" which could also be detected through other information channels.

Once an initial decomposition is done, parallel sub-processes can be started for the various sub-hypotheses. As an example, assuming that an analyst believes that someone needs to have both intent and capability in order to commit a terror attack, one sub-process can focus on looking for possible intent (e.g., based on radical postings made by the individual) while the other one is focusing on capability (e.g., web sites discussing how to make bombs). The results from the various sub-processes are then fused and can be used to assess whether someone has an increased likelihood of committing an act of terror, resulting in a list of potentially dangerous actors that might be subject to further analysis. It is important to note that since we consider digital traces that are left on the Internet, it is only possible to detect aliases that might have an increased risk of committing an act of terror, but how the physical person behind the alias can be detected is another problem that is outside the scope of this article.

In this work we focus our attention on the problem of finding out whether someone has the intent to commit an act of terror. In the section "Techniques for analyzing data" we describe techniques that can be utilized in order to detect digital traces that can be used as evidence for some of the identified indicators supporting that someone has the intent of committing a terror attack.

Users

As mentioned previously, this article describes concepts and prototypes that could be implemented in an operational system for web analysis of extremist behavior. The potential user of this system is a law enforcement officer

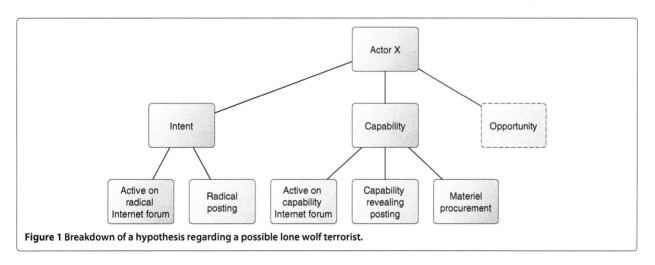

Figure 1 Breakdown of a hypothesis regarding a possible lone wolf terrorist.

who today investigates web extremism by browsing well-known extremist web sites and manually searches for signs of planned terror attacks or individuals that have to be investigated more closely. By developing a better support system for this, it will be possible to analyze more data and reduce the risk for false negatives. It is important that the potential introduction of such systems is accompanied by clear regulations regarding what data the user is, and is not, allowed to investigate. Prototype systems such as the one developed by the project described herein could be an important help for legislators and human rights organizations to evaluate the consequences of allowing or banning different kinds of automatic analyses.

It is important that the users of web analysis systems are properly trained. In addition to the training in legal, privacy and integrity issues that was touched upon above, they must also have proper training in decision theory to be able to avoid as many as possible of the human biases that might otherwise induce them to construct non-objective analysis models and markers. Total impartiality when constructing these if of course a chimera. Hence it is necessary to include checks and balances in the system, both in the technology and in the form of peer reviews of both analysis models (including markers) and the results of analyses.

We believe that serious gaming [18,19] training could be an important component to help ensure that the users of the system meet these requirements. By making the training as realistic as possible, it will be easier to train the analyst to detect their own biases. This is, however, just an idea that has not yet been tested and will not be elaborated upon further in the article.

Seed identification and topic-filtered web harvesting

The amount of content on the Internet is enormous and it does not make sense to try to search for digital traces from potential lone wolf terrorists without any guidance. Therefore, it is necessary to limit the search and instead focus on a smaller subset of the Internet. Although there are large portions of the web that are not reachable using search engines such as Google, many extremist web sites are well-known, since part of the idea is to communicate ideologies and other messages to the larger masses. Moreover, a majority of extremist web sites contain links to other extremist sites, according to a study presented in [20]. Hence, it makes sense to use well-known extremist sites as seeds[1], and then try to identify other interesting forums and sites that in some way are connected to the web sites, by using the seeds as a starting point (it is not necessarily so that only extremist web sites are of interest, also "normal" web sites containing information regarding an indicator may be interesting to watch).

The process of systematically collecting web pages is often referred to as crawling. Usually, the crawling process starts from one or more given source web page(s) (the seeds described above) and follows the source page hyperlinks to find more web pages [21]. The crawling process is repeated on each new page and continues until no more new pages are discovered or until a certain number of pages (that have been determined beforehand) have been collected. By treating the collected web sites as nodes in a graph, and by creating an edge between two web sites each time a hyperlink is found between them, it becomes possible to create a (large) network that can be analyzed further to find out which the most interesting web sites are. By using hyperlink analysis a large number of potential extremist forums can be found. However, many of the web sites will be perfectly normal, making them rather uninteresting for intelligence analysts. Hence, it is of uttermost interest to be able to automatically separate web sites with interesting content from the ones with normal, uninteresting content (that is, from a counterterrorist perspective). In order to make this kind of analysis, natural language processing (NLP) and text mining can be of great use. As a first step, we suggest having a predefined list of keywords to search for on the crawled web pages. If enough of the terms are encountered on a web page, it is marked as interesting and the web site is added to the queue. However, if they are marked as irrelevant, the web page becomes discarded, and no links are followed from it. The same holds true for URLs that are part of a *white list*, to which the analyst can choose to add web sites matching the keywords but are judged not to be relevant for further analysis (e.g., web sites with the purpose of countering extremist propaganda). While crawling the web it is also possible to discard links that are broken. If a web site is inaccessible due to password protection, the analyst can be asked to either choose to discard the link, or to manually create a user login and enter the user credentials to access material on the site. Our suggested approach is in many ways similar to the approach used for identifying online child pornography networks in [22].

To evaluate our web mining approach, we have implemented a proof-of-concept web spider. The goal is to create a network consisting of web sites, forums (discussion boards), forum posts and aliases. An example of such a network can be found in Figure 2. As can be noted, the network becomes very large and therefore it is important to prune the network using natural language processing techniques. The spider is based on the crawler Crawler4J[2] and extended with methods for Internet forum information extraction.

Given a set of seeds (web page URLs), the web spider expands the network by following all links that can be found on the page that meet a set of conditions. First of

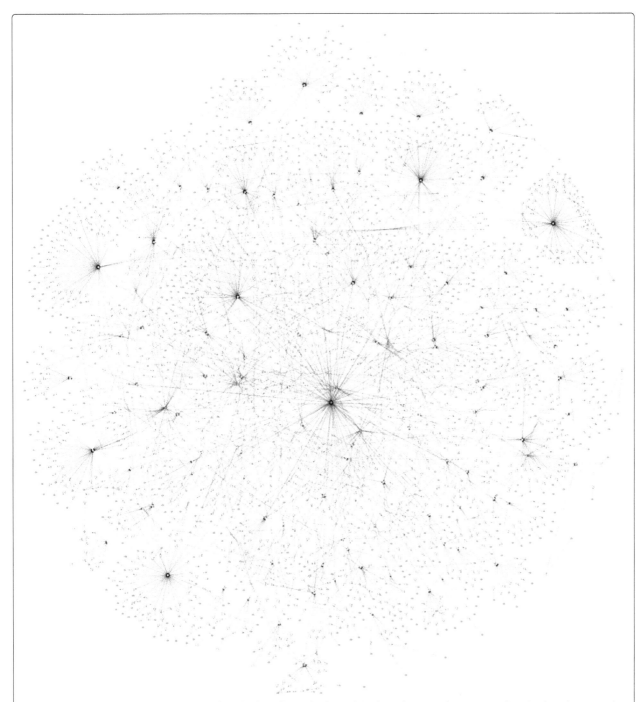

Figure 2 A network graph created by our web spider based on a single seed. Nodes in the network represent a discussion board, posts, and aliases.

all the link should point to a web page, and secondly the content of the web page should be classified as interesting (matching a list of one or several predefined keywords). If the page represents a discussion forum, tailored content extraction algorithms are applied. The algorithms extract the user aliases and their posts, and add this information to the network (to be further used in the web

site and alias assessment phases). In our initial proof-of-concept implementation, we have developed information extraction algorithms for a specific representative Internet forum.

In a real-world setting, one needs to address the fact that Internet forums or web sites may have significantly different structures. Hence, a flexible strategy for learning the structure of a new site is desirable. One way to overcome this obstacle is to let an algorithm guess the structure, try to extract relevant information and let a human (the analyst) verify the results. Another way is to let humans analyze the hypertext representation and locate specific tags that can be used as markers for where to find relevant information and how to separate posts.

Techniques for analyzing data

Once the collection of relevant data from the Internet is done the content of the web site and forums needs to be analyzed. In this section we present techniques that can be used by intelligence analysts to analyze data with the aim of discovering indicators supporting that someone has intent to commit an act of terror. The goal of the process described in this section is to obtain a list of potential lone wolf terrorists that need further investigation. Comparing our suggested approach to related work already described in existing research literature (see, e.g., [23-25]), two main differences can be identified: 1) our focus on lone wolf terrorists rather than terror organizations, and 2) our focus on semi-automated tools for supporting the analyst, rather than fully automated tools. While it obviously is interesting to construct fully automatic tools for web analysis, it is more realistic to consider a web analysis system that consists of a human user that is supported by tools such as those described in this article. In addition to the problems of making reliable automated tools, there are also cultural and ethical requirements that make it interesting to consider semi-automated tools [5].

From the topic-filtered web harvesting, a set of interesting web sites or forums are collected. The idea is to make a deeper analysis of these sites by making use of natural language processing and text mining techniques. One type of text mining known as affect analysis has earlier been identified as being useful for measuring the presence of hate and violence in extremist forums [26]. To be able to use natural language processing techniques, it is necessary to first preprocess the retrieved content from the web sites. This preprocessing step for example includes removing HTML tags and tokenizing the text into sentences. From the collected data, all aliases are extracted and a model is created for each alias. The fact that all identified aliases are active on web sites that are considered radical qualifies them as candidates for further investigation.

Intent

We have in [16] identified a set of indicators for someone having the intent to commit an act of terror and becoming a lone wolf terrorist. The list of indicators is not comprehensive and we use it to illustrate how it is possible to automatically detect evidence for indicators using text analysis techniques. The indicators that we use are:

- the fact that someone is active on a radical web page,
- radical expression in postings,
- leakage,
- identification,
- fixation.

In the following sections we describe techniques that can be used to automatically detect these indicators from text.

Active on radical web pages

The fact that someone is active on a radical web page can be revealed by identifying any kind of activity on the set of web pages that are collected using the topic-filtered web harvesting. The web pages that are collected are all considered to be radical in some sense and therefore we can assume that all users that are active on any of the web pages may be considered radical. This assumption does not necessarily hold true in practice since people may post things on extremist web pages without being extremists themselves. In such cases it is however unlikely that other indicators will be activated for the person anyway.

Radical expression in postings

Classifiers for estimating the level of radical content or other types of interestingness in a text (e.g., a blog post or a tweet) can be built in various ways. One alternative is to manually create a discriminant-word lexicon that can be used for classifying the text; the higher fraction of terms in the text present in the lexicon, the higher the level of interestingness. To manually create such a list may be a tricky task, and it may also be necessary to update the list with regular intervals, as the popular words to express radical opinions or other kinds of topics may change over time. Within the research field of text mining, it has been shown that handcrafted lexicons are often not the best alternative for text classification tasks. Instead, various unsupervised and supervised learning algorithms are more frequently used. Irrespectively of which type of technique that is used, some input will be needed from an expert. In case a handcrafted list of words is used, the actual terms to use have to be specified by experts. In the case of an unsupervised approach, a list of seed terms has to be suggested by the experts which then can be used to automatically find and classify other terms that, e.g., are synonyms or antonyms to the manually labeled terms, or in other ways are co-occurring with terms with a known label. Finally, in the supervised case, the expert has to manually classify a number of text samples into the classes *radical* and *non-radical* (or *interesting* and *non-interesting* in the more general case). It can be expected that the supervised approach will yield the best performance, but this comes with a cost of finding useful data for training purposes, and the manual annotation of the training data. This kind of methods have previously been proposed in [26].

One type of classifier that is often used for various supervised natural language classification tasks is the naïve Bayes classifier. This is the classifier we currently intend to use in our system. The classifier, however, still needs to be learned using representative training samples, which remains as future work. An advantage of such an approach is that it is easy to interpret for humans, making it possible to verify that a learned model looks reasonable. Furthermore, it is more computationally effective than many alternative algorithms, making the learning phase faster. In order to use such a classifier for discriminating between texts with *radical* and *non-radical* content, a natural first step would be to tokenize the text. By extracting features such as unigrams (single words), bigrams (pairs of words) or trigrams (triples of words) from the tokenized text, this can be used for training the classifier and to classify new texts once the classifier has been trained. Since there would be very many features if allowing for all possible unigrams and bigrams, a necessary step would be feature reduction, in which the most informative features $f_1, \ldots, f_n$ are selected from the training data and used as leaf nodes in the resulting classifier. By extracting features from new texts to be classified, we can according to Bayes' theorem calculate the posterior probability of the text having a certain label (e.g., *radical* or *non-radical*) as:

$$P(label|f_1, \ldots, f_n) = \frac{P(label)P(f_1, \ldots, f_n|label)}{P(f_1, \ldots, f_n)}. \quad (1)$$

Now, by using the conditional independence assumption of the naïve Bayes model, this is reduced to:

$$P(label|f_1, \ldots, f_n) \propto P(label) \prod_{i=1}^{n} P(f_i|label). \quad (2)$$

This conditional independence assumption is rather strong and does not necessarily hold in practice. Given the class label, the occurrence of a word is not independent of all other words, even though this is assumed in Equation 2. This may result in that conditionally dependent words can have too much influence on the classification. Despite this, naïve Bayes methods have been shown to work well for many real-world problems. The needed probabilities on the right side of Equation 2 can easily be estimated from the training data (using Laplace smoothing to account for zero counts).

Other popular choices for text classification tasks is the use of maximum entropy classifiers (relying on the principle of choosing the most uniform distribution satisfying the constraints given by the training data) or support vector machines. Regardless of the choice of classifier, the most important part is to get hold of enough training data of good quality. Once this is solved, the next big question is which features to use. To use unigrams as features is the most straightforward way and will most likely be enough to separate terrorism-related discussions from many other

kinds of discussions of no relevance to the subject matter. However, it is not obvious that unigrams are enough for more fine-grained classification, e.g., separating between postings where terrorist acts are discussed or reported on, and where intentions to actually commit terrorism acts are expressed. It may therefore be beneficial to use bigrams or trigrams to allow for a less shallow analysis. The feature set to be used in our implementation will be decided in future experiments.

It should be noted that what ought to be taken to constitute radical behavior is often in the eyes of the beholder. However, since such judgements are made by analysts already today (although manually), creation of algorithms that classify posts according to the same criteria would be no different from todays' situation (except for that the classification of texts then can be made on a much larger scale).

Leakage

A notable characteristic of lone wolf terrorists is that they often announce their views and intentions in advance. In the samples of school shooters (a phenomenon closely related to lone wolf terrorism) analyzed in [27], it can be seen that a majority of the perpetrators revealed their intentions in social media before carrying out their attacks. Leakage is the communication to a third party of an intent to do harm to a target. Leakage can be either intentional or unintentional and more or less specific regarding the actual attack [17].

Leaked information of intent is likely to contain auxiliary verbs signaling intent (i.e., "…will …," "…am going to …," "…should …") together with words expressing violent action, either overtly or, perhaps more likely, through euphemisms. Based on these observations, leakage can potentially be detected by using a simple approach where the analyzed text after stemming or lemmatization (reducing the end of a word in order to return the word's common base form) is matched against a predefined word list of violent actions. Since there is a large number of synonyms that can be used for the verbs signaling a violent intent, the use of an ontology such as the lexical database WordNet[3] in which semantic relations between synonym sets are expressed can be used. An example of such a semantic relation would be that the verb "massacre" belongs to the same synonym set as the words "mow down" and "slaughter." By using such semantic relations, the number of words that must be explicitly defined in the word list of terms to search for can be decreased. Since the occurrence of a single word expressing a violent action is far from enough for classifying a sentence as being a linguistic marker for leakage, part-of-speech tagging should also be taken into account when searching for indications of leakage. This kind of text analysis methods obviously has a hard time coping with ironic statements, leading to a risk of false positives where jokes are classified as a potential marker or leakage. However, by restricting the attention to sites or forums that through automated content analysis or prior knowledge are known to contain content related to violent extremism, false positives can most likely be kept at an acceptable level.

Example To illustrate leakage we use a sentence from Anders Behring Breivik's manifesto "2083—A European Declaration of Independence":

> *We will ensure that all category A and B traitors, the enablers of Islamization and the destroyers of our cultures, nations and societies, will be executed.*

In the sentence, a verb signalling intent such as "...will..." is followed by an expression of violent action ("executed"). In WordNet, "executed" belongs to the same synonym set as "put to death."

Identification

The warning behavior called identification is defined as a behavior indicating a desire to be a "pseudo-commando," have a warrior mentality, closely associate with weapons or other military or law enforcement paraphernalia, identify with previous attackers or assassins, or identify oneself as an agent to advance a particular cause [16]. This rather broad definition shows the complexity of the phenomenon. To make it more manageable, we follow [17] and divide identification into two subcategories: identification with radical action and identification with a role model. Group identification is considered an essential part of the radicalization of lone wolves as well as organized terrorists.

Identification with a group or cause can be expressed for instance by a usage of positive adjectives in connection with mentioning of the group. Similarly, a usage of negative adjectives in connection with mentioning of a group or person may indicate negative identification. To find out which positive or negative sentiments that are present in a text, or which kinds of emotions that are expressed, sentiment and affect analysis techniques can be used. References to the group can be detected by investigating the use of first person plural pronouns ("we" and "us"), while much use of third person plural pronouns (e.g., "they" and "them") according to [28] can be used as an indicator of extremism. In [28] the software LIWC is used to analyze the content of al-Qaeda transcripts.

Identification with a warrior, the so-called warrior mentality, can be spotted through the use of a certain terminology, while a sense of moral obligation can be expressed through the usage of words related to duty, honor, justice, etc.

Identification with another radical thinker can, aside from frequent quoting and mentioning, be expressed by a similarity in language. It is common that the same terminology as the role model is used and there is a possibility that even a similar sentence structure is used. In these cases it is possible to use author recognition techniques to identify similarities.

Example There are many examples of images and videos posted on the Internet where lone wolf terrorists pose with weapons long before the attack, such as the pictures of Anders Behring Breivik wearing a compression sweater and pointing an automatic weapon against the camera. Other examples of identification can be found among school shooters. One such example is Matthew Murray who killed four people at a church and a missionary training school in Colorado. Murray compared himself to the Columbine shooter Harris and Hui (who was responsible for the shooting at Virginia Tech University) in an Internet posting.

Fixation

The warning behavior fixation indicates a preoccupation with a person or a cause, for instance increasing perseveration on the object of fixation, increasingly strident opinion, or increasingly negative characterization of the object of fixation [17].

Fixation can be observed as a tendency to repeatedly comment on an issue or a person, which in written communication would result in text wherein one person, group or issue is mentioned by the subject with a significantly higher frequency than it is mentioned by other discussants. Also, frequent combinations of certain key terms, for instance "jew" and "communism," can reveal a fixation with a certain idea. Fixation taking the form of extensive fact-gathering can only be detected in communication if a person chooses to share some of the information.

In order to find this kind of fixation in text, the relative frequency of key terms relating to named entities such as persons, organizations, etc., can be counted. To find out which words that relate to named entities, algorithms for named entity recognition can be used. Implementations of such algorithms are available in free natural language processing toolkits such as NLTK and GATE.

Example An example text where fixation can be detected can again be found in Anders Behring Breivik's manifesto "2083—A European Declaration of Independence":

> *It is not only our right but also our duty to contribute to preserve our identity, our culture and our national sovereignty by preventing the ongoing Islamisation. There is no Resistance Movement if individuals like us refuse to contribute... Time is of the essence. We have only a few decades to consolidate a sufficient level of*

resistance before our major cities are completely demographically overwhelmed by Muslims. Ensuring the successful distribution of this compendium to as many Europeans as humanly possible will significantly contribute to our success. It may be the only way to avoid our present and future dhimmitude (enslavement) under Islamic majority rule in our own countries.

In the text, it can be noted that words related to Islam ("Islamisation," "Muslims," and "Islamic") are mentioned with a high frequency.

Ranking and assessment of aliases

After collecting relevant data using the topic-filtered web harvesting, the data is analyzed. The first part of the analysis is to identify all aliases that are present in the collected data. Thereafter the data is analyzed using techniques described in the previous section while searching for indicators for intent of committing an act of terror.

Online instantiation of model templates

Once an alias is identified in the collected data, the alias is added to a list of aliases that need to be analyzed further. Naturally, one indicator for intent is not enough to classify the alias as a potential lone wolf terrorist with good reliability. However, having observed one indicator is a good reason to start looking for other indicators. In order to make a more detailed assessment of the alias, a threat model template (Figure 1) is instantiated for the alias. When a threat model for an alias has been instantiated, all relevant information related to the alias is connected to the indicators in the model. The threat model defines how to combine indicators of intent as well as other relevant indicators and can be used to do a summarized assessment. Moreover, the threat model can be used to determine which indicators we should collect more information about in order to improve the assessment.

Combined indicator assessment

Since one indicator alone is insufficient for classifying an alias as a potential lone wolf terrorist with certainty, we need to combine the information of several indicators in order to make an adequate assessment. There are several potential ways to combine the indicators of intent that we have described in this article. One way is to require that we need positive evidence for all indicators in order to be able to say that the alias has an evil intent with sufficient credibility. Another way is to use a weighted average model where some of the indicators are more important than others. A third way is to demand that a certain number of indicators, e.g., three out of five, are sufficient in order to say that an alias has intent. A fourth way is to use a more advanced tailored statistical model such as Bayesian belief networks which makes it possible to define complex

relationships between indicators. Since the statistical relationship between the indicators presented in this article are unexplored, the use of such a model is not feasible at the moment.

In addition to the current degree of belief that an alias has an intent to commit a terror attack, the change over time in the degree of belief may provide valuable information. For example, an alias for which we have identified two indicators and the degree of belief is increasing slowly but surely, might be as interesting as an alias for which we have identified three indicators and the degree of belief is unchanged or decreasing.

Representing indicator states/values

The current state of an indicator can be represented in numerous ways. One way is to represent the current state by a binary value that expresses if we have evidence for the indicator or not. Another way is to use discrete values such as "unknown," "weak," "moderate," and "strong." A third way is to let a continuous value represent the probability (or belief mass, if we are using Dempster-Shafer theory) that the indicator is true. Non-binary approaches allow a more detailed way of describing the current state of an indicator but requires a method (manual or automatic) that specifies how to set the indicator state based on available evidence. For example, three radical message board entries are required to set the indicator value to moderate.

Alias matching

One problem that arises when analyzing data from the Internet is the fact that people may use several different aliases. There are many potential reasons for an individual to use multiple aliases. It could be the case that the first alias has been banned on the forum, or that the author simply forgot the password to the original account. It could also be the case that an alias has lost the others' trust in the discussions, or that the author has developed bad personal relationships with other individuals at the forum. Another potential reason is that the author creates multiple aliases in order to be able to write messages that support his or her own arguments. No matter what the reason is for having multiple aliases, the fact that many people use several aliases makes an analysis more difficult since it is harder to fuse weak signals generated by a single user (individual) that is using multiple aliases.

Alias matching refers to techniques that can be used to identify a user that has several different aliases. If a user is active on a number of web sites, forums, or other kinds of social media and uses several different aliases, alias matching can be very difficult. In [29] and [9], techniques for detecting multiple aliases in discussion boards are described. Some of the components that can be used to detect multiple aliases are:

- similarities in alias name,
- stylometry,
- temporal information,
- similarities in networks (social networks or network of threads).

If a user is using the same alias everywhere it is simple, and if there are only small variations in user names, entity matching approaches such as the Jaro-Winkler distance metric [30] can be useful. However, if a user uses aliases which are more or less arbitrarily selected, the actual alias name as such cannot be used for the matching process.

Stylometry or analysis of writing style makes use of the assumption that every person has a more or less individual "writeprint" (cf. fingerprint) that is based on the way we write. A writeprint is created using different characteristics that can be discovered in text. Such characteristics could for example be choice of words, language, syntactic features, syntactical patterns, choice of subject, or different combinations of these characteristics [31]. Internet-scale authorship identification based on stylometry is described in [32]. Temporal information can also be used to identify users with multiple aliases. Temporal information could be information about what time of the day messages are posted or frequency of messages during longer time periods. Social network analysis (SNA) [33,34] could also be used to help in the identification of authors by computing structural similarities between different aliases. If two aliases post to the same forums, on the same topics, and regularly comment on the same type of posts, it is more likely that they are in fact the same. It is also possible to use abstraction techniques such as simulation [35] to determine the likelihood with which two aliases are the same. By combining various information about the aliases and the messages written by aliases the possibility to identify users with multiple aliases increases. In [9] we have shown that the combination of temporal information and stylometric information can yield good accuracy when detecting the use of multiple aliases in web forums. The problem of alias matching is important for the system proposed herein since we have to combine all aliases that are used by the user of interest in order to estimate the likelihood that an Internet user has intent to become a lone wolf terrorist.

Identifying the physical person behind an alias is another, although related, problem. If messages have been posted on non-radical forums it might be possible for police or intelligence services to get information about the IP address that has been used when making the posting, but this cannot be expected to be retrieved from extremist forums. Moreover, the IP address may not necessarily be of interest, since people can use dynamic IP numbers, use computers at Internet cafes, connect through VPNs, etc.

The FOI Impactorium fusion platform

The FOI Impactorium fusion platform [6-8] is a prototype implementation that can be used to fuse information from heterogenous sources. Impactorium can be used to create top-down threat models as the one presented earlier in the section entitled "Analysis model." The threat models can be constructed using a graphical user interface or by using Impactorium's RESTful webservice API. The API makes it possible to create threat models or instantiate model templates as part of an automated process. The API can be used to instantiate a threat model such as the one depicted in Figure 1, when an alias that is active on a radical forum is detected. The API can also be used to update the threat model or add evidence to indicators. For example, an algorithm that performs alias matching can use the API to merge two threat models. Impactorium also provides a subscription mechanism which can be used to instantaneously receive a notification when a model component, such as an indicator or evidence, has been updated or added. This functionality can be used to notify an analyst when the degree of belief that an alias is a potential terrorist exceeds a threshold or to notify other analysis tools that new models have been created.

In Impactorium the values of the different indicators are fused in order to come up with an answer to the original problem, i.e., to which degree the collected evidence or weak signals support the hypothesis that an individual is (or will become) a lone wolf terrorist. A screen shot exemplifying how the values of a threat model are inferred in the Impactorium tool is shown in Figure 3. In the figure, the problem of deciding whether someone has the intent to commit a terror act is broken down into five indicators: active (on a radical web site), radical expression (in a posting), leakage, identification, and fixation. In the figure, evidence for the indicators "active on a radical web site" and "radical expression" has been identified.

Various combination functions such as min, max, average, or weighted sum can be used to make inferences. Except for combining the various digital traces that have been collected, Impactorium also allows for fusion of information coming from other sources, such as intelligence reports or data from sensors. As an example, if customs provide information that an individual has bought large quantities of fertilizers, this information can be inserted into the threat model calculations. In Figure 3, the likelihood that an actor has intent to become a lone wolf terrorist has increased since evidence for two (of the five) indicators are found.

When monitoring extremist web sites, a threat model is created for each alias and information about each alias is gathered. Based on the results of the fusion, a list of aliases worth monitoring more closely is created. An example of such a list is shown in Figure 4. The list can be used by

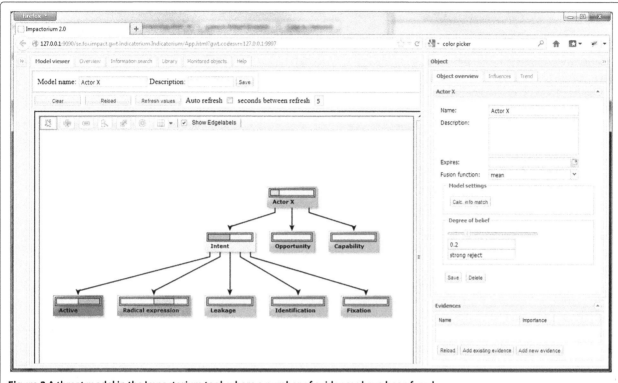

Figure 3 A threat model in the Impactorium tool, where a number of evidences have been fused.

an analyst to direct further investigations and resources to the aliases on the list that have the highest likelihood of becoming lone wolf terrorists.

The analysis models in Impactorium are meant to be continuously updated and adapted to the current situation. It is thus easy for the user to change them if, e.g., too many false positives are detected. Both the structure of the models and the model parameters (e.g., how much evidence that is needed before an individual is indicated as a potential lone wolf) can be changed. An indicator or

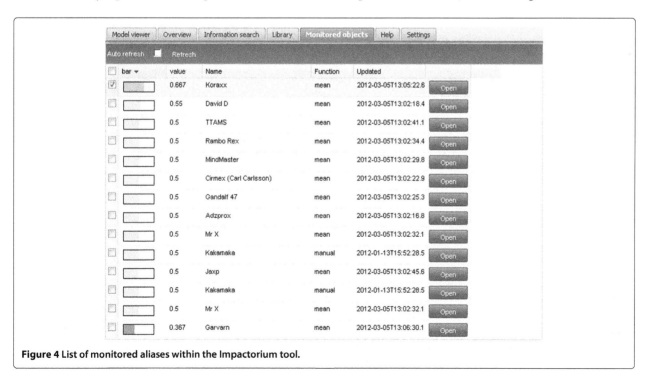

Figure 4 List of monitored aliases within the Impactorium tool.

marker that has been determined to no longer be useful can also be forgotten.

Since the content of web sites such as extremist forums is not static, the overall process has to be repeated over and over again. The first stages can however be done more seldom than the later phases, since forums and web sites of interest will pop up or become obsolete on a much slower rate than the change in content within the web sites. It is also important to note that duration of time is a significant factor in this process. It is very likely that becoming a lone wolf terrorist is not something that happens over night, but is rather a process that can take several years.

Discussion

The search for digital traces on Internet that can be fused in order to try to find potential lone wolf terrorists must be considered a fine balance between people's security at the one hand, and people's privacy on the other hand. To automatically search through large masses of text and use text mining techniques to try to identify whether a piece of text should be treated as radical or not can by some people be seen as a violation of privacy. The needs of the law enforcement and intelligence communities and the privacy concerns must be balanced. It should, however, be noted that analysts are already checking extremist forums as of today. It is always a human analyst that should check the reasons for why a user has been classified as having a motive or intent of being a potential lone wolf terrorist, and whether actions should be taken to bind an alias to a physical person, and to collect more information using other means. The analyst can also always decide whether an alias should be removed from the list of "suspect" individuals. This highlights the need for a mixed-initiative [36,37] system with a human-in-the-loop as a central component.

Having such a human-in-the-loop makes it possible to tolerate a higher number of false positives than would be acceptable in a fully automated system. Since there is a trade-off between false positives and false negatives, the increase of false positives should decrease the number of false negatives (i.e., classifying weak signals from potential terrorists as non-interesting). Hence, the suggested method should be thought of as a help for the analyst to filter out a smaller set of data to look at, rather than a method to be fully automated.

In the description of the suggested methodology, we have discussed how many indicators that are needed in order to say something about the intent of an individual, but there is also a question of how much material that is needed in order to trigger a single indicator. This is not a question with an easy answer since it most probably will vary for different indicators. Several radical posts are clearly more interesting than a single radical post,

but several leakages are not necessarily worse than a single one. It also depends on whether binary, discrete, or continuous states are used, as mentioned earlier. The thresholds to use for deciding when, or how strongly, an indicator should be triggered remains as future work.

The analysis models and markers and indicators used will need to be continuously updated and adapted, both to keep track of changing behavior on the Internet and in order to, for instance, remove markers and models that have wrongly identified someone as a lone wolf terrorist. It is important that the tools used include ways of doing this, similar to the model adaptation tools that are implemented in the Impactorium tool.

While we have focused on analyzing text in this article, it is worth noticing that a lot of material posted to web sites and social media is not text. On extremist forums, it is not unusual with video clips showing executions, bomb making instructions, etc. There is much ongoing research on image and video content analysis, as well as content-based image retrieval (CBIR, see [38] for an overview) that can be useful in the future, but as far as we know, no mature techniques for identifying radical content in video with good precision exists as of today. Another possibility is to automatically extract speech from audio and video content and transcribe it into text. Such technology is, e.g., available in a beta version for certain English-language videos on YouTube. The technology is still far from perfect, but it can be expected that it will work well in the foreseeable future, and then also for other languages than English.

The techniques we have proposed in this article are not constrained to work for a single language. The classifiers we are suggesting to use for classifying content as being radical or not can work for any language. However, they need to be learned with representative samples for each language of interest. Moreover, many resources for text mining (such as WordNet) are language dependent and only works for English. One way to deal with content in several languages is to develop separate lexicons for the various languages of interest. Another way that demands less resources is to preprocess the text using automatic machine translation into a common language, and then use the preprocessed text as input to the classifier. Such an approach will probably give worse precision, but demand less resources.

Lastly, it is important to point out that the concept tools presented here are research suggestions and not an operative system. The described concept tools are part of an ongoing fusion framework development effort and are partially implemented within that platform, where they will be used for research experiments in the future. A full implementation of support tools for web analysis will need to include support for privacy and integrity control as well as training support to avoid human biases when constructing the analysis models and identifying the indicators.

Conclusions

One of the major problems when it comes to detecting possible lone wolf terrorists is that there is no consistent or typical profile of a lone wolf. Moreover, the lone wolves are hard to capture using traditional intelligence methods since there are no physical groups to infiltrate or wiretap. However, there are many concrete actions and activities (that are not necessarily illegal) taken by an individual that can be treated as weak signals and that combined may indicate an interest in terrorism acts. Recognizing and analyzing digital traces from online activities of possible lone wolf terrorists is one key to the difficult problem of detecting lone wolf terrorists before they strike. We have presented a framework for working with such digital traces through the use of techniques such as topic-filtered web harvesting and content analysis using natural language processing. Parts of the proposed system have been implemented, while work remains to be done for other parts.

It is important to highlight that the proposed system is not intended to be fully automatic. The central component of the system will be the human analyst, but this analyst will be supported in the work of finding, analyzing, and fusing digital traces of interest for finding potential lone wolf terrorists. In the future, we would like to perform more detailed experiments with the prototype system, to more properly evaluate the extent to which it is useful for law enforcement officers.

Endnotes

[1] The actual seeds to use are up to the analyst to define and are outside the scope of this article.

[2] http://code.google.com/p/crawler4j/

[3] http://wordnet.princeton.edu/

Competing interests
The authors declare that they have no competing interests.

Authors' contributions
All authors drafted, read and approved the final manuscript.

Acknowledgements
This research was financially supported by the Swedish Governmental Agency for Innovation Systems (VINNOVA) through the VINNMER program, and by the R&D program of the Swedish Armed Forces.

References

1. R Spaaij, The enigma of lone wolf terrorism: an assessment. Stud. Confl. Terrorism. **33**(9), 854–870 (2010)
2. COT, Lone-Wolf Terrorism. Tech. Rep., Instituut voor Veiligheids- en Crisismanagement (2007)
3. M Sageman, *Leaderless Jihad: Terror Networks in the Twenty-First Century.* (University of Pennsylvania Press, 2008)
4. T Stevens, PR Neumann, Countering Online Radicalisation: A Strategy for Action. Tech. Rep., International Centre for the Study of Radicalisation and Political Violence (2009)
5. J Brynielsson, A Horndahl, L Kaati, C Mårtenson, P Svenson, in *Proceedings of the 14th International Command and Control Research and Technology Symposium (14th ICCRTS).* Development of Computerized Support Tools for Intelligence Work, (Washington, District of Columbia, 2009)
6. P Svenson, T Berg, P Hörling, M Malm, C Mårtenson, in *Proceedings of the Tenth International Conference on Information Fusion (FUSION 2007).* Using the impact matrix for predictive situational awareness, (2007)
7. R Forsgren, L Kaati, C Mårtenson, P Svenson, E Tjörnhammar, in *Skövde Workshop on Information Fusion Topics (SWIFT 2008).* An overview of the Impactorium tools 2008, (2008)
8. P Svenson, R Forsgren, B Kylesten, P Berggren, WR Fah, MS Choo, JKY Hann, in *Proceedings of the 13th International Conference on Information Fusion (FUSION 2010).* Swedish-Singapore studies of Bayesian Modelling techniques for tactical Intelligence analysis, (2010)
9. F Johansson, L Kaati, A Shrestha, in *Proceedings of the 2013 International Symposium on Foundations of Open Source Intelligence and Security Informatics (FOSINT-SI 2013).* Detecting Multiple Aliases in Social Media, (2013)
10. F Burton, S Stewart, The 'Lone Wolf' Disconnect. Terrorism Intell. Rep., Stratfor (2008)
11. L Kaati, P Svenson, in *Proceedings of the 2011 European Intelligence and Security Informatics Conference (EISIC 2011).* Analysis of Competing Hypothesis for Investigating Lone Wolf Terrorists, (2011), pp. 295–299
12. M Fredholm, in *Stockholm Seminar on Lone Wolf Terrorism.* Hunting Lone Wolves – Finding Islamist Lone Actors Before They Strike, (2011)
13. A Bergin, SB Osman, C Ungerer, NAM Yasin, Countering internet radicalisation in Southeast Asia. Tech. Rep. 22, (ASPI, 2009)
14. R Abcarian, in *Los Angeles Times* January 29. Scott Roeder convicted of murdering abortion doctor George Tiller, (2010)
15. Anti-Defamation League, James Von Brunn: An ADL Backgrounder (2009). http://www.adl.org/main_Extremism/von_brunn_background.htm
16. K Cohen, F Johansson, L Kaati, J Clausen Mork, Detecting Linguistic Markers for Radical Violence in Social Media. Accepted Publ Terrorism Pol. Violence (2013)
17. J Reid Meloy, J Hoffmann, A Guldimann, D James, The role of warning behaviors in threat assessment: an exploration and suggested typology. Behav. Sci. Law. **30**(3), 256–279 (2012)
18. C Aldrich, *The Complete Guide to Simulations and Serious Games.* (Pfeiffer, 2009)
19. H Mouaheb, A Fahli, M Moussetad, S Eljamali, The serious game: what educational benefits? Procedia – Soc. Behav. Sci. **46**, 5502–5508 (2012)
20. PB Gerstenfeld, DR Grant, CP Chiang, Hate online: a content analysis of extremist internet sites. Analyses Soc. Issues Public Policy. **3**(1), 29–44 (2003)
21. MR Henzinger, Hyperlink analysis for the Web. IEEE Internet Comput. **5**(1), 45–50 (2001)
22. K Joffres, M Bouchard, R Frank, B Westlake, in *Proceedings of the 2011 European Intelligence and Security Informatics Conference (EISIC 2011).* Strategies to Disrupt Online Child Pornography Networks, (2011), pp. 163–170
23. L Yang, F Liu, JM Kizza, RK Ege, in *Proceedings of the IEEE Symposium on Computational Intelligence in Cyber Security (CICS 2009).* Discovering topics from dark websites, (2009)
24. E Reid, J Qin, W Chung, J Xu, Y Zhou, R Schumaker, M Sageman, H Chen, in *Proceedings of the Second Symposium on Intelligence and Security Informatics (ISI 2004).* Terrorism Knowledge Discovery Project: A Knowledge Discovery Approach to Addressing the Threats of Terrorism, (2004), pp. 125–145
25. (H Chen, E Reid, J Sinai, A Silke, B Ganor, eds.), *Terrorism Informatics: Knowledge Management and Data Mining for Homeland Security, Volume 18 of Integrated Series in Information Systems.* (Springer, 2008)
26. A Abbasi, H Chen, in *Proceedings of the Fifth IEEE International Conference on Intelligence and Security Informatics (ISI 2007).* Affect Intensity Analysis of Dark Web Forums, (2007), pp. 282–288
27. A Semenov, J Veijalainen, J Kyppö, Analysing the presence of school-shooting related communities at social media sites. Int. J. Multimedia Intell. Secur. **1**(3), 232–268 (2010)

28. JW Pennebaker, CK Chung, in *The Content Analysis Reader*. Computerized
     Text Analysis of Al-Qaeda Transcripts (Sage, 2008)
29. J Dahlin, F Johansson, L Kaati, C Mårtenson, P Svenson, in *Proceedings of
     the 2012 International Symposium on Foundations of Open Source
     Intelligence and Security Informatics (FOSINT-SI 2012)*. Combining Entity
     Matching Techniques for Detecting Extremist Behavior on Discussion
     Boards, (2012), pp. 850–857
30. WE Winkler, in *Proceedings of the Section on Survey Research Methods*.
     String Comparator Metrics and Enhanced Decision Rules in the
     Fellegi-Sunter Model of Record Linkage, (1990), pp. 354–359
31. S Kim, H Kim, T Weninger, J Han, in *Proceedings of the ACM SIGKDD
     Workshop on Useful Patterns*. Authorship Classification: A Syntactic Tree
     Mining Approach, (2010), pp. 65–73
32. A Narayanan, H Paskov, NZ Gong, J Bethencourt, E Stefanov, ECR Shin,
     D Song, in *IEEE Symposium on Security and Privacy*. On the Feasibility of
     Internet-Scale Author Identification, (2012), pp. 300–314
33. J Scott, *Social Network Analysis: A Handbook*. (London, Sage Publications,
     2 edition, 2000)
34. S Wasserman, K Faust, *Social Network Analysis: Methods and Applications*.
     (Cambridge University Press, 1994)
35. J Brynielsson, L Kaati, P Svenson, Social positions and simulation relations.
     Soc. Netw. Anal. Mining. **2**(1), 39–52 (2012)
36. MA Hearst, JF Allen, CI Guinn, E Horvitz, Trends & controversies:
     mixed-initiative interaction. IEEE Intell. Syst. **14**(5), 14–23 (1999)
37. G Tecuci, M Boicu, C Ayers, D Cammons, in *Proceedings of the First
     International Conference on Intelligence Analysis*. Personal Cognitive
     Assistants for Military Intelligence Analysis: Mixed-Initiative Learning,
     Tutoring, and Problem Solving, (McLean, Virginia, 2005)
38. J Ahlberg, F Johansson, R Johansson, M Jändel, A Linderhed, P Svenson,
     G Tolt, Content-based image retrieval – An introduction to literature and
     applications. Tech. rep., Swedish Defence Research Agency (2011)

13

Using publicly visible social media to build detailed forecasts of civil unrest

Ryan Compton[1*], Craig Lee[1], Jiejun Xu[1], Luis Artieda-Moncada[1], Tsai-Ching Lu[1], Lalindra De Silva[2] and Michael Macy[3]

Abstract

We demonstrate how one can generate predictions for several thousand incidents of Latin American civil unrest, often many days in advance, by surfacing informative public posts available on Twitter and Tumblr.

The data mining system presented here runs daily and requires no manual intervention. Identification of informative posts is accomplished by applying multiple textual and geographic filters to a high-volume data feed consisting of tens of millions of posts per day which have been flagged as public by their authors. Predictions are built by annotating the filtered posts, typically a few dozen per day, with demographic, spatial, and temporal information.

Key to our textual filters is the fact that social media posts are necessarily short, making it possible to easily infer topic by simply searching for comentions of typically unrelated terms within the same post (e.g. a future date comentioned with an unrest keyword). Additional textual filters then proceed by applying a logistic regression classifier trained to recognize accounts belonging to organizations who are likely to announce civil unrest.

Geographic filtering is accomplished despite sparsely available GPS information and without relying on sophisticated natural language processing. A geocoding technique which infers non-GPS-known user locations via the locations of their GPS-known friends provides us with location estimates for 91,984,163 Twitter users at a median error of 6.65km. We show that announcements of upcoming events tend to localize within a small geographic region, allowing us to forecast event locations which are not explicitly mentioned in text.

We annotate our forecasts with demographic information by searching the collected posts for demographic specific keywords generated by hand as well as with the aid of DBpedia.

Our system has been in production since December 2012 and, at the time of this writing, has produced 4,771 distinct forecasts for events across ten Latin American nations. Manual examination of 2,859 posts surfaced by our method revealed that only 108 were discussing topics unrelated to civil unrest. Examination of 2,596 forecasts generated between 2013-07-01 and 2013-11-30 found 1,192 (45.9%) matched exactly the date and within a 100 km radius of a civil unrest event reported in traditional news media.

Keywords: Information retrieval; Data and text mining; Computational social science

Introduction

Widespread adoption of social media has made it possible for any individual to rapidly communicate with an audience of thousands [1]. Unlike traditional news media, where several difficult time-consuming steps must be carried out prior to publication and the possibility of censorship by media owners is ever-present, information in social media becomes publicly available within a few seconds of its creation and often circumvents attempts at content filtering.

Recently, the speed and flexibility of publication on social media have motivated its use as a tool for the organization and announcement of strikes, protests, marches and other demonstrations to the public (hereinafter collectively referred to as "civil unrest") [2]. In this work, we show in detail how it is now possible to examine social media and report on a large number of civil unrest events prior their occurrence, while they are still in their planning stages. We restrict our attention to pub-

*Correspondence: rfcompton@hrl.com
[1] Information and System Sciences Laboratory, HRL Laboratories, 3011 Malibu Canyon Road, 90265 Malibu, CA, USA
Full list of author information is available at the end of the article

licly visible data only. In fact, we restrict our analyses only to data that has been explicitly flagged as public by its creator. Information such as IP addresses (which can be used for geolocation) or connection speed (which may correlate with large protests [3]) is ignored in this study.

Early detection of civil unrest events is valuable for several industrial and government applications. For example, if a port is likely to shut down due to a riot, shipping companies may opt to redirect freight in order to prevent unexpected losses. If a massive protest is planned to happen in front of an embassy, governments may elect to postpone diplomatic visits in order to ensure the safety of their politicians. The value of civil unrest forecasting has recently caught the attention of researchers from a wide variety of disciplines [4-7].

Predicting international protests by mining Twitter for mentions of future dates was first done in [8] (which this work is an extension of). Later research by Kallus [9] adapted the future date heuristic to forecast unrest in additional languages and developed a new evaluation methodology. Research by Xu et al. in [10] demonstrated results focused specifically on Tumblr.

Alternative methods for civil unrest forecasting are based on physical models describing large-scale theories of population behavior (e.g. [6,7,11]). Often relying on time series (or "trends"), these methods take into account a small amount of information from millions of posts, treating as social media as a sensor of population sentiment. While time series analysis may lead insight into collective social dynamics, relying on millions of tweets to generate predictions for the next day's events is not practical when the number of events is high and detailed information from each forecast is important. Time series based methods suffer a major disadvantage when an auditor seeks additional information about a given prediction. Expecting all auditors to fully grasp the models employed to generate the prediction is unreasonable; having the auditors examine all posts that were used to generate the time series is impossible.

The distinguishing feature of our approach is direct extraction and analysis of a small number of highly relevant posts, treating social media as a "news source" rather than a "sensor". This allows us to easily generate a large number of predictions each day and allows an auditor to easily read through all the posts associated to each prediction.

The data input to our system consists of all public posts on Twitter and Tumblr. Our decision to work with Twitter and Tumblr and not, say, Facebook, Google+,

LinkedIn, or Orkut, is primarily motivated by the fact that high-volume data feeds consisting of public posts on Twitter and Tumblr are readily available from several data providers [12,13]. Additionally, Twitter has recently gained much notoriety as an organizational tool for activism after its central role in 2011 Arab Spring protests [14,15]. Tumblr, however, has not yet been the focus of much research and little is known about its structure or utility. We will show that, while the number of forecasts we generate with Tumblr is eclipsed by Twitter, much information about future civil unrest is in fact present and easily retrievable from Tumblr.

The focus of our work is Latin America. Widespread use of Twitter and Tumblr, numerous strikes and protests, absence of government censorship, and only two languages throughout the region make this an ideal location to study social media signal prior to civil unrest events. Our research is distributed across ten major nations: Argentina, Brazil, Chile, Colombia, Ecuador, El Salvador, Mexico, Paraguay, Uruguay, and Venezuela.

This paper is organized as follows: section 'Method' describes each step of our technique in detail. Section 'Results' showcases our user interface and has information about the system's past performance. Finally, section 'Conclusion' discusses future work and concluding remarks.

Method

Our goal is to generate forecasts of the form:

```
{date, location, population, event_type,
 probability}
```

Where "population" describes the demographic of the event participants (eg education, labor, agriculture), "event_type" gives further detail about the reason for the event (eg employment, housing, economic policies), "date" is the date the event is forecast to occur on, "location" is the city where we expect the event to occur, and "probability" is how likely it is that the event will actually happen.

We extract informative social media posts via the application of several filters (cf Alg. 1) designed to reduce the number of posts we analyse down from hundreds of millions to dozens. The posts identified by alg. 1 are often rich in information about upcoming civil unrest. We believe that a single human auditor could easily read all posts in t_5 for a given day and be well-informed about several announced events. In the following subsections we describe the filters to reach t_5 in detail.

Algorithm 1: Future event detection

Input: hundreds of millions of today's posts from twitter.com and tumblr.com

Output: a few dozen posts relevant to upcoming events

t_1 = posts with text containing unrest keywords

t_2 = posts in t_1 with text containing future dates

t_3 = posts in t_2 which have passed through a logistic regression classifier

t_4 = posts in t_3 whose retweets/reblogs localize within nations of interest or whose text contains mentions of specific locations

t_5 = posts in t_4 with more than a specified number of retweets/reblogs

Return: t_5

Keyword searches

The first filter a tweet must pass is a simple check for mentions of Latin American civil unrest keywords. We have manually identified a collection of 44 keywords which we believe are highly relevant to civil unrest (e.g. "protesta", "huelga", "marcha"). The advantage of this filter is that it is possible to apply it to the entirety of Twitter and Tumblr with minimal effort.

Future date searches

Simple checks for keyword mentions are poor indicators of content. A quick experiment has shown that, in both English and Spanish, only about 20% of posts that contain a civil unrest keyword are indeed about civil unrest. Furthermore, it is unclear how to forecast an event date from only posts with certain keywords. We thus apply a second filter, one for mentions of future dates, to the posts containing unrest keywords.

Our temporal expression tagger searches first for month names and abbreviations in Spanish and Portuguese and second for numbers less than 31 within three whitespace separated tokens from each other. Thus, an example matching date pattern would be "10 de enero". Four-digit years are rare in tweets, in order to determine the year of the mentioned date we use the year which minimizes the number of days between the mentioned date and the tweet's post time. In our example, if a tweet mentions "10 de enero" on 2012-12-29 we assume the user is talking about 2013-01-10 as 2013-01-10 is closer in time to 2012-12-29 than 2012-01-10 is. Additionally, we tag colloquial date expressions (e.g. "el martes próximo") with basic string searches. Despite the simplicity of this approach, we find that many posts can be annotated with our date tagger. More advanced temporal expression taggers, such as Heideltime [16] may be used in place of our method for Spanish text, but are currently not available in Portuguese.

Once we have extracted dates from the text, we assert that the mentioned dates occur after the tweets post time.

When the future date filter is applied the number of tweets is reduced substantially, a quick experiment on 144,167 tweets containing unrest keywords collected on 2013-03-01 found that only 1,512 of these tweets also contained future dates.

Social media text is remarkably short. On Twitter there is a hard limit of 140 characters per tweet, and Tumblr posts (which are primarily focused on images) rarely exceed the length of tweets. When an unrest keyword is mentioned alongside a future date there is little room left to obscure the topic of the post away from civil unrest. We find this comention filter to be highly informative.

For each tweet passing this filter we tentatively issue a forecast for the mentioned date.

Logistic regression classification

Comentions of keywords with future dates, however, does not guarantee that a particular post is indeed about civil unrest. For Twitter, we have developed two classifiers to classify tweets based on their relevance to a civil unrest event. Our first classifier is a standard logistic regression classifier trained on tweets. The features for the classifier were unigrams and bigrams that surpassed a frequency threshold of 3 in the training data. The training data was acquired using three annotators through Amazon Mechanical Turk and they annotated 3000 tweets for their relevance to a civil unrest event (pairwise inter-annotator agreement ranged from 0.68 to 0.74).

Our second classifier makes use of recent work we have done establishing that tweets from organizations are roughly three-times more likely to be civil unrest-related than similar tweets from individuals [17]. In order to exploit this concept, we designed an auxiliary classifier that classifies the source user type of a tweet into two categories - organizations and individuals. For this classifier, we make use of an ensemble framework for user type identification based on heuristics, an *n-gram* classifier, and a linguistic classifier. The heuristics were designed to capture two strong cues that are characteristic of organization tweets - 1) they almost always contains a URL and 2) organizational tweets rarely contain replied tweets (tweets beginning with @user mentions). The *n-gram* classifier was based on unigrams and bigrams and the linguistic classifier captures several types of linguistic features that are characteristic of tweets in either category. These three components in the ensemble are then utilized in linear combination using another logistic regression classifier to determine the user type of any given tweet. After we have identified the posting user as individual/organization using this classifier, we adjust the forecast probability accordingly, by incorporating the likelihoods to derive the posterior probability of a tweet being civil unrest-related given its user type.

Event geocoding

Identification of event locations is central to the goal of this project. We infer the location of an upcoming event with two different methods, one text based and the other social network based.

Our text based location assignment is a straightforward search for mentions of cities or monuments from a manually compiled list of unambiguous location names. For Tumblr, where GPS information is never public, event geocoding is solely textual. For Twitter, where GPS information is public, but extremely rare, we are able to use social network based techniques to infer additional user locations (see 3 for detail on our user geocoder).

For each tweet passing the logistic regression filter, we identify user IDs of all the tweet's retweeters. User IDs are then fed into our user geocoder and filtered based on whether or not they center in Latin America. We assign a latitude and longitude to the forecast event using a robust estimate of the center of the retweeter's locations, i.e. the forecast location is the $l1$-multivariate median [18] of the retweeter locations.

To be precise, let $\mathcal{U}$ be the set of all retweeter locations and d the geodesic distance measured using Vincenty's formulae [19]. We compute the $l1$-multivariate median of $\mathcal{U}$ as:

$$\underset{x}{\text{argmin}} \sum_{y \in \mathcal{U}} d(x,y) \qquad (1)$$

and use the solution to eq. 1 for event location.

The success of our geocoding depends on communicative locality in Twitter, which is currently an unsettled research direction. Work supporting the idea that social ties in Twitter are grounded in geography can be found in [20-23]. Similar work on the Facebook social network was done in [24]. These papers study communicative locality by restricting attention to subsets of the social networks where all users locations are known. Results of [20] demonstrate that @mentions are unlikely to align with geography unless the @mentions have been reciprocated.

Research showing that Twitter contact is not grounded in geography can be found in [25], where the author examines a 32.5 million GPS-known retweet pairings and finds an average distance of 749 miles between users. Averages, however, are sensitive to outliers which may be present in the social media data studied. In this work, we will make use of robust statistics (i.e. the $l1$-multivariate median and median absolute deviation) to estimate center and spread for sets of locations.

The papers mentioned thus far have been focused on user geocoding and do not guarantee that event location

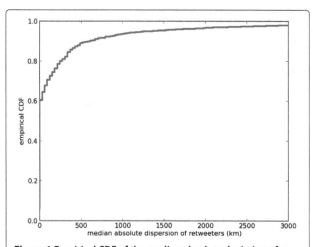

Figure 1 Empirical CDF of the median absolute deviation of retweeter locations of 4,004 forecasts generated by our model. With over 80% probability the retweeters are dispersed by less than 500 km.

can be learned from social media sharing patterns. Predicting an event location from retweeter location is only possible for tweets containing event announcements (which are the focus of this work).

We quantify the dispersion of a set locations using the median absolute deviation,

$$\widetilde{\mathcal{U}} = \text{median}_i \left(d(u_i, \, l1\text{-median}(u_j)) \right) \qquad (2)$$

Examining 4,004 forecasts generated by our model with more than 3 geocodable retweeters shows us that the vast majority of tweets used to generate forecasts have localized retweeters. In Figure 1 we show the empirical CDF of the median absolute deviation of retweeter locations, the data indicates that there is over an 80%

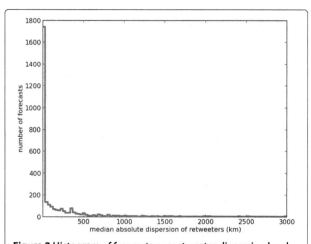

Figure 2 Histogram of forecasts per retweeter dispersion level. Retweeters typically localize within a small radius. We take the center of the retweeter locations to be the forecast location.

Retweeter Locations:

Data used for warning generation:

link:
postTime:
unrestTerm:
isRetweet:

originalUserName:
originalUserId:

retweetingUserName:
retweetingUserId:

originalTweetId:
retweeters: |
                              ]
retweetersGPSInfo: [

                  ]

Figure 3 Example forecast. A march related to Petroleos Mexicanos (Pemex) is planned for March 18 in Mexico City. Our system detected the event on March 5th. The interactive map provides end-users with links to retweeter accounts.

probability the retweeters are dispersed by less than 500 km. While the 500 km figure may be too large to disentangle neighbouring cities, the number of tweets surfaced by our method is small enough that a human could manually read through them before any action is taken.

In Figure 2 we examine the same 4,004 forecasts and plot the number of forecasts at each dispersion level, the histogram shows that a large number of forecasts have retweeters localizing within a small radius. An example of this phenomenon is visible in Figure 3, where we see that all retweeters discussing the upcoming march are localized within Mexico City.

We note here that this filter is remarkably difficult to pass. Of the 1,512 tweets collected in the previous step in our example, only 36 passed the geocoding filter.

We also remark that, unlike much research in social media analysis, our event geocoding technique is entirely language independent. Which opens up the possibility of expanding our method to a global scale.

User geocoding

We identify retweeter locations with our previously developed Twitter geocoder [20,23]. In this section we briefly explain how our geocoder works, more detail is available in [20] and [23].

The distinguishing feature of our geocoder is that we iteratively infer a non-GPS user's location based on the locations of their friends. This is accomplished by solving the convex optimization:

$$\min_{\mathbf{f}} |\nabla \mathbf{f}| \text{ subject to } f_i = l_i \text{ for } i \in L \text{ and } \tilde{\nabla} f_i \leq \gamma \quad (3)$$

where f encodes a location estimate for each user, L denotes the set of users who opt to make their GPS locations, l_i, public, the total variation, $|\nabla \mathbf{f}|$, on the Twitter @mention network is defined by:

$$|\nabla \mathbf{f}| = \sum_{ij} w_{ij} d\left(f_i, f_j\right) \quad (4)$$

Here, the edge weights, w_{ij}, are equal to the minimal number of reciprocated @mentions between users i and j. The quantity $\tilde{\nabla} f_i$ is the median absolute deviation of the users distances to their friends, defined by

$$\tilde{\nabla} f_i = \text{median}_j \left(w_{ij} d\left(f_i, f_j\right)\right) \quad (5)$$

The parameter γ defines how dispersed we allow a user's friends to be and is set to 100 km in our code.

In summary, we seek a network such that the sum over all geographic distances between connected users is as small as possible, subject to a constraint on the dispersion of each user's friends.

Our geocoding technique falls under the category of transductive learning and shares some similarity with "label propagation" [26]. However, unlike label propagation, our labels (latitude/longitude pairs) are continuously valued. Equation 3 exploits this additional structure with geodesic distance and total variation, which has demonstrated superior performance as an optimization heuristic for several information inference problems across a wide variety of fields [27-29].

We begin by extracting home locations for users based on the number of times they have tweeted with public GPS. When we observe 3 or more tweets from a user within a 30 km radius we use the geometric median of those tagged tweets to establish the user's home location. This provides us with home locations for 10,590,474 users. We extract self-reported locations when a users enters an unambiguous location name into their profile. The number of users we find from self-reports is 9,466,251, of these 8,057,879 were not using GPS publicly. We hold out 10% of GPS users for testing. By combining self-reports with non-test GPS users we obtain locations for 17,589,170 Twitter users. These 17M users are used for L in eq. 3.

The total variation functional is nondifferentiable. Solving a total variation-based optimization is thus a formidable challenge and vastly different methods have been proposed for several decades [30].

We employ "parallel coordinate descent" to solve eq. 3. Most variants of coordinate descent cycle through the domain sequentially, updating each variable and communicating back the result before the next variable can update. The scale of the data we work with necessitates a parallel approach, prohibiting us from making all the communication steps required by a traditional coordinate descent method.

At each iteration, our algorithm simultaneously updates each user's location with the $l1$-multivariate median of their friend's locations. Only after all updates are complete do we communicate our results over the network.

Note that the argument that minimizes $|\nabla_i(\mathbf{f}^k, f)|$ is the $l1$-multivariate median of the locations of the neighbours of node i. Thus, we iteratively update each user's location with the median of their friends locations, provided that their friends are not too dispersed.

We have no convergence proof for Alg. 2. Empirically, Alg. 2 converges, providing us with estimates of home locations for 91,984,163 Twitter users. Comparison with the 10% hold-out GPS users shows a median error of 6.65 km, and a mean error of 300.06 km with a standard deviation of 1,131.83 km.

Algorithm 2: Parallel coordinate descent iterations for geocoding

---

Initialize:$f_i = l_i$ for $i \in L$ and parameter γ
while *not converged* **do**
    foreach *node i* **do**
        if $i \in L$ **then**
            $f_i^{k+1} = l_i$
        end
        else
            if $\widetilde{\nabla} f_i \leq \gamma$ **then**
                $f_i^{k+1} = \underset{f}{\mathrm{argmin}}|\nabla_i(\mathbf{f}^k, f)|$
            end
            else
                no update
            end
        end
    end
end

Demographics and event code assignment

We condense duplicate forecasts for the same date/location into one forecast by averaging their probabilities.

Language experts have provided us with lists of terms relevant to several demographics and event types in Latin America. Additionally, we greatly expand our lists using DBpedia. As an example, entering the below query into http://dbpedia.org/snorql/?query= will provide a list of all political parties in Argentina or Venezuela.

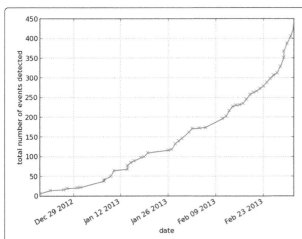

450
400
350
300
250
200
150
100
50
0

total number of events detected

Dec 29 2012   Jan 12 2013   Jan 26 2013   Feb 09 2013   Feb 23 2013

date

Figure 4 Cumulative sum of the number of forecasts generated since 2012-12-17. The increased number of warnings per day in November 2013 was due primarily to improvements in date tagging.

Table 1 Number of forecasts generated for each country

Number of events forecast	Nation
500	Argentina
778	Brazil
317	Chile
557	Colombia
134	Ecuador
69	El Salvador
1235	Mexico
128	Paraguay
65	Uruguay
985	Venezuela

Mexico is highly active on twitter.com and receives the most coverage from our system. Timeframe: 2012-12-17 until 2014-01-14.

```
SELECT * WHERE {
?uni rdf:type <http://dbpedia.org/ontology/
PoliticalParty> .
?uni dbpedia2:country ?country .
FILTER(?country = "Argentina"@en ||
?country = "Venezuela"@en )
OPTIONAL{ ?uni rdfs:label ?label .}
OPTIONAL{?uni dbpedia2:name ?name .}
OPTIONAL{?uni dbpedia2:nativeName
?nativename .}
}
```

Entering the following query will provide a list of all universities in Argentina or Venezuela.

```
SELECT * WHERE {
?uni rdf:type <http://dbpedia.org/ontology/
University> .
?uni dbpedia2:country ?country .
FILTER(?country = :Argentina ||
?country = :Venezuela )
?uni rdfs:label ?name .
}
```

The two above queries provide us with keywords allowing us to distinguish between politics and education.

To assign a demographic to each forecast we collect the tweet histories of every retweeter of every tweet associated with a forecast and search our lists of terms.

Table 2 Total number of forecasts generated by our system

Data feed	Number of forecasts	Average lead time
Twitter only	5150	3.91
Tumblr only	198	6.38
Both	1298	2.93
Total	6596	3.81

Timeframe: 2012-12-17 until 2014-03-10.

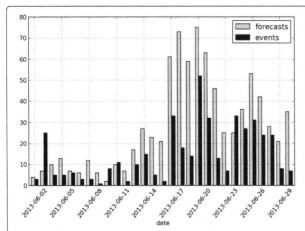

Figure 5 Number of events forecast to happen per day in Brazil during June 2013. Our system under reported the initial wave of protests, but successfully captured a major uptick in late June. Average lead time: 5.58 days.

The most commonly occurring classes of terms are used to assign our forecast's demographic and event code.

Results

Successful end-user interpretation is important. By approaching this problem from the viewpoint of data mining rather than time series analysis we can provide an easily interpretable audit trail with minimal effort. For each forecast generated we provide the tweets used, the retweeter locations, the keywords matched, and links to all retweeter accounts. (cf Figure 3).

Our system has been in place since 2012-12-17 (cf Figure 4, Table 1, and Table 2), in that time the rate at which forecasts are generated has been steadily increasing as we continue to improve our algorithms and keyword lists.

Assessing the performance of our system is relatively straightforward given the audit trails. Manual examination of 2,859 posts surfaced by our method revealed only 108 that were discussing topics related to sporting events, concerts, other public functions, or simple chatter.

It is possible to evaluate such a system without the use of our audit trail. Manually searching major news media for articles describing Latin American civil unrest provided us a ground truth dataset of 4,825 articles describing distinct events between 2013-07-01 and 2013-11-30. In this time frame we generated 2,596 forecasts. We align forecasts with news articles when the forecast date matches exactly with the event date and the forecast location is within 100 km of the event location. We find that 1,192 forecasts could be aligned in this way. A complete description of the manually annotated data used for evaluation can be found in [31].

A completely automated evaluation is possible with the aid of the GDELT dataset [32]. Briefly, the GDELT project aims to automatically extract and annotate all English news articles describing societal-scale events. GDELT uses the CAMEO coding system, where code "14" can be taken to mean civil unrest. Of our 2,596 forecasts, only 583 aligned with GDELT events within 100 km and on the exact date. It is not yet clear why the precision is lower here. Possibilities may be due to differences in publishing criteria between Latin American social media and English traditional news media, geocoding and date tagging inaccuracies, or the fact that our keyword lists are generated without taking into account CAMEO coding. We hope to improve precision on GDELT in future work.

We examine forecasts generated by our method in June 2013. This time period encompasses the "Brazilan Spring" where massive protests swept across the nation. The number of real events per day as well as the number of events forecast to happen per day is shown in Figure 5. These protests generated substantial signal in Twitter. In Brazil, our geocoder reported over 2M tweets from Brazil containing the Portuguese term "protesto" during the month with a peak of over 400,000 per day in late June. A visualization of these tweets is available in Additional file 1.

Tumblr results

Recall that our system consists of a set of filters. The Venn diagrams in Figure 6 show the numbers of resulting

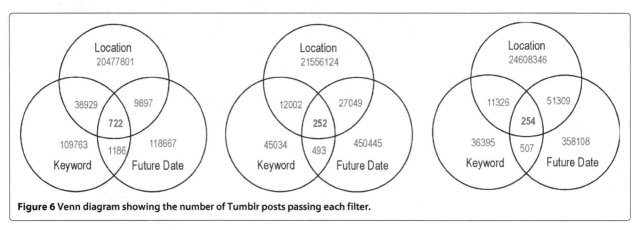

Figure 6 Venn diagram showing the number of Tumblr posts passing each filter.

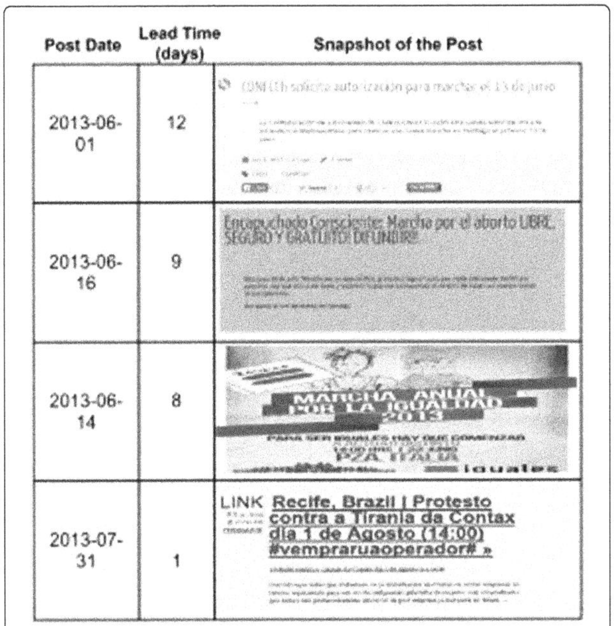

Figure 7 Snapshots of Tumblr posts (detected by our system) showing planned future civil unrest events.

Tumblr posts which pass each filter. The number of posts is substantially smaller and more manageable when compared with the original size of input data. The surfaced posts are easy to read and highly informative, cf. Figure 7.

Forecasts from Tumblr and Twitter are fused together when they are forecast to occur on the same date and within the same city. After fusion, we find that roughly 12.7% of our forecasts are visible in both Twitter and Tumblr (cf. Table 2). Interestingly, when restricting to June 2013 there is minimal overlap between Twitter and Tumblr (cf Table 3).

In the same manner as before, we evaluate matches against news articles during the 2013-07-01 until 2013-11-30 period. There were 138 warnings based only on Tumblr during this period, 56 (40.5%) could be aligned with a manually annotated news articles while 32 (23.1%) matched GDELT. There were 11 warnings based on both Twitter and Tumblr, 7 (63.6%) of these matched manually annotated news while 3 (27.2%) matched GDELT.

Table 3 Number of forecasts generated for June 2013 from the different data feeds

Data feed	Number of forecasts	Average lead time
Twitter only	525	5.57
Tumblr only	51	5.98
Both	4	2.75
Total	580	5.58

Surprisingly, of the 580 forecasts, only 4 were visible in both Twitter and Tumblr.

Conclusion

Social media has become a powerful tool for the organization of mass gatherings of all types. However, the shear volume of Twitter and Tumblr make it difficult to automatically identify new and valuable information in a reasonable amount time. In this work we have provided a straightforward approach for the detection of upcoming civil unrest events in Latin America based on successive textual and geographic filters.

Traditional news media is often assumed to be perfectly accurate and can therefore only report on events once they have occurred. The fact that it is now possible to relax the assumption of perfect accuracy and report on events before their occurrence is remarkable and continued work on this project is already in progress.

Immediate future work includes more advanced tweet classification using larger training sets, associated user IDs, our @mention network, and dictionary-based approaches. We also plan to analyse the links shared in tweets for further information on upcoming events.

Additional file

Additional file 1: Visualization of 2M tweets containing the term "protesto" during June 2013.

Competing interests

The authors declare that they have no competing interests.

Acknowledgements

Supported by the Intelligence Advanced Research Projects Activity (IARPA) via Department of Interior National Business Center (DoI / NBC) contract number D12PC00285. The U.S. Government is authorized to reproduce and distribute reprints for Governmental purposes notwithstanding any copyright annotation thereon. The views and conclusions contained herein are those of the authors and should not be interpreted as necessarily representing the official policies or endorsements, either expressed or implied, of IARPA, DoI/NBE, or the U.S. Government.

Author details

[1]Information and System Sciences Laboratory, HRL Laboratories, 3011 Malibu Canyon Road, 90265 Malibu, CA, USA. [2]Department of Computer Science, University of Utah, Salt Lake City, Utah, USA. [3]Social Dynamics Laboratory, Cornell University, Ithaca, New York, USA.

References

1. H Kwak, C Lee, H Park, S Moon, What is twitter, a social network or a news media? WWW (2010)
2. J Skinner, Social media and revolution: The arab spring and the occupy movement as seen through three information studies paradigms (2011)
3. C Anderson, Dimming the internet: Detecting throttling as a mechanism of censorship in iran. arXiv preprint arXiv:1306.4361 (2013)
4. E Stepanova, The role of information communication technologies in the "arab spring". PONARS Eurasia Policy Memo No. 159 (2011)
5. F Chen, J Arredondo, RP Khandpur, C-T Lu, D Mares, D Gupta, N Ramakrishnan, Spatial surrogates to forecast social mobilization and civil unrests. Position Paper in CCC Workshop on "From GPS and Virtual Globes to Spatial Computing-2012" (2012)
6. D Braha, Global civil unrest: contagion, self-organization, and prediction. PLoS One (2012)

7. NF Johnson, P Medina, G Zhao, DS Messinger, J Horgan, P Gill, JC Bohorquez, W Mattson, D Gangi, H Qi, P Manrique, N Velasquez, A Morgenstern, E Restrepo, N Johnson, M Spagat, R Zarama, Simple mathematical law benchmarks human confrontations. Sci. Rep. **3** (2013)

8. R Compton, C Lee, T-C Lu, L De Silva, M Macy, Detecting future social unrest in unprocessed twitter data:"emerging phenomena and big data", in *Intelligence and Security Informatics (ISI), 2013 IEEE International Conference On* (IEEE, 2013), pp. 56–60

9. N Kallus, Predicting crowd behavior with big public data. arXiv preprint arXiv:1402.2308 (2014)

10. J Xu, T-C Lu, R Compton, D Allen, Civil unrest prediction: A tumblr-based exploration, in *International Social Computing, Behavioral Modeling and Prediction Conference. SBP'14*, (2014)

11. N Johnson, S Carran, J Botner, K Fontaine, N Laxague, P Nuetzel, J Turnley, B Tivnan, Pattern in escalations in insurgent and terrorist activity. Science (2011)

12. http://gnip.com

13. http://datasift.com

14. http://www.wired.com/magazine/2013/04/arabspring

15. PN Howard, A Duffy, D Freelon, M Hussain, W Mari, M Mazaid, Opening closed regimes: what was the role of social media during the arab spring? (2011)

16. J Strötgen, M Gertz, Heideltime: High quality rule-based extraction and normalization of temporal expressions, in *Proceedings of the 5th International Workshop on Semantic Evaluation*. (Association for Computational Linguistics, Uppsala, Sweden, 2010), pp. 321–324. http://www.aclweb.org/anthology/S10-1071

17. LD Silva, E Riloff, Exploiting the textual content of tweets for user type classification. ICWSM (submitted) (2013)

18. Y Vardi, C-H Zhang, The multivariate l1-median and associated data depth. Proc. Natl. Acad. Sci. **97**(4), 1423–1426 (2000)

19. http://www.geodesy.org

20. D Jurgens, Inferring location in online communities based on social relationships. HRL Technical report (2013)

21. J Aelterman, HQ Luong, B Goossens, A Pižurica, W Philips, Augmented Lagrangian based reconstruction of non-uniformly sub-Nyquist sampled MRI data. Signal Process. **91**(12), 2731–2742 (2011). doi:10.1016/j.sigpro.2011.04.033

22. Y Yamaguchi, T Amagasa, H Kitagawa, Landmark-based user location inference in social media, in *Proceedings of the First ACM Conference on Online Social Networks. COSN '13* (ACM New York, NY, USA, 2013), pp. 223–234. http://doi.acm.org/10.1145/2512938.2512941

23. R Compton, D Jurgens, D Allen, Geocoding social networks with total variation minimization (2014)

24. L Backstrom, E Sun, C Marlow, Find me if you can: improving geographical prediction with social and spatial proximity, in *Proceedings of the 19th International Conference on World Wide Web* (ACM, 2010), pp. 61–70

25. K Leetaru, S Wang, G Cao, A Padmanabhan, E Shook, Mapping the global twitter heartbeat: the geography of twitter. First Monday. **18**(5) (2013)

26. X Zhu, Z Ghahramani, Learning from labeled and unlabeled data with label propagation. Technical report, Technical Report CMU-CALD-02-107, Carnegie Mellon University (2002)

27. L Rudin, S Osher, E Fatemi, Nonlinear total variation based noise removal algorithms. Physica D: Nonlinear Phenomena. **60**(1-4), 259–268 (1992). doi:10.1016/0167-2789(92)90242-F

28. E Candes, J Romberg, T Tao, Stable Signal Recovery from Incomplete and Inaccurate Measurements arXiv : math / 0503066v2 [math . NA] 7 Dec 2005. Science. **40698**, 1–15 (2005)

29. T Goldstein, S Osher, The Split Bregman Method for L1-Regularized Problems. SIAM J. Imaging Sci. **2**(2), 323 (2009). doi:10.1137/080725891

30. T Goldstein, X Bresson, S Osher, Geometric Applications of the Split Bregman Method: Segmentation and Surface Reconstruction. J. Sci. Comput. **45**(1-3), 272–293 (2009). doi:10.1007/s10915-009-9331-z

31. N Ramakrishnan, P Butler, S Muthiah, N Self, R Khandpur, P Saraf, W Wang, J Cadena, A Vullikanti, G Korkmaz, C Kuhlman, A Marathe, L Zhao, T Hua, F Chen, C-T Lu, B Huang, A Srinivasan, K Trinh, L Getoor, G Katz, A Doyle, C Ackermann, I Zavorin, J Ford, K Summers, Y Fayed, J Arredondo, D Gupta, D Mares, 'Beating the news' with, EMBERS: Forecasting Civil Unrest using Open Source Indicators (2014). arXiv:1402.7035

32. K Leetaru, PA Schrodt, Gdelt: Global data on events, location, and tone, 1979–2012, in *Paper Presented at the ISA Annual Convention*, vol. 2, (2013), p. 4

14

Emerging issues for education in E-discovery for electronic health records

Shuai Yuan*, Raghav H Rao and Shambhu Upadhyaya

Abstract

In order to provide a foundation for education on e-discovery and security in Electronic Health Record (EHR) systems, this paper identifies emerging issues in the area. Based on a detailed literature review it details key categories: Development in EHR, E-discovery policy and strategy, and Security and privacy in EHR and also discusses e-discovery issues in cloud computing and big data contexts. This may help to create a framework for potential short course-design on e-discovery and security in the healthcare domain.

Keywords: Electronic Health Record; E-discovery; Security and Privacy

Introduction

Electronic Health Record (EHR) systems are the aggregate electronic record of health-related information on individuals "created and gathered cumulatively across more than one health care organization and managed and consulted by licensed clinicians and staff involved in the individual's health and care" (National Alliance for Health Information Technology (NAHIT[a]) [1]. EHR has been strongly recommended for adoption in the healthcare industry in the U.S. The increased use of EHR systems has assisted health care professionals in medical practices by storing patients' medical and diagnosis information, exchanging laboratory reports and radiologic images, and also providing decision support tools for the physicians and communication methods with patients [2,3]. The American Recovery and Reinvestment Act of 2009 (ARRA)'s goal was to computerize all Americans health records by 2014 by dedicating nineteen billion dollars to the promotion of health information technology [4,5]. However, EHR systems also bring new liability and litigation risks such as the inappropriate use of the systems, privacy breaches, and inadvertent data disclosures, which in turn may impose heavy costs in terms of preservation of electronic information and potential litigation issues [6].

E-discovery refers to discovery of information, often for civil litigations, that is stored in electronic format, known as Electronically Stored Information (ESI). In 2006, amendments were made to federal rules to facilitate ESI discovery. This resulted in changes to traditional e-discovery rules [7]. To comply with the new rules, healthcare providers are required to establish and update policies and procedures in terms of information governance and EHR systems along with advanced technologies that may also be needed to be developed to facilitate e-discovery.

EHR adoption will require significant efforts with regard to workforce since it is a complex and large initiative in healthcare industry. This calls for expansion of today's education system to cover topics of security, security technology and policy, and privacy issues. The primary purpose of this study is to lay a foundation for topics in both security issues and e-discovery challenges involving EHR system use. To achieve this purpose, we categorize the emerging issues based on in-depth literature review, into three categories: Development in EHR, E-discovery policy and strategy, and Security and privacy in EHR. We also discuss some key issues related to e-discovery raised from the new technologies of cloud computing and big data contexts. A major contribution of this paper is the development of a framework for education. The outcome of this study can be used to design short courses on security and e-discovery regarding EHR systems in the healthcare domain.

The rest of the paper is organized as follows. Section 2 provides discusses three categories- Development in EHR, E-discovery policy and strategy, and Security and privacy in EHR. Section 3 studies new and emerging

* Correspondence: shuaiyua@buffalo.edu
SUNY at Buffalo, Buffalo, NY 14260, USA

issues associated with e-discovery when cloud computing and big data are becoming prevalent. Section 4 concludes with a discussion on the course-design framework for faculty members.

Literature review of E-discovery in EHR
Developments in EHR
EHR systems that contain patients' medical data and information, have not only been used in healthcare delivery, but are relevant to litigation and are subject to ESI discovery due to amendments that were passed in 2006. As the adoption of EHR systems in hospitals and other healthcare sectors is increasing, providers and legal counsel must be aware of the advances in EHR technology, get a better understanding of the information they can acquire and retrieve from EHR systems, and prepare e-discovery provisioning requirements [8]. The development of techniques in EHR systems would facilitate e-discovery. In addition, healthcare providers naturally have a wide choice as to how engaged their medical practice will be with EHR technology and which EHR system will be used [8]. With national benchmarks to measure EHR systems in terms of certification and meaningful use, the quality of the system outcomes as well as the functionalities associated with e-discovery request need to be guaranteed. Furthermore, particular EHR technologies, for instance, metadata search algorithms, are necessary to facilitate the review process for e-discovery use. Healthcare providers and legal counsel might not be technology experts in EHR development, however, the knowledge of where relevant ESI exists and how to preserve such information to satisfy e-discovery obligations is a necessary requirement.

Techniques in EHR systems to facilitate e-discovery
Advanced techniques in EHR systems to facilitate e-discovery process are needed, otherwise e-discovery will be inefficient and costly, leading to heavy burden to stakeholders involved. For instance, the 2006 amendments have expanded the use of a "legal hold" for preservation of paper documents as well as ESI document. Healthcare organizations should suspend routine document retention and destruction policy to ensure the preservation of all forms of relevant information avoiding sanctions for ESI spoilage, at the time when the organization receives a notice of litigation [9]. There is a documented lack of efficient technology in EHR systems to establish a legal hold on patients' records and it is costly to put a legal hold on one particular patient in EHR systems [10]. Further, sometimes legal counsels do not have sufficient knowledge in techniques to acquire valuable data from EHR systems. This calls for education about functions of EHR systems.

Information sharing and data interoperability
There is an increasing need to build a national health information infrastructure (NHII) to connect users and manage knowledge of healthcare so that provides functions for information sharing among different EHR systems. There are three main reasons why the NHII is required [11]: First, professionals and researchers face substantial growth and much more complex health data about patients as they encounter more types of illnesses and simultaneously improving diagnostic capabilities; Second, data standardization fulfilled by NHII will facilitate data manipulation so that costs and turnaround times are reduced and last but not least, a platform is needed to assure the benefits of cutting edge technology and method diffuse to different stakeholders in healthcare domain. For instance, large datasets are needed to acquire the knowledge regarding the molecular underpinning of disease through intensive computing capabilities. Such data sets can be one feature of the NHII. In order to achieve the goal to build a NHII connected participants in healthcare, series of agreements on standardization of technology, data, processes and rules need to be reached as well. The quantity and quality of data to support decision-makings in health care delivery are important for implementation of a complete NHII [8]. Each of these issues is critical for system related education.

Data interoperability is a key ability in NHII implementation that two or more EHR systems can exchange and share information. This feature has also been indicated in "meaningful use" stage 1 requirements such that key patient data can be exported to a common format. Currently two formats have been developed: Continuity of Care Records (CCR) and Continuity of Care Documents (CCD) but neither of them has been used to export entire patient's EHR records, since abbreviations and terminology vary among practice [12]. In order to facilitate e-discovery, first, the format used by the export feature must be able to provide a complete record of a patient for production during discovery. In addition, the EHR data should be viewable by a lawyer in a similar layout as viewed by medical professionals since, "A party must produce documents as they are kept in the usual course of business..." Finally, it is necessary for the feature to be able to export specific data required for production such that the lawyer is capable to produce only relevant data for discovery purposes [12].

Metrics for EHR systems quality control
Without appropriate mechanisms and metrics to control the quality of diverse EHR systems in the market, healthcare organizations are at risk of investing large amounts on poorly designed systems which may not improve the outcomes. Therefore, developing national benchmarks to

measure not only the technology but systems in terms of certification, meaningful use, and implementation specification, etc. are mandatory [13,14].

Here, it is also worth noticing the difference between certification and meaningful use on EHR systems [15]. Certification of EHR systems ensures that the particular system meets functionality standards. In June 2010, the Office of the National Coordinator for Health Information Technology (ONC) defined the temporary criteria for testing and certifying EHRS functionality [16]. Subsequently in January 2011, ONC issued the final rule on a Permanent Certification Program for Health Information Technology, for functional testing requirement, cases and tools. Meaningful use implies "providers need to show they're using certified EHR technology in ways that can be measured significantly in quality and in quantity", corresponding to quality of the adoption of EHR systems [17]. Identification of these issues is important for educational programs.

Clinical practice guidelines to optimize EHR system use

Clinical practice guidelines (CPG)s assist in decisions about special circumstances in healthcare. CPGs in terms of diagnostic and treatment practices have been developed by professional societies over a long time period. The standard of care is a key to successful defense in medical malpractice litigation since it reveals whether the defendant "proceed [ed] with the reasonable caution that a prudent man would have exercised under such circumstances" [13]. Compliance with well-established CPGs, similar to expert testimony, can be utilized as proof that the defendant met the standard of care, "at least as evidence of a practice that is accepted by a respectable minority". However, at the early age of EHR system development and adoption, few authoritative CPGs exist regarding the design and use of EHR systems, and even less in the litigation context [13]. Any educational program related to e-discovery in health needs to include such CPGs.

Audit trails/ metadata search techniques

Audit trails are the records about "who did what and when" in order to meet requirements on "system integrity, recoverability, auditing, and requirements". Effective audit trails on EHR systems should keep all relevant system input and output not only for the purpose of system validation and problem diagnosis, but also to understand how EHR systems are operating. The audit trails can then serve as unbiased evidence of medical practice for potential litigation use [13].

A key component of the functioning of audit trails is Metadata - which is generated to track how an electronic document has been manipulated. Metadata has been viewed as non-hearsay evidence by the courts because it can be considered to have integrity - it is automatically generated without human intervention [10]. Metadata can also be used as a tool to reveal what documents have been actually created, reviewed, modified and deleted. Federal courts have held that when an electronic document is discoverable, it is to be produced "in native format...with their metadata intact" [10]. E-discovery with metadata would generate a huge amount of ESI. This calls for effective search techniques and strategies to facilitate the review process [13]. Therefore, search techniques for metadata and an understanding of metadata need to be covered in e-discovery courses.

Advances in health 2.0

Health 2.0. has been defined as the phenomenon in which Web 2.0 Technologies provide members of the health community–health professionals, health consumers, and health science students–with new and innovative ways to create, disseminate, and share information both individually and collaboratively. It is a new concept of health care that employs social software and other Web-based tools to promote collaboration between patients, their caregivers, medical professionals, and other stakeholders in health care to create a better, more knowledgeable and cost effective environment for better well-being [18]. Health 2.0 is the use of a set of Web tools (blogs, Podcasts, wikis, etc.) in health care by doctors, patients, and scientists. For example, websites like PatientsLikeMe [19] use knowledge from users the network from social media to personalize health care and promote health education [20].

One key difference between traditional models of medicine and Health 2.0 is the knowledge of patient records and related control. In traditional models, patients' records could only be kept and accessed by medical professionals; while in newer models patients obtain more control and deeper insight into their own information. Web 2.0/technology, patients, professionals, social networking, health information/content, collaboration, and change of health care are the topics closely related to the definition of Health 2.0 [18].

Therefore, any curriculum for Health 2.0 should also include, for instance: 1) the stakeholders involved, e.g. patients/consumers, professionals/caregivers, and biomedical researchers, 2) the emerging methods and technology, e.g. web 2.0 and virtual-reality tools, 3) the change of relationship between stakeholders, such as the improved collaboration and communication between professionals and patients, and 4) the impact on the development of health care system like improvement on safety, efficiency and quality of old system. In addition, inaccurate online information is another concern in Health 2.0. Although research has found that online information is often accurate or can be corrected rapidly, many practitioners believe "the consequences could be disastrous for any inexperienced trainee following the advice" [21]. The use of Health 2.0 raises a challenge for healthcare organizations to serve e-discovery requests. Since the information in Health 2.0 associated with privacy, ethical, and ownership issues is in the scope of discovery as well, failing to preserve relevant information due to un-updated usage and electronic data management policy and techniques could lead to potential sanctions. It is important that students are exposed to each one of these, since these could drive e-discovery lawsuits.

E-discovery policy and strategy

Policies and processes for electronic records management

Electronic health records are composed of types of information within the boundary of the health organization, e.g. email, text messages, and even legacy information systems [22]. Health Information Management and IT professionals need to work together to fulfill the tasks of determining organizational document storage, retention, and destruction schedules as well as for digital information to avoid potential sanctions resulting from failure to preserve relevant documents in e-discovery cases.

For instance, the updated policies and processes should indicate where and in what type of format the electronic health records should be stored, how often to maintain such records, and when to destroy them. Updated policies and processes for electronic medical records are required for healthcare organizations to comply with federal, state requirements to facilitate e-discovery.

Economics of cost

Recently, courts have started to limit ESI discovery based on cost-benefit analysis. Under the Discovery Scope and Limits in Rule 26 of The Federal Rules of Civil Procedure, ESI discovery could be limited if "the burden or expense of the proposed discovery outweighs its likely benefit, considering the needs of the case, the amount in controversy, the parties' resources, the importance of the issue at stake in the litigation, and the importance of the proposed discovery in resolving the issues". For example, in Lorranie v. Markel American Insurance Co., Judge Grimm denied the parties' competing motions for summary judgment by opining that "it makes little sense to go to all the bother and expense to get electronic information only to have it excluded from evidence or rejected from consideration during summary judgment because the proponent cannot lay a sufficient foundation to get it admitted [23]". Therefore, it is important for students to understand how organizations should establish a means for determining the actual costs for

production of ESI, and for detecting if this production would be over burdensome in which case such ESI would be out of the scope of discovery [10].

Legal hold policies to handle preservation of relevant documents

Legal hold indicates that a party "must suspend its routine document retention/destruction policy" for the purpose of making sure the preservation of relevant document including ESI, once the party receives a notice of litigation [24]. In order to comply with the preservation obligation, in addition to appropriate techniques, healthcare organizations need to understand the legal hold policy to handle this process, e.g. the instructions and corresponding workflow so that the regular automatic retention/destruction policy would not execute automatically. These issues would fit into an understanding of both law and workflow systems.

Security and privacy issues

Information privacy and data confidentiality

For an information system in any area and domain, security is of crucial concern. Further, information privacy is one key issue that has serious influence on the adoption of EHR systems since all the patients' healthcare information are stored, shared and communicated among different EHR systems and healthcare sectors. Any privacy breach and abuse of data may prohibit the intention to use EHR systems in spite of numerous benefits. Privacy issues have not been addressed sufficiently at either technical or business process level, e.g., in a nationwide survey conducted in February 2005 by Harris Interactive of Rochester, N.Y., 70 percent of people were somewhat or very concerned that personal medical information would be leaked due to weak data security [25].

Data is the primary resource in EHR systems thus its confidentiality is significant for information privacy. Personal information obtained in physician-patient relationship should not be revealed to others unless the patient understands and consents to disclosure [26]. The trend of data sharing among EHR systems and healthcare organizations is inevitable, as a result, innovative management techniques and policies on data confidentiality should be taught to keep in step.

Access controls and policies for EHR

While maintaining information privacy matters, obtaining patients' healthcare information on demand from EHR systems for caregivers like hospitals and doctors is critical as well. There is a trade-off between accessibility to patients' information and privacy concerns, especially when some EHR systems are based on web services which make the information more easily to access while at the same time give rise to potential privacy issues. Therefore, a challenge raised is to develop access control policies that can provide required protection on privacy while keeping flexibility to accommodate authorized users so that only a set of users can access certain level of patient information [27], e.g. which portions of a patient's record can access by whom for a specific period of time. In general, attribute-based access control (ABAC) and role-based access control (RBAC) are the two main approaches to control access to EHR systems [28,29]. ABAC divides the system into subcomponents and for each subcomponent, access policy has been stored as an attribute of the data, while RBAC constructs a hierarchy of roles that can be assigned to each user, through which to authorize privileges to each role instead of each user. Both approaches have their own benefits and shortcomings. Thus understanding existing access control method and policy to ensure both flexibility and security is urgent for any student of e-discovery.

Management of patient consent

As we mentioned earlier, without patient's awareness and consents to disclosure, private information in EHR systems should not be revealed to others, thus consent of patient plays a vital role. Individual patients should know and understand the contents of records in terms of effective notification and truly informed consent for disclosure, which also implies that the particular patient is fully informed of his/her medical status and gives voluntary agreement to permit access to their healthcare information [26]. Failure to truly inform patient's awareness of disclosure, e.g. using implied consent, would lead to unethical issues.

Patients either implicitly or explicitly consent to information disclosure according to different consent models. For example, two types of consent models are considered: General Consent with Specific Denials and General Denial with Specific Consent [30]. Obviously the latter can maintain information at a high level of confidentiality while at the same time, it might hinder the workflow of healthcare providers. Therefore, an understanding of effective consent and control mechanisms are needed that can give patients control for their own healthcare information as well as not impede regular healthcare delivery process.

HITECH and HIPAA privacy and security rules

Significant modifications have been made to Health Information Technology for Economic and Clinical Health Act (HITECH) and Health Insurance Portability and Accountability Act (HIPAA) Privacy and Security Rules. For instance, substantial incentives and grants are provided in the HITECH Act for the adoption of EHR systems and information exchange to improve both quality and efficiency of healthcare. On the other hand, for the HIPAA Privacy and Security Rules, mandatory federal security breach reporting requirements, criminal and civil penalties for noncompliance are established [31,32]. These extensions and enforcements are aimed at continually improving the effect of HITECH and HIPAA rules – clearly an important area of knowledge for the student.

Issues on E-discovery in cloud and Big data

The cloud is the place where various users including patients and physicians on EHR systems have started to share resources [33]. E-discovery becomes more complex in the context of the cloud environment. First, the data are preserved by a cloud service provider, which may lead to the consequence that some ESI might be outside the scope of discovery, or alternately, some data may fall under e-discovery but may not be controlled by firms facing a discovery request. The other reason is, since data from various users is intermingled in the cloud controlled only by the service provider, retrieving and placing a hold on one user's information for anticipated litigation request may affect other users who are not involved [34]. Therefore, some unique issues are needed to be understood in the context of e-discovery in cloud as well.

Cloud services support the basic infrastructure and platform for EHR systems, and would be instrumental in the harvesting of big data. Organizations are experiencing exponential growth in the amounts of data they create, capture, and retain within their in-house facilities, as well as that are maintained in the cloud in the current big data world, thus call for advanced analytics techniques dealing with them [35]. E-discovery also relies on high performance analysis tools to reduce the time and cost, but due to the nature of big data more powerful tools will be needed to identify, organize, and analyze big data. In addition to the technical tools, comprehensive policy and strategy according to e-discovery are also required to accommodate the "big" world. Developing guidelines, procedures, and workflows for the creation, storage and destruction of ESI with potential big data involved in litigation procedures for compliance with federal and state regulations has been considered urgent and necessary as well as a big challenge [36].

In addition, cloud computing service and big data interact with each other. Therefore, they have in common some critical issues, e.g. data preservation and analytics techniques in e-discovery, as well as usage policies and "thresholds" of relevancy for evidence to be admissible.

Data analytics

The volume of data, velocity with which data is generated and variety of data-pictures, messages, audio files, text files, in e-discovery procedures, makes it nearly impossible to review them by humans. Data mining along with predictive analytics plays an important role in e-discovery for legal purposes. For instance, text mining, as well as image mining can discover hidden patterns and relationship between people and events that can be used as evidence in litigations [37].

Predictive coding as the service that can rank and code relevant documents might be used in an anticipated litigation through machine learning algorithms and pattern recognition methods built-in. It is increasingly recognized as a field of inquiry and capability development and could reduce the extent of human involvement in the e-discovery process [38]. A hybrid method combining both predictive coding and data mining techniques with extra attention by human review on the most important ESI would help best practice results in e-discovery. Such skills are important for an e-discovery scholar.

Data preservation and control policies
Data in the cloud provides additional difficulties in data preservation since ESI from one particular user can be stored across multiple physical storage locations due to the nature of cloud. Thus, in order to implement preservation, specific cloud resources need to be isolated [34,39]. Data in the cloud are under custody and control by the cloud service provider which means users may not have actual powerful control over them that can serve as key evidence in litigation [34]. When litigation is anticipated, it is required to put a legal hold on relevant ESI as well in the cloud. Failing to maintain relevant ESI, e.g. deletion by routine operation policy, would result in potential spoliation claims.

Further, the users of EHR data have access and control of their accounts and the information. However, it is possible they may delete some information without realizing that such information could be relevant to anticipated legal issues and should be preserved. Under this circumstance, it is necessary to determine whether the users have a duty to preserve the information and whether it is reasonable to foresee that the information is in the scope of discovery [40].

These issues regarding data preservation in cloud environment by the third party service provider and data control are not taught in many universities as of yet and we suggest that they should be required.

Thresholds of relevancy for evidence to be admissible
Courts are determining on a case-by-case basis whether a person's claim of privacy is reasonable [33]. Courts have continued to be opposed to the notion that any protectable privacy interest exists in material posted on social network websites related to health record, for example, in Fawcett v. Altieri, the court reasoned that, "if

you post a tweet, [it is] just like you scream it out the window, [and] there is no reasonable expectation of privacy." Effective and efficient approaches to determine a "threshold" showing of relevancy for evidence to be admissible are required when concerned about the impact of privacy interests.

Review and Conclusions
This review indicates that there are some "common" issues shared with e-discovery in EHR systems, cloud computing and big data, particularly the attention and emphasis on the needs for organizational policy updates for integrating e-discovery requirements into regular operations and workflows while advances on technical and information privacy are the other two sides. Information is the core in any discovery-related procedure, thus information governance composed of technical and managerial issues would be important for students to understand. We summarize the above discussion in a framework (See Table 1). The framework can be used for potential short course-design on e-discovery and security in the healthcare domain.

This study provides a broad view and better understanding of the critical and urgent issues on e-discovery

Table 1 Framework of key issues for e-discovery in EHR

Domains		Key issues
EHR Systems	Development in EHR	Techniques in EHR systems to facilitate e-discovery
		Information sharing and data interoperability
		Metrics for EHR systems quality control
		Clinical practice guidelines (CPGs) to optimize EHR system use
		Audit trails/metadata search techniques
		Advances in Health 2.0
	E-Discovery policy and strategy	Policies and processes for electronic records management
		Economics of cost
		Legal hold policies to handle preservation of relevant documents
	Security and privacy	Information privacy and data confidentiality
		Access controls and policies for EHR
		Management of patient consent
		HITECH and HIPAA privacy and security rules
Cloud Computing and big data		Data analytics
		Data preservation and control policies
		Thresholds of relevancy for evidence to be admissible

and security focusing on EHR systems. The list of issues can also help healthcare industry for better training of personnel.

It is important to mention that this study was not intended to capture "all of the issues" within given contexts. Nevertheless, it offers an opportunity to build consensus on what is significant and what is urgent in this field. Furthermore, this study would also contribute to developing guidelines for design of courses on e-discovery in the healthcare domain. In the long term with the increasing rate of EHR adoption and EHR meaningful use achievement, new issues and challenges would emerge. Experts from healthcare organizations, legal institutes, and IT professions as well as privacy and data management communities should work closely to draw a detailed education map for this field by sharing different ideas from various orientations.

Endnotes

[a]NAHIT ceased operations in 2009, but it concluded several major US health related initiatives before it ceased. (http://www.healthcareitnews.com/news/nahit-no-more).

Competing interests
The authors declare that they have no competing interests.

Authors' contributions
Author SY carried out the review under the guidance of HRR and SU. All authors participated in the writing of the paper. All authors read and approved the final manuscript.

Acknowledgements
The authors thank the guest editors and reviewers for critical comments that have improved the paper. This research was supported in part by the National Science Foundation under grant # DUE-1241709. The usual disclaimer applies.

References

1. Gensinger Jr RA, Introduction to healthcare information enabling technologies. Chicago: Healthcare Information and Management Systems Society (HIMSS); (2010)
2. C Chen, T Garrido, D Chock, G Okawa, L Liang, The kaiser Permanente electronic health record: transforming and streamlining modalities of care. Health. Aff. **28**, 323–333 (2009)
3. JA Handler, CF Feied, K Coonan, J Vozenilek, M Gillam, PR Peacock, R Sinert, MS Smith, Computerized physician order entry and online decision support. Acad. Emerg. Med. **11**, 1135–1141 (2004)
4. D Blumenthal, Stimulating the adoption of health information technology. N. Engl. J. Med. **360**, 1477–1479 (2009)
5. Strobel CD, American recovery and reinvestment act of 2009 (ARRA09). J Corp Account Finance 20(5):83-85 (2009) (111th US Congress)
6. R Kaushal, AK Jha, C Franz, J Glaser, KD Shetty, T Jaggi, B Middleton, GJ Kuperman, R Khorasani, M Tanasijevic, Return on investment for a computerized physician order entry system. J. Am. Med. Inform. Assoc. **13**, 261–266 (2006)
7. G Paul and B Nearon, The Discovery Revolution: e-Discovery Amendments to the Federal Rules of Civil Procedure, American Bar Association, Chicago, Illinois (2006)
8. Fulton-Cavett AM, Electronic Health Records: Federal E-Discovery Rules and Case Law Are Guides for State Litigation. The Brief, 40 (2011)
9. KB-S Reich, E-discovery in healthcare: 2010 and beyond. Annals. Health. L. **19**, 173 (2009)
10. TR McLean, EMR metadata uses and E-discovery. Annals. Health. L. **18**, 75 (2009)
11. DE Detmer, Building the national health information infrastructure for personal health, health care services, public health, and research. BMC. Med. Informatics. Decision. Making. **3**, 1 (2003)
12. JL Masor, Electronic medical records and E-discovery: with New technology come New challenges. Hastings. Sci. Tech. LJ. **5**, 245 (2013)
13. S Hoffman, A Podgurski, E-Health hazards: provider liability and electronic health record systems. Berkeley. Tech. LJ. **24**, 1523 (2009)
14. S Hoffman, A Podgurski, Meaningful use and certification of health information technology: what about safety? J. Law. Med. Ethics. **39**, 77–80 (2011)
15. R Drummond, EHR certification: getting comfortable with the concept. Health. Manag. Technol. **32**, 26 (2011)
16. Certification Process for EHR Technologies. [http://www.healthit.gov/providers-professionals/certification-process-ehr-technologies]
17. Meaningful Use Definition & Objectives. [http://www.healthit.gov/providers-professionals/meaningful-use-definition-objectives]
18. Van De Belt TH, Engelen LJ, Berben SA, Schoonhoven L: Definition of Health 2.0 and Medicine 2.0: a systematic review. J. Med. Internet. Res.**12**, 2 (2010)
19. Patientslikeme [http://www.patientslikeme.com/]
20. Health 2.0 in Wikipedia. [http://en.wikipedia.org/wiki/Health_2.0]
21. Hughes B, Joshi I, Wareham J: Health 2.0 and Medicine 2.0: tensions and controversies in the field. J. Med. Internet. Res. 2008, **10**, 3 (2008)
22. C Dimick, E-discovery: preparing for the coming rise in electronic discovery requests. J. AHIMA. **78**, 24 (2007)
23. Lorraine v. Markel American Insurance Company, 241 F.R.D 534 (D.Md. May 4, 2007)
24. RC Goss, Hot issues in electronic discovery: information retention programs and preservation. Tort. Trial. Ins. Prac. LJ. **42**, 797 (2006)
25. Ray P, Wimalasiri J: The need for technical solutions for maintaining the privacy of EHR. In Engineering in Medicine and Biology Society, 2006 EMBS'06 28th Annual International Conference of the IEEE; New York City. IEEE. 4686–4689 (2006)
26. KT Win, A review of security of electronic health records. Health. Information. Manag. **34**, 13–18 (2005)
27. Norman C: Advances and Challenges in Secure EHR Access. CEISARE's Information Assurance Program 2012, (2012)
28. Yuan E, Tong J: Attributed based access control (ABAC) for web services. In Web Services, 2005 ICWS 2005 Proceedings 2005 IEEE International Conference on IEEE; Los Alamitos. IEEE. (2005)
29. Ferraiolo D, Cugini J, Kuhn DR: Role-based access control (RBAC): Features and motivations. In Proceedings of 11th annual computer security application conference. IEEE Computer Society Press; Los Alamitos. IEEE. 241-248 (1995)
30. E Coiera, R Clarke, e-Consent: The design and implementation of consumer consent mechanisms in an electronic environment. J. Am. Med. Inform. Assoc. **11**, 129–140 (2004)
31. MM Richards, Electronic medical records: confidentiality issues in the time of HIPAA. Professional. Psychol. Res. Practice. **40**, 550 (2009)
32. PLC CGSB, Client Alert: HITECH Act Expands HIPAA Privacy and Security Rules. In Book Client Alert: HITECH Act Expands HIPAA Privacy and Security Rules. Coppersmith Gordon Schermer & Brockelman PLC; Phoenix (2009)
33. Ashish S. Prasad, Cloud computing and social media: Electronic discovery considerations and best practices. Metropolitan. Corporate. Counsel. 26–27 (2012)
34. Alberto G. Araiza, Electronic Discovery in the Cloud, 10 Duke Law & Technology Review 1–19 (2011)
35. Singh S, Singh N: Big Data analytics. In Communication, Information & Computing Technology (ICCICT), 2012 International Conference on; 19–20 Oct. 2012. IEEE; Mumbai. IEEE. 1–4 (2012)
36. Ingram B: Controlling E-discovery costs in a big data world. Peer Peer. http://www.lexisnexis.com/pdf/Litigation/ArticleILTAPeer2Peer-ControllingEDSCCostsinaBigDataWorld-Ingram032013.pdf (2013)
37. JG Browning, Digging for the digital dirt: discovery and use of evidence from social media sites. SMU. Sci. Tech. L. Rev. **14**, 465 (2010)
38. A Sanfilippo, N Gilbert, M Greaves, Technosocial predictive analytics for security informatics. Security. Informatics. **1**, 1–3 (2012)
39. C Pham, E-discovery in the cloud Era: what's a litigant to do. Hastings. Sci. Tech. LJ. **5**, 139 (2013)
40. 2013 Year-End Electronic Discovery and Information Law Update. [http://www.gibsondunn.com/publications/pages/2013-Year-End-Electronic-Discovery-InformationLaw-Update.aspx]

15

Automated deception detection of 911 call transcripts

Mary B Burns[1*] and Kevin C Moffitt[2]

Abstract

This study is a successful proof of concept of using automated text analysis to accurately classify transcribed 911 homicide calls according to their veracity. Fifty matched, caller-side transcripts were labeled as truthful or deceptive based on the subsequent adjudication of the cases. We mined the transcripts and analyzed a set of linguistic features supported by deception theories. Our results suggest that truthful callers display more negative emotion and anxiety and provide more details for emergency workers to respond to the call. On the other hand, deceivers attempt to suppress verbal responses by using more negation and assent words. Using these features as input variables, we trained and tested several machine-learning classification algorithms and compared the results with the output from a statistical classification technique, discriminant analysis. The overall performance of the classification techniques was as high as 84% for the cross-validated set. The promising results of this study illustrate the potential of using automated linguistic analyses in crime investigations.

Keywords: Automated Linguistic Analysis; Deception Detection; 911 Calls

Introduction

In part due to a natural "truth bias," humans (including those with special training) can generally detect deception at a rate only slightly better than chance, at around 54% [1,2]. This inability to accurately separate truth from deception can have serious consequences; this is particularly true in the case of law enforcement. Not only do criminal investigators have to be concerned with deception that is not detected (false negatives), but they must also take into account the serious outcome of labeling truth tellers as deceivers (false positives). Thus, there is a critical need for more reliable and accurate methods of identifying deception, especially in the earliest contact between a suspected perpetrator and law enforcement. In this study, we evaluate linguistic cues extracted from transcriptions of 911 homicide[a] calls as potential indicators of deception.

As a dataset, 911 calls may be ideal for deception detection research because they occur in a real-world setting, are relatively unrehearsed, occur soon after the crime in question, and are part of emotionally charged situations [3,4]. In contrast, in laboratory settings where deception is

often sanctioned, the consequences of lying and getting caught are minor, and incentives to deceive are artificial (e.g., [5,6]). Thus, as Mann et al. [7] suggest, these low-stakes laboratory environments may not induce feelings of guilt or elicit behavior found in real settings; as a result, they may adversely affect researchers' ability to accurately judge credibility, and therefore diminish the external validity of the results. Thus, it is important to add real-world scenarios to the collection of deception research data.

Deception studies using real-world person-of-interest statements begin to address the research gap identified above [8–10]. Person-of-interest statements are written explanations of crimes by a person who has not been formally charged with a crime but who is "of interest" to law enforcement in an investigation. Studies have been conducted using pre-polygraph interviews, which also involve real-world data [11]. However, relative to 911 calls, the time between the crime and the statements in pre-polygraph interviews is much longer, giving deceivers time to rehearse their responses. Additionally, such datasets may be influenced by investigative procedures or the deceiver's contact with acquaintances between the incident and the statement [4,12]. Thus, 911 calls may be considered a less biased dataset because the interaction with authorities occurs much sooner after the crime and the individual's

---

* Correspondence: mary.burns1@montana.edu
[1]Jake Jabs College of Business & Entrepreneurship, Montana State University, P.O. Box 173040, 59717-3040 Bozeman, MT, USA
Full list of author information is available at the end of the article

words have been less affected by outside influences. Therefore, this dataset provides researchers an unusual opportunity for an unfiltered look at deception.

A subset of 911 calls reporting homicides are available on the Internet because they are high-profile crimes. The calls can be corroborated for ground truth by examining the associated court outcomes. Establishing ground truth is one of the most difficult aspects of research into deception detection [13]. Because initial homicide reports, subsequent investigations, legal proceedings, and judgments are covered widely by news media, it is possible to substantiate ground truth to a high degree of certainty for these types of 911 calls. Although 911 homicide calls represent an extremely small fraction of total 911 calls, they can serve as a proxy for calls made reporting other high-profile crimes such as arson, bomb threats, and sexual assault.

Data mining techniques, including text mining, linguistic feature mining, and classification by text features, can be used to analyze the "caller side" of the transcripts of these calls. Text mining involves looking for hidden patterns or cues in texts, while linguistic feature mining refers to dissecting texts with respect to specific linguistic categories, such as words associated with positive affect. Text mining is a multidisciplinary research area that combines approaches used in the fields of computer science, linguistics, mathematics, communication, and psychology. It focuses on using computing power to process unstructured human language in spoken or written form [5]; furthermore, text mining has been used to process text data to discover linguistic cues or features in order to classify documents, including fraudulent versus non-fraudulent financial statements [14,15] or deceptive versus truthful statements in instant messages, email exchanges, or person-of-interest statements [6–10,16].

In this study, we applied linguistic feature mining to evenly matched (i.e., deceptive matched with truthful) transcripts of 911 homicide calls via Linguistic Inquiry and Word Count (LIWC). LIWC 2007, a general-purpose psychosocial linguistic dictionary comprising 4,500 words and word stems, has been used by researchers to quantify linguistic cues for deception [16–19].

This paper contributes to research streams in security informatics, deception detection, and crime analysis in the following ways:

1) Using a truthful/deceptive matched convenience data set of fifty 911 calls, we identify linguistic cues based on deception theories that may be used to discriminate between deceptive and truthful 911 calls;
2) We extract useful information from unstructured text comprised of transcribed 911 calls to demonstrate that the largely unexploited data of 911

calls can be analyzed for further investigative work; and
3) The classification results achieve up to 84% accuracy.

The remainder of this paper proceeds as follows: we first review deception theories and previous research involving automated or manual deception detection; we then examine advantages and disadvantages of using 911 calls as a data source and discuss linguistic cues of deceptive and truthful 911 callers as we develop our research question and hypotheses; next we describe our methodology, and finally we present and discuss the results, research contributions, limitations of the study, and future research directions.

Literature review

Deception is defined as purposefully concealing the truth, either by omission or commission. In the present study, our general hypothesis is that 911 callers who deceive exhibit systematic differences in the words they use compared to 911 callers who are telling the truth. Possible underlying causes for the differences in deceptive speech are described by deception theories, including four factor theory [20], interpersonal deception theory (IDT) [21], information manipulation theory [22], and reality monitoring [23]. Deception detection researchers rely on theory to identify strategically employed clues that can discriminate between those who deceive and those who do not. In this study, we rely on four factor theory and IDT because they best fit the interpersonal context of a 911 call.

Four factor theory [20] delineates four processes or factors that underlie deceivers' behaviors. *Control*, the first process, describes how deceivers control or suppress their behavior to try to conceal their deception. For example, in 911 calls, deceivers will manage the linguistic and paralinguistic features of their interaction with the dispatcher in order to appear as truthful as possible and not to induce suspicion. The second factor, *arousal*, refers to various autonomic arousal responses of the deceiver's central nervous system that coincide with the deceptive behavior or story. *Felt emotion*, the third factor, encompasses various emotions that deceivers experience, specifically guilt, anxiety, and/or satisfaction in pulling the wool over others' eyes (i.e. "duping delight"). For instance, because of the negative feelings associated with guilt, deceivers try to disassociate themselves from their crime by referring to others rather than to the self through a greater use of through the use third-person pronouns. Anxiety may also impair the quality of the control that deceivers use to conceal their deception. Finally, due to the fourth factor, *cognitive processing*, deceivers have an increased cognitive load as they fabricate and maintain lies. This factor ties into a proposition of IDT, specifically that high cognitive load may be detrimental to a liar's performance and increase the chances of detection. Because of this, deceivers in 911 calls may shorten their responses and use a smaller set of words.

According to IDT [21,24], deception is goal-oriented and strategic. Arising out of interpersonal communication and deception research, IDT predicts the behaviors of senders and receivers in an interactive context[b]. The theory acknowledges the "superordinate role" of the context and relationship within which the interaction occurs. For example, the situational factors of a 911 homicide call will influence how deceptive exchanges play out, and consequently, the hypotheses regarding these exchanges. IDT proposes that the behavior of the deceiver will vary systematically with the spontaneity of the interaction (i.e., lying to a 911 operator requires more dexterity than lying in a written letter) and the immediacy of the context. In 911 calls, the interaction is spatially non-immediate, but temporally immediate. IDT also predicts that deceivers are strategic in managing the information they send, their image, and their behavior; as a result, however, they experience nonstrategic byproducts including dampened affect, noninvolvement, and performance decrements. In the current study, callers should experience increased cognitive loads relative to most contexts, making deception even more difficult. The increased stakes and spontaneity of the conversation may impair deceptive performance.

These theories lend support to the feasibility of using linguistic analysis to carry out deception detection. To discern these deceptive patterns in communication, many recent studies involving automated linguistic cue analyses have leveraged a general-purpose, psychosocial dictionary such as LIWC [5,8-10,25-27]. LIWC contains predefined categories composed of words related to a particular construct, such as Anxiety or Negative Emotion. Depending on the context in which deception occurs, deceivers have been found to display elevated uncertainty and affect, share fewer details, provide more spatiotemporal details, and use less diverse and less complex language than truth tellers [17,26,28]. Researchers have also documented cases in which deceivers use more words, group references and use more informal, non-immediate language than truth tellers [6,9,29].

Researchers who have conducted manual content analyses have also documented linguistic markers of deception [30]; for example, perpetrators of homicide or kidnapping may use past tense (vs. present or future) when discussing the victim, and deceivers may try to distance themselves from the crime by using "they" rather than "I" in statements [4]. Law enforcement researchers [3,4] were successful in manually coding verbal indicators to classify 911 homicide callers as "guilty" or "innocent." In these studies, the key verbal indicators of guilt included extraneous information, inappropriate politeness, a lack of plea for help, and evasion. In an earlier study, Olsson [31] analyzed emergency calls made to report fires in London, UK. He found that hoax calls could be discriminated from truthful ones based on how the caller described or implied his/her relationship to the emergency and the urgency and cooperation of the caller.

The original mode of communication (i.e., written vs. spoken language) is particularly important with respect to linguistic cues that distinguish between truth tellers and deceivers. As noted in IDT, deception is strategic and the spontaneity of the interaction is important [21,24]. Thus, for example, a team tasked with writing the text to include with financial statements has months in which to develop a document that may include strategic misrepresentation or obfuscation via increasing word count and employing words of more than three syllables [14,15]. On the other hand, a person calling a 911 operator after committing a crime has far less time for strategic wordsmithery and may use fewer, simpler words to suppress or control verbal cues for deception.

Research question and hypotheses

Contrary to media hype regarding highly publicized crimes, most 911 calls are not full of drama, excitement, and/or rich descriptions of the crime, crime scene, or victim(s). The 911 operator is trained to elicit information to deploy the right emergency resources as quickly as possible. Although a dramatic outpouring of emotion may be observed in some calls, most 911 calls comprised a great deal of mundane information gathering and information passing to clarify names, addresses, and directions; give life-saving instructions (such as the steps to perform cardiopulmonary resuscitation (CPR)); and ask questions that only require a one-word answer (e.g., "is the victim breathing?").

There are several key advantages to using automated linguistic analysis techniques to detect deception in transcripts of 911 homicide calls. First, 911 calls represent the initial contact between a caller and an emergency response team, including law enforcement, leaving callers little time to prepare or to settle down for the encounter. Moreover, as noted above, the caller's statement has not yet been corrupted by contact with criminal investigators or lawyers [4]. Furthermore, because callers do not perceive 911 operators to be members of law enforcement, deceptive callers may exhibit less controlled behavior and more cues of deception; consequently, 911 callers may become more engaged in interpersonal communication and be less guarded because 911 operators interview rather than interrogate. Due to the temporal immediacy of the crime in relation to the 911 call, there may also be more active stress on the caller, in turn causing the caller to display more deceptive cues. Another advantage for comparison of truthful and deceptive responses in emergency calls is that 911 operators use a structured interview style that was similar across calls.

On the other hand, there are a number of issues with 911 calls that make them a less than ideal source for linguistic analysis. First, these calls can be very short. In the dataset used for this study, calls ranged from less than thirty seconds to over ten minutes in length. On average, the calls were about three to four minutes. Another problem is that there can be a lot of dead air time while the 911 operator puts the caller on hold to coordinate with the rest of the emergency team; such gaps cannot be used in linguistic analyses. Third the sound quality of the calls can make them difficult to transcribe. Fourth, dispatchers, operators, callers, and rescue workers may talk simultaneously. Fifth, certain sounds such as sobs, shrieks, or gasps of pain cannot be easily transcribed and/or analyzed using current linguistic feature dictionaries. Finally, a caller may be poised to offer what could prove to be valuable clues to future investigators, but 911 operators may have to interrupt them to elicit the best information for timely dispatching of the right resources. Consequently, to accomplish their primary mission, the operators who perform both call-taking and dispatching functions may restrict "telling" cues or information [32].

The strengths of the dataset ultimately outweigh the potential weaknesses of the dataset. Thus, we analyzed cues in transcribed 911 calls using the same approach that other researchers have adopted to analyze unstructured texts with a view to distinguish between deceivers and truth tellers. Based on IDT, four factor theory, and previous research, we considered that deceivers may try too hard to cover up what they perceive to be deceptive cues. For example, in a face-to-face context, deceivers may try to limit fidgeting and/or posture shifts, thereby displaying more "stillness" during a lie in an attempt to inhibit overt signs of deception [28]. In the circumstances of this study, where callers are not visible, deceptive 911 callers may restrict their verbal responses, exhibiting low affect or shortened responses when compared to truth tellers. This may be observed in a higher rate of negation and assent words (e.g., "no" and "yes") that may be used by deceivers to limit and control answers. Deceivers may also feel emotions such as guilt, anxiety, and/or duping delight [33]. To lessen these feelings, they may attempt to distance themselves from the situation. The use of first-person singular constructs implies that the speaker "owns" the statement. However, because liars try to distance themselves [34] from the crime or bad situation, they include fewer self-references in retelling stories [17]. Thus, we should find that

deceptive 911 callers use more third-person plural to share the blame.

Four factor theory posits that cognitive effort is required to not only lie, but also to maintain the lie. Vrij, Fisher, Mann, and Leal [35] expand upon this claim and outline all of the tasks a deceiver undertakes that increase cognitive load, including developing a plausible lie, self-monitoring for credibility, monitoring the listener, and remembering the details of the lie while concealing the truth. In short, they argue that lying requires strategic intent and more cognitive effort than truth telling. To mitigate these effects, a liar may rehearse his or her story to keep the facts and details in order. However, because deceptive 911 callers have often had little opportunity to rehearse between the time of the crime and the time of the call, they may face extreme cognitive overload. Thus, these callers may compensate by supplying shorter, controlled statements, sharing fewer details with emergency responders (such as those that would be helpful in locating the physical address of the victim), and asking the 911 operators to "hold on" or "wait" when the operator gives instructions.

Based on these theories and building on previous research on deception detection using linguistic cue analysis, our research question is as follows:

Can automated linguistic analysis techniques accurately classify deceptive versus truthful callers in transcripts of 911 homicide calls?

To define the types of cues that can be examined for deception or truthfulness in 911 calls, we suggest that truth tellers will exhibit more *immediacy* through greater use of first-person singular and first-person plural words. On the other hand, we expect deceivers will show more *non-immediacy*, a distancing from what is said, by referencing others in the third-person singular or plural. To *control* verbal output, or to suppress reactions or answers, deceivers will tend to answer more frequently with shorter, simpler "yes" or "no" answers. Because deceivers tend to suppress reactions, we expect that truth tellers will display more *felt emotion*. On the other hand, we anticipate that deceivers will use more swear words because instances of swearing can be perceived as more credible [36]. Thus, deceivers may include swear words as a way to appear to be emotionally connected to an incident while suppressing their true emotions. Relative to deceivers, truth tellers have a lower *cognitive overload* that allows them to give more location details, such as house numbers and generic information about location. Truth tellers want to provide many clues to get rescue teams to their location as quickly as possible, and will therefore provide specific addresses and phone numbers more clearly, as well as giving more details about the location, such as whether it is a house or apartment building. Finally, due to cognitive overload deceivers may be reluctant, or find it difficult to follow life-saving instructions given by the dispatcher even though not doing so would seem suspicious.

Formally stated, the hypotheses in this study are as follows:

Deceptive 911 callers will display:
(a) higher use of third-person plural, (b) higher use of third-person singular, (c) more assent terms, (d) more negation terms, (e) more emotionally-charged swearing, (f) more inhibition words, and
(g) lower use of first-person plural, (h) lower use of first-person singular, (i) less negative emotion, (j) less anxiety, (k) lower use of numbers, and (l) lower use of generic location details than truthful 911 callers.

Methodology

Our dataset represented a convenience sample obtained from publicly available sources found on the Internet. The majority of the calls came from Dispatch Magazine On-Line (911dispatch.com). This resource contains a tape library of public domain 911 and other emergency calls that have been collected since 2006. The website contains documentation about the calls that enables the user to determine the outcome of the case.

Because we do not have control over the chain of custody of these 911 calls, we cannot state to what degree they were edited. For the most part, personally identifying information has been redacted, but we have no reason to believe that the calls were edited otherwise. However, the inability to state this conclusively is a potential limitation of this convenience dataset. Still, the archive presents a unique opportunity to access this type of real-world data.

The final dataset of 50 transcribed 911 calls was equally split between truthful and deceptive callers. The size of the dataset was restricted by the number of publicly available deceptive calls for which ground truth could be established. To establish ground truth, we corroborated subsequent arraignment, prosecution, and/or admission of guilt via news articles about the crimes based on the information at the source website and other websites as necessary. Once we had identified 25 deceptive calls, we randomly chose 25 calls from our set of transcribed truthful calls to create a matched set. After transcribing the calls and removing the 911 operators' side of the conversations, we analyzed the caller side of the transcripts using LIWC. LIWC normalizes the data by dividing category counts by the number of words in each document.

As summarized in Table 1, the various constructs that we examined comprised one to several linguistic cues as defined in LIWC. The *immediacy* of truth tellers was

Table 1 Constructs and corresponding LIWC categories

Constructs	LIWC categories
Immediacy	1st person plural, 1st person singular
Non-immediacy	3rd person singular; 3rd person plural
Control	Assent; Negate
Felt Emotion	Negative emotion; Anxiety
Lack of felt emotion	Extreme swearing
Cognitive overload	Inhibition
Lack of cognitive overload	Numbers; Leisure (location-related)

anticipated to be observable in greater use of First-Person Plural and First-Person Singular terms (LIWC categories). Conversely, we expected deceivers to show more *non-immediacy* by referencing others in the Third-Person Singular or Third-Person Plural (LIWC categories). Deceivers would also tend to answer with more Negation terms (LIWC category) or more Assent terms (LIWC category) answers as part of *control*. We expected that truth tellers would display more *felt emotion* via the LIWC categories of Negative Emotion and Anxiety than deceivers. In contrast, we anticipated that deceivers, who would attempt to fake an emotional connection while suppressing their true emotions, would use more swear words (LIWC category = Sexual (includes emotionally-charged swear words)). Also due to *cognitive overload*, deceivers might be reluctant to initiate CPR or other first aid efforts (LIWC category = Inhibition). Meanwhile, the lack of *cognitive overload* would enable truth tellers to give more location details such as house numbers (LIWC category = Number) or location-related words such as "garage" or "apartment" (the LIWC category that includes these location words = Leisure).

The first step for identifying significant linguistic cues was to run a one-tailed independent sample t-test for each linguistic cue to compare truth tellers with deceivers. We considered each 911 call transcript to be an independent observation, since it represented one call placed by a unique caller.

Next, we trained various machine-learning classification algorithms on the cues and tested their classification accuracy using 10-fold cross-validation as a bootstrap technique to increase the validity of the results. The following machine-learning algorithms were selected to classify the 911 calls because of their theoretically diverse foundations: logistic model tree induction, naïve Bayes, neural network, and random forest. Classification by one statistical technique, discriminant analysis, was also performed. Table 2 reports the results for each classification method.

Each machine-learning algorithm builds a model based on a different set of theoretical premises. Logistic tree

Table 2 Results of Classification Algorithms

Classification methods	Logistic model tree induction		Naïve Bayes		Random forest		Neural network		Discriminant analysis	
	Training	Cross-valid	Training	Cross-valid	Training	Cross-valid	Training	Cross-valid	Training	Cross-valid
Overall performance	98%	82%	90%	78%	100%	70%	82%	74%	96%	84%
Truth performance	100%	82%	88%	76%	100%	64%	84%	64%	96%	88%
Deception performance	96%	84%	92%	80%	100%	76%	80%	84%	96%	80%

model induction is a classifier for building logit models using regression functions as base learners [37]. A simple naïve Bayes is a probabilistic classifier based on Bayes' theorem. A neural network is a "black box" that performs a classification using hidden layers. A random forest is a type of decision tree that applies decision rules to divide an overall dataset into smaller classification sets. Using these theoretically diverse algorithms, we reduce the likelihood of relying on the results of one algorithm that over-learns the data and fails to generalize to a broader population.

Results and discussion

Table 3 includes the original hypothesis for each construct and associated variable (LIWC category), as well as the results from each one-tailed independent samples t-test. In this way, it gives a comparison of linguistic differences in the deceptive and truthful conditions.

On average, compared to truthful calls, deceptive 911 calls exhibited greater use of "they" ($t_{(50)} = 1.802$, $p < .05$). They also involved more negation ($t_{(50)} = 2.031$, $p < .05$) and assent terms ($t_{(50)} = 1.905$, $p < .05$). Furthermore, they displayed a higher rate of inhibition terms ($t_{(50)} = 2.428$, $p < .05$). In contrast, truthful callers used more numeric words ($t_{(50)} = -2.417$, $p < .05$) and leisure (location-related) words ($t_{(50)} = -2.109$, $p < .05$). The transcripts for truthful calls contained more negative emotion words ($t_{(50)} = -1.915$, $p < .05$), terms for anxiety ($t_{(50)} = -1.975$, $p < .05$), and leisure (location-related) terms ($t_{(50)} = -2.109$, $p < .05$). Table 2 reports the results of the classification algorithms for both a training set and a cross-validation set.

The overall performance of the classification techniques was very strong and ranged from 70% to 84% for the cross-validation tests. The results yielded predictive models with much higher accuracy than that of unaided humans, which, as mentioned above, is 54% [1,2]. The best classification method used was discriminant analysis, followed by logistic model tree induction.

Table 4 lists each variable name (LIWC category) with examples from the transcripts that conform to the results. In part, the accurate classification performance of this study may be due to high motivation exhibited by the callers. DePaulo et al. [28] point out that cues to

deception are more evident when individuals are striving to carry out deception successfully.

The results suggest that truthful callers display more negative emotion and anxiety than deceivers, who tend to display flat affect. Although we had hypothesized that deceivers would use more swear words as an attempt to appear more credible through a faked emotional response, we actually discovered that truth tellers used more extreme swearing (the mean for truthful swearing = .0652; the mean for deceptive swearing = .0000). Emotionally charged swearing was another way for truth tellers to convey negative emotion or frustration during the calls. This finding corresponds to previous research that demonstrated that the primary reason that people swear is to express negative emotions or frustration [38,39].

Honest callers also tended to refer to others in third-person singular. To aid emergency responders, truth tellers used more numbers related to addresses and/or phone numbers and used names of locations, such as "apartment" or "garage".

Deceivers used third-person plural at a higher rate, perhaps to distance themselves from an incriminating situation. However, contrary to our hypotheses, they also demonstrated more immediacy than truth tellers by using both first-person singular (the mean for truthful first-person singular = .2964; the mean for deceptive first-person singular = 1.1760) and first-person plural pronouns (the mean for truthful first-person plural = 9.4136; the mean for deceptive first-person plural = 10.6788).

Deceivers' use of negation and agreement words may have represented their need to suppress or contain their own verbal responses and/or affect. Finally, deceivers tended to tell the 911 operator to "wait" or "hold [on]" (inhibition terms) at a higher rate than truth tellers. This occurred in the 911 calls when the operator asked them to do something they were reluctant to do, such as CPR.

The aim of this research was to expand the understanding of how we can analyze 911 call transcripts for crime analysis and solving. Thus, this study makes three major contributions. First, it has advanced deception detection research by applying linguistic feature mining methods to a unique corpus, namely, transcripts of 911 homicide calls, which represents extremely raw and

Table 3 Analysis of constructs/variables (LIWC categories) in transcripts

Constructs	Associated variables (LIWC categories)	Predicted	Actual	Truthful mean	Truthful Std Dev	Deceptive mean	Deceptive Std Dev
Immediacy	1st person plural	T > D	D > T	.2964	.50586	1.1760	2.15572
	1st person singular	T > D	D > T	9.4136	3.42226	10.6788	4.67963
Non-immediacy	3rd person singular	D > T	T > D*	5.4756	3.84711	3.7344	3.06803
	3rd person plural	D > T	D > T*	.6280	1.16957	1.2652	1.32602
Control	Negation	D > T	D > T*	3.7160	2.18237	4.9892	2.25060
	Assent	D > T	D > T*	4.8160	3.52826	6.9232	4.25887
Felt emotion	Negative emotion	T > D	T > D*	1.5980	1.48383	.8736	1.17341
	Anxiety	T > D	T > D*	.3632	.63672	.0904	.26723
	Extreme swearing (Sexual)	D > T	T > D	.0652	.15075	.0000	.0000
Cognitive overload	Number	T > D	T > D*	5.5628	5.71633	2.5760	2.34458
	Leisure	T > D	T > D*	.7564	.65370	.3560	.68811
	Inhibition	D > T	D > T*	.1748	.27091	.4648	.53210

*Significant at p-value < = 0.05.

largely unrehearsed human communication. We determined that deceivers use language and linguistic cues differently than truth tellers in a high-stakes, real-world corpus of 911 homicide calls. Thus, this study represents a successful proof of concept of using automated linguistic analysis to classify deceptive versus truth telling 911 homicide calls accurately, quickly, and objectively in comparison to manual methods of content analysis, which involve extensive training, time-consuming analyses, and subjectivity. Through analysis of 911 calls, law enforcement could detect deceptive, guilty perpetrators earlier in the investigative process and use that information for crime analysis. Second, we extracted useful information from unstructured text comprising transcribed 911 calls to demonstrate that these largely unexploited data can be analyzed for further investigative work. Third, this study provided strong classification results of up to 84%

accuracy (cross-validated). These results approach the highest reported accuracy of field-based polygraph tests which is 92% [40,41]. Combined with speech-to-text software, automated deception detection techniques could be used to monitor 911 calls in real time. Although the mission of the 911 operators would remain the same, automated monitoring of 911 calls could enable law enforcement and rescue workers to focus efforts and resources more successfully on post-hoc crime solving and analysis.

Limitations and conclusion

Despite these contributions discussed above, the convenience sample of 50 archived 911 homicide calls downloaded from the Internet represents a limited dataset. The size of the current dataset was restricted by the number of publicly available deceptive calls for which

Table 4 Variables (LIWC Categories) with Examples from Transcripts

Variable Name	Direction	Truthful Transcript	Deceptive Transcript
3rd person singular	T > D	**She's** right on the floor. **She's** not breathing.	
3rd person plural	D > T		Yes, **they** said, **they** said if **they** heard anything **they** were going to my house.
Negation	D > T		**No, nothing**, he's gone.
Assent	D > T		Okay, **they're here.**
Negative emotion	T > D	There was a **fight**. It was **terrible**.	
Anxiety	T > D	I found out about an hour ago and I've been in a **panic** ever since.	
Number	T > D	**Five seventeen** West Doty Street	
Leisure	T > D	I see her in her **garage** right now.	
Inhibition	D > T		[conversation while the operator is trying to give CPR instructions] **Hold** on, I have to throw up, please **hold** on.

Note: Bold-faced type in transcript columns indicates words associated with each respective variable.

ground truth could be established. Furthermore, the 911 calls were taken from the Internet, not the original source. As a result, some information—such as names—may have been blocked out to protect the privacy of the caller when the 911 call was released to the public. An additional limitation arises from the fact that we did not control the chain of custody over the 911 calls. Thus, we are not able to establish whether or to what degree the 911 calls had been edited. Moreover, only certain states currently release 911 calls to the public, so the geographic origin of the calls could be skewed. Finally, the calls were restricted to those placed by English-speaking callers located in the U.S. To counter these limitations in the future, audio files and/or transcripts should be collected directly from law enforcement in subsequent research to validate our results, and sampling from diverse geographical locations should be carried out.

Accurate, credible assessment decisions are critical for law enforcement personnel, who may not detect deception, may act on false positives, or may use incorrect information for crime analyses. Moreover, other clues for deception, such as vocalic cues, should be studied in conjunction with linguistic cues for a practical decision support tool that includes combined analyses. In the future, an integrated system for deception detection that can be used in real time in high-stakes 911 calls could be added to law enforcement's overall crime-solving and crime-analysis strategy. Text mining tools could also be used to analyze 911 calls linguistically as part of a portfolio of crime-solving techniques to enable law enforcement and rescue workers to focus their efforts and resources more successfully.

This study's findings provide critical knowledge about how deceivers communicate during typically unrehearsed verbal exchanges and expand the usefulness of deception models from a low-stakes, laboratory setting into a high-stakes, real-world environment where there are serious consequences not only for the deceiver, but also for law enforcement. The next step for this research will be to validate these results using a larger real-world dataset. Additionally, when we use a larger dataset, we can conduct testing of revised hypotheses for 1st person plural (D > T), 1st person singular (D > T), and swearing (T > D) to establish if new results are significant in the revised directions. Current and future quantitative models and decision aids could assist law enforcement in detecting deception.

Endnotes

[a]In this paper, the term "homicide" includes not only murders, but also accidents that were later deemed by investigators to be homicides, reports of kidnapping that masked an underlying homicide or neglectful death, and murder-suicides.

[b]A unique characteristic of this dataset that may not be true in others is that 911 deceivers are treated implicitly as truthful by the dispatcher. A 911 dispatcher operates under the assumption that the caller is telling the truth. Therefore, a deceptive caller may never change his story based on his perception that the operator is suspicious of it.

Competing interests
The author(s) declare that they have no competing interests.

Authors' contributions
MB conceived of the study, participated in its design, obtained funding for the project, gathered the audio data files and transcribed the files into text, performed the statistical analysis and interpretation of the data, and drafted the manuscript. KM participated in the design of the study, participated in obtaining funding for the project, performed the parsing of the data into linguistic cue categories, participated in the overall analysis and interpretation of the data, and helped to draft the manuscript. Both authors read and approved the final manuscript.

Acknowledgements
We are pleased to acknowledge the generous support from a Center for Identification Technology Research (CITeR) Grant for funding the data collection and analysis phases of this project.

Author details
[1]Jake Jabs College of Business & Entrepreneurship, Montana State University, P.O. Box 173040, 59717-3040 Bozeman, MT, USA. [2]Accounting and Information Systems, Rutgers Business School, Rutgers, The State University of New Jersey, 100 Rockefeller Road, 08854 Piscataway, NJ, USA.

References
1. CF Bond, BM DePaulo, Accuracy of deception judgments. Personal. Soc. Psychol. Rev. **10**, 214–234 (2006)
2. M Aamodt, H Custer, Who can best catch a liar? Forensic Examiner **15**, 6–11 (2006)
3. SH Adams, T Harpster, 911 homicide calls and statement analysis. FBI Law Enforce. Bull. **77**, 22–31 (2008)
4. T Harpster, SH Adams, JP Jarvis, Analyzing 911 homicide calls for indicators of guilt or innocence. Homicide Stud. **13**, 69–93 (2009)
5. L Zhou, JK Burgoon, DP Twitchell, T Qin, JF Nunamaker Jr, A comparison of classification methods for predicting deception in computer-mediated communication. J. Manag. Inf. Syst. **20**, 139–165 (2004)
6. L Zhou, JK Burgoon, JF Nunamaker Jr, DP Twitchell, Automating linguistics based cues for detecting deception in text based asynchronous computer mediated communication: an empirical investigation. Group Decis. Negotiation **13**, 81–106 (2004)
7. S Mann, A Vrij, R Bull, Suspects, lies, and videotape: an analysis of authentic high-stake liars. Law Hum. Behav. **26**, 365–376 (2002)
8. CM Fuller, DP Biros, M Adkins, JK Burgoon, JF Nunamaker Jr, S Coulon, Detecting Deception in Person-Of-Interest Statements, in *Lecture Notes in Computer Science*, vol. 3975 (Springer, Berlin/Heidelberg, 2006), pp. 504–509
9. CM Fuller, DP Biros, D Delen, Exploration of Feature Selection and Advanced Classification Models for High-Stakes Deception Detection, in *Proceedings of the 41st Hawaii International Conference on System Sciences (HICSS)* (Waikoloa, Big Island, HI, 2008)
10. CM Fuller, DP Biros, RL Wilson, Decision support for determining veracity via linguistic-based cues. Decis. Support. Syst. **46**, 695–703 (2008)
11. ML Jensen, E Bessarabova, B Adame, JK Burgoon, SM Slowik, Deceptive language by innocent and guilty criminal suspects: the influence of dominance, question, and guilt on interview responses. J. Lang. Soc. Psychol. **30**, 357–375 (2011)
12. VA Sandoval, Strategies to avoid interview contamination. FBI Law Enforce. Bull. **72**, 1–12 (2003)

13. A Nijholt, RC Arkin, S Brault, R Kulpa, F Multon, B Bideau, DR Traum, H Hung, E Santos Jr, D Li et al., Trends and controversies. IEEE Intell. Syst. **27**, 60–75 (2012)

14. S Humpherys, KC Moffitt, MB Burns, JK Burgoon, WF Felix, Identification of fraudulent financial statements using linguistic credibility analysis. Decis. Support. Syst. **50**, 585–594 (2011)

15. KC Moffitt, MB Burns, *What does that mean?* Investigating Obfuscation and Readability Cues as Indicators of Deception in Fraudulent Financial Reports, in *Fifteenth Americas Conference on Information Systems* (San Francisco, CA, 2009), p. 2009

16. JT Hancock, LE Curry, S Goorha, M Woodworth, On lying and being lied to: a linguistic analysis of deception in computer-mediated communication. Discourse Process. **45**, 1–23 (2008)

17. ML Newman, JW Pennebaker, DS Berry, JM Richards, Lying words: predicting deception from linguistic styles. Personal. Soc. Psychol. Bull. **29**, 665–675 (2003)

18. JW Pennebaker, ME Francis, RJ Booth, *Linguistic Inquiry and Word Count* (Erlbaum Publishers, Mahway, NJ, 2001)

19. YR Tausczik, JW Pennebaker, The psychological meaning of words: LIWC and computerized text analysis methods. J. Lang. Soc. Psychol. **29**, 24–54 (2010)

20. M Zuckerman, BM DePaulo, R Rosenthal, Verbal and Nonverbal Communication of Deception, in *Advances in Experimental Social Psychology*, ed. by L Berkowitz, vol. 14 (Academic, New York, NY, 1981), p. 60

21. DB Buller, JK Burgoon, Interpersonal deception theory. Commun. Theory **6**, 203–242 (1996)

22. SA McCornack, Information manipulation theory. Commun. Monogr. **59**, 1–16 (1992)

23. M Johnson, C Raye, Reality monitoring. Psychol. Rev. **88**, 67–85 (1981)

24. JK Burgoon, DB Buller, Interpersonal deception: III: effects of deceit on perceived communication and nonverbal behavior dynamics. J. Nonverbal Behav. **18**, 155–184 (1994)

25. CM Fuller, DP Biros, JK Burgoon, M Adkins, DP Twitchell: An analysis of text-based deception detection tools. In *AMCIS 2006 Proceedings*. 2006: Paper 418

26. T Qin, JK Burgoon, JP Blair, JF Nunamaker Jr, Modality Effects in Deception Detection and Applications in Automatic Deception Detection, in *Proceedings of the 38th Hawaii International Conference on Systems Sciences (HICSS)*, 2005

27. L Zhou, DP Twitchell, T Qin, JK Burgoon, JF Nunamaker Jr, An Exploratory Study into Deception Detection in Text-Based Computer-Mediated Communication, in *Proceedings of the 36th Hawaii International Conference on Systems Sciences (HICSS '03)*, 2003

28. BM DePaulo, JJ Lindsay, BE Malone, L Muhlenbruck, K Charlton, H Cooper, Cues to deception. Psychol. Bull. **129**, 74–118 (2003)

29. L Zhou, JK Burgoon, DP Twitchell, A Longitudinal Analysis of Language Behavior of Deception in E-Mail, in *Intelligence and Security Informatics: First NSF/NIJ Symposium, ISI 2003, Tucson, AZ, USA, June 2-3, 2003 Proceedings*, ed. by H Chen, R Moore, D Zeng, J Leavitt, vol. 2665/2003 (Springer, Berlin / Heidelberg, 2003), pp. 102–110. Lecture Notes in Computer Science

30. LN Driscoll: A validity assessment of written statements from suspects in criminal investigations using the scan technique. Police Stud: Int. Rev. Police Dev. **17**, 77–78 (1994)

31. J Olsson, *Forensic Linguistics: An Introduction to Language, Crime, and Law* (Continuum International Publishing Group, London, 2004)

32. SJ Tracy, When questioning turns to face threat: an interactional sensitivity in 911 call-taking. West. J. Commun. **66**, 129–157 (2002)

33. P Ekman, Mistakes when deceiving. Ann. N. Y. Acad. Sci. **364**, 269–278 (1980)

34. A Vrij, *Detecting Lies and Deceit: Pitfalls and Opportunities*, 2nd edn. (Wiley, Chichester, West Sussex, England, 2008)

35. A Vrij, R Fisher, S Mann, S Leal, A cognitive load approach to lie detection. J. Investig. Psychol. Offender Profiling **5**, 39–43 (2008)

36. E Rassin, S van der Heijden, Appearing credible? Swearing helps! Psychol. Crime Law **11**, 177–182 (2005)

37. M Sumner, E Frank, M Hall, Speeding up Logistical Model Tree Induction, in *9th European Conference on Principles and Practice of Knowledge Discovery in Databases*, 2005, pp. 675–683

38. E Rassin, P Muris, Why do women swear? An explanation of reasons for and perceived efficacy of swearing in Dutch female students. Personal. Individ. Differ. **38**, 1669–1674 (2005)

39. T Jay, K Janschewitz, The pragmatics of swearing. J. Politeness Res. Lang. Beh. Cult. **4**, 267–288 (2008)

40. PE Crewson, *Comparative analysis of polygraph with other screening and diagnostic tools. No. DODPI01-R-0003* (Research Support Service, Ashburn, VA, 2001)

41. CR Honts, DC Raskin, A field study of the validity of the directed lie control question. J. Police Sci. Adm. **16**, 56–61 (1988)

16

Pathways to identity: using visualization to aid law enforcement in identification tasks

Joe Bruce[1*], Jean Scholtz[1], Duncan Hodges[2], Lia Emanuel[3], Danaë Stanton Fraser[3], Sadie Creese[2] and Oriana J Love[1]

Abstract

The nature of identity has changed dramatically in recent years and has grown in complexity. Identities are defined in multiple domains: biological and psychological elements strongly contribute, but biographical and cyber elements also are necessary to complete the picture. Law enforcement is beginning to adjust to these changes, recognizing identity's importance in criminal justice. The SuperIdentity project seeks to aid law enforcement officials in their identification tasks through research of techniques for discovering identity traits, generation of statistical models of identity and analysis of identity traits through visualization. We present use cases compiled through user interviews in multiple fields, including law enforcement, and describe the modeling and visualization tools design to aid in those use cases.

Keywords: Identity; Attribution; Enrichment; Visual analysis; Modeling; Wizard; Law enforcement; Visualization; Data transformation

Background and related work

The complexity of identities has increased dramatically in recent years, particularly with the introduction and widespread adoption of social networks and broader online activities [1]. The complexity presents challenges for law enforcement, especially given the massive volumes of data being generated [2]. Identity is a key enabling factor in almost everything in the 21st century [3]; successfully identifying individuals underpins almost every secure and private system. Important systems such as banking, international travel, and commerce all rely on identity; many interpersonal services rely on individuals identifying themselves (e.g., email, information technology services, etc.)[4].

Gathering a more complete picture of an individual (identity enrichment) and tracing an activity back to the acting party (identity attribution) are tasks complicated by the diversity of identifying information. However, the glut of data can also aid law enforcement in their investigative tasks if they can take advantage of it [5]. Furthermore, new connections and investigative paths are accessible if the research can be materialized into operational procedures [6].

Law enforcement decision makers are now recognizing the importance of using social networks in their investigations. The International Association of Chiefs of Police (IACP) conducted a survey in 2012 that showed that 92.4% of the 600 law enforcement agencies polled were using social media [7]. Law enforcement personnel can use social media for prevention of crime as well as investigation of crime. Information about plans for protests often can be found online as can discussions and photographs of activities that have occurred [8]. As identity spans both the natural and the cyber worlds, it is important that law enforcement have the tools to establish and pursue identities as they flow across the domain boundaries; no longer is it sufficient to explore identities purely in one domain [3].

The SuperIdentity project is designed to accomplish just that: provide the tools that pursue identities across domains. SuperIdentity is a collaborative effort among six UK universities and a US national laboratory conducting research in a variety of domains that can aid in attribution and enrichment investigative tasks. This paper presents a visual analytic application developed at the Pacific Northwest National Laboratory (PNNL) that provides a visual interface to a complex statistical model of identity, developed at the University of Oxford. The model encapsulates research performed at the collaborating universities in

* Correspondence: joe.bruce@pnnl.gov
[1]Pacific Northwest National Laboratory (PNNL), Richland, WA, USA
Full list of author information is available at the end of the article

the United Kingdom and generates analytic pathways that can lead an investigator from that which is known to that which is unknown but essential to the investigative task.

The pathways generated by the model, and the visualization that makes them accessible, will enable law enforcement to take full advantage of the interconnected elements of identity in our modern world. From the beginning, the SuperIdentity project has used a user-centric design approach. An early activity in the SuperIdentity project was the collection of use cases (*Developing the use cases* Section) to explore how various law enforcement roles could interact with the model. The aim of this activity was twofold. The initial aim was to understand how various types of end users undertook the task of identifying individuals, including the data used, the initial evidence that was usually available, the desired outcome of the identification, and the amount of uncertainty that could be tolerated. Secondly, the information obtained in these use cases helped to guide the development of the model for identity and the visualization to support those same end users. The use cases were collected through interviews with law enforcement personnel and illustrate difference scenarios in identifying individuals or in enriching the identification of an individual. These use cases helped researchers understand how law enforcement personnel go about doing identification tasks and problems and constraints in this work. Exemplar use cases were developed from current use cases and illustrate how new types of identity traits could facilitate identification tasks. The application has been developed using exemplar use cases that have helped identify useful visualization techniques. A user-centered evaluation is also planned for later in the year and will be discussed in the *Future Work* section.

Research in identity attribution and enrichment is beginning to explore how this process may span the physical and cyber world divide. For instance, links between biometric physical features and avatar recognition for identity authentication and enrichment are being explored [9]. There has been a focus on authorship attribution, for example, to determine if the content of multiple online social network identities belongs to a single author [10] or extracting identity features in tracing cybercrime [11].

Several active research consortiums are exploring how to mine and model identity data in more comprehensive ways. The Collaborative information, Acquisition, Processing, Exploitation and Reporting project (CAPER) is one of the larger ongoing projects [12]. This active consortium is focused on enabling law enforcement agencies across the EU to work together, with a focus on the ability to use and share open source intelligence to detect and prevent organized crime. The development process of the Caper Regulatory Model (CRM) has taken a user-centric approach in involving law enforcement users in

the function, legality, and visualization of the model. The project has been guided by the goals to enable analysts to collaboratively collect, connect, and work with multiple data types (e.g., audio, text, video) to enrich identity information, while allowing analysts to fuse their own closed source data with open source on a site-by-site basis. However, much of the project's focus has been developing the former (enhancing open source web mining/analysis capabilities) to provide "early warning" trends for organized crime across cyber-space. Although there is some discussion on the inclusion of physical domain identity attributes, such as biometric data, there is no indication of cross-domain links or inference capabilities beyond big data pattern detection within CRM.

The Uncertainty of Identity multidisciplinary project has been capitalizing on the wealth of location information now available in the cyber world [13]. Specifically, this project looks at how geo-social networks can provide spatio-temporal information linking physical and virtual identities. Although this approach allows for large-scale links between physical and cyber domains, the identity attributes that can be inferred from cyber location data are currently limited to online social networks and relatively shallow identity descriptors. For instance, the project has developed a method to model and geographically visualize Twitter activity. From this, the user is able to infer names, ethnicity, gender of Twitter users, and temporal activity patterns across different physical locations (e.g., London, Paris, and New York) [14].

Much of the previous attribution work has centered on author attribution and cyber intrusion attribution, e.g., [15-17]. This work is heavily weighted toward automated, machine-learning solutions. Moreover, the attribution efforts do not cross identification domains.

For many applications, a holistic approach to understanding identity is needed. A holistic approach would span and link physical and cyber domains and be organized in such a way that individuals working with identification tools could intuitively understand, organize, manipulate, and infer unknown from known pieces of information about an individual or group. This paper introduces the SuperIdentity approach to these issues and describes the user-centric methods used in the development of the SuperIdentity model and visualization interface.

Developing the use cases

Use case development was an early activity in the SuperIdentity project. It is important to note that the majority of these use cases were obtained in the United States and hence some of the constraints discussed here are based on the legal framework applicable in the United States. However, researchers in the SuperIdentity project are looking at differences in laws in different countries, and indeed the resulting model allows the encapsulation of differing legal, cultural, and ethical frameworks [4].

Use cases were collected for several reasons. First, use cases provided insight into how analysts who have the task of identifying individuals currently work, including information they usually know, information they need to know, the certainty needed in identifications, resources used, and obstacles encountered, such as time constraints and inability to access certain resources. Secondly, understanding current work provided insights about what identity attributes would be useful and how to present this information to the end-users.

Individuals were recruited from three analysis domains: intelligence analysis, cyber security investigations, and law enforcement. PNNL works with a number of different agencies and law enforcement departments, so individuals in some of these organizations were contacted to help recruit participants. In the United Kingdom, recruitment was facilitated by one of the project sponsors. In the law enforcement domain, we interviewed individuals from the county sheriff's office, a police chief, and city law enforcement officers working in a fusion center. The individuals who participated were interviewed about their work in identifying individuals.

Questionnaires were also developed to elucidate the types of information that were used and how important the various information types were to the identification work. After the semi-structured interviews, participants were asked to look at information in different domains and identify those elements they commonly used in their work. For example:

Demographics/physical attributes: age, gender, ethnicity, handedness, facial biometrics
Work and extra-curricular activities: hobbies/interests, travel plans, group affiliations
Financial information: owned assets, banking information
Court/council records: arrests, tickets/fines, current/past addresses
Cyber attributes: email addresses, social network user names, personal websites

Overall, 21 individual use cases were developed. Commonalties were identified in these individual use cases, which resulted in the generation of several generic use cases, such as going from an online user name to an actual name. In addition, a number of exemplar use cases were generated, illustrating how different types of information can be combined to augment what we know about a person, including cyber (e.g., IP address), biometric (e.g., fingerprint), biographic (e.g., home address), and psychological (e.g., personality traits) information.

In this paper, the focus is on the issues involved in law enforcement. Besides gathering information to generate use cases, additional information about policies and procedures in law enforcement was obtained, providing valuable insights into the context in which software tools need to work. The following paragraphs contain information about the context in which identification tasks often take place. It should be noted that the majority of this information is based on interviews done in the US states of Oregon and Washington.

Much of the public-facing law enforcement work is done in real time and in close proximity to the individual being identified—e.g., during traffic stops. However, for some officers there is also other investigative work that, while it does not have to be completed in real time, has a requirement for the task to be completed as efficiently as possible.

Real-time law enforcement work, such as traffic stops, can have many constraints. While a law enforcement officer may stop a car or an individual, there has to be a valid reason, such as a traffic violation. The driver of the car or the individual stopped does have to talk to the law enforcement officer, but the discussion must focus only on the reason the individual was stopped. The individual detained can refuse to answer questions, but it is illegal to lie to a law enforcement officer. The individual stopped can only be detained for a short period of time; a traffic stop that lasts for more than 20 minutes is unreasonable. If passengers are in the car, they cannot be asked for identification or questioned unless the officer has seen them break a law.

Having stopped an individual, the law enforcement officer has information about the vehicle (if driving), the driver's license of the individual driving the vehicle, and a physical description of the individual. This information can be communicated via radio or a computer and additional information obtained, such as the owner of the vehicle, the name and aliases of the driver, whether there are outstanding warrants for the arrest of the driver, and possibly information as to whether the driver has a history of being "unfriendly to law enforcement." If there is a warrant out for arrest of an individual with this name, date of birth, and matching physical characteristics, the officer is justified in taking the individual to the police station and taking fingerprints to increase the certainty of the identification. It is currently not legal to obtain a DNA sample.

In general, law enforcement officers preferred to err on the side of caution. It is better to take a person in for more questioning than to miss picking up a person who has outstanding warrants. When officers provide data on the stopped individual to a police database "near misses" are returned if there is no direct match. Sorting out a number of near misses may consume too much time, so the officer may take the individual back to the police station for full identification.

In investigative work, officers have more time to conduct their investigation but also lack the richness of information (physical and recorded) that officers in real-time situations have. There may be physical descriptions from eyewitnesses and a description of a vehicle and/or a license plate number. Items may be left behind, including notes, fingerprints, and footprints. The goals are to locate the individual(s) who were involved in the crime being investigated and to place them at the scene of the crime with enough certainty to make an arrest.

In addition to the work done by Law Enforcement Divisions, the United States has created a number of fusion centers in response to the September 11, 2001 terrorist attacks. These fusion centers, located in urban areas, comprise representatives from the major intelligence agencies and state and local law enforcement agencies. They can share information to help with law enforcement, prevent terrorist activities, and respond to emergency situations [18]. The analysts that work in these fusion centers are a very rich resource for our use cases as they deal with many different types of data, from different sources, with differing confidence levels; hence, several interviews were conducted with analysts from fusion centers.

In the 21 use cases we collected, 10 were from the law enforcement domain and the rest were from intelligence domain. Here we focus on the law enforcement use cases. Of these 10, three could be classified as strictly attribution tasks: a crime has happened and the task is to identify who did it. Four could be classified as enrichment tasks: an individual is known but it is unknown if this individual is a danger to police. Three others could be classified as both attribution and enrichment: is this person really who they say they are, and what else is known about that person? Even attribution tasks are often more complex that just going from a crime to a name. We might have several similar crimes and want to determine if the same individual is responsible for all crimes. Of the use cases involving enrichment, two were descriptions of real-time incidents; law enforcement officers have an individual in front of them and want to understand who that person is and if that person poses a danger to them.

A typical use case is the Property Crime: Someone has broken into a car and stolen some items. There is a small amount of evidence, e.g., some fingerprints, a footprint, and perhaps a description of the person from a passerby. The police want to find out who is responsible. They need to find the name of the individual and the individual's current location.

The use cases, such as the examples discussed above, provided a good understanding of the tasks, resources and constraints that law enforcement officers face. Using this information a number of exemplar use cases were developed. Similar themes in use cases were identified and merged into an exemplar use case. As the individual use cases are based on what is currently done, the exemplar case studies were augmented to utilize the work in SuperIdentity. These use cases are being used in developing the visualizations to demonstrate to end users the different possibilities for obtaining the desired information given their starting information, the various resources available to them, and the certainty required in their identification. The visualization work will be discussed in the *SuperIdentity model and visualization* Section and will use the exemplar use case below.

The exemplar use case described below is based on a real homicide case. We have added a second homicide to illustrate how the model can be used to in connecting information between two crimes. We have also added an iPhone to introduce new types of information used by the model.

Two homicides occurred in a particular town within two weeks. The police are trying to find a possible suspect or suspects and motives. They have several pieces of information. At the scene of the first homicide, a witness saw a car leave the area and is able to recall a partial license plate. An iPhone was dropped at the second scene and police believe it is reasonable to assume that the phone is not associated with the victim or the victim's friends or family.

Using the description of the car and the partial license plate number, the police have located a set of a dozen suspects. Of these, only four were anywhere close to the area of the crime scenes. None of these four have any police records. However, the phone number of one of these persons was listed as a recent call on the cell phone left at the scene.

The license plate information and car description are typically what would be expected for information as are the contents of the cell phone, such as recent online activity and fingerprints on the phone. In the next section, the model will suggest other information that may be obtained. If a suspect can be identified and brought in for questioning, it may be possible to determine if the suspect was responsible for both homicides.

SuperIdentity model and visualization
The exemplar use case described in the previous section demonstrates the requirement to consider identity as complex phenomena crossing many different domains. SuperIdentity considers identity across four complementary domains: an individual's biological makeup, biographical information, online presence (cyber domain), and mental makeup (psychological domain). These cross-domain characteristics are used to evaluate the holistic identity associated with individuals.

There are projections of identity in the natural world; the physical projections of identity include things like biometrics, an individual's description (height, sex, weight, hair color, etc.) are important as these are used by humans to help recognize individuals in the natural world. In addition to these physical projections of identity, biographical information provides factual information about the individual, such as home address, occupation, social security numbers, work address, etc. This information is often used to locate or identify a single individual.

Over the last 20 years, online projections of identity have emerged; these projections in cyber-space are now pervasive throughout society. Society uses cyber-space for everything from very personal activities (such as engaging with friends, documenting our lives, expressing our creativity), to learning and developing opinions, to very practical concepts such as travel planning, commerce, and banking [19]. All online activities leave a trail of identity pieces scattered throughout cyber-space, whether through conscious disclosures (e.g., on social networks), subconscious disclosures (such as exploited in textual-content analysis), or through technology-level leakages (e.g., through cookies) [20]. Meta-data associated with online activities also exists, such as IP addresses, account names, etc., which can all be related to an individual's identity.

The final identification domain that is important to consider when discussing identity is the psychological domain. This involves the psychological profile of an individual. Measures like the Big-5 [21] and the Dark Triad [22] give insight into concepts such as extraversion, conscientiousness, Machiavellianism, etc. These personality elements often drive behaviors in different spaces and as such are important to understand when investigating an individual.

All four of these identification domains are important to consider. This is clear from the exemplar use case in the *Developing the use cases* Section. Starting with a mobile phone, much of the data available is likely to be related to the cyber domain, and much of the investigation may involve gathering online data. But the investigator likely wants to explore more about the motive of the individual and indicators of intent. Both psychological traits and content posted on the Internet will be contributing factors. The license plate will provide contradictory information to that of the phone: the owners are not the same person. This investigation will draw in social contacts, physical residence, and temporal location. Leveraging all this data to yield a more complete picture of the individuals involved requires the collective use of data from all four domains.

To this end, we use an intuitive modeling approach that, in an investigative mode, allows the capture of these rich identities in addition to documenting both the processes by which the pieces of identity were derived and the confidence associated with each piece. To illustrate, consider the partial license plate gathered as evidence from the exemplar use case. Any identification performed

will have a moderate level of uncertainty attached to it because the correctness of the license plate is in question. Inferences suffer the same potential uncertainty, depending on the nature of the inference. An investigator might infer a relationship between a phone's owner and a person listed in the contact list, but uncertainty exists about the nature and strength of that relationship. Knowing how the inferences were made (their derivation) and their associated confidence is necessary to yield a complete picture of what is known, and what is unknown, about a particular identity.

The model is built around two simple concepts: elements of identity and inferences. An element of identity is a single piece of information that is representative or indicative of an identity; it does not need to be unique (i.e., an individual's height), it may be unique in a given context (i.e., a Twitter user name is unique on Twitter, but the same user name may be used by another individual on Instagram) or it may be globally unique (e.g., a MAC address). Each element has an associated confidence that is related to the uncertainty associated with an element.

As part of the SuperIdentity project, a simple taxonomy of these elements of identity has been created with the top layer of the hierarchy representing the four identification domains discussed previously (biological, biographical, cyber, and psychological). The folksonomy was created as a joint-design exercise amongst the SuperIdentity consortium. The cross-disciplinary expertise within the consortium was exploited in order to identify both the elements of identity across all projections of identity and then place the elements into a hierarchy. The hierarchy that resulted from this exercise contained four distinct levels the top-level representing the four domains (as discussed previously), the level below this representing a sub-division within this domain (for example within Cyber there are subdivisions for devices (e.g. smartphone, laptop, etc.), generic technologies (e.g. e–mail) and personas (an individual's use of a site)). The penultimate level of the hierarchy represents the space where the element of identity is exposed (for example elements are exposed in a Facebook account, other elements are exposed in a hand). The final element of the hierarchy is the actual data point – this represents the element that is explicitly measured or captured (for example within Facebook, the username, the avatar, the friendslist etc. all represent elements that can be captured, for a hand the fingerprints can be captured, the fingerlength can be measured, etc.) Figure 1 illustrates Facebook and hand identity elements as examples within the context of the SuperIdentity hierarchy. Summarizing statistics related to the model as a whole can be found in Table 1.

This hierarchy allows control of the fidelity around the elements of identity, e.g., an investigator may be interested in anything about the individual's work-life rather

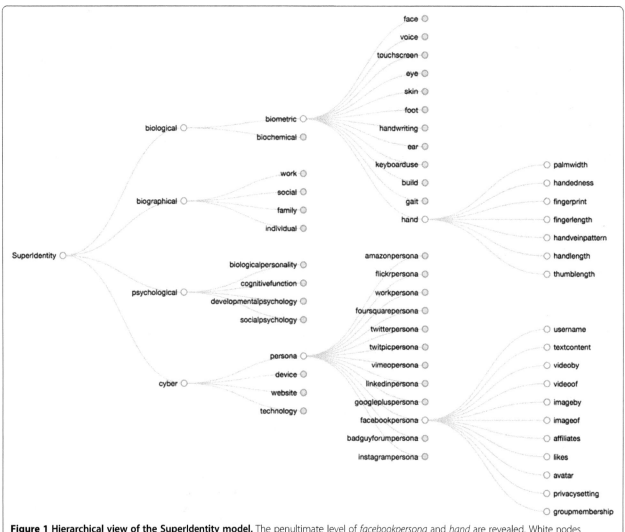

Figure 1 Hierarchical view of the SuperIdentity model. The penultimate level of *facebookpersona* and *hand* are revealed. White nodes represent fully expanded portions of the hierarchy and blue nodes represent collapsed portions of the hierarchy.

than his or her specific occupation [23]. The model is completely agnostic of any particular taxonomy—meaning any taxonomy of elements can be used, and it is expected that individual organizations will tailor the taxonomy of elements to their context.

Simply having a bag of elements of identity is not enough to satisfy the exemplar use case previously outlined. To this end, we introduce the second core concept of the model: inferences. These allow the creation of a new, previously unknown element of identity from a known element of identity; these can be simple, automated transforms (e.g., using a Twitter username to infer the corresponding Twitter avatar), more complex inferences that use statistical correlations (e.g., the estimation of height from foot-length), or other inferences that involve using databases of information the investigator may have available (e.g., the ability to infer a name from a home address using a local authority database). Each inference

has an associated description, which explains how to perform the inference; in essence, what process does an investigator need to perform the inference?

Confidence can be propagated along an inference. In other words, given an input element, it is possible to calculate the probable confidence of the result of the inference. The discussion of this is beyond the scope of this paper, but the reader is referred to [24,25].

The model results in a directed graph with the vertices representing elements of identity and the edges representing inferences. The inferences are annotated; these annotations are dimensions that are used to describe a number of the inferences' characteristics, for example, whether a transform can be automatable, how long it takes to perform the inference, whether the inference uses classified technology, etc.

The model provides a guide as to how to perform the identity attribution or enrichment tasks; while the model

Table 1 General statistics from the super identity model

Number of elements	297
Elements in the Biographical Domain	56
Elements in the Biological Domain	50
Elements in the Cyber Domain	157
Elements in the Psychological Domain	34
Number of transforms	**1853**
Source Element in the Biographical Domain	275
Source Element in the Biological Domain	74
Source Element in the Cyber Domain	1413
Source Element in the Psychological Domain	91
Average size of SuperIdentity*	
At 70% Confidence	5.81
At 50% Confidence	14.45
At 20% Confidence	24.27

*The number of elements that can be populated beginning from each element and following transforms until the confidence is lower than the given confidence.

can provide a description as to how to perform the task, the model will not, at present, perform an inference. The model can be thought of as a recipe book that allows users to explore identity in a number of different ways.

Casting an identification activity into the model results in a set of known elements (representing an investigator's starting knowledge, e.g., the evidence from an investigator) and a set of desired elements (representing the final knowledge required). Given this bound, the model queries the graph to work out all routes through the graph from the known elements to the unknown elements. Individual paths can then be chosen based on the paths that provide the desired elements with the greatest confidence or by using the vertex labels (e.g., the route that provides the fastest answer, routes that don't require the use of the internet, etc.).

Once a set of possible routes has been chosen, it is then possible to use the routes and the descriptions associated with each inference to lead an investigator through the steps required to perform the tasks. This output from the model then provides the guide that the investigator can use.

The model has a number of other uses in both privacy and capability management [23,25], including the ability to allow investigators' gut instinct to jump around the graph, effectively creating their own ad-hoc inferences [24,26].

The SuperIdentity visualization complements the Super-Identity model by helping the user explore and traverse the model, encapsulating the computations performed over the model, and organizing gathered data for review and dissemination. The visualization is a workflow management

application and is designed to lead the user through a step-by-step process with the model supporting the underlying computation. In this way, using the application is much like route planning. In fact, the visualizations used draw inspiration from transit maps (e.g., the London Tube Map) [27]. The user has a starting point, a desired destination, and potentially many intermediate points. By using such a metaphor, we hope to help the user anticipate the flow of the application.

The application comprises a series of screens that represent stages of an investigative process: establishing a context for the inquiry, recording known quantities and desired quantities, exploring routes from that which is known to that which is desired, navigating those routes to arrive at a result, and reviewing the results of the inquiry. Each of these is depicted in order from top to bottom in Figure 2. The application leads users through these screens with animated transitions (panning from left to right) as the investigation progresses from one stage to the next. More detailed images of each stage are provided below as the stages are discussed.

The context for an inquiry is termed a *project* in the application. A project has no associated data to begin with but accumulates data as the user begins to record his or her findings. Any data discovered, either as a desired result or an intermediate result, is recorded in the context of the project and recalled whenever the project is opened. Computations performed by the model are stored and recalled as well, but they have no effect on any other project.

Primarily, data is collected as discrete entities called *nodes*. Nodes that are constructed from values known a priori are called *seeds*. They represent the knowledge with which the user begins. Nodes constructed without a known value but that represent what the user would like to know are called *targets*. The user's interaction with the application will be a progression from seeds to targets. The first screen, then, represents the dichotomy of seeds and targets (Figure 3). This dichotomy is reinforced visually by the vertical divide in the central circle of the second screen; the circle represents the whole of the identity, with seeds on the left and targets on the right. An investigative process is a movement, using information transformations from left (the seeds) to right (the targets).

The application aids the user in recording seeds and targets by listing the representative elements from the model. Once a suitable element is chosen, if the node is a seed, the user is given the opportunity to record the known value and an approximate confidence in the accuracy of the data. Users' confidence may vary with their confidence in the source. No further data is recorded for targets because none is known; the application is designed to aid in its discovery.

Confidence is stored in the model as a percentage value. The visualization maps these percentages into ranged categories of confidence: Very Low, Low, Medium, High, Very High, and Certain. The ranges and the terminology are configurable. Kesselman [28] shows that users make poor use of numeric ratings, so we have adjusted our visualization accordingly. To record their confidence, users select a category from a dial. The selected confidence is highlighted. The same terminology and representation of confidence are repeated throughout the interface.

Once the endpoints are established, the application can suggest paths through the model (traversals of the graph) that will lead the user from a seed to a target. Every path is composed of two or more nodes; a seed and a target are required. Nodes may be of any identification domain, as long as a transform exists between the source and the immediate target. If a direct transform exists (from the seed directly to the final target), then the path will be two nodes long. Otherwise, the model will employ intermediate nodes to complete the path.

Every transform from one node to another incurs some measure of error and thus some loss in confidence in the result. By their nature, longer paths tend to yield a lower confidence result. Paths are generated for all seeds and targets provided as inputs and a default final confidence is computed based on the encoded loss in confidence incurred by each transform. Paths are then sorted by their final confidence and presented in descending order. The paths that are likely to result in the highest confidence result are presented first.

There are times when no paths will be available from the provided seeds to the provided targets or when the paths provided are low confidence, undesirable, or nonexistent. In such cases, the model is able to suggest other seeds that may yield a higher confidence result. The user can engage those seeds by adding them on the previous screen and seeking out the necessary data, if

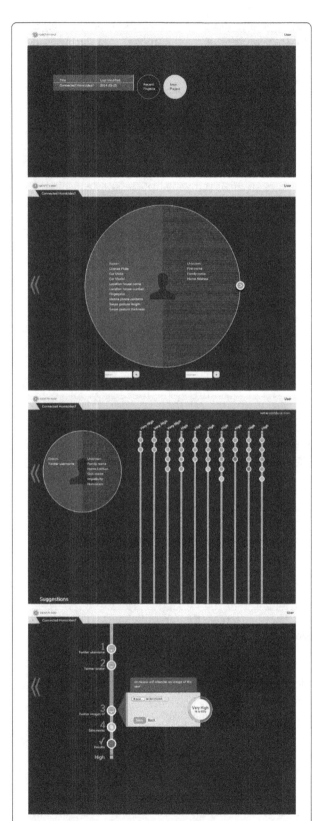

Figure 2 All four screens of the SuperIdentity application. From top to bottom: Project Create/Open, Seeds & Targets, Path Overview, and Path Walkthrough. The user progresses from left to right within the application, returning to the Overview after completing a walkthrough.

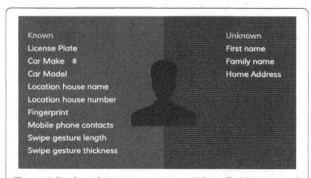

Figure 3 Seeds and targets entry screen (Also called Knowns and Unknowns). Examples of seeds and targets enumerated to populate the visualization. Seeds can have associated data and confidences; Targets have none and will be discovered through interaction.

accessible. The model will then recalculate the paths, including the added seeds, returning the higher confidence paths. Alternate seed suggestions will prefer seeds that share the closest possible relationship to existing seeds (e.g., a Facebook username seed, *John Doe*, might generate a suggestion for a Twitter username seed, *@johndoe*). If close relationships are unfruitful, the suggestions will reach out as far as a related sub-domain but no farther. For example, the Facebook username might generate a suggestion of website address but not physical address, because physical address is considered to be of a different identification domain.

The color of the nodes encodes the domain of origin (i.e., cyber, biometric, biographic, and psychological), which is reinforced with a symbolic representation when the user selects a path. A selected path presents the name of each node, its identification domain, and the order in the path. After inspecting the details, the user can progress to a detailed walkthrough of the path or select an alternate path. A selected path, with other paths juxtaposed, is depicted in Figure 4. The path is read from the top down, starting with the expected final confidence, followed by a seed, intermediate elements, and concluding at a target. "Select" takes the user to the Path Walkthrough screen for that path.

Once a path is chosen, the user walks through the path, following one transform after another, acquiring data for each node until arriving at the target node. The user interface aids in this process by presenting each node in a linear progression mimicking the Path Overview screen described earlier but providing more detail and isolating the selected path. In this view, a dialog is presented at each step that allows the user to record findings and rate confidence in the result (Figure 5).

Users are not required to enter data or record a confidence to progress. The data field is left blank; a blank data field only prevents automatable transforms from performing their task and later information retrieval (e.g., for reporting). In every other respect, the model can still function. The default confidence set is that provided by the model based on the confidence of the previous node in the path and the confidence loss due to the transform. If the user elects not to specify a confidence, this default confidence is used.

To aid the user in performing non-automated transforms, the model supplies a descriptor of means for performing the transform. As an example, to transform from the length of a person's hand to their gender, the model supplies *"Handlength and Gender are correlated—men tend to have longer hands,"* which provides a basis for inference. Some transforms are more complicated than others, but all transforms are intended to be a single step. This is where the linear nature of the walkthrough is most clearly beneficial: it dramatically simplifies the reasoning process

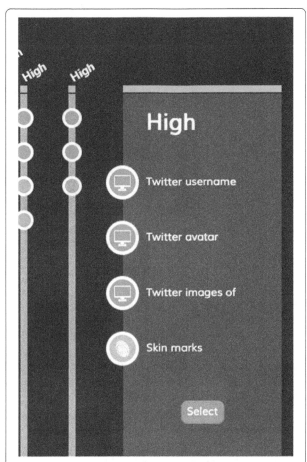

Figure 4 Paths as presented in the overview. A user can see the expanded view (right side) by clicking on a collapsed path (left side). "Select" progresses the user to the Walkthrough.

for the user, allowing them to focus on the transform tasks (which a machine cannot perform).

It may be prudent here to discuss transforms that require multiple input elements but yield a single output element. For example, biometrics on multiple attributes of a person's voice can yield inferences about certain personality traits [29]. In such cases, the path is a composite path and begins at bifurcated sub-paths that join at a later node. The linear progression is preserved by leading the user down one sub-path, then the other, and finally completing the transform at the merge node before progressing to the target node.

At the end of the walkthrough, the user is presented with a summary of the result: the user-populated target node and its confidence, other target nodes that have been populated in previous walkthroughs, and the opportunity to return to the Path Overview to pursue a new target. (The Path Overview is updated to give preference to unpopulated target nodes.) A path can be visited more than once, and a target node can be populated multiple times with potentially conflicting results.

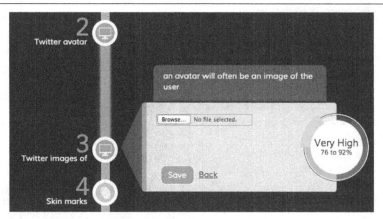

Figure 5 One transform in the Walkthrough, from "(#2) Twitter avatar" to "(#3) Twitter images of." The value and confidence are recorded in the dialog. The means of performing the transform are described above the dialog. After the final transform in a path, the dialog displays a summary of the acquired targets and their confidences.

This capability should encourage the user to explore further paths to high confidence data for the target node.

Application to use cases and future work

The construction of the model and the design of the interface are intended to support the identity attribution use cases identified through interaction with the targeted communities. To illustrate, we now consider the role of the visualization in support of the "Connected Homicides?" use case.

The connected homicides use case does not have a strong temporal element as other law enforcement cases typically have. There is sufficient information that can be considered *known items* including the partial license plate, description of the car, and geolocation, as well as data that can be retrieved from the phone recovered: swipe gesture, fingerprints, contacts, user names, and other content. The unknown items of identity revolve around identifying information to discover any correlations between the perpetrators. In particular, the user wants to know if the perpetrator in each case is really the same person.

These known items form the start points in the model; the model is queried to provide the possible paths from the start points to required information. The output of the model is the set of paths that can be followed in order to solve the problem, as described in the *SuperIdentity model and visualization* Section. The current instantiation of the model emphasizes cross-domain transforms—that is, making connections from one identity domain to another. For example, the model suggests connections from the contents of the phone to a probable home address. To accomplish this, the model presents a path leading from the phone to photos taken by the user that are geo-tagged to a location or area that has a strong grouping. Other examples of paths provided by the model, with the given seeds and targets, are in Table 2. This set of paths provides not only simple paths that an investigator is used to using but also unconventional paths that an investigator may not be used to using. This is particularly useful should an investigation stall or an investigation not proceed as expected.

The phone and the car establish an interesting pair. From the license plate, the user should be able to acquire the vehicle registration, and then the name of the person to whom the car is registered. The phone should also yield a name, stemming from the account with the phone company. Given the scenario, these names will not match, which will lead the investigator down an uncertain path: Were both people involved? How? Who should be brought in for questioning? What other evidence can be gathered in support of one or another suspect?

The model yields further paths that can aid in this process, and alternative paths can be suggested that use alternate start points. This capability can aid stalled investigations by suggesting other evidence that can be gathered to unlock new paths. Alternatively, the model

Table 2 Conceptual paths that demonstrate prototypical model output

Path	Confidence
Phone contents → Geo-tagged photos → Home address	Medium
Phone number → Cellular account → Person name	Certain
License plate → Car registration → Person name	Certain
Phone contents → Social media account names → Content of recent posts* → Indicators of mental health	Low
Phone contents → Social media account names → Content of recent posts* → Indicators of motive or intent	Low
Phone → Swipe gesture arc → Handedness	High
Phone contents → Contact List → Association with victim	Medium

*This assumes the information is either publicly available or legally accessible.

can suggest other paths that can be used to clarify who was involved in the homicides by taking multiple independent paths and providing consensus over a particular element of identity.

We have explored the use of this application to address a use case provided by law enforcement. In the process, both its strengths and weaknesses were revealed. In revealing cross-domain opportunities to complete either attributive or enriching identity tasks, the results were good. These are investigative pathways not often used by law enforcement. The application also benefits from its simple, linear progression, reducing the complexity of the statistical model to a form friendly to all users.

It is good to recall, however, that the application is designed with more than just law enforcement in mind. The collection of use cases came from analysts in intelligence, cyber security, and law enforcement. While there is some overlap in the use cases and similarity in the identification needs of each community, there are also significant differences. This application seeks to benefit all attribution and enrichment tasks in a general way. This generic approach can have negative impacts on particular use cases. As an example, in the "Connected Homicides?" exemplar use case considered, the car and the phone produced two individuals of interest, but the application provided no support for dividing the investigation or otherwise associating some pieces of identity with one individual, and others with another.

The model and the visual representation are sufficiently modular and general to be repurposed for applications targeted at particular communities or even particular investigative methodologies. Considering the use case example presented here, one could envision customized applications that contain legal aspects pertinent to a particular law enforcement region or task. This approach would facilitate the choice of paths based on what information is acceptable as evidence. We did not investigate those possibilities in this body of work and consider them an exercise for future work. The following sections discuss future work with the aim to consider further iterations of the model in the modular or general sense, rather than a strictly law enforcement focus.

Critical path

An overview of the collection of paths leading from all seeds to all targets is essential to grasp the broader picture of an investigation; it is termed the *critical path*. It highlights the nodes that are essential for a user to complete his or her task and reveals transforms that suffer greater losses in confidence. Some nodes have a greater number of paths that pass through them. Some edges have a higher possible confidence when transforming to the next node in the path. Critical information for the user might be intermediate nodes that are required for all paths to a

target or collections of transforms that are necessarily weak, with no alternatives. For instance, Table 1 showing conceptual paths for the "Connected Homicides?" use case suggests that social media account names may be an essential node for inferring information about phone content, albeit with a low confidence. Such information reveals both the strengths and weaknesses of the investigators' position and can help them adjust to accommodate.

Automated transforms

Many transforms can be automated. Some transforms are simple, like approximating height from hand length or acquiring a social media avatar given a user name; they're simple functions that are easily performed by a computer. More importantly, they are rudimentary tasks for a user, and they should be relieved of such duties. Some transforms are not simple but can still be automated—for example, performing facial recognition or social network traversals. From our use case, automating the transformation from the swipe gestures on a phone to indicate handedness is automatable but would require specialized software. Transforms of this category require more sophisticated automation engines and likely more sophisticated interfaces for the user to interact with. Some transforms cannot be reasonably automated.

Every automated transform incurs some loss in confidence, just as when a user performs the same transform, they may be more or less confident in the result. A username to an account avatar is a high-confidence transform, while facial recognition software is beneficial but far from perfect, yielding perhaps a moderate to low confidence depending on the quality of the inputs. When users engage an automated transform, they are also notified of the resulting confidence, allowing them to compensate or reconsider their investigative trajectory.

The present work has planned for the presence of automated transforms, but they have not yet been introduced to the user interface and exposed as an executable option. As more research from the UK institutions in the consortium matures, we hope to introduce more opportunities for users to engage automated processes to complete portions of their work.

Review screen(s)

At present, the SuperIdentity application provides for a shallow review of gathered data for the user: the seed-target summary at the end of a path walkthrough. While this is a beneficial reminder to the user of overall progress, it is insufficient for important tasks like reconciling element discrepancies and report generation. When the user encounters multiple results for a single element, there will need to be some means of exploring the evidence supporting or refuting each. Little work has been done yet to design an approach, and it is unclear what level of detail is required for effective use. Requirements may be gathered in further interactions with the various user bases.

Reporting is supported in the sense that the model retains all the nodes and their relationships to each other. It also preserves node provenance, including metadata (e.g., whether the node was populated by the user or an automated transform). So the means are there to recall any and all data users require to generate reports of their findings, but no user interface requirements have been compiled or considered as yet. This is another topic for follow-up interactions with users.

Evaluation

Both the described exemplar use cases as well as others developed will be used in evaluating the utility and usability of this research. For each of the three analysis domains (intelligence, law enforcement, and cyber security) five to seven experts will be recruited for each evaluation study. In the studies, the experts will be asked how they would currently do the task, the resources they would use, the certainty they would have in the result assuming the necessary information needed could be obtained. Using the SuperIdentity model and visualizations, a set of experts will explore and evaluate the model's capabilities through solving the exemplar use cases. During the exercise, the experts will be asked to talk out loud, providing a more immediate evaluation of the model as they move through the exemplar use cases. They will be asked which paths they will take and the rationale for their decision, including their views on the confidence levels associated with pathways in the model. After the walkthrough, participants will be asked to rate both the utility of the model and the usability of the various visualization components. This information will be used by the visualization and model teams to make appropriate changes. It is also important to get reactions as to which information the experts feel comfortable using now, what information they deem to be problematic, and how they may be able to use their valuable tacit knowledge while using the model.

Conclusion

In conclusion, we have presented a collaborative effort from PNNL and Oxford, as well as other UK institutions, that seeks to provide a capability to investigators for enriching identities and attributing actions to individuals. Oxford has developed a robust model for traversal of paths between interconnected identity elements, statistical computation of approximate levels of confidence in data, and maintenance of investigative provenance. PNNL has developed a visual analytic interface to make the model accessible, so that investigators can leverage its capabilities without fully comprehending the complex nature of the model.

These pieces were designed and built from requirements gathered through interviews with analysts from multiple domains. We explored those for law enforcement, highlighting one particular use case that could demonstrate the capabilities of the model. It not only revealed particularly how the model can cross identity domains but also revealed opportunities for specialization of the tool in future iterations. We also discussed plans for improvement and evaluation going forward.

Abbreviations

EPSRC: Engineering and physical sciences research council; PNNL: Pacific northwest national laboratory; CAPER: The collaborative information, acquisition, processing, exploitation and reporting project; CRM: Caper regulatory model; IACP: International association of chiefs of police.

Competing interests

The authors declare that they have no competing interests.

Authors' contributions

JB: Development of user interface, writing of introduction, visualization, application, and future work sections, and conclusion; lead author. JS: Conducted and compiled user interviews, writing of use case section, and general editing. DH: Development of the model, writing of the model section. LE: Conducted and compiled user interviews, writing of use case and related work sections. DSF: User interviews, minor writing contributions. SC: Research oversight. OL: User interviews, user interface design, research oversight. All authors read and approved the final manuscript.

Acknowledgments

Work performed at PNNL (user interviews and visualization) was supported by the US Department of Homeland Security. PNNL is managed for the US Department of Energy by Battelle under Contract DE-AC05-76RL01830. The work performed at Oxford (user interviews and model development) and Bath (user interviews) was performed under the Engineering and Physical Sciences Research Council (EPSRC) grant EP/J004995/1. The SuperIdentity project is investigating the interactions between offline and online identities; the cross-disciplinary consortium ranges from innovative new biometric measures through to management of online identities. The authors would like to thank our colleagues in the Cyber Security Centre at the University of Oxford, particularly Michael Goldsmith, Jason Nurse, Thomas Gibson-Robinson, and Elizabeth Phillips, whose early work developing a transitivity model for relating identity elements has been instrumental in developing the SuperIdentity model. We would also like to thank Chris Bevan, who helped with the early design of the protocol for the interviews. Our thanks also to colleagues at PNNL: Bill Pike for his innovative leadership, Dee Kim for her contributions to user interface design, and Art McBain for his development efforts.

Author details

[1]Pacific Northwest National Laboratory (PNNL), Richland, WA, USA. [2]Oxford University, Oxford, UK. [3]University of Bath, Bath, UK.

References

1. AE Marwick, Online Identity, in *A Companion to New Media Dynamics*, ed. by J Hartley, J Burgess, A Bruns (Wiley-Blackwell, Oxford, UK, 2013), pp. 355–364
2. J James, How Much Data is Created Every Minute? in *Domosphere*, 2012. http://www.domo.com/blog/2012/06/how-much-data-is-created-every-minute/
3. The Government Office for Science, *Foresight Future Identities (2013) Executive Summary*, 2013. https://www.gov.uk/government/uploads/system/uploads/attachment_data/file/273968/13-524-future-identities-changing-identities-summary.pdf
4. S Saxby, The 2013 CLSR-LSPI seminar on electronic identity: The global challenge – Presented at the 8th International Conference on Legal, Security and Privacy issues in IT Law (LSPI) November 11–15, 2013, Tilleke & Gibbins International Ltd., Bangkok, Thailand. Comput. Law Secur. Rev. **30**, 112–125 (2014)

5. Caper, in http://www.fp7-caper.eu/
6. Secure Identity Across Borders Linked (STORK), in https://www.eid-stork.eu/)
7. 2012 IACP Social Media Survey, in http://www.iacpsocialmedia.org/Portals/1/documents/2012SurveyResults.pdf
8. Social Media and Tactical Considerations For Law Enforcement, in https://info.publicintelligence.net/COPS-SocialMedia.pdf
9. ML Gavrilova, RV Yampolskiy, Applying Biometric Principles to Avatar Recognition, in *2010 International Conference on Cyberworlds (CW)*, 2010, pp. 179–186
10. K Gani, H Hacid, R Skraba, Towards Multiple Identity Detection in Social Networks, in *Proceedings of the 21st International Conference Companion on World Wide Web* (ACM, New York, NY, USA, 2012), pp. 503–504. WWW '12 Companion
11. R Zheng, Y Qin, Z Huang, H Chen, Authorship Analysis in Cybercrime Investigation, in *Proceedings of the 1st NSF/NIJ Conference on Intelligence and Security Informatics* (Springer-Verlag, Berlin, Heidelberg, 2003), pp. 59–73. ISI'03
12. C Aliprandi, A Marchetti, Introducing CAPER, a Collaborative Platform for Open and Closed Information Acquisition, Processing and Linking, in *HCI International 2011 – Posters' Extended Abstracts*, ed. by C Stephanidis (Communications in Computer and Information Science, vol. 173, Springer Berlin Heidelberg, 2011), pp. 481–485
13. The Uncertainty of Identity Multidisciplinary Project, in http://www.imprintsfutures.org/about/
14. M Adnan, G Lansley, PA Longley, A geodemographic analysis of the ethnicity and identity of Twitter users in Greater London, in *Proceedings of the 21st Conference on GIS Research UK (GISRUK)*, 2013
15. P Juola, Authorship Attribution. Found. Trends. Inf. Retrieval. **1**, 233–334 (2007)
16. DA Wheeler, GN Larsen, *Techniques for Cyber Attack Attribution* (Institute for Defense Analyses, Alexadria, VA, 2003)
17. J Hunker, B Hutchinson, J Margulies, Role and challenges for sufficient cyber-attack attribution, in *Institute for Information Infrastructure Protection*, 2008
18. State and Major Urban Area Fusion Centers, in http://www.dhs.gov/state-and-major-urban-area-fusion-centers
19. UK Cabinet Office, *Cyber Security Strategy*, 2011
20. S Creese, M Goldsmith, JRC Nurse, E Phillips, A Data-Reachability Model for Elucidating Privacy and Security Risks Related to the Use of Online Social Networks, in *2012 IEEE 11th International Conference on Trust, Security and Privacy in Computing and Communications (TrustCom)*, 2012, pp. 1124–1131
21. RR McCrae, PT Costa, Validation of the five-factor model of personality across instruments and observers. J. Pers. Soc. Psychol. **52**, 81–90 (1987)
22. DL Paulhus, KM Williams, The dark triad of personality: Narcissism, Machiavellianism, and psychopathy. J. Res. Pers. **36**, 556–563 (2002)
23. D Hodges, S Creese, Building a better intelligence machine: A new approach to capability review and development, in *2013 IEEE International Conference on Intelligence and Security Informatics (ISI)*, 2013, pp. 113–115
24. D Hodges, S Creese, M Goldsmith, A Model for Identity in the Cyber and Natural Universes, in *Intelligence and Security Informatics Conference (EISIC), 2012 European*, 2012, pp. 115–122
25. D Hodges, S Creese, Breaking the Arc: Risk control for Big Data, in *2013 IEEE International Conference on Big Data*, 2013, pp. 613–621
26. D Hodges, J Nurse, M Goldsmith, S Creese, *Identity attribution across CyberSpace and the Natural Space*, 2012
27. J Vertesi, Mind the Gap: The London Underground Map and Users' Representations of Urban Space. Soc. Stud. Sci. **38**, 7–33 (2008)
28. RF Kesselman, Verbal Probability Expressions in National Intelligence Estimates: A Comprehensive Analysis of Trends from the Fifties through Post 9/11, in *MCIIS Theses in Intelligence Studies. Mercyhurst College Institute for Intelligence Studies (MCIIS)*, 2008
29. G Mohammadi, A Vinciarelli, M Mortillaro, The voice of personality: Mapping nonverbal vocal behavior into trait attributions, in *Proceedings of the 2nd international workshop on Social signal processing. ACM*, 2010, pp. 17–20

17

Bridging the perceptual gap: variations in crime perception of businesses at the neighborhood level

Valerie Spicer[*], Justin Song and Patricia Brantingham

Abstract

Current research on fear of crime reveals a recurrent theme of disorder in explanations of fear of crime and perceptions of security. This disorder is scalable, ranging from proximal cues associated with specific encounters between people or defined micro locations through to distal feelings of fear about areas, activity nodes, or major pathways. The research presented here compares two samples (n = 235) of businesses surveyed during the summer of 2012 in Grandview-Woodland, a diverse neighborhood, in the City of Vancouver, Canada. A visualization technique is presented to demonstrate how aggregate cognitive maps about perception of crime can be created and used by civic agencies when determining strategies aimed at reducing fear of crime. The results show that although both samples are taken from the same geographical neighborhood, their specific location within the community generates two very distinct perceptual patterns. Differences between the impact of proximal and distal cues on perception is explored. Other variations in perception are studied including differences between males and females, business owners and employees and those who have been victims of property crime versus personal crime. The results are presented and future research directions discussed.

Keywords: Business security; Fear of crime; Disorder; Cognitive

Introduction

Business communities are unique in their experience of the urban domain. They occupy both social and physical spaces that present different opportunities for victimization. Understanding these dynamics and implementing crime prevention strategies that mitigate victimization can help to foster healthier business communities. In particular, the perception of crime and disorder can instigate adverse feelings and generate fear thus altering how people behave in the urban domain potentially increasing subsequent victimization. The research presented in this paper aims to discover perceptual variations within a business community located in Grandview-Woodland, Vancouver, Canada.

While there are numerous factors that impact perception of crime such as age, gender, ethnicity, social economic status and level of education, the spatial dynamics of perception of crime can elicit new information about this phenomenon [1-4]. In particular, spatially locating perception of crime within business communities can be done using a mapping technique in which either employees or business owners working in a particular neighborhood are presented with an area map, and then asked to indicate the area(s) where they perceive there is a higher level of crime. Precision in defining specific places depends on multiple factors including the size of the study area and the individual's relative knowledge of local problems. Visualizing this geographical information can improve clarity and assist civic agencies and urban planners to enhance security plans thus assisting business communities in improving safety within the neighborhood.

Public disorder generates environmental cues that impact individuals when navigating their environment in particular at the pedestrian level. Studies on disorder such as those conducted under the Broken Windows theory have shown how individuals within urban communities are affected by public disorder [5-8]. Disorder encompasses both the physical and social manifestations of human behavior in the urban environment that are generally perceived as problematic. Studies have also shown how markers of disorder are both linked to fear and the perception of crime and can therefore influence pedestrian behavior [8-15]. Individuals in vehicles experience the environment differently depending on their knowledge of an

* Correspondence: vspicer@sfu.ca
Institute of Canadian Research Studies, Simon Fraser University, Burnaby, BC, Canada

area and the disorder cues that are impactful to individuals in vehicles are scalable to those experienced by pedestrians [13]. For example discarded syringes or condoms can be seen by pedestrians, but not by vehicle commuters. For pedestrians, tpublic disorder cues can act as a warning to crime problems such as public drug use, drug trafficking and solicitation.

Distal and proximal perception can be used to analyze the spatial distribution of perception of crime in the urban domain [16]. While these terms can describe the actual physical distance, they can be expanded and used to further explain proximal experiences of disorder, such as aggressive panhandlers outside the respondent's business, and the impact of distal landmarks such as mass transportation hubs. From a perception of crime and disorder perspective, proximal perception would be varied at the individual level and dependent on personal experiences and location of experiences, whereas distal perception in the aggregate may form very structured patterns centered on known areas and landmarks.

No published research explores the mapping of perception of crime and disorder in the business community. Geographic information systems (GIS) are an effective method of visualizing a particular problem [11,12,17,18]. From a theoretical perspective, problem exploration through detailed visualization can lead to a better comprehension of the core elements that formulate a particular situation. Hotspot mapping that identifies concentrations of crime are usually represented using Kernel Density Smoothing to transform address level data to surface data. This technique has been used extensively in the policing world, yet it has almost uniquely been applied to reported crime data [19].

On the other hand, the mapping of crime perception may yield promising results [20]. In particular, business communities can benefit from this type of exploration because it helps to expose local dynamics and problems related to perceptions of security within the specific context of businesses. This paper explores a community survey approach and a visualization technique that can be used to analyze composite fear maps generated from drawings such as those shown in the following figures. This paper also presents a theoretical framework grounded in environmental criminology for the cognitive maps of fear produced by business owners and employees.

Theoretical orientations

Environmental criminology concerns itself with the everyday effect of the urban environment on the people who populate it. Perception of crime and security can be explored using principles from environmental criminology that are most often applied to criminal activity and events. The following theories are most often used to explain perception of crime and feelings of security within the analysis of space and time [21]:

- Routine Activity Theory
- Rational Choice Theory
- Geometry of Crime
- Pattern Theory

Routine activity theory

The Routine Activity Theory suggests the minimal elements for a criminal event to occur are a motivated offender, a suitable target and a non-capable guardian, but the inclusion of these elements does not mean a crime will always occur [22]. Furthermore both motivated and unmotivated individuals may commit crimes depending on the situation.

Within the context of perception of crime, this theory can be used to explain both perception of crime and feelings of security: individuals conduct their daily routines and during these activities, they are presented with situations where there is a perceived motivated offender and a lack of capable guardianship. The interaction of the three elements that form the Routine Activity Theory (victim – offender – location) can trigger a crime occurrence, but also create a fearful situation.

The temporal aspect of human movement is of particular importance because certain activities have to occur at a certain time and through a defined space. This is especially true within business communities where owners and employees have to commute to a designated place at a defined time. When locked into certain routes and times, individuals may feel more vulnerable within their environment [10]. When mass transportation is part of these movement patterns, the relationship between the transit system and the urban domain surrounding this system can create complex urban dynamics [12,23].

From the routine activity perspective, perception of crime at the aggregate level will occur where there is an intersection between human movement patterns in the urban domain, reduced guardianship and increased public display of criminality. This is both location and time specific as this theory includes the temporal dimension as the intersection of the three elements must occur in both a geographical place, and in a temporal space [22].

Furthermore, businesses owners and employees can play both the role of capable guardian and at the same time supply suitable targets in the environment. Therefore, these individuals are likely very attuned to the daily routines of neighborhoods as business owners and employees form an integral part of these routines and can also interrupt or intercept the routines that trigger crime occurrences.

Rational choice theory

The Rational Choice Theory assumes that individuals are rational and a decision-making process occurs prior to the commission of an offence. When individuals find themselves in a position to commit a crime, they will weigh the situation, considering both the potential risks associated with the act and the benefits resulting from the act [24].

This theory can be reversed and applied to people operating in the urban domain and who are making choices about activities and the potential victimization related to these choices. When presented with alternatives, the person in the potential victim position relies upon rational choice. There is a choice impasse when people are locked into a route and cannot make a rational decision to practice avoidant behavior [10]. These would be situations where the person engaged in the activity, is aware of the potential ramifications of his or her actions, but has few choices in relation the chosen activity. The individual in fact, is locked into a choice where crime avoidance is difficult and where victimization is probable. Mass transportation hubs are a good example of a choice impasse because people are reliant on this form of transportation and quite often do not have a viable alternative [4,25]. Therefore, they are locked into going to a very specific area even though they may be fully aware of potential victimization.

Within the business community, owners and employees are locked into many circumstances both temporally and geographically. The location of businesses determined by client base, and there are other factors some of which beyond their control such as problem premises near by or macro urban planning decisions that impact micro business communities. Owners and employees are guided by temporal patterns usually occupying regular business hours thus forecasting potential victimization. These factors are imbedded in individual decision making processes that guide how these individuals behave and perceive their environment.

Geometry of crime
Geometry of Crime Theory is based on human geography where decision-making about criminal offending is related to urban spatial dimensions. The environment produces cues that offenders pick up on and translate into perceived opportunities [21,26]. Offender movement patterns should not be assumed to differ considerably from the movement of the non-criminal population [27]. At the aggregate level, crime will be concentrated in locations where there is a convergence of environmental factors that relate to the general movement of offenders with the availability of suitable targets [28].

This theory can be applied to the perception of crime. Individuals in society have activities bringing them from one location to another. As people go through daily routines they develop an activity space that is related to an awareness space. However, rather than concentrating on perceived opportunities for the commission of a crime, they will develop an awareness around perceived opportunities for victimization. At the aggregate level, cues that generate the perception of crime may emanate more strongly in some areas and be linked to very specific displays of criminality and disorder.

Business owners and employees can be particularly attuned to perceived opportunities for victimization. For example, they may know and recognize prolific shoplifters operating in the area and be scanning customers looking for these individuals. Indeed, they are often in possession of viable targets and by virtue of this role are placed between potential offenders and their targets. As such, they can become more perceptive of cues in the environment that attract potential offenders. Their perception of the environment, especially near their place of employment is likely more intense and detailed as it may serve as a protective mechanism against victimization.

Crime pattern theory
The offender's awareness space is a geographical area surrounding travel paths that go between places such as a home, work or entertainment locations [21]. As the offender travels from place to place, they receive cues from the environment assisting them in the identification of suitable targets [28]. Offenders build an offending template taking into account these factors and eventually, this template stabilizes and becomes fixed, therefore leading to the predictability of offending patterns [28].

This theory can be inversed and applied to the perception of crime and rather than developing crime templates, individuals who act in a protective manner develop *safety templates* [20]. The term *safety template* is defined here as a new concept based on the concept of crime template formulated in Crime Pattern Theory. While a crime template is linked to the awareness space of a specific offender and used in criminal offending, individuals who navigate the urban domain and want to avoid victimization form *safety templates* [20].

Individuals in urban places travel from one location to the next in their daily routines and create awareness spaces around these travel paths. They will read cues in the environment and develop cognitive maps that include the information emitted from the environment. Feelings of safety and security will vary throughout the course of their travels depending on the cues they receive and how these relate to the locations they are attending. Over time, these cues will form fixed *safety templates* with some predictable cues and others linked to specific places or activities [20]. Within the *safety template* individuals will have both distal and proximal experiences with crime and disorder that will tie into their perception of crime. Distal experience will centered on areas where crime and disorder are more likely occur, whereas proximal experiences are individualized and defined through daily routines.

Business owners and employees often have regular travel patterns to and from their work environment. They can also have a strong sense of their micro work environment. As these patterns evolve, feelings of safety in the workplace can be liked to a workplace *safety template* and new or different cues an indication of potential victimization.

Summary of theory
These four theories help define how perception of crime and feelings of security are displayed in the geographical urban space. While at the aggregate level there exists generalized patterns of perception within the urban domain, subcategories of individuals will experience the environment differently as the places where they reside, operate businesses or travel to work may vary significantly from the norm. Understanding these variations in perception and fear of crime can improve crime control techniques and assist in urban planning decisions [29]. Therefore, determining the specific perceptual dynamics of subcategories of individuals within the business community can assist in enhancing feelings of security in the urban domain. Within the business community, these theories help to understand the unique perceptual patterns of these individuals.

Research study
Survey instrument
The instrument used for this business survey was originally developed and implemented in 1997 by the Grandview-Woodland Community Policing Centre (GWCPC), located in Grandview-Woodland, Vancouver, Canada. The purpose of this survey is to gauge local perception of disorder problems occurring in the neighborhood and how this relates to perception of crime. The survey is designed so it could be filled out in a short amount of time. Therefore subjects can be polled on the street, in parks, at community events and business owners and employees with limited time would also be compelled to complete it. On the front of the survey, there are 30 questions about quality of life issues in the neighborhood varying from significant disorder problems such as aggressive panhandling to issues likely considered positive community attributes such as mural and outside café seating [20].

The back of the survey contains general demographic questions such as age, gender, location of residence as well as questions about victimization. At the bottom of this page, a map is included and respondents asked to circle the area on the map where they feel there is the highest level of crime. This survey instrument was implemented on several occasions including three times in Grandview-Woodland (1997–2007 – 2010). The 1997 and 2007 version of this survey remained identical as the purpose was to gauge differences that occurred in this 10 year period. The 2010 survey instrument was modified to include current issues affecting the neighborhood as reported to the GWCPC. The business survey instrument that was implement in this study utilized a similar format and the questions modified to reflect the business perspective as reported to the GWCPC.

The instrument was also modified to represent the needs of three other Vancouver communities and subsequently implemented. The survey results have guided community policing efforts and civic decisions in these neighborhoods [20].

Survey implementation
In 2012, the GWCPC wanted to obtain more detailed information on the business community in the Grandview-Woodland neighborhood so that specific programming could be develop to address their safety and security needs. The survey instrument was the same as the previous implementations containing 30 questions on the front, and demographics with a mapping component on the reverse. This business survey was distributed to every business in the study area. Figure 1 shows the study area. It is 4 km from the centre of the study area to downtown Vancouver.

The Grandview-Woodland neighborhood is 448 hectares large and contains a mix of land use including residential single family and multiple dwelling, industrial and commercial. The neighborhood is anchored by Commercial Drive where there are multiple shops, cafés, restaurants and pubs. There is a community center in the middle of this neighborhood and at the time it was built, was one of North America's largest facilities containing a high school, elementary school, library, and recreation center designed to accommodate the very mixed population in this area. This community center is adjacent to Grandview Park that covers a one block area and is a focal point. The southern part of this neighborhood contains the largest public transit station in British Columbia where two A Skytrain routes connect and funnel into cross-town buses. The Skytrain is a light rapid metro system that is mostly above ground and elevated servicing the metro Vancouver region. The northern part of Grandview-Woodland is predominantly industrial.

The composition of this neighborhood creates two distinct business communities within the same geographical area. The first community is located on Commercial Drive. This area attracts people to businesses for entertainment and shopping, and is used by both local residents and people coming to the area from elsewhere in the city. The second business community is located off Commercial Drive with most business in the northern section of the study area. This business community is more industrial based offering specialized services. The survey was implemented with the intent to target these two distinct business communities. Half the sample was taken from businesses located on Commercial Drive. The other half

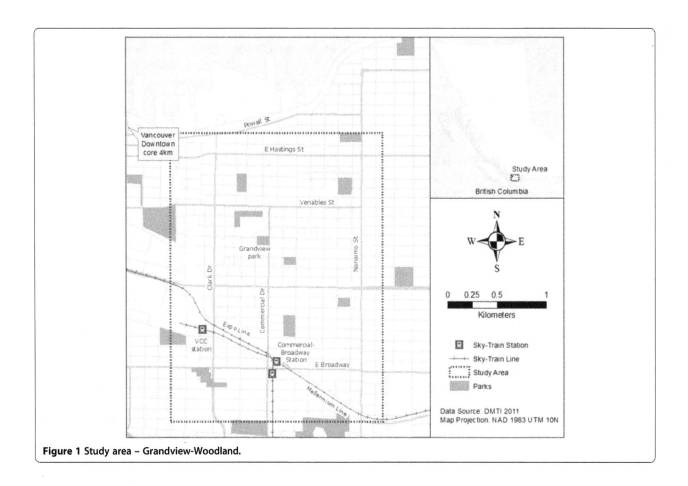

Figure 1 Study area – Grandview-Woodland.

was taken from businesses located off Commercial Drive. Businesses included in the study were street accessible and open to the general public such as grocery stores, specialty shops, pubs, cafes and restaurants.

Surveys were hand delivered by a GWCPC volunteer to every business located in the study area. This occurred during regular business hours from Monday to Friday between 9:00 AM and 5:00 PM. The completed surveys were collected a week later. Businesses that did not complete their survey were given an additional three days. This process occurred over two months (July and August) during the summer of 2012. Respondents were asked to complete this two-page survey that included 30 questions about crime and disorder in the neighborhood on the front page, demographic information on the second page, with a map of the study area where respondents were asked to circle the area they felt had the most crime.

As a result, 236 surveys were delivered with 99 completed surveys collected from Commercial Drive, 135 completed surveys collected from businesses off Commercial Drive. Two surveys that were delivered were not returned. This means that of the 236 surveys delivered and 234 were completed. This represents a 99.1% completion rate with 99 surveys in this study collected from the business

community on Commercial Drive and 134 from businesses off Commercial Drive. The perception of crime mapping data from the surveys in this study is analyzed and presented in this paper.

Perceptual business data and GIS analysis

The completed surveys were analyzed and those with a completed map extracted from the sample. There were 47 crime perception maps completed by businesses located on Commercial Drive and 49 crime perception maps completed by businesses located elsewhere in the study area. The polygons drawn on the maps were manually entered and digitized using ArcGIS.

The polygons where then run through the raster function using a program loop to maximize this process. This program loop is described in Figure 2. Through this process the polygons were divided into rasters 10 by 10 meters squares. The raster function was selected as the most precise way to transcribe the drawn polygons into an analytical method of visualization. The 10 by 10 meter size was selected because it is small enough to capture both the smallest drawn polygons while at the same time providing incremental variation at the aggregate level when multiple polygons are overlapped.

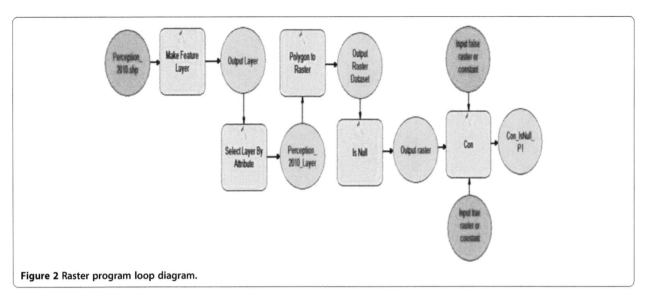

Figure 2 Raster program loop diagram.

Results

Perceptual business maps

The survey was implemented over a two-month period, July and August 2012. This lag in the survey implementation occurred as a result of the systematic hand delivery process through a trained volunteer. The goal was to obtain a high survey retrieval rate, which in this study is 99.1% of surveys delivered were collected. This time lag may impact results as experiences of crime and disorder will have varied throughout the study period.

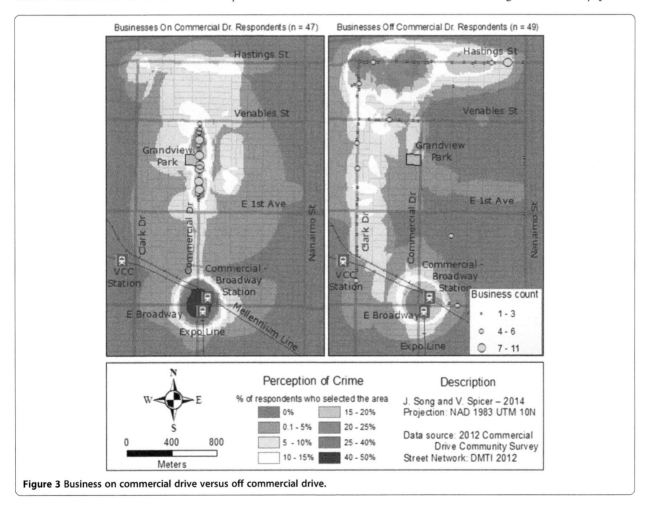

Figure 3 Business on commercial drive versus off commercial drive.

However, it should be noted that during this study period many factors remained consistent including the seasonal impact on street life, crime and disorder.

The two perceptual maps represented in Figure 3 show very distinct patterns. This first perceptual map compares the cognitive maps from businesses on Commercial Drive to businesses located off Commercial Drive. The average distance between the businesses on Commercial Drive to the Skytrain station is 1195 meters whereas this distance between businesses off Commercial Drive and the Skytrain station is 1518 meters. The average distance to the Skytrain station is of importance to this study because results from previous studies using this survey instrument show a significant hotspot around this station [27]. Therefore this station may have greater impact on the businesses that are more closely linked to this place. In particular, the businesses on Commercial Drive are directly tied to this location as this street extends to the intersection where the Skytrain station is located.

In Figure 3, two hotspots emerge in this map of businesses located on Commercial Drive. The first hotspot is located where the majority of surveyed businesses are located. The second hotspot is located at the south

end of the study area and is substantially more pronounced with over 40% of respondents selecting an area covering 43,800 square meters. This area contains a mass transportation hub that connects two Skytrain lines and feeds express buses that travel along a major thoroughfare that bisects Vancouver. Commercial Drive is pedestrian oriented where public disorder is more prominent both the street activities and the influence on the Skytrain station impact perception of crime for these businesses.

The businesses off Commercial Drive display a significantly different perceptual pattern and select a very different area. Unlike businesses located on Commercial Drive, the focus is less concentrated at the south end of the study area where the major transportation hub is located. Rather, these businesses select a more diffused area located in the northwest sector. This is an area that is predominantly industrial where there are fewer walk-in shops and residences. These businesses are less affected by the residual effect of the Skytrain area and more aware of the potential crime problems relating to the industrial section of the study area.

The average surface area of the drawn polygons for businesses on Commercial Drive is 197,366 square meters

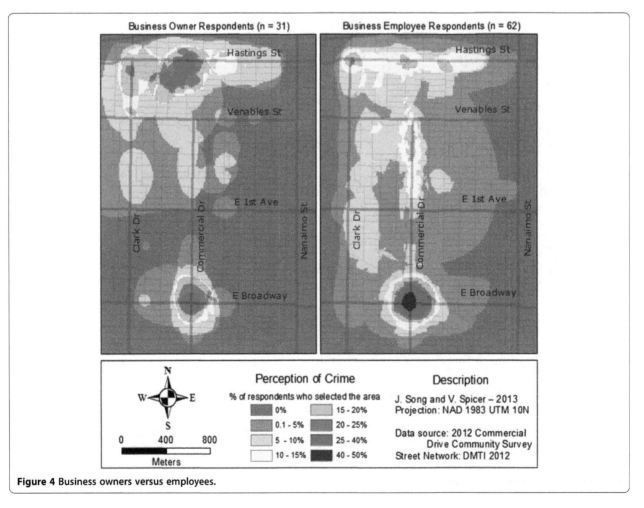

Figure 4 Business owners versus employees.

whereas business off Commercial Drive on average are larger drawn polygons 235,565 square meters. It is also interesting that the distance between the respondent's business and the respondent's drawn polygon is closer from businesses on Commercial Drive – 651.2 meters between the business and the drawn polygon – versus 704.4 meters for businesses off Commercial Drive.

Figure 4 displays the perceptual patterns for business owners and employees. These two vary significantly with employees more focused on the transit hub and business owners selecting two predominant areas. As well, employees pick a more concentrated area likely associated to generalized movement patterns linked to mass transportation. While business owners appear to have a perceptual pattern more likely associated with vehicle-based transportation. Future perception survey should take into account primary transportation mode as part of the data collection.

Figure 5 explores the difference between male and female respondents. In this case, females have a much more condensed perception of crime located at the Skytrain station. Over 40% of these respondents selected a very small area at the intersection of Broadway and Commercial Drive where

this transportation hub is located. Males, on the other hand, seem to have a more diffused perception of crime and the two hotspot split between the northern section and the Skytrain station. Several hypotheses could explain these differences that could be further researched. The northern section of the study area is predominantly industrial and would not be travelled as much on foot. Given this is a business study, the male respondents might be more likely employed in this area, utilize vehicles to attend and therefore familiar with the crime dynamics in this location. Whereas the female respondents more likely to be employed in the businesses on Commercial Drive and therefore more likely to access the Skytrain. Future iteration of this study should include questions about mode of transportation in order to further explore this hyposthesis.

A second hypothesis may be related to the formation of *safety templates* and gender differences that can occur in this formation. *Safety templates* are formed during routines activities and experiences with crime and disorder cues. These experiences can be varied and include real experiences, perceived risk, and can be supplemented by information gathered in the media or through social ties. For the females in this sample, the Skytrain station

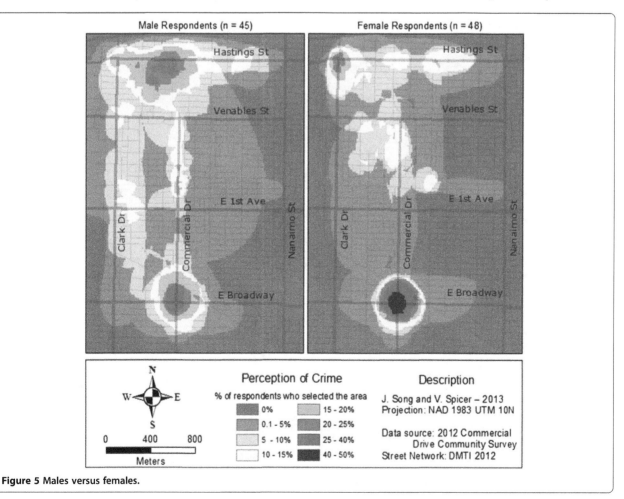

Figure 5 Males versus females.

may be a very defined crime generator with intense reson- ance. Therefore this location may emanate very strongly in the aggregate and demonstrate how locations can be- come fixed within a *safety template*. Future research could delve into these differences to explore how different loca- tions or landmarks can factor into the gendered formation of *safety templates.*

Figure 6 compares respondents who were victims of property crime to those who were victims of personal crime. These are two different perceptual patterns. Respondents who were victims of property crime con- tinue to focus on the Skytrain station. Comparatively, victims of personal crime have more diffused perception likely associated to their personal experience. It should be noted that very few respondents (n = 18) were victims of personal crime.

Finally, Figure 7 demonstrates another method to visualize these results. Since the raster function is uti- lized in the analysis, it is possible to create an accurate street chart to further explore variations in perception. The raster size of 10 meters by 10 meters allows for an accurate interpretation of results at the neighborhood level. This Figure 7 clearly shows that significant difference

between these two business communities. Businesses on Commercial Drive are much more focused on the Skytrain station and the main shopping area. Whereas business off Commercial Drive appear more concerned with the northern section of the studies area.

Conclusion

Heightened perception of crime can have a negative impact on business in general and reduces feelings of security for business owners, employees and clients. The results in this study show a heightened perception of crime that is both proximal and distal. These two distinct business communities select a proximal area close to the majority of the businesses in the sample while at the same time selecting a distal area located at a mass transportation hub. Future research should focus on furthering this spatial analysis by looking at how these two business communities differ in their experience of disorder. In particular, the responses from the 30 questions about crime and dis- order included in this survey could be compared and used to further understand the perceptual patterns.

This study supports the theoretical propositions founded in environmental criminology. Indeed, proximal perception

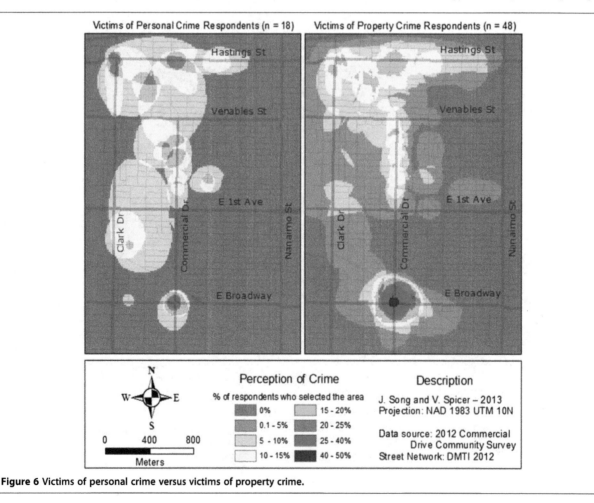

Figure 6 Victims of personal crime versus victims of property crime.

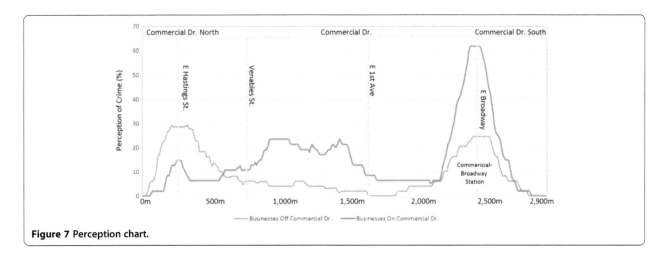

Figure 7 Perception chart.

is individualize and linked to cues in the environment while distal perception associated with routine activities that form aggregate patterns of perception as related to the generalized movement of citizens in the urban domain. In order to enhance feelings of security within the business community, civic agencies need to optimize their strategies along well-travelled routes while also addressing the local needs of micro business communities. These strategies should include measures that mitigate the effects of disorder associated with mass transportation that also impact pedestrian based streets such as Commercial Drive.

In particular, the concept of *safety templates* is introduced in this paper. These varied perceptual patterns indicate that variations can be linked to a number of factors including the location of the business, the work function in the business, gender, prior victimization as well as other factors not included in this instrument. Future research needs to further define and explore the concept of *safety templates* as this could assist in formalizing this concept and transforming it into a preventative strategy that can be shared within the business community. The concept of *safety templates* can be improved on in future research to determine the relationship between place of residence and place of employment. As well, the respondents' characteristics could help in describing the various factors impacting the formation of *safety templates.*

This study shows how two very distinct patterns emerge with one micro area linked to the businesses surveyed on Commercial Drive where there is high pedestrian traffic, and the other area connected to an industrial zone where other problems create a more diffused sense of perception. Future research will focus on extracting more precise information on the areas selected, including the associated movement patterns of the person drawing the map, additional testing of the fear generating cues, and the relationship of these factors with actual crime in the area. This will help to further elucidate environmental factors that trigger a heightened perception of crime

and with further testing could lead to a business fear generation measurement tool to be used by police and civic agencies.

Acknowledgements
We are grateful to the support from the Grandview-Woodland Community Policing Centre for implementing this business survey and in particular Baljit Bhullar who was integral during the data collection phase of this project.

References
1. J Flatley, S Moley, J Hoare (eds.), *Perceptions of Anti-Social Behavior: Findings from the 2007/08 British Crime Survey* (Home Office, London, 2008)
2. BK Scarborough, TZ Like-Haislip, KJ Novak, WL Lucas, LF Alarid, Assessing the relationship between individual characteristics, neighborhood context, and fear of crime. J. Crim. Justice 38(4), 819–826 (2010)
3. P Smith, TL Phillips, RD King, *Incivility: The Rude Stranger in Everyday Life* (Cambridge University Press, Cambridge, 2010)
4. N Yavuz, EW Welch, PS Srijaj, Individual and Neighborhood determinants of perceptions of bus and train safety in Chicago: An application of hierarchical linear modeling. Trans. Res. Rec. 2034, 19–26 (2007)
5. JM Gau, TC Pratt, Revisiting broken windows theory: examining the sources of the discriminant validity of perceived disorder and crime. J. Crim. Justice 38(4), 758–766 (2010)
6. A Park, *Modeling the Role of Fear of Crime in pedestrian Navigation* (Simon Fraser University, 2008). PhD dissertation
7. A Park, J Clare, V Spicer, PL Brantingham, T Calvert, G Jenion, Examining context-specific perceptions of risks: Exploring the utility of "human-in-the-loop" simulation models for criminology. J. Exp. Criminol. 8(8), 29–47 (2012).
8. RJ Sampson, SW Raudenbush, Seeing disorder: neighborhood stigma and the social construction of "broken windows". Soc. Psychol. Q. 67, 319–342 (2004)
9. T Armstrong, C Katz, Further evidence on the discriminant validity of perceptual incivilities measures. Justice Q. 27(2), 280–304 (2009)
10. KF Ferraro, *Fear of Crime Interpreting Victimization Risk* (State University of New York Press, Albany, New York, 1995)
11. JH Ratcliffe, A temporal constraint theory to explain opportunity-based spatial offending patterns. J. Res. Crime. Delinquency 43(3), 261–291 (2006)
12. J Robinson, L Goridano, M Andresen, B Kinney (eds.), *Spatial Interplay: Interaction of Land Uses in Relation to Crime Incidents Around Transit Stations. Patterns, Prevention, and Geometry of Crime* (Routledge, London, 2011)
13. RJ Sampson, SW Raudenbush, Systematic social observation of public spaces: a new look at disorder in urban neighborhoods. AJS 105(3), 603–651 (1999)
14. G Valentine, Living with difference: reflections on geographies of encounter. Prog. Human Geogr. 32(3), 323–337 (2010)
15. JL Worrall, The discriminant validity of perceptual incivility measures. Justice Q. 23(3), 360–383 (2006)

16. E Brunswick, *The Conceptual Framework of Psychology. International Encyclopedia of Unified Science, Vol. 1(10)* (The University of Chicago Press, Chicago, 1952)
17. S Chainey, J Ratcliffe, *GIS and Crime Mapping* (Wiley, Hoboken, NJ, 2005)
18. T Satur, ZQ Liu, A contextual fuzzy cognitive map framework for geographic information systems. IEEE Trans. Fuzzy Syst. **7**(5), 481–494 (1999)
19. S Chainey, Tompson, S Uhlig, The utility of hotspot mapping for predicting spatial patterns of crime. Secur. J. **21**, 4–28 (2008)
20. V Spicer, *The Geometry of Fear: An Environmental Perspective on Fear and the Perception of Crime* (Simon Fraser University, 2012). PhD Dissertation
21. PJ Brantingham, PL Brantingham, Notes on the geometry of crime, in *Environmental Criminolgy*, ed. by PJ Brantingham, PL Brantingham (Waveland Press, Prospect Heights, 1981)
22. LA Cohen, M Felson, Social change and crime rate trends: a routine activity approach. Am. Sociol. Rev. **44**, 598–608 (1979)
23. AD Newton, Crime on public transport: 'Static' and 'non-static' (moving) crime event. West. Criminol. Rev. **5**(3), 25–42 (2004)
24. DB Cornish, RV Clarke (eds.), *The Reasoning Criminal: Rational Choice Perspectives on Offending* (New York Springer-Verlag, New York, 1986)
25. N Yavuz, EW Welch, Addressing fear of crime in public space: gender differences in reaction to safety measures in train transit. Urban Stud. **47**(12), 2491–2515 (2010)
26. PJ Brantingham, PL Brantingham, A theoretical model of crime site selection, in *Crime, Law and Sanction*, ed. by M Krohn, RL Akers (Sage Publications, Beverly Hills, California, 1978), p. 1978
27. J Song, V Spicer, P Brantingham, Richard Frank, *Crime Ridges: Exploring the relationship between crime attractors and offender movement.* Conference Proceedings – European Intelligence and Security Informatics Conference EISIC (2013), (IEEE, Uppsala, Sweden, 2013)
28. PL Brantingham, PJ Brantingham, Environment routine and situation: toward a pattern theory of crime. Adv. Criminol. Theor. **5**, 259–294 (1993)
29. PJ Brantingham, PL Brantingham, Understanding and controlling crime and fear of crime: conflicts and trade-offs in crime prevention planning, in *Crime Prevention at a Crossroads*, ed. by SP Lab (Anderson Publishing Co., Cincinnati, Ohio, 1997), p. 1997

18

Language use in the Jihadist magazines inspire and Azan

David B Skillicorn[1][*] and Edna F Reid[2]

Abstract

The language of influence or propaganda has been studied for a century but its predictions (simplification, deceptiveness, manipulation) can now be examined empirically using corpus analytics. Semantic models for intensity of belief and use of gamification as a strategy allow novel aspects of influence to be taken into account as well. We develop a semi-automated approach to assess the quality of the language of influence using semantic models, and singular value decomposition as a middle ground between high-level abstract analysis and simple word counting. We then apply this approach in a significant intelligence application: examining the use of the language of influence in the jihadist magazines *Inspire* and *Azan*. These magazines have attracted attention from intelligence organizations because of their avowed goal of motivating lone-wolf attacks in Western countries. Our approach enables us to address questions like: How good are the authors and editors of these magazines at producing influential language (and so how great is the impact of these magazines likely to be)? How does this change with time, and as a reaction to world events, and what does this tell us about competence and strategic goals? What is the impact of changes in authorship?

Keywords: Language model; Jihadist language; Integrative complexity; Gamification; Deception; Propaganda; Corpus analytics

Introduction

Inspire magazine is an online jihadist magazine, written in English. At the time of writing, twelve issues have appeared, the first in the middle of 2010 and the most recent in Spring 2014. The first eight issues were edited by Samir Khan, with substantial assistance from the charismatic preacher, Anwar al-Awlaki. Issue 8 did not appear until well after their deaths in 2011, but had clearly been written by them. Issues 9–12 are the product of different, so far unknown, editors.

The goal of *Inspire* appears to be to motivate lone-wolf attacks in Western countries by diaspora jihadists. Such potential attackers are assumed to have little Arabic, and so the magazine is written in English; to be familiar with high-quality publications, and so the magazine has high production values, including significant attention paid to layout and presentation; and to have had limited exposure to religion and particularly the religious language endemic in much of the Middle East. *Inspire* is thus much more "Westernized" than the typical discussions in, for example, Islamist forums. Intelligence agencies have taken *Inspire*'s role as a recruiting tool very seriously [1]. Indeed, it is against the law to possess copies in the United Kingdom, and several people have been convicted for this offence; an Australian man has also been charged with a similar offence.

Azan magazine resembles *Inspire* in "look and feel" and appears to share many of the design elements, so it seems reasonable to assume that it was modelled on *Inspire*. At the time of writing, five issues have appeared, the first in March 2013 and the fifth early in 2014. Its focus is more on a South Asian (English-speaking) readership, but its goal is apparently also to encourage self-initiated attacks in Western countries. The magazine's authorship is not known but the topics covered suggest concerns centered in Pakistan and Afghanistan, particularly a focus on the threat from drones. The textual content of issues of *Azan* is typically between three and four times longer than the textual content of issues of *Inspire*, and issues are appearing much more often so their author/editor is noticeably more productive.

*Correspondence: skill@cs.queensu.ca
[1] Queen's University, Kingston, Canada
Full list of author information is available at the end of the article

The effect of these magazines is difficult to judge. Several lone-wolf attackers have had copies in their possession; but it is also clear that the magazines are widely read in their target communities. There has not been a noticeable uptick in lone-wolf attacks since they began appearing, so it is difficult to conclude that they have had much effect. We investigate whether magazines such as these meet their goals or not. We focus on the language patterns used in these magazines and what they can tell us about the aims and perceptions of the authors, and the constraints on their success.

The contribution of this paper is threefold:

1. A mapping of high-level descriptions of the language of influence or propaganda into hypotheses about the ways in which particular, measurable language elements are expected to be used in documents intended to influence.
2. A computational methodology for instantiating models of particular kinds of language in terms of extracted word frequencies and variational analysis using singular value decomposition. This enables model intensity of different documents to be compared, especially for each of the magazines across time, and hypotheses about expected language use to be validated or falsified.
3. This, in turn, allows questions about the potential success of these jihadist magazines to be answered: how well they are able to deploy influence (how dangerous these magazines are), and how they react to world events and their own successes and failures (how professional or strategic they are). We are also able to determine authorship of individual issues.

We conclude that both magazines deploy the language of influence fairly well, although *Inspire* seems to have difficulty staying "on message". More worryingly, the intensity of jihadist language is rapidly increasing in *Inspire*.

We assume that intelligence analysts are assisted by automated or semi-automated analytic methodologies to carry out tasks such as extracting text and applying various language models to it, a task we carry out by hand. We make no special effort to handle issues that arise from the conversion process from Portable Document Format to text, or those that arise from automated part-of-speech labelling and word frequency extraction, on the assumption that a scalable version of this methodology should be robust in the presence of these issues.

Background

There is a long history of modelling the language of influence or, more pejoratively, propaganda, and these analyses provide indications of what to expect of the language patterns of documents whose primary purpose is influence. Martin [2] defines propaganda this way: "an organized deliberate attempt to influence many people, explicitly or implicitly". It is clear that *Inspire* and *Azan* meet these criteria. The essence of propaganda is that it is intended to be opinion forming, and the essence of its mechanism is that it is manipulative. Martin suggests that propaganda is characterized by: simplification, attractive visuals, deceptiveness of some kind, and psychological techniques that weaken or bypass rationality. Work in corpus analytics has made it possible to instantiate these characterizations in terms of particular sets of words and how they are used in documents and corpora.

We apply models with a semantic component: Rayson's models of informative language and imaginative language [3], Suedfeld's model of integrative complexity [4], Pennebaker's model of deception [5], Koppel's model of jihadist language [6], and a model for gamification developed by the authors. Gamification is being used as a strategy for motivation in business settings, but it has only just begun to be considered as a potential strategy for influence or propaganda.

Previous analysis of the approach and content of *Inspire* has focused on four questions: how does the content address the avowed purpose; what mechanisms are used to increase the "stickiness" of the message; what choice model for the readers is assumed; and are there contradictions inherent in the goal of the magazine? *Azan* has not yet received much academic attention, but the same four questions invite answers.

There are three audiences who appear to be addressed, at least implicitly, by these magazines. The most obvious and important are those sympathetic to jihadist ideology who are capable of being convinced to carry out attacks. Content for this audience consists of coercion towards carrying out attacks, and information about targeting and methodologies to support this. The second audience is the jihadist community itself who need to be shown that steps are being taken, who can point to the magazine as something to be proud of, and who can use it as a tool in their own recruiting. Content for this audience might be framed as morale building. The third audience is the population of Western countries at large. Content for this audience is intended to create terror by suggesting the presence of large numbers of motivated lone-wolf extremists in their midst, hard to identify and ready to strike anywhere without detectable precursors. A detailed analysis of the content of *Inspire* (up to Issue 7) was carried out by Ford [7]. She argues that the messaging in *Inspire* is consistent with themes in other Al Qaeda communication, emphasizing: a clash of civilizations, Muslim unity, the necessity of (violent) jihad, religious justification, Al Qaeda's superiority, and glorification of martyrdom and hero worship. Interestingly, issues of *Azan* have also (somewhat plaintively) asked for help from a fourth audience, anyone with knowledge of drone operations to help them develop countermeasures.

The second aspect is how the authors attempt to make their messages "sticky", that is both standing out in the noisy media environment of the West, and compelling to the intended audiences. One major part of this is the use of narrative, both narratives of past successes, and biographies of previous heroes and martyrs of the movement. This is intended to create identification, to make abstract possibilities seem plausible and realistic, and perhaps even to create envy. Another part is the high production values of the magazine itself, making it more readable and serious-looking for Western eyes, used to the production quality of mass-market magazines. Considerable attention is paid to pictures and layout.

The contrast between *Inspire* and typical Islamist discussion forums, which also attempt to motivate attackers and attacks, is striking. There has also been research suggesting that crowdsourcing and gamification are being used in *Inspire* as a motivational strategy and to desensitize readers to the human consequences of violent attacks [8,9].

The third aspect is the choice model that is assumed by the writers and editors, that is what is supposed to go through the mind of a reader on the path towards willingness for violent action [10]. A rational choice model is implausible since the intention is to influence individuals towards actions that will result in their deaths or long terms of imprisonment. Two choice models have been suggested. The first is bounded rational choice, in which the available choices are made to appear constrained, either by controlling the available information, or the amount of resource available to make a decision. In settings where the consequences to the individual of taking action are severe, for example in the military, appeals to honor and community are often made, and these magazines use the same strategy. The second choice model is situational action theory, which models the process as the infection of vulnerable individuals. There is some empirical evidence to support this – it explains the *rates* of lone-wolf attacks well – but it does not have much explanatory power as a way of predicting *which* individuals may become infected [11]. Overall, those who are convinced to act in a violent way do not themselves enjoy the results of their actions. Accordingly, those who want to convince them must feel pressure to express the outcomes in abstract terms, and the goals in terms of what they are against, rather than what they are for.

The fourth aspect is the inherent contradiction in producing documents intended to convince *others* to carry out violent acts at a cost to themselves, an argument that

has been made in detail by Ramsay [10]. If it is acceptable to contribute to jihad by writing for and producing magazines, then it must also acceptable for magazine readers to contribute to jihad in less-lethal ways, perhaps recruitment and fund raising. This may go some way to explaining why the effects of *Inspire* and *Azan* have apparently been so modest.

Lemieux *et al.* [12] have described *Inspire* from the perspective of the Information, Motivation, and Behavior (IMB) framework. This framework suggests that causing others to act requires providing them with information, providing them with motivation, and teaching them behavioral skills that will be required for the desired actions. They show that the issues match this framework quite well – for example, the most famous article in *Inspire*, "Build a bomb in the kitchen of your Mom" is a recipe book for building a certain kind of IED. The IMB framework may be used intuitively, but it is also possible that Khan and al-Awlaki had some informal psychological background and deployed this strategy consciously.

The theory of the language of influence or propaganda, and the specific theories that have been raised for magazines such as *Inspire* and *Azan*, suggest several hypotheses about the language patterns to be seen in these magazines.

- Informative language intensity will be high as the magazines try to train their readers in both targeting and techniques. (This is slightly unexpected: conventional theories of propaganda tend to emphasize transmission of ideas, rather than of actionable knowledge about, for example, bomb making).
- Imaginative language intensity will be high to increase emotional drivers of motivation, and perhaps as a way to bypass rationality.
- Integrative complexity will be consistent with other kinds of Western magazines – the goal is not to provide a textbook; but neither is it to become too overtly simplistic.
- Deceptive language intensity will be high because of the inherent difficulty of convincing others to carry out actions that are not in their individual interest, and because influence tends to become manipulative.
- Jihadist language intensity will be high, reflecting the mindset of the authors.
- Gamification language intensity will be non-negligible as as a way to drive action via rewards from the process itself, and to provide emotional distance between acts and consequences.

We investigate empirically whether these hypotheses are supported. The temporal variation in intensity of these semantic models is of particular interest for two reasons: it provides us with insight about how author/editor strategy changes in relation to what happens in the outside world; and it allows us to gauge whether, for example, the danger posed by these magazines is increasing or decreasing.

Empirical evidence from Islamist forums has shown that high levels of jihadist language tends to be associated with low levels of deception [13,14]. The validation of the hypotheses relating to jihadist and deceptive language intensity will shed light on whether these magazines resemble forum language or not.

Since authorship is fairly reliably detectable from text, we can also investigate whether magazine issues are written by the same author(s). We expect the first 8 issues of *Inspire* to display consistent language; and we can address questions of authorship for the remaining issues of *Inspire* and all of the issues of *Azan*.

Approach

A language model measures some high-level property of the documents in a corpus by counting the occurrence frequencies of words that are associated with that property. At its simplest, the total number of occurrences of a given set of words can be computed for each document and treated as a score – for example, counting the number of adjectives in a document to measure its 'colorfulness'.

We compute a number of such measures for the magazine issues in what follows. Given a set of relevant words, either explicitly as a list, or by capturing all occurrences of a given part-of-speech, we compute a document-word matrix. Each row corresponds to a magazine issue, each column corresponds to a word of the particular language model, and the entries describe the frequency of each such word in each document.

The entries in each row of such a matrix could simply be summed to approximate the intensity of the language in each document. However, frequencies are necessarily larger in longer documents, so the rows must at least be normalized by dividing by the total number of word occurrences (that is, the length of the document), converting word frequencies into word rates.

In most language models, individual words are not equally significant markers of the property being considered, but summing across rows implicitly assumes that they are. Instead, we refine the analysis of a language model by transforming the space spanned by the words into a lower dimensional one, and embedding the (rows corresponding to the) documents as points in this space. If the language model describes only a single-factor property, this embeds the documents in a 1-dimensional space with documents that have the greatest intensity of the language model at one end, and those with the weakest

intensity at the other. In other words, the embedding creates a ranking of documents by the intensity of the property. Even when the language model consists of more than one underlying factor, a ranking can be constructed by projecting onto a a vector that captures variation along more than one axis.

A representation of the documents (and the words) in a 2- or 3-dimensional space allows the results to be visualized, and similarities and differences exposed. When there is a time sequence to the set of documents, as there is for the issues of these two magazines, we can also glean information from the trajectory over time of the intensity of each kind of language.

We use a singular value decomposition of the document-word matrix to carry out this embedding. Given an $n \times m$ document-word matrix, A, the singular value decomposition [15] expresses it as a product

$$A = USV'$$

where k is the minimum of n and m, U is $n \times k$, S is an $k \times k$ diagonal matrix whose non-increasing entries indicate the amount of variation in each dimension of the embedding, and V' is $k \times m$. The superscript dash indicates matrix transposition. U describes the coordinates of each document with respect to axes defined by V and, simultaneously and symmetrically, V describes the coordinates of each word with respect to axes defined by U. The decomposition can be truncated at values smaller than k, say 2 or 3, with minimal loss of structure, and then plotted so that structures can be visualized.

For the semantic language models, we create two artificial documents to represent both strong and weak language patterns. Before computing the SVD, word frequencies are converted to z-scores. Therefore we create an artificial document (matrix row) all of whose entries are $+1$ and another all of whose entries are -1. These represent documents that appear as if they use every word of the language model at one standard deviation above (resp. below) the mean usage rate in each corpus. These documents do not participate in the computation of the SVD, but are inserted into the resulting space by postmultiplying them (as row vectors) by $V * S^{-1/2}$. The resulting positions approximate where a document with intense use of the language model being considered would lie (indicated by an "H"), and where one with weak use of the language model would lie (indicated by an "L"). This is useful in two ways. First, the line joining "L" to "H" indicates the direction in which the language intensity is increasing, and so orients the roles of the other points (documents). Second, it allows us to claim that levels of particular language are high when many of the journal issues fall near or above the "H" level, since this means that many words of the corresponding model must occur more than one standard deviation above the mean, *even within such a small corpus.*

Document-word matrices were extracted from versions of the magazines converted from Portable Document Format to plain text. This conversion, especially for such visually rich documents, introduces a number of artifacts. We remove only the most obvious of these, since a typical intelligence analysis pipeline would typically not have the resources to clean the text files extensively. Enough investigation was carried out to suggest that the remaining artifacts have negligible effects on the results.

Results

Three issues of *Inspire* are of particular interest in what follows:

- Issue 3 – bombs aboard cargo planes, claim of bringing down a UPS plane in Dubai that is widely believed to be untrue;
- Issue 5 – Arab spring;
- Issue 7 – 9/11 anniversary.

The results presented in this section for each semantic model are plots with one point corresponding to each document, placed at coordinates derived from the first three columns of the U matrix. These three columns define a three-dimensional space in which the cloud of points

is centered around the origin (because of the normalization to z-scores). Its axes are linear combinations of all of the word frequencies; these are not directly interpretable and so we omit them from the images, and the space is isotropic so that distances in all directions are equally meaningful. This space captures the variation among documents derived from the variations in the way that they use the set of words of each model. Distance from the origin is a surrogate for significant variation, and points in the same direction from the center use the set of words with similar frequencies. Thus closeness corresponds to semantic similarity. For issues of *Azan* and for the first 8 issues of *Inspire* which were written by the same authors, we connect the points corresponding to issues in time order so that variation with time (trends) can be seen.

Informative language

Rayson's informative language model [3] represents how a document succeeds in conveying ideas in a rational fashion; in our context, how well a document represents a call to action based on convincing arguments. It is based on the rate of use of nouns, adjectives, prepositions, and conjunctions.

Figure 1 shows the informative language model applied to the issues of *Inspire*. Issues 1 to 12 are connected by a line in time order, while variation is shown in two dimensions. Thus we can see that most of the issues are quite similar to one another, but Issues 3 and 7 vary substantially

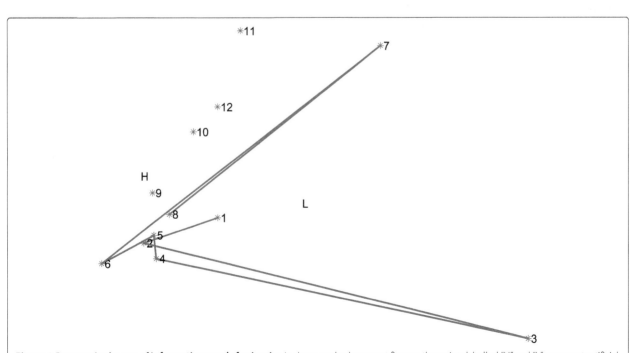

Figure 1 Patterns in the use of informative words for *Inspire*. In these, and subsequent figures, the points labelled "H" and "L" represent artificial documents with levels of the language pattern well above and well below the mean rate in the corpus.

from these typical issues, and from one another. The issues by new authors also show a trend with time, and one that differs from the earlier trends.

The points marked as high ("H") and low ("L") intensity are the inserted artificial documents – documents that use every word of the model at one standard deviation above or below the mean rate. The line between these points defines the gradient from lower to higher intensity and so shows that informative language intensity increases from right to left. Issues 3 and 7, which we earlier commented were triumphalist, are also least informative, which seems consistent.

Figure 2 shows the issues of *Azan*, with most informative at the left of the figure and least informative at the right.

Figure 3 shows the combined plot, with informative intensity increasing from right to left. *Azan* clearly ranks higher overall on informativeness.

Imaginative language

Rayson's imaginative language model, in contrast, tries to convince by appealing to the imagination [3]. It is based on the use of verbs, adverbs, and pronouns. Figure 4 shows the structure of *Inspire* issues based on imaginative language, with intensity increasing from right to left. From this and Figure 1, we see that Issues 3 and 7 are both the least informative and the least imaginative. Note also that the recent issues exhibit a different, orthogonal pattern of informative language: similar in intensity to the other issues, but different in form.

Figure 5 shows the structure for *Azan* with imaginative intensity also increasing from right to left. Figure 6 shows the comparative imaginative intensity across both magazines. *Azan* is slightly more imaginative than *Inspire* across the board.

These results show that informative and imaginative language are not necessarily antithetical – it is possible for a document to be high in both, in just one, or in neither.

Integrative complexity

The integrative complexity model [4,16] measures the intellectual complexity of the content of a document. It can be further subdivided into two aspects: dialectic complexity, the awareness that concepts can be considered from more than one point of view, and elaboration, the awareness that concepts can contain more than one simple idea [17]. Integrative complexity is measured on a 7 point scale; its usefulness has been considerably advanced by the development of an automatic scoring algorithm which we use here [18].

The integrative complexities, shown in Figure 7 show a steady increase with time for *Inspire*, except for the anomalous Issues 10 and 12. *Azan*, in contrast, has an almost constant integrative complexity. Almost exactly the same patterns are visible for dialectic and elaborative complexities (Figures 8 and 9), indicating that the arguments being made include *both* an awareness of contrasting points of view *and* of depth within any single point of view.

It is interesting to consider how these values compare with values for other kinds of writing. Table 1 shows comparable values for randomly chosen articles in mainstream magazines. The values for *Inspire* and *Azan*'s integrative complexity and dialectical complexity are in the mid range compared to these magazines;

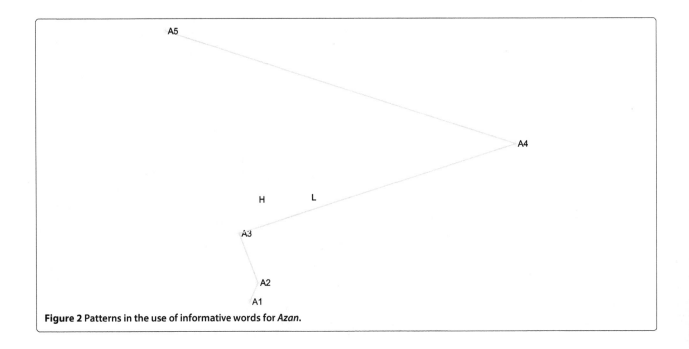

Figure 2 Patterns in the use of informative words for *Azan*.

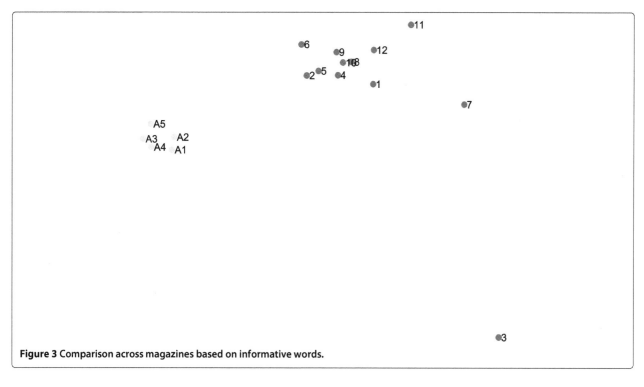

Figure 3 Comparison across magazines based on informative words.

their elaborative complexity scores are perhaps slightly lower.

Deceptive language
Deception is a broad spectrum property that includes both outright factual falsehoods and attempts to deceive by creating an impression that is knowingly not true to the facts. Settings all the way from propaganda to advertising contain some measure of deception. We measure deception using characteristic changes in the frequencies of a set of words that were originally determined empirically but have since been verified in a large number of domains [5]. Deception is signalled by:

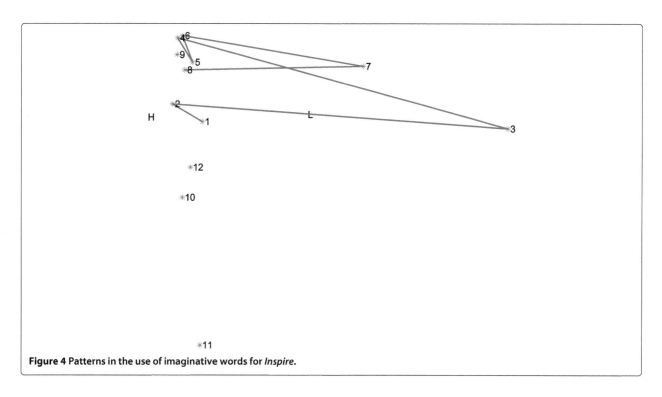

Figure 4 Patterns in the use of imaginative words for *Inspire*.

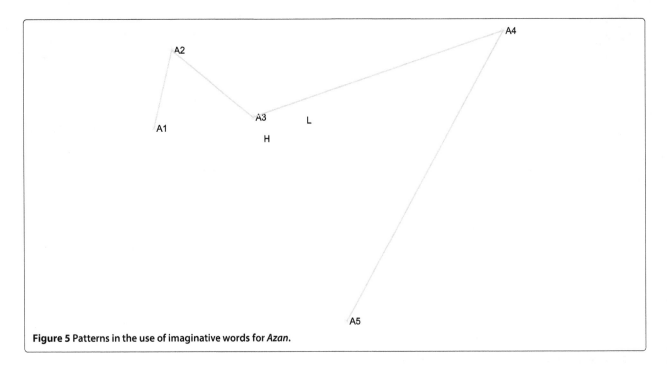

Figure 5 Patterns in the use of imaginative words for *Azan*.

- Decreases in first-person singular pronouns ("I", "mine");
- Decreases in exclusive words, words that signal increasing refinement of the thought being expressed ("but" and "or");
- Increases in negative emotion words ("hate", "angry"); and
- Increases in action verbs ("go", "make").

Because intensity of deception is signalled by *decreases* in the frequencies of some words, word rates are mapped to z-scores, and those in the first two categories are then multiplied by −1 so that increasing magnitude is consistently associated with increasing deception. A singular value decomposition is then applied to the resulting matrix.

Figure 10 shows the structure of the *Inspire* issues based on the deception model. In this figure, deception increase from bottom to top, so that Issue 7 is by far the most deceptive among them.

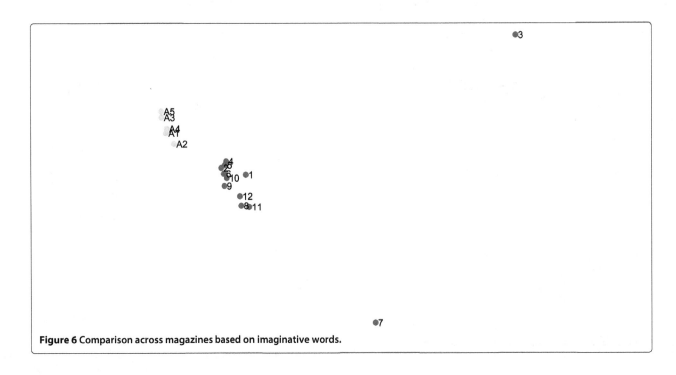

Figure 6 Comparison across magazines based on imaginative words.

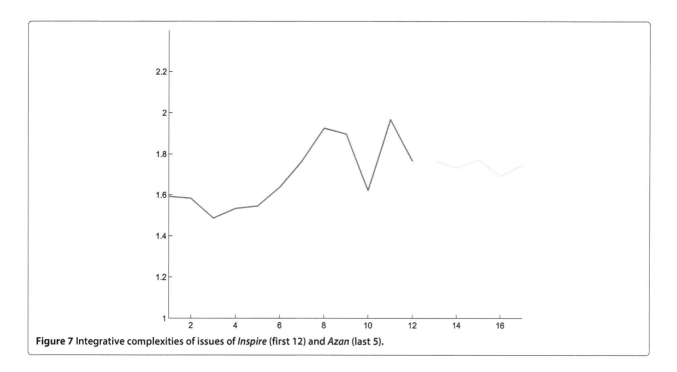

Figure 7 Integrative complexities of issues of *Inspire* (first 12) and *Azan* (last 5).

Figure 11 shows the ranking by deceptive language for the *Azan* issues. Deception increases from lower right to upper left in this figure, so Issue 4 is the least deceptive.

Figure 12 shows the deception ranking for both magazines. The issues of *Azan* are all less deceptive than the issues of *Inspire*. However, the separation between the two magazines is not as great as for some previous word categories.

Jihadist language

Koppel *et al.* [6] developed a language model that measures the intensity of jihadist language. Again, the model was developed empirically. The model words were originally in Arabic; we use English versions obtained using Google Translate. The resulting 85 English words have been shown in other contexts to produce a strong single-factor ranking of Islamic forum postings, suggesting that, although the construction

process is somewhat cavalier, the results are usable [13,14].

Figure 13 shows the ranking of *Inspire* issues based on this model, with intensity increasing from right to left. Thus the newer Issues 9–12 have much higher levels of jihadist language than the earlier issues. Some of the words associated with this increased intensity are "jihad", "mujahideen", and "killing". Figure 14 shows the ranking of *Azan* issues based on this model, with intensity also increasing from right to left.

Figure 15 shows the levels of jihadist language across the two magazines. The issues of *Azan* are at about the same level as the majority of issues of *Inspire*.

The results from the deception and jihadist language models are similar to previous analysis of Islamist forum posts [13,14]. There it was argued that a reasonable explanation was that high levels of jihadist language were plausibly associated with high sincerity, and so low levels of deception. The recent issues of *Inspire*, which have especially high levels of jihadist language, have levels of deception that are in the mid-range, or perhaps even a little lower than that, suggesting that the same relationship may be present.

Gamification language

Gamification has been used in many different settings, for example in business and learning, to increase the attraction of the desired process by adding elements of a game (goals, competition) to them. There are signs that a similar approach has begun to be used in jihadist propaganda as a way to change the calculus of carrying out an attack whose consequences are substantial, by focusing

Table 1 Integrative complexity scores for randomly chosen articles in mainstream magazines

Document	IC	DIAL	ELAB
Atlantic	2.44	1.97	1.63
Chatelaine	2.08	1.60	1.53
Harpers	1.63	1.50	1.28
National Geographic	1.70	1.50	1.26
New Yorker	1.68	1.44	1.28
Readers Digest	2.23	1.78	1.54

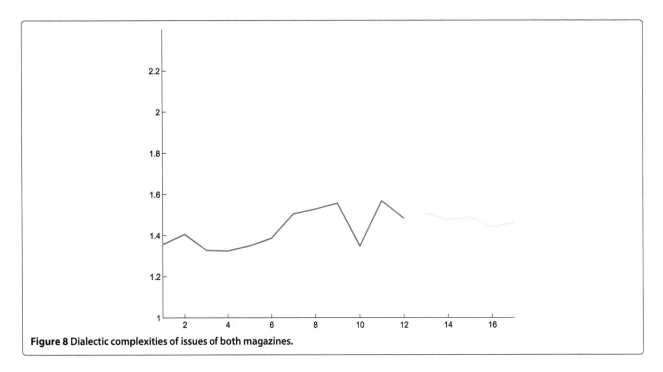

Figure 8 Dialectic complexities of issues of both magazines.

on the process rather than the consequences. In other words, gamification attempts to motivate individuals to take actions towards proximate goals, and perhaps in competition with others, providing notional real-world goals while at the same time blurring or down-playing the real-world consequences associated with achieving them.

We constructed a gamification lexicon using the commonest words from McGonigal's book [19] extended with words from some popular gamification web sites.

Figure 16 shows the intensity of gamification language for the issues of *Inspire*, with intensity increasing from lower right to upper left. As we have already seen, Issues 3 and 7 bask in the success of previous attacks; these results suggest that this comes at the expense of motivating new attacks, so it is not surprising that they show the lowest levels of gamification language. Figure 17 shows the intensity of gamification language for the issues of *Azan*, with the same orientation.

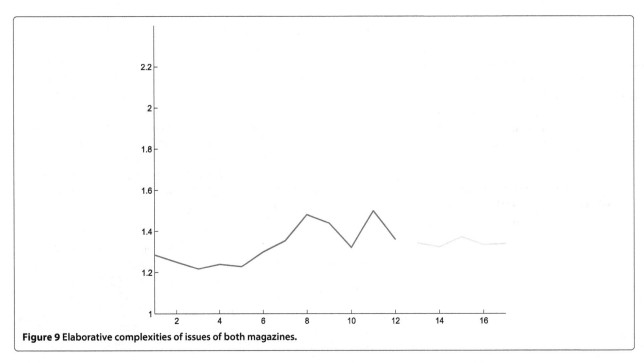

Figure 9 Elaborative complexities of issues of both magazines.

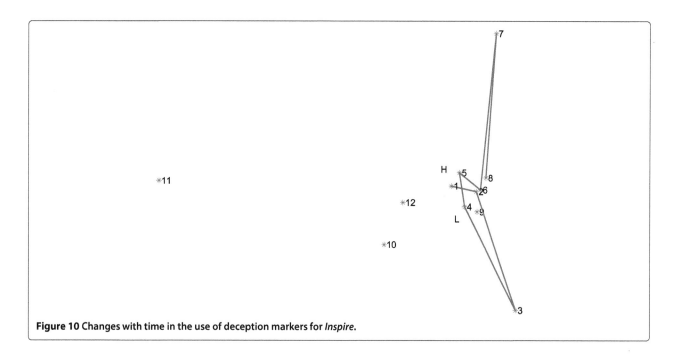

Figure 10 Changes with time in the use of deception markers for *Inspire*.

Figure 18 shows the ranking by gamification intensity across both magazines, with intensity increasing from lower right to upper left. There is considerable variation in the observed levels of gamification language, making it hard to judge whether there are attempts to use gamification, but in an uncertain way, or whether the ideas underlying gamification are being used unconsciously.

It is striking that the recent issues of *Inspire* differ so markedly from the others with respect to this model. *Azan* shows consistently higher levels of gamification language than *Inspire* does. So little is known of the authors and editors that it is hard to judge whether this represents intentional or accidental deployment of this style of language.

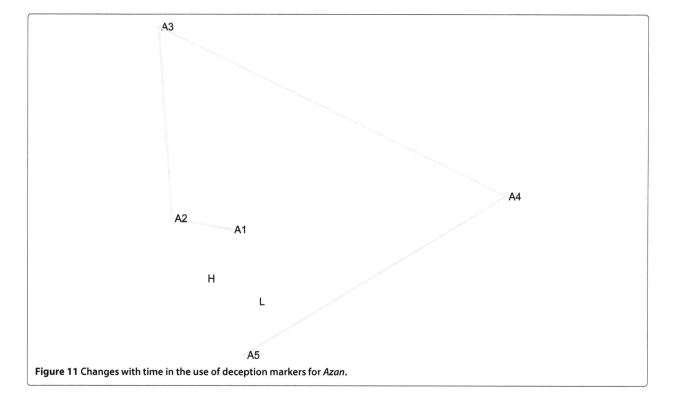

Figure 11 Changes with time in the use of deception markers for *Azan*.

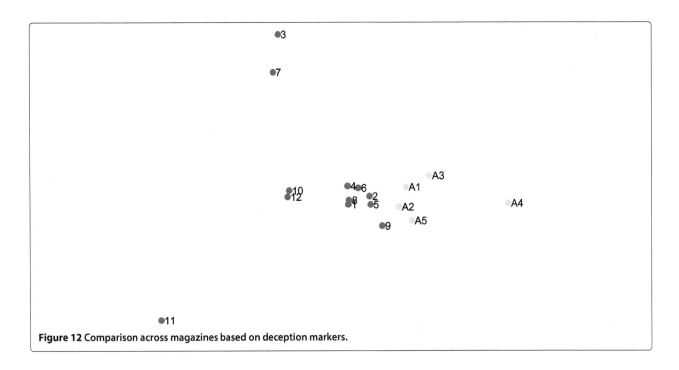

Figure 12 Comparison across magazines based on deception markers.

Discussion

We now revisit our hypotheses, given the results of the empirical analysis. We justify claims of the form "intensity with respect to this particular language model is high" by appealing to the placement of the artificial documents in relation to the magazine issues. In particular, the document indicated by the point labelled "H" represents a document containing occurrences of every word of the model at rates one standard deviation above the mean. Such a document represents extremely high intensity, especially for the informative, imaginative, and gamification models where the 1000 most-frequent words are used. Thus a magazine issue that lies above the level of the "H" document must use the corresponding language at extremely high levels.

For the hypotheses we posited, we reach the following conclusions from the results:

- *Informative language intensity will be high.* This is supported; *Azan* is clearly better in this dimension, and *Inspire* wanders from informative to triumphalist several times.
- *Imaginative language intensity will be high.* This is partly supported; most issue lie just below the "H" marker. The issues of *Inspire* that were lowest on informative language also have low levels of imaginative language.
- *Integrative complexity will be consistent with other magazines.* This is supported; levels of complexity vary but remain in the general range of mass-market

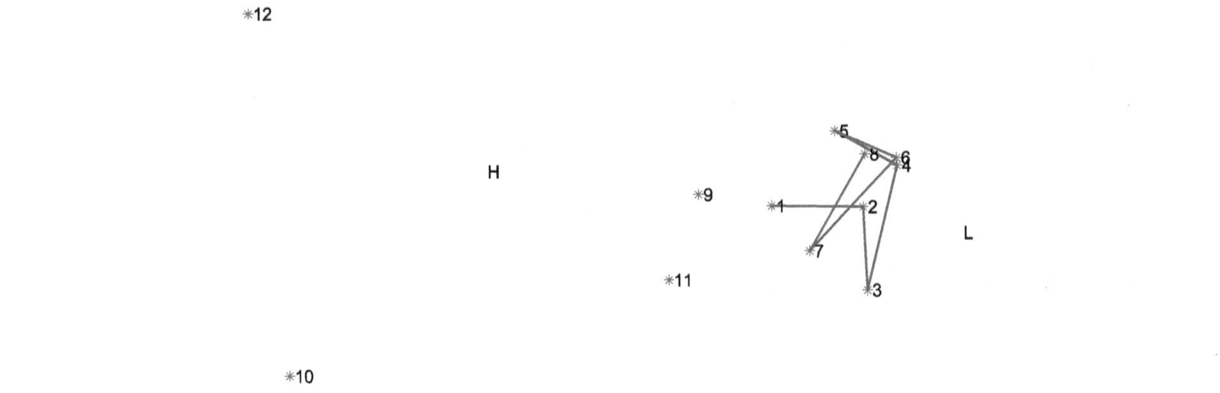

Figure 13 Changes with time in the use of jihadist language for *Inspire*.

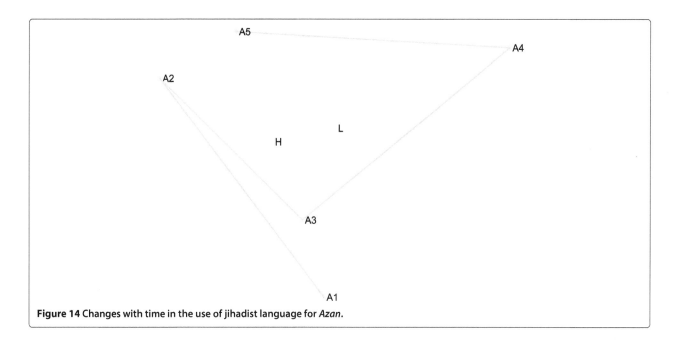

Figure 14 Changes with time in the use of jihadist language for *Azan*.

Western magazines. This is counter-evidence to the perception that Islamist propaganda is necessarily simplistic.

- *Deceptive language intensity will be high.* This is partially supported – most issues of *Inspire* are in the mid-range, with issues of *Azan* noticeably higher.
- *Jihadist language intensity will be high.* This is partially supported. Again, the issues of *Azan* have higher intensities than the older issues of *Inspire*, but the three most recent issues of *Inspire* show the highest levels overall.

- *Gamification language intensity will be non-negligible.* Some issues have very high levels of gamification, but others have very low levels, and there is no temporal pattern. The results suggest that gamification is being attempted, but with unsure technique leading to inconsistent levels.

The results based on these semantic language models are consistent with expectations of propaganda and the language of influence. Thus jihadists have adopted the

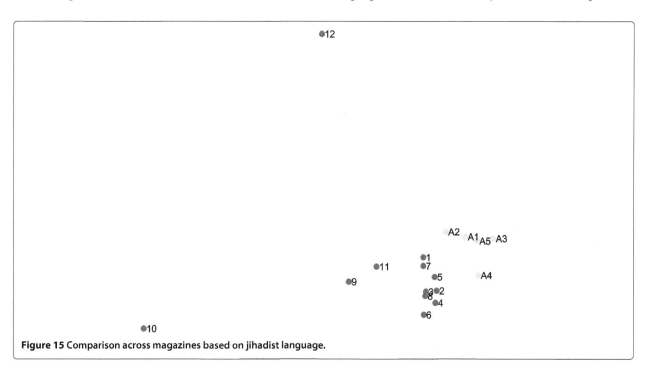

Figure 15 Comparison across magazines based on jihadist language.

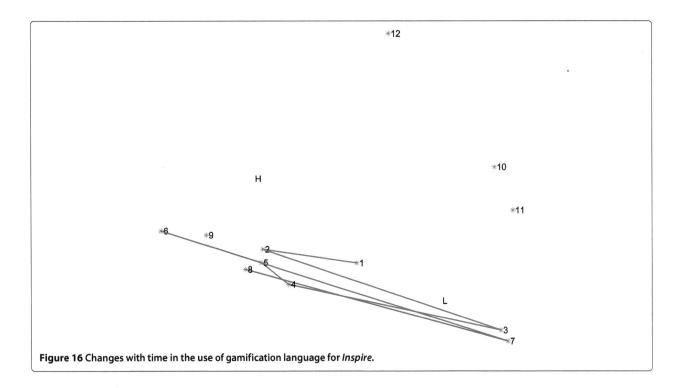

Figure 16 Changes with time in the use of gamification language for *Inspire*.

playbook of governments, as they try to influence readers to adopt a jihadist ideology and, more importantly, to act on it.

Authorship is detectable. We can certainly discriminate the first 8 issues of *Inspire* from Issues 9–12, although Issues 3 and 7 are substantially different from the other earlier ones. The early issues may have been a collaborative effort between Khan and al-Awlaki, with the balance shifting depending on subject matter. All of the issues of *Azan* appear to be the work of a single author (despite the different author names associated with individual articles).

Azan issues are more consistent than those of *Inspire*, which shows a tendency to focus opportunistically on the issues of the moment, rather than on a strategic plan to convince and develop lone-wolf attackers. *Azan's* admitted small number of issues have been focused and consistent, which speaks to tight editorial control, and intentionality. The early issues of *Inspire* were

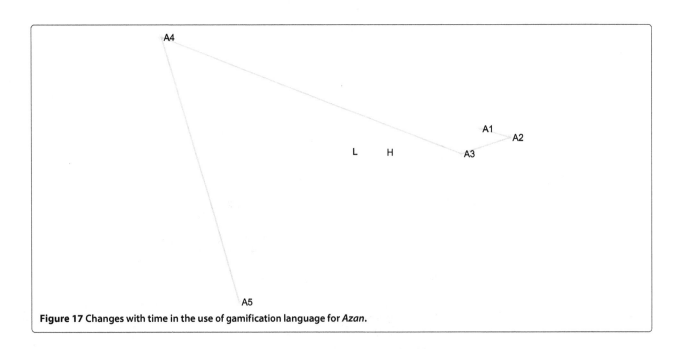

Figure 17 Changes with time in the use of gamification language for *Azan*.

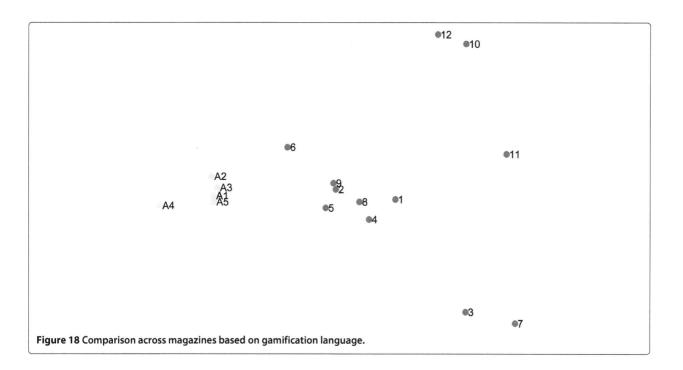

Figure 18 Comparison across magazines based on gamification language.

not nearly as focused or consistent; rather they tend to use current events as a jumping off point for each issue. This may be, to some extent, deliberate but it suggests the lack of a strategic and intentional view of the goals of the magazine. The more recent issues have been different from one another, but the common structures relating them in the various figures suggest that there is some deeper consistency that is now in play. This may some background figure who is exercising a kind of pseudo-editorial control, or it may reflect the homogeneity of the community from which it emanates.

It has been suggested that competition is one of the factors that might cause *Inspire* to become more strident [20]. The intensity of *Inspire* is visibly increasing, but there has only been minimal overlap in time of the two magazines, so it is too early to examine this conjecture.

We have demonstrated a methodology that can be applied to a corpus in at least a semi-automated way to extract data relevant to a set of language models; and to visualize the properties of the documents in the corpus with respect to these language models. Consideration of similarity/variation and temporal changes allow us to see aspects of the authors and of their mindsets.

From an intelligence perspective, this methodology allows us to draw conclusions about the changing editors at *Inspire* after the deaths of its founding editors; and the pool of authors and editors associated with *Azan*. We are also able to judge, to some extent, the sophistication of the authors and editors as they deploy persuasion techniques, visible via some of these language models. We are also

able to judge intensity of properties such as informativeness, imaginativeness, deception, and (most significantly perhaps) jihadist language.

Author details

[1]Queen's University, Kingston, Canada. [2]James Madison University, Harrisonburg, USA.

References
1. G Weimann, Lone wolves in cyberspace. J. Terrorism Res. **3**(2) (2012)
2. R Martin, *Propaganda and the Ethics of Persuasion*, 2nd edn. (Broadview Press, 2013)
3. P Rayson, A Wilson, G Leech, Grammatical word class variation with the British National Corpus sampler, in *Twenty First International Conference on English Language Research on Computerized Corpora*, (2000), pp. 295–306
4. P Suedfeld, P Tetlock, Integrative complexity of communications in international crises. J. Conflict Resolution. **21**, 169–184 (1977)
5. ML Newman, JW Pennebaker, DS Berry, JM Richards, Lying words: predicting deception from linguistic style. Pers. Soc. Psychol. Bull. **29**, 665–675 (2003)
6. M Koppel, N Akiva, E Alshech, K Bar, Automatically classifying documents by ideological and organizational affiliation, in *Proceedings of the IEEE International Conference on Intelligence and Security Informatics (ISI 2009)*, (2009), pp. 176–178
7. SA Ford, Inspiring a narrative: a content analysis of Al Qaeda's English-Language Inspire magazine. Master's Research Essay, Carleton University (2012)
8. EF Reid, AQAP *Inspire* magazine: implications for crowdsourcing and gamification. Technical report, Research Paper, National Intelligence University (NIU), Washington, D.C. (2012)
9. EF Reid, Crowdsourcing and gamification techniques in inspire (aqap online magazine), in *IEEE International Conference on Intelligence and Security Informatics (ISI)*, (2013), pp. 215–220
10. G Ramsay, Targeting, rhetoric and the failure of grassroots jihad. J. Terrorism Res. **3**(1) (2012)

11. J Woo, J Son, H Chen, An SIR model for violent topic diffusion in social media, in *Proceedings of 2011 IEEE International Conference on Intelligence and Security Informatics, ISI 2011*, (2011)

12. AF Lemieux, J Brachman, J Levitt, J Wood, *Inspire* magazine: a critical analysis of its significance and potential impact through the lens of the information, motivation, and behavioral skills model. Terrorism Pol. Violence. **1**(1), 1-18 (2014)

13. DB Skillicorn, Lessons from a jihadi corpus, in *Foundations of Open-Source Intelligence FOSINT 2012*, (2012)

14. DB Skillicorn, Applying interestingness measures to Ansar forum texts, in *Proceedings of KDD 2010, Workshop on Intelligence and Security Informatics*, (2010), pp. 1–9

15. GH Golub, CF van Loan, *Matrix Computations*, 3rd edn. (Johns Hopkins University Press, 1996)

16. P Suedfeld, PE Tetlock, S Streufert, Conceptual/integrative complexity, in *Motivation and Personality: Handbook of Thematic Content Analysis* (Cambridge University Press, 1992), pp. 393–400

17. LG Conway III, F Thoemmes, AM Allison, KH Towgood, MJ Wagner, K Davey, A Salcido, AN Stovall, DP Dodds, K Bongard, KR Conway, Two ways to be complex and why they matter: implications for attitude strength and lying. J. Pers. Soc. Psychol. **95**(5), 1029–1044 (2008)

18. L Conway III, KR Conway, LJ Gornick, SC Houck, Automated integrative complexity. Pol. Psychol. (2012). in press

19. J McGonigal, *Reality Is Broken*. (Penguin Books, 2011)

20. DB Skillicorn, C Leuprecht, Improving the language of influence, in *Proceedings of Foundations of Open Source Intelligence, at Advances in Social Network Analysis and Modelling (ASONAM)* (ACM & IEEE, 2013), pp. 1028–1033

Permissions

All chapters in this book were first published in SI, by Springer; hereby published with permission under the Creative Commons Attribution License or equivalent. Every chapter published in this book has been scrutinized by our experts. Their significance has been extensively debated. The topics covered herein carry significant findings which will fuel the growth of the discipline. They may even be implemented as practical applications or may be referred to as a beginning point for another development.

The contributors of this book come from diverse backgrounds, making this book a truly international effort. This book will bring forth new frontiers with its revolutionizing research information and detailed analysis of the nascent developments around the world.

We would like to thank all the contributing authors for lending their expertise to make the book truly unique. They have played a crucial role in the development of this book. Without their invaluable contributions this book wouldn't have been possible. They have made vital efforts to compile up to date information on the varied aspects of this subject to make this book a valuable addition to the collection of many professionals and students.

This book was conceptualized with the vision of imparting up-to-date information and advanced data in this field. To ensure the same, a matchless editorial board was set up. Every individual on the board went through rigorous rounds of assessment to prove their worth. After which they invested a large part of their time researching and compiling the most relevant data for our readers.

The editorial board has been involved in producing this book since its inception. They have spent rigorous hours researching and exploring the diverse topics which have resulted in the successful publishing of this book. They have passed on their knowledge of decades through this book. To expedite this challenging task, the publisher supported the team at every step. A small team of assistant editors was also appointed to further simplify the editing procedure and attain best results for the readers.

Apart from the editorial board, the designing team has also invested a significant amount of their time in understanding the subject and creating the most relevant covers. They scrutinized every image to scout for the most suitable representation of the subject and create an appropriate cover for the book.

The publishing team has been an ardent support to the editorial, designing and production team. Their endless efforts to recruit the best for this project, has resulted in the accomplishment of this book. They are a veteran in the field of academics and their pool of knowledge is as vast as their experience in printing. Their expertise and guidance has proved useful at every step. Their uncompromising quality standards have made this book an exceptional effort. Their encouragement from time to time has been an inspiration for everyone.

The publisher and the editorial board hope that this book will prove to be a valuable piece of knowledge for researchers, students, practitioners and scholars across the globe.

List of Contributors

Xiaofeng Wang
Predictive Technology Laboratory, University of Virginia, Charlottesville, Virginia, USA

Donald E Brown
Predictive Technology Laboratory, University of Virginia, Charlottesville, Virginia, USA

Michael C Madison
Pacific Northwest National Laboratory, 902 Battelle Boulevard, 999, MSIN K7-28 Richland, WA 99352, USA

Andrew J Cowell
Pacific Northwest National Laboratory, 902 Battelle Boulevard, 999, MSIN K7-28 Richland, WA 99352, USA

R Scott Butner
Pacific Northwest National Laboratory, 902 Battelle Boulevard, 999, MSIN K7-28 Richland, WA 99352, USA

Keith Fligg
Pacific Northwest National Laboratory, 902 Battelle Boulevard, 999, MSIN K7-28 Richland, WA 99352, USA

Andrew W Piatt
Pacific Northwest National Laboratory, 902 Battelle Boulevard, 999, MSIN K7-28 Richland, WA 99352, USA

Liam R McGrat
Pacific Northwest National Laboratory, 902 Battelle Boulevard, 999, MSIN K7-28 Richland, WA 99352, USA

Peter C Ellis
State of Washington, 735B Desoto Ave, Tumwater, WA 98512, USA

Paul Ormerod
Volterra Partners LLP, London, UK

Xuning Tang
College of Information Science and Technology, Drexel University, Philadelphia, USA

Christopher C Yang
College of Information Science and Technology, Drexel University, Philadelphia, USA

Arvind Verma
Department of Criminal Justice, Indiana University, Bloomington, USA

Ramyaa Ramyaa
Department of Computer Science, Indiana University, Bloomington, USA

Suresh Marru
Department of Computer Science, Indiana University, Bloomington, USA

Andrew J Park
Institute for Canadian Urban Research Studies (ICURS), Simon Fraser University, Burnaby, BC, Canada and Thompson Rivers University, Kamploops, BC, Canada

Herbert H Tsang
Trinity Western University, Langley, BC, Canada

Mengting Sun
Interdisciplinary Research in the Mathematical and Computational Sciences (IRMACS) Centre, Simon Fraser University, Burnaby, BC, Canada

Uwe Glässer
Interdisciplinary Research in the Mathematical and Computational Sciences (IRMACS) Centre, Simon Fraser University, Burnaby, BC, Canada

Victor Asal
University at Albany, New York, USA

Kristin Glass
Sandia National Laboratories, New Mexico, USA

Richard Colbaugh
Sandia National Laboratories, New Mexico, USA

Neal Holtschulte
Department of Computer Science, University of New Mexico, Albuquerque, USA

Melanie Moses
Department of Computer Science, University of New Mexico, Albuquerque, USA

Bruce A Desmarais
Department of Political Science, University of Massachusetts at Amherst, Amherst, Massachusetts 01003, USA

Skyler J Cranmer
Department of Political Science, University of North Carolina at Chapel Hill, Chapel Hill, North Carolina 27599, USA

Colby L Valentine
Dominican College, 470 Western Highway, Orangeburg, New York 10962, USA

Carter Hay
Florida State University, College of Criminology and Criminal Justice, 634 W. Call Street, Tallahassee, Florida 32306-1127, USA

Kevin M Beaver
Florida State University, College of Criminology and Criminal Justice, 634 W. Call Street, Tallahassee, Florida 32306-1127, USA

Thomas G Blomberg
Florida State University, College of Criminology and Criminal Justice, 634 W. Call Street, Tallahassee, Florida 32306-1127, USA

Amir H Ghaseminejad
Institute for Canadian Urban Research Studies, Simon Fraser University, Vancouver, Canada

Paul Brantingham
Institute for Canadian Urban Research Studies, Simon Fraser University, Vancouver, Canada

Patricia Brantingham
Institute for Canadian Urban Research Studies, Simon Fraser University, Vancouver, Canada

Zhenyu Cheryl Qian
Interaction Design, Purdue University, 552 W. Wood Street, 47907 West Lafayette IN, USA

Yingjie Victor Chen
Computer Graphics Technology, Purdue University, 402 S. Grant Street, 47907 West Lafayette IN, USA

Philippe J Giabbanelli
Interdisciplinary Research in the Mathematical and Computational Sciences (IRMACS) Centre, Simon Fraser University, 8888 University Drive, V5A 1S6 Burnaby, Canada

Joel Brynielsson
FOI Swedish Defence Research Agency, SE-164 90 Stockholm, Sweden

Andreas Horndahl
FOI Swedish Defence Research Agency, SE-164 90 Stockholm, Sweden

Fredrik Johansson
FOI Swedish Defence Research Agency, SE-164 90 Stockholm, Sweden

Lisa Kaati
FOI Swedish Defence Research Agency, SE-164 90 Stockholm, Sweden

Christian Mårtenson
FOI Swedish Defence Research Agency, SE-164 90 Stockholm, Sweden

Pontus Svenson
FOI Swedish Defence Research Agency, SE-164 90 Stockholm, Sweden

Ryan Compton
Information and System Sciences Laboratory, HRL Laboratories, 3011 Malibu Canyon Road, 90265 Malibu, CA, USA

Craig Lee
Information and System Sciences Laboratory, HRL Laboratories, 3011 Malibu Canyon Road, 90265 Malibu, CA, USA

Jiejun Xu
Information and System Sciences Laboratory, HRL Laboratories, 3011 Malibu Canyon Road, 90265 Malibu, CA, USA

Luis Artieda-Moncada
Information and System Sciences Laboratory, HRL Laboratories, 3011 Malibu Canyon Road, 90265 Malibu, CA, USA

Tsai-Ching Lu
Information and System Sciences Laboratory, HRL Laboratories, 3011 Malibu Canyon Road, 90265 Malibu, CA, USA

Lalindra De Silva
Department of Computer Science, University of Utah, Salt Lake City, Utah, USA

Michael Macy
Social Dynamics Laboratory, Cornell University, Ithaca, New York, USA

You Chen
Department of Biomedical Informatics, School of Medicine, Vanderbilt University, Nashville, TN, 37203, USA

Steve Nyemba
Department of Biomedical Informatics, School of Medicine, Vanderbilt University, Nashville, TN, 37203, USA

Wen Zhang
Department of Electrical Engineering and Computer Science, School of Engineering, Vanderbilt University, Nashville, TN, 37203, USA

Bradley Malin
Department of Biomedical Informatics, School of Medicine, Vanderbilt University, Nashville, TN, 37203, USA
Department of Electrical Engineering and Computer Science, School of Engineering, Vanderbilt University, Nashville, TN, 37203, USA

Shuai Yuan
SUNY at Buffalo, Buffalo, NY 14260, USA

Raghav H Rao
SUNY at Buffalo, Buffalo, NY 14260, USA

Shambhu Upadhyaya
SUNY at Buffalo, Buffalo, NY 14260, USA

Mary B Burns
Jake Jabs College of Business & Entrepreneurship, Montana State University, P.O. Box 173040, 59717-3040 Bozeman, MT, USA

Kevin C Moffitt
Accounting and Information Systems, Rutgers Business School, Rutgers, The State University of New Jersey, 100 Rockefeller Road, 08854 Piscataway, NJ, USA

Joe Bruce
Pacific Northwest National Laboratory (PNNL), Richland, WA, USA

Jean Scholtz
Pacific Northwest National Laboratory (PNNL), Richland, WA, USA

Duncan Hodges
Oxford University, Oxford, UK

Lia Emanuel
University of Bath, Bath, UK

Danaë Stanton Fraser
University of Bath, Bath, UK

Sadie Creese
Oxford University, Oxford, UK

Oriana J Love
Pacific Northwest National Laboratory (PNNL), Richland, WA, USA

Valerie Spicer
Institute of Canadian Research Studies, Simon Fraser University, Burnaby, BC, Canada

Justin Song
Institute of Canadian Research Studies, Simon Fraser University, Burnaby, BC, Canada

Patricia Brantingham
Institute of Canadian Research Studies, Simon Fraser University, Burnaby, BC, Canada

David B Skillicorn
Queen's University, Kingston, Canada

Edna F Reid
James Madison University, Harrisonburg, USA

Printed in the USA
CPSIA information can be obtained
at www.ICGtesting.com
JSHW052021301024
72690JS00004B/126

9 781682 85108